## Praise for *Managing Windows® with VBScript and WMI*

"This is the 'must-have' scripting guide for administrators of all levels. It shows what you need to get the job done and how."

—Joseph Niemi, Systems Engineer

"Finally, a step-by-step VBScripting book to make you look like a programmer, without the time and sweat! Don't waste your time searching the Internet for examples; this book does it for you!"

—Greg A. Marino, Senior Systems Engineer and Consultant
Westtown Consulting Group, Inc.

"Each chapter is like having a personal tutor at your side through the iterative process of scripting, no matter what your experience level. Whether you are writing complex scripts or simply automating repetitive tasks, I found this book truly hits the mark as the right tool to get the job done."

—Joel Yoker, Program Manager
Microsoft Corporation

"This book will provide any technical reader with a real-world understanding of how to use VBScript with WMI. The examples are clear and pertinent to the needs of the day-to-day system administrator."

—Bob Reselman, Principal
Cognitive Arts and Technologies

# Managing Windows® with VBScript and WMI

# Microsoft Windows Server System Series

Books in the **Microsoft Windows Server System Series** are written and reviewed by the world's leading technical authorities on Microsoft Windows technologies, including principal members of Microsoft's Windows and Server Development Teams. The goal of the series is to provide reliable information that enables administrators, developers, and IT professionals to architect, build, deploy, and manage solutions using the Microsoft Windows Server System. The contents and code of each book are tested against, and comply with, commercially available code. This series should be an invaluable resource for any IT professional or student working in today's Windows environment.

## TITLES IN THE SERIES

Paul Bertucci, *Microsoft SQL Server High Availability,* 0-672-32625-6 (Sams)

Peter Blackburn and William R. Vaughn, *Hitchhiker's Guide to SQL Server 2000 Reporting Services,* 0-321-26828-8 (Addison-Wesley)

William Boswell, *Learning Exchange Server 2003,* 0-321-22874-X (Addison-Wesley)

Bill English, Olga Londer, Shawn Shell, Todd Bleeker, and Stephen Cawood, *Microsoft Content Management Server 2002: A Complete Guide,* 0-321-19444-6 (Addison-Wesley)

Don Jones, *Managing Windows® with VBScript and WMI,* 0-321-21334-3 (Addison-Wesley)

Sakari Kouti and Mika Seitsonen, *Inside Active Directory, Second Edition: A System Administrator's Guide,* 0-321-22848-0 (Addison-Wesley)

Shyam Pather, *Microsoft SQL Server 2000 Notification Services,* 0-672-32664-7 (Sams)

**For more information please go to www.awprofessional.com/msserverseries**

# Managing Windows® with VBScript and WMI

*Don Jones*

Addison-Wesley

Upper Saddle River, NJ • Boston • Indianapolis • San Francisco
New York • Toronto • Montreal • London • Munich • Paris • Madrid
Capetown • Sydney • Tokyo • Singapore • Mexico City

The publisher offers excellent discounts on this book when ordered in quantity for bulk purchases or special sales, which may include electronic versions and/or custom covers and content particular to your business, training goals, marketing focus, and branding interests. For more information, please contact:

U.S. Corporate and Government Sales
(800) 382-3419
corpsales@pearsontechgroup.com

For sales outside the U.S., please contact:

International Sales
international@pearsoned.com

Visit us on the Web: www.awprofessional.com

*Library of Congress Cataloging-in-Publication Data*

Jones, Don.
Managing Windows with VBScript and WMI / Don Jones.
p. cm.
Includes index.
ISBN 0-321-21334-3 (pbk. : alk. paper)
1. Microsoft Windows (Computer file) 2. Operating systems (Computers)
3. VBScript (Computer program language) I. Title.

QA76.76.O63J6623 2004
005.4'4682—dc22

2003026069



ISBN 0-321-21334-3
Text printed in the United States on recycled paper at Courier in Stoughton, Massachusetts.
Fourth printing, October 2005

*This is for Chris.*
*For seven years, you've given me nothing but love, support, and encouragement, and I can never thank you enough.*

# Contents

# Preface

Microsoft introduced Visual Basic, Scripting Edition—commonly known as VBScript—in the mid-'90s, positioning it as a native replacement for Windows' aging command-line batch language, which was based on Microsoft's earliest operating system, MS-DOS. VBScript was intended to be easy to learn, powerful, and flexible. The language was included as an add-on to Windows 95 and Windows NT 4.0, was an optional installation component included in Windows 98, and was included in all editions of Windows Me, Windows 2000, Windows XP, and Windows Server 2003.

Software developers immediately seized upon VBScript for Web programming, particularly in Active Server Pages, Microsoft's rapid-development programming framework for the Web. However, Windows administrators—one of VBScript's initial target audiences—were left cold. VBScript seemed to be much more complicated than administrators' beloved MS-DOS-based batch language, and many didn't see the need to learn an entirely new batch language.

When Windows 2000 and Active Directory came along, however, administrators found that Windows administration had become a great deal more complex. Suddenly, administrators were searching for Resource Kit and other utilities that offered automated administration, especially for repetitive tasks. Active Directory enabled the use of VBScript for logon and logoff scripts, which seemed to promise more advanced use environment manipulation. At around the same time, Microsoft's naïveté in releasing a powerful language like VBScript with absolutely no security controls resulted in a huge wave of high-impact VBScript-based viruses, forcing administrators to lock down their environments and remove VBScript as an option both for viruses and for administrative tools.

As a regular speaker at some of the country's top technical conferences that focus on Windows technologies, including MCP TechMentor, the past few years I've given half- and full-day sessions on VBScripting for Windows administrators, and the sessions have been incredibly popular. In these sessions, I try to provide just enough VBScript experience to make scripting possible, and then concentrate on accomplishing common administrative tasks with VBScript. I also cover the security concerns of VBScript and provide administrators with the means for safely using VBScript in their environments. This book is essentially a written form of those sessions, greatly expanded with more coverage of Windows Management Instrumentation and other advanced topics, and with more coverage of VBScript security issues and resolutions.

I'm not out to turn you into a programmer. In fact, one of the real successes of VBScript is that you don't *need* to be a programmer to use it. Most of what you'll be doing in this book involves using VBScript to tell Windows to do things for you; you'll be able to ignore much of VBScript's complexity, using it as a sort of electronic glue to combine various operating system functions.

## Who Should Read This Book?

The only assumption I have about you is that you already know how to administer some version of Microsoft Windows. You'll find that most of the material in this book is suitable for Windows NT, Windows 2000, and Windows Server 2003 environments, and it will continue to be useful through future versions of Windows. I do not assume that you have any background in programming, and I'm not going to give you a programming background.

You should have a desire to learn how to use what I call "the batch language of the twenty-first century" and a wish to move away from clumsier—and often more complex—batch files based on the MS-DOS batch language. Although some folks like to refer to batch files as scripts, I don't; and when you see how easy and flexible VBScript is, you'll understand why!

## How to Use This Book

You can read this book in order from the Introduction to the Appendix. However, if you already have some experience with VBScript, or if you just want to dive right into the more complete example scripts, you can skip around as much as you like. I've organized this book in the same way that I organize my live VBScripting sessions at conferences, so you may feel that it's some time before you really get into the meat of scripting. I assure you, though, that each example in this book—starting in Chapter 1—is focused on Windows administration. You'll get your feet wet right away!

I've also included In This Chapter elements at the start of each chapter and Coming Up elements at the end of each chapter. These are brief paragraphs that are intended to help set the stage and help you decide if you need to read a particular chapter or not. They'll also help you decide which chapter to read next based on your individual needs and interests. I hope that these elements—along with the cross-references I've included in each chapter—will help you zip straight to the scripting information that you need most.

To help you decide where to start, here's a brief overview of each chapter.

## Part I: Introduction to Windows Administrative Scripting

Part I serves as an introduction to the world of scripting and provides you with a methodology for approaching administrative tasks from a scripting standpoint. One of the most difficult parts about producing new scripts from scratch is the "Where do I start?" factor, and I'll provide you with a framework for figuring that out every time.

### *Chapter 1: Scripting Concepts and Terminology*

As I've already implied, administrative scripting isn't hard-core programming. Instead, it's using VBScript as a sort of electronic glue to secure various bits of the Windows operating system together. In this chapter, I'll introduce you to those various bits and set the stage with some basic terminology that you'll use throughout this book.

### *Chapter 2: Running Scripts*

Writing a script isn't much fun if you can't run the script, and so this chapter will focus on the technologies used to execute scripts. You might be surprised to learn how many different Microsoft products support scripting. In this chapter, I'll show you how far your scripting skills can really take you. I'll also introduce you to some scripting tools that can make writing and debugging scripts a bit easier.

### *Chapter 3: The Components of a Script*

In this chapter, I'll present a complete administrative script, and then break it down line-by-line to explain its various components. Although this chapter isn't necessary to learning administrative scripting, it will help you write scripts that are more reliable and easier to troubleshoot.

### *Chapter 4: Designing a Script*

As I've mentioned already, one of the toughest aspects about scripting can be figuring out where to start. In this chapter, I'll provide you with a framework that you can use as a starting point for every new scripting project. I'll also introduce you to some concepts that many scripting books ignore, such as planning for errors and creating a useful "resource kit" of script components that you can reuse throughout your scripting projects.

## Part II: VBScript Tutorial

Here's your official crash course to the VBScript language: just enough to make administration via script a possibility! The best part is that I won't use the trite "Hello, world" examples that books for software developers often start out with. Instead, I'll make every example useful to you as a Windows administrator. That means you'll be producing simple, useful scripts at the same time you're learning VBScript. What could be better?

### *Chapter 5: Functions, Objects, Variables, and More*

In this chapter, I'll show you the basic building blocks of any script and introduce you to some sample scripts that use each building block in a particular administrative task. This is really the meat of administrative scripting, and you'll be able to write useful scripts when you're finished with this chapter.

### *Chapter 6: Input and Output*

You can make your scripts more flexible by adding the ability to dynamically change computer, user, and domain names, along with other information. In this chapter, I'll show you how your script can collect information it needs to run and dynamically alter itself to take advantage of that information.

### *Chapter 7: Manipulating Numbers*

This chapter will explain how scripts can manipulate numbers, making it easier to create scripts that work with numeric data, such as user account data. I'll also introduce you to VBScript's numeric data handling and conversion commands, putting you on the path to some great scripting techniques.

### Chapter 8: Manipulating Strings

Strings—a fancy word for *text data*—are at the heart of most scripting tasks. In this chapter, I'll show you how VBScript deals with strings and how you can easily integrate them into your scripts.

### Chapter 9: Manipulating Other Types of Data

Aside from text and numbers, your scripts may need to deal with dates, times, bytes, and other forms of data to accomplish specific administrative tasks. In this chapter, I'll show you how VBScript handles these other data types and how you can use them in your own scripts.

### Chapter 10: Controlling the Flow of Execution

The best administrative scripts can respond to changing conditions with internal logic, called *control-of-flow*. In this chapter, I'll show you how your scripts can be made to evaluate various conditions and respond accordingly, perform repetitive tasks, and much more.

### Chapter 11: Built-in Scripting Objects

Much of VBScript's power comes from its capability to join various operating system objects, and in this chapter, I'll introduce you to your first set of those objects. You'll learn how to manipulate network information, map drives, and much more—pretty much everything you need to write effective logon scripts.

### Chapter 12: Working with the File System

A common use of scripting is to manipulate files and folders, and in this chapter, I'll introduce you to the VBScript FileSystemObject, which provides a complete object model for working with the file system. You'll learn to build a utility that scans IIS log files for error messages, a useful script for any environment!

### Chapter 13: Putting It All Together: Your First Script

This is where you'll put everything from Part II together. You'll be creating a script that rotates IIS log files, keeping the past 30 days' worth of files in a special archive folder. I'll guide you through the complete process of designing, writing, testing, and troubleshooting the script. In fact, I'll deliberately introduce some logic errors into the script so that you can see the debugging process in action.

## Part III: Windows Management Instrumentation and Active Directory Services Interface

With the glue of VBScript under your belt, I'll dive into the two most powerful technologies for administering Windows: Windows Management Instrumentation (WMI) and the Active Directory Services Interface (ADSI). These technologies provide administrative access to, and control over, nearly every aspect of the Windows operating system, from Windows NT to Windows Server 2003.

### *Chapter 14: Working with ADSI Providers*

Despite its name, ADSI isn't just for Active Directory. In this chapter, I'll show you how ADSI can be used to interface with NT, Active Directory, Novell NDS, Exchange Server, and other types of directory services. I'll provide some basic examples of the types of tasks you can perform with ADSI to get you started.

### *Chapter 15: Manipulating Domains*

With the ADSI basics out of the way, I'll focus on manipulating domain information in a script. You'll learn how to query domain information, modify domain policies like password length, and much more.

### *Chapter 16: Manipulating Users and Groups*

In this chapter, you'll learn how to write scripts that query and modify user and group information. This is one of the most common tasks you'll perform with VBScript, and I'll include plenty of useful examples.

### *Chapter 17: Understanding WMI*

WMI provides a hook into just about every portion of the Windows operating system, making it an incredibly useful tool for administrative scripts. In this chapter, I'll introduce you to WMI and show you a preview of what you can use it for in your environment.

### Chapter 18: Querying Basic WMI Information

Do you want to find out which users in your organization have a Pentium 4 computer? This chapter will show you how to write your own basic WMI queries, including those that involve remote machines. You'll also learn basic WMI manipulation, which lets you modify local and remote machine settings from within a script.

### Chapter 19: Querying Complex WMI Information

Some WMI queries are more complex, such as querying the IP addresses from multiple network adapters in multiple remote computers. This chapter provides clear examples of these more complex WMI tasks, helping you learn to write enterprise management scripts.

### Chapter 20: Putting It All Together: Your First WMI/ADSI Script

This is where it all comes together. I'll walk you through the process of designing, writing, testing, and debugging a complete WMI/ADSI script from scratch. You'll finish this chapter with a concrete example of the administrative capabilities of these technologies, and then you'll be ready to start writing your own scripts.

## Part IV: Creating Administrative Web Pages

One popular use of Web technologies inside corporate networks is to provide user self-service pages, such as a simple Web page where users can reset their own passwords, if necessary. In Part IV, I'll give you a crash course on IIS and Active Server Pages (ASP) and show you how to start building your own administrative Web pages.

### Chapter 21: Active Server Pages Crash Course

ASP is a great way to create effective administrative Web pages. I'm not going to try to make you a Web developer or an HTML expert; the Web pages you'll create in this chapter won't be pretty, but they'll be incredibly effective.

### *Chapter 22: Adding Administrative Script to a Web Page*

After you have a basic Web page ready, you can start adding script to it to make the Web page perform administrative tasks. I'll provide examples of real-world tasks that you can start using in your environment right away.

### *Chapter 23: Web Page Security Overview*

Web pages have special security concerns, which I'll focus on in this chapter. I'll explain how IIS 5.0 and 6.0 process Web pages, what you can and cannot easily accomplish from within a Web page, and how you can create a secure, stable environment for Web-based administrative scripts.

### *Chapter 24: Putting It All Together: Your First Administrative Web Page*

You're now ready to design, write, run, test, and debug your own administrative Web pages, and in this chapter, I'll step you through the entire progression. When you're finished, you'll not only have a ready-to-run administrative Web page to use, you'll also be ready to start creating your own Web pages from scratch. Again, they might not be pretty, but they'll be incredibly functional and useful.

## Part V: Advanced Scripting Techniques

As you become a more experienced scripter, you'll be ready to start saving time and be more secure, with advanced techniques like script encryption, scripting components, script security, and so forth. In this part of the book, I'll give you a comprehensive look at each of these technologies and show you how to put them into use in your own environment.

### *Chapter 25: Modular Script Programming*

If you find yourself cutting and pasting code—or worse, retyping it—this is the chapter for you. I'll introduce you to modular scripting concepts, which make it easier to reuse code between various scripts, saving you time and effort! By way of example, we'll start with a complex script that contains lots of useful code, and then break it down into easily reused modules.

### Chapter 26: Using Script Components

Windows Script Components are the easy way to create your own fully encapsulated chunks of script, each of which performs a useful task. Building on the examples in Chapter 25, I'll show you how to create and use script components to make administrative scripting faster and easier. You'll come away with a whole library of script components that you can start using immediately!

### Chapter 27: Encoded Scripts

Are you worried that others will peek into your scripts and steal your ideas? Scripting encryption helps protect your scripts from both Peeping Toms and potential misuse, so I'll show you how to set up, deploy, and use script encryption within your environment in this chapter.

### Chapter 28: Scripting Security

Some folks think Microsoft made a huge mistake when it included VBScript in the Windows operating system, but I disagree. Properly configured, scripting can be as safe as any other type of application. In this chapter, I'll explain scripting security concepts and introduce you to the tools that can make scripting a safe and valuable part of any computing environment.

## Part VI: Ready-to-Run Examples

I figured a great way to wrap up the book would be a whole section on ready-made example scripts that you can start using in your own environment. Additionally, these scripts—like every other script in this book—will have complete, line-by-line explanations, making them a perfect reference guide as you start to create your own scripts from scratch.

### Chapter 29: Logon and Logoff Scripts

I'll use this chapter to present more complex logon and logoff scripts and to give you some ideas for how scripting can make these important scripts more effective. Of course, the line-by-line explanations will make each script a useful reference for customizing your own scripts.

#### *Chapter 30: Windows and Domain Administration Scripts*

Automating domain administration is probably one of the big reasons you started looking at scripting in the first place, so I'll use this chapter to present a number of examples of tasks that scripts can perform. The detailed explanations with each script will help you rip them apart and customize them for your own use.

#### *Chapter 31: Network Administration Scripts*

Network administration is ideally suited for scripting, and in this chapter, I'll provide a handful of examples that will show you what's possible. The line-by-line explanations will make it easy to put these into use in your own environment.

#### *Chapter 32: WMI and ADSI Scripts*

These can be the toughest scripts to write due to the complexity and flexibility of WMI and ADSI. In this chapter, I'll provide you with several ready-to-use scripts for common tasks like querying WMI, creating users and groups, and more. These scripts can be easily modified and incorporated into your own scripts, saving you scripting time!

### Part VII: Appendix

#### *Appendix: Administrator's Quick Script Reference*

One of the toughest parts about VBScript is that it contains so much functionality. It's usually pretty easy to figure out *what* you want a script to do; the tough part is often figuring out *how* to make VBScript do it! In this appendix, I'll provide you with an alphabetical list of common tasks and give the VBScript commands that perform each task. You can use this reference along with the VBScript documentation to make designing and writing scripts much easier.

## Preparing to Use This Book

Before you dive in, you should make sure that your computers are ready for VBScript. Fortunately, any computer with Windows 2000 or later is ready to go out of the box, and I'll assume that you're doing your development work on either a Windows 2000–, Windows XP–, or Windows Server 2003–based computer.

## Typographical Elements

Books on programming can benefit a great deal from easy-to-understand typestyles and elements like the ones I'll explain here. These typestyles and elements are designed to make the text easier to follow and to call your attention to special concerns.

Boldfaced type will be used to set off material that should be typed into the computer; boldfaced also will be used to signify onscreen menu and/or dialog box selections. For example, "select **Run** from the Start menu, type **wbemtest**, and click **OK**" sets off the menu selection, what you need to type onscreen, and what should be clicked from the dialog box.

Blocks of code and code lines that appear within the text will appear in a monospaced font, as in, "to change the contents of a variable, you can use something like `Var1 = Trim(Var1)`."

---

**TIP** Tips will provide shortcuts and other "insider advice" about scripting that you'll find valuable.

---

**NOTE** Notes will provide cautions and other clarifications that will help you avoid problems or further clarify complex concepts.

---

I'll also direct you to material that more thoroughly explains particular concepts, VBScript commands, and so forth. Although I'm not a big fan of flipping back and forth through a book, these cross-references will allow you to remain focused within each chapter and will guide you to more detailed explanations, when appropriate.

Finally, there are times when it is necessary to present an extended explanation of something that isn't critical to the task at hand. In those cases, I'll use a sidebar. A sidebar is a cue that the information is useful, but it's not really key to the main text; you're welcome to skip the sidebar and come back to it later if you like.

### Sidebars

Sidebars make it easier to cover slightly off-topic information without distracting you from the main text.

### ➤➤ Sample Scripts

Obviously, a book on scripting is going to have many code listings. To make these as useful as possible, I introduce each example script with a special head style, and present it in a listing by itself with no comments.

**Listing P.1** *A Sample Script.* Accepts a name, and then redisplays that name.

```
'Get the user's name
sName = InputBox("What is your name?")

'Display the user's name
MsgBox "Your name is " & sName
```

After I present each script, I'll briefly review any changes you might need to make to get the script running in your environment, such as changing computer or domain names. You'll find each complete script included on the CD that accompanies this book. I've created a separate folder for each chapter and named the script files by their listing number for easy reference.

### ➤➤ Sample Scripts—Explained

For each script in this book, I'll include a line-by-line explanation of the script, so that you understand exactly what's going on. For example:

First, the sample script will display a dialog box where the user can type his name. By default, this dialog box includes an **OK** and **Cancel** button; I'm not providing any way to detect the **Cancel** button in this script, so I'm assuming the user will type something and click **OK**.

```
'Get the user's name
sName = InputBox("What is your name?")
```

Finally, the script uses the `MsgBox` statement to redisplay the user's name. Notice the use of the ampersand operator (`&`) to tack on the contents of the variable `sName`, which stores whatever the user typed into the input box.

```
'Display the user's name
MsgBox "Your name is " & sName
```

Walk-throughs like this one will help you become more familiar with VBScript, what each command does, and exactly how each example script works.

# Acknowledgments

Books never seem to write themselves, no matter how much money I leave out for the elves at night. Fortunately, behind every author like myself stands an incredible team of professionals, and the folks behind this book were truly at the top of their industry. So, special thanks to my literary agent at Studio B, Neil Salkind, and my acquisitions editor at Addison-Wesley, Sondra Scott: Thanks so much for your hard work in taking this book through the acquisitions process! I'd also like to offer a special thanks to technical editors Bob Reselman and Scott Worley for what was probably the most professional, thorough review of any book I've written. And a big thanks to all the other behind-the-scenes folks at Pearson Education who worked so hard to bring this book to market.

On a more personal level, I'd like to thank the folks in my life who make a project like this worthwhile: My parents, Rhonda and John; my ferrets, Clyde, Ziggy, Buffy, Pepper, and little Tigger; and my close and supportive friends, Sonya, Chris, Spencer, George, and Tom. I'd also like to thank my business partner, Derek Melber, who has been so patient while I've been devoting time to this book. I'd also like to thank Keith, Dian, and Kris at *Microsoft® Certified Professional Magazine* for all of their personal and editorial support. Finally, I'd like to thank all the folks at Microsoft that I've enjoyed working with through the years: Amy, Dr. Todd, Mary Beth, Ben, Harold, Kris, Christine, Kim, Steve, Deb, Chuck, Peggy, Bucky, Barb, Alice, Joel, and Andy.

Don Jones
BrainCore.Net, LLC
February 2004

# About the Author

**Don Jones** is an independent consultant, speaker, and author, and a founding partner of BrainCore.Net, the world leader in exam development and exam delivery technologies for the information technology industry. Don's focus has always been on high-end Windows administration topics, and his recent books include *Special Edition Using Microsoft® .NET Enterprise Servers* (published by Que) and *Windows® Server 2003 Weekend Crash Course* (published by Wiley). Don is also the creator and series editor of the Delta Guides, a series of books published by Sams designed to help experienced administrators quickly come up to speed on new versions of Microsoft server technologies. Don coauthored the first book in the series, *Windows Server 2003 Delta Guide*. Don is now firmly based in Las Vegas, Nevada, after spending more than two years traveling the United States in a 40-foot RV.

PART I

# Introduction to Windows Administrative Scripting

CHAPTER 1

# Scripting Concepts and Terminology

**IN THIS CHAPTER**

Completely new to scripting? This is the chapter for you! You'll learn how scripts work, what they are, and how Windows uses them. You'll also learn about key security issues, which will be covered in more detail in later chapters.

In the past few years, scripting has become increasingly popular with Windows administrators. Visual Basic, Scripting Edition—commonly known as VBScript—has become especially popular, due to its ease of use and incredible flexibility. Unfortunately, most books on scripting seemed to be focused toward developers, or at least toward Windows administrators with a strong software development background. The result is that most administrators think that scripting is too complex for them, which simply isn't true. In this book, I'll introduce you to scripting from a purely administrative standpoint, starting with this chapter, where I'll explain exactly what I mean by "scripting," and how it all fits into Windows administration.

## What Is Scripting?

*Scripting* means different things to different people. Some folks, for example, would define *script* as any series of computer commands that are executed in a sequence, including so-called scripts written in the MS-DOS batch language. These batch files were the mainstay of administrative automation for many years, and many administrators still rely heavily upon them today. Other people define scripting as small computer programs written in a high-level scripting language, such as VBScript.

Nobody's really wrong, and scripting can mean all of these things. Personally, I fall into the latter camp, believing that it has to be written in

VBScript, JavaScript, or some other high-end language to earn the name *scripting*. Although batch files are certainly a means of automating administrative tasks in Windows, they don't really have the power or flexibility of modern scripting languages—nor should you expect them to. Batch files are based on a command language that's two decades old!

For the purposes of this book, *scripting* will refer to the act of creating, executing, and utilizing small computer programs that are written in a high-end scripting language, specifically VBScript.

## Script Hosts

Scripts start out life as simple text files. Try this: Open Windows Notepad on a Windows XP computer, and type the following text:

```
Set SNSet = GetObject("winmgmts:").InstancesOf
  ("Win32_OperatingSystem")
for each SN in SNSet
 MsgBox "The serial number for the installed OS is: " & SN.SerialNumber
next
```

Save the file as "SampleScript.vbs." Be sure to include the filename in double quotation marks, or Notepad will append a TXT filename extension. Now, locate the file in Windows Explorer. Make sure it has a VBS filename extension and double-click it. Provided you're running Windows XP and VBScript hasn't been disabled on your computer, you should see a small dialog box containing the serial number of your operating system. Congratulations, you've just scripted!

---

**NOTE** For the time being, you don't need to worry about how this script does what it does. In later chapters, I'll explain what each of these four lines of code accomplishes. If you just can't wait, jump to Chapters 17 through 19, where I demonstrate how to use Windows Management Instrumentation to retrieve serial numbers and other operating system information.

---

What actually happens when you double-click the VBS file? You can find out easily enough. From any Windows Explorer window, select **Folder Options** from the **Tools** menu. Select the **File Types** tab and locate VBS in the list. As shown in Figure 1.1, the VBS filename extension is associated

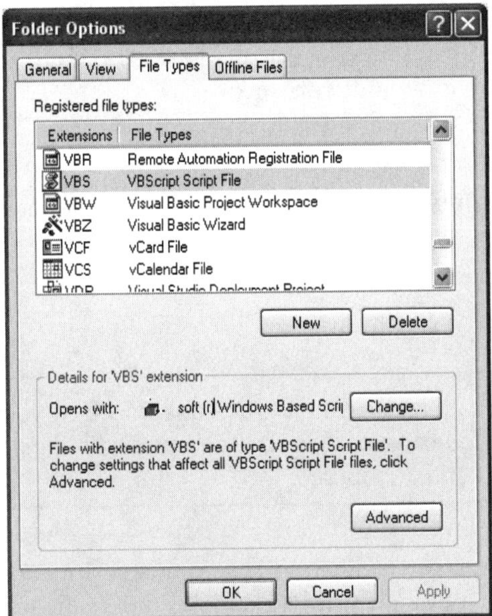


**Figure 1.1** File association for the VBS file type

with the Microsoft Windows Based Script Host. Whenever you double-click a VBS file, Windows fires up the Script Host, tells it which script you double-clicked, and lets the Script Host run the script. It's similar to what happens when you double-click a DOC file: Windows fires up Microsoft Word, tells it which file to open, and your document appears.

So, what is the Microsoft Windows Based Script Host (WSH)? It's a built-in component of Windows 2000, Windows XP, and Windows Server 2003. In fact, it's under Windows File Protection for those operating systems, meaning you can't delete or remove the WSH executable, `Wscript.exe`. WSH is also included with Windows Me, is an optional installation component in Windows 98, and can be added to Windows NT 4.0 and Windows 95 through a free download from www.Microsoft.com/scripting.

---

**TIP** The latest version of WSH is 5.6, and you can download it for free from www.Microsoft.com/scripting. WSH is packaged in a Windows Installer file (MSI), so you can easily deploy it to your client computers via Windows Group Policy.

---

WSH isn't included with some versions of Windows. In fact, WSH is present in many Microsoft products, in various versions. Here's where you can find WSH, along with the default versions:

- Windows 98 (optional), v1.0
- Windows NT 4.0 Option Pack, v1.0
- Windows 2000, v2.0
- Windows XP, v5.6
- Windows Server 2003, v5.6

---

**NOTE** For the purposes of this book, I'll always assume that you're running v5.6 of WSH. If you aren't, you can upgrade for free by downloading the newest version from www.Microsoft.com/scripting.

---

WSH is simply a Windows application that reads scripts and executes them. Interestingly, VBScript is *not* implemented right within `WScript.exe` itself. WSH is actually intended to be extensible, and it supports a number of scripting languages besides VBScript.

WSH does have a number of built-in functions, which is why it's nice to have the latest version—newer versions of more built-in functions. WSH can, for example, map network drives, connect to printers, work with environment variables, and modify the registry—all useful things to be able to do from within an administrative script.

---

**NOTE** Other applications—such as Internet Explorer, Exchange Server, SQL Server, and IIS' Active Server Pages—can serve as script hosts, too. The nice part about learning to create Windows administration scripts in VBScript is that you can quickly learn to create SQL scripts, Exchange scripts, or even Active Server Pages, all using the same scripting language.

---

## ActiveX Scripting Languages

VBScript is just one of many *ActiveX Scripting Languages.* These languages are written to a specification developed by Microsoft, and scripts written in these languages can be executed by WSH. Each ActiveX Scripting Language is implemented by a *scripting engine.* Usually, this DLL file interfaces with `WScript.exe` to interpret scripts, one line at a time, so that WSH can execute them. Microsoft maintains two ActiveX Scripting Languages: VBScript and JScript. JScript is Microsoft's implementation of ECMA-Script, which is the industry-standard version of Netscape's JavaScript scripting language.

---

**NOTE** Ignoring company copyrights, trade names, and other legal matters, JScript, ECMAScript, and JavaScript are more or less interchangeable terms.

---

The scripting engines are maintained separately from WSH and carry their own version numbers. However, both the latest version of VBScript and JScript are included with the basic WSH installation, so you don't need to worry about getting them individually.

Other companies have produced ActiveX Scripting Languages, too. For example, VideoScript is an independent scripting language that works with WSH (www.videoscript.com). PerlScript and LiveScript are other popular ActiveX Scripting Languages.

Scripting languages all have a few common characteristics.

- They are *interpreted.* That means the scripting engine reads each line of script, one at a time, and then executes it. Execution requires the WSH to translate the scripted instructions into native Windows API calls. Interpreted languages are slower than *compiled* languages like Visual Basic 6.0, where the compiler translates the entire program into native Windows code all at once, saving time later when the program is executed.
- They are text based. In other words, you can create scripts with a simple text editor like Notepad. The downside is that anyone can read your script with Notepad, too. Most software applications' code is compiled into a native binary format, making it very difficult for end-users to read the code. Microsoft does offer an encryption utility (discussed in Chapter 27) that allows you to protect your source code from prying eyes.
- They are *native.* In other words, your scripts will only execute on Windows, because WSH itself will only execute on Windows. Contrast this with languages like Java, which can be compiled and executed on any platform for which a Java Virtual Machine (JVM) is available.
- They are easy to deploy. Unlike compiled Visual Basic 6.0 applications, scripts don't usually require a bunch of DLLs and other files

that you have to deploy, register, and so forth. Scripts can generally be copied from one computer to another and executed as-is.

Perhaps the most powerful feature of VBScript is its capability to interface with Microsoft's Component Object Model.

### VBScript and .NET: What Does the Future Hold?

I'm often asked how the release of VB.NET and the .NET Framework will affect VBScript. After all, you don't hear much mention of "VBScript.NET!"

It's a complicated question. The easy answer is this: Microsoft invested a lot of time and money getting administrators to use VBScript, and administrators are using it. WSH will probably be included in new releases of Windows for some time to come, even if Microsoft doesn't do any further development. However, Microsoft did release a new version of WSH for Windows XP, when .NET was still under development, so it's quite possible that VBScript will have a parallel life with .NET.

Keep in mind, though, that .NET is, in many ways, a scripting language itself. It isn't compiled in the same sense that Visual Basic 6.0 applications were compiled, and new versions of Windows—starting with Windows Server 2003—will come with the .NET Common Language Runtime (CLR), essentially .NET's version of WSH. Therefore, administrators will be able to use language like VB.NET to produce easily deployed administrative scripts.

.NET makes it easier to do a lot of administrative tasks, because it exposes so much of Windows' native functionality. However, the .NET learning curve is quite a bit steeper than VBScript's, so I definitely expect administrators to stick with the easier scripting language, at least for the time being.

VBScript—and JScript even more so—has a long life ahead of it in Web browsers. Web browsers, including Microsoft Internet Explorer, can't execute client-side .NET code, leaving VBScript and JScript as the only viable options for client-side Web programming. Although that type of programming isn't the focus of this book, it demonstrates that VBScript is far from obsolete and remains a powerful, viable administrative tool.

## The Component Object Model (COM)

Software developers have always been encouraged to develop reusable code. Imagine that you created some piece of code that retrieves the TCP/IP settings of a remote computer. Many administrators might want to use that code again. So how do you make your code available to them in an easy-to-use way?

Microsoft's answer is COM, the Component Object Model. COM is a specification that describes how code can be packaged into *objects*, making them self-contained, easy (relatively speaking) to deploy, and easy for other developers to use. Physically, COM objects are usually implemented in DLL files—which, if you check out the contents of a Windows computer's System32 folder, should tell you how pervasive COM is!

VBScript is completely capable of utilizing COM objects. That's a powerful feature, because most of Windows' functionality—and most other Microsoft applications' functionality—is rolled up into COM components. Working with e-mail, Active Directory, Windows Management Instrumentation, networking, the registry, and more is all possible through COM components, and therefore through VBScript. I'll cover objects in more detail, including examples of how to use them in script beginning in Chapter 5, and show you how to really take advantage of them in Chapter 11.

VBScript is even capable of creating COM components. That means you can use VBScript to create your IP-retrieval software, package that software as a COM component, and distribute it to other administrators. This feature of scripting is called *Windows Script Components.* Chapter 25 is all about modular script programming, including Windows Script Components.

## Critical Scripting Security Issues

Sadly, Microsoft implemented VBScript without much thought for the consequences. Windows XP, Microsoft's newest client operating system, shipped with full scripting capability built-in and enabled by default. The power of VBScript can be used not only for beneficial administrative tasks, but also for malicious hacking, and many viruses are based on VBScript or another ActiveX Scripting Language.

Administrators have reacted to the security threat of scripts in a number of ways.

- Deleting `WScript.exe`. Unfortunately, this doesn't work on Windows 2000 or later, because `WScript.exe` is under Windows File Protection. Delete it and it just comes back.

- Disassociating the VB, VBS, JS, and other WSH file extensions, or re-associating them to simply open in Notepad rather than in WSH. This effectively disables scripting.
- Deploying antivirus software, such as Norton AntiVirus, which detects script execution and halts it.

Regrettably, disabling scripting usually disables it for good, meaning you can't use scripting for logon scripts, administrative tasks, and other beneficial purposes. There's a middle road that you can take however, which authorizes only certain scripts for execution. This middle road helps protect you against scripts written by hackers, while still allowing scripts to be used for administrative and logon purposes.

Fortunately, Microsoft's come to the table with security improvements that can make scripting safe again, and I've devoted Chapter 28 to the topic of scripting security.

## Review

VBScript is one of many available ActiveX Scripting Languages. The scripts that you write are executed by the Windows Script Host (WSH), which is physically implemented as `WScript.exe` and available for (or included with) all 32-bit Windows operating systems. VBScript—like other ActiveX Scripting Languages—is especially powerful because it can interface with COM, Microsoft's Component Object Model. COM allows VBScript to be infinitely extended to perform other functions, including the majority of the Windows operating system's functions. In fact, COM integration sets VBScript apart from other so-called scripting technologies like old MS-DOS-style batch files.

However, VBScript does bring up some important security issues that you'll need to learn to deal with in your environment. Microsoft's regrettable lack of planning when it comes to scripting has resulted in a huge number of script-based viruses, making scripting a tool for both good and evil. Nonetheless, you can learn to configure your environment so that only approved ("good") scripts run, allowing you to use the power and flexibility of script-based administration, while protecting your environment from malicious scripts.

**COMING UP**

Chapter 2 focuses on running scripts, editing scripts, and writing scripts. You'll learn about basic and more advanced script authoring tools, and the various ways that you can launch scripts within Windows.

CHAPTER 2

# Running Scripts

**IN THIS CHAPTER**

It is time to start running—and more importantly, editing—scripts. In this chapter, you'll learn the various ways to execute a script, and learn about the ins and outs of creating and editing scripts. You'll also have your first experience with an administrative script!

Suppose you have several scripts ready to run—what do you do with them? Do you load them into Visual Basic and compile them? How do you distribute them to your users for use as logon scripts? What about when you're ready to start writing your own scripts? What tools are available, and how well do they work? This chapter is designed to introduce you to your scripting toolbox, the bits you'll need to write, run, edit, and debug your administrative scripts.

## Windows Script Host

The most common way to run scripts is to use `WScript.exe`, the graphical version of the Windows Script Host (WSH), which I introduced in Chapter 1. WScript is registered to handle common scripting file extensions, so simply double-clicking a .VB or .VBS file will normally execute `WScript.exe`, then ask it to execute the double-clicked script.

To see WScript in action, try this:

1. Right-click your desktop and select **New**; then point to **Text File**.
2. Rename the new text file to Sample1.vbs.
3. Right-click the file and choose **Edit.** By default, Windows registered Notepad as the handler for the Edit action, so a blank Notepad window will open.
4. Type **WScript.Echo "Displaying Output"** and save the file.
5. Close Notepad.

6. Create another new text file on the desktop, and name this one Sample2.vbs.
7. Edit Sample2.vbs and enter the following:

```
Wscript.Echo "Here we go..."

Dim V
V = InputBox("What is your name?")
MsgBox "Hello, " & V
```

These aren't terribly complex scripts, but they'll serve to illustrate some important concepts. First, double-click Sample1.vbs. If your system is properly configured, you'll see a dialog box like the one in Figure 2.1. Click **OK** on the dialog box to dismiss it and end the first script. Now, double-click Sample2.vbs. It'll start with a similar dialog box, as shown in Figure 2.2. Then, as shown in Figure 2.3, you'll be prompted to enter your name.

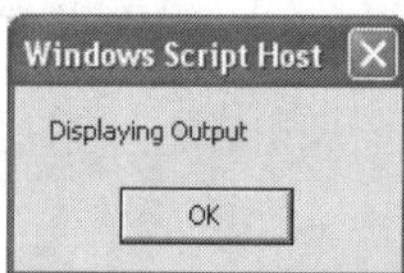


**Figure 2.1** Basic graphical dialog box from a script

**Figure 2.2** Starting dialog box

**Figure 2.3** Prompting you for your name

**Figure 2.4** Addressing you by name

Finally, Figure 2.4 shows the last dialog box, which addresses you by name.

**TIP** What you've just seen is the sum total of VBScript's user interface capabilities. If you were hoping to use VBScript to create complex dialog boxes and graphical controls, forget about it! You'll need a full programming language, like Visual Basic 6.0 or VB.NET, to create a more complex user interface.

What does all this buy you? First, you've experienced the type of graphical user interface that VBScript can provide: simple input and output. You can get a tad more complex and create dialog boxes with Yes and No buttons, or Abort, Retry, and Ignore buttons, but that's about the extent of it.

This script is simple enough that you should be able to figure out exactly what each line of code is doing. `Wscript.Echo` obviously displays a dialog box with some text in it, and was used in both scripts. `Dim V` creates a new variable named "`V`" (more on those in Chapter 5), and the `InputBox` function collects some information and places it into the variable. Finally, `MsgBox` seems to duplicate `Wscript.Echo`, displaying some specified information in a dialog box.

The big question on your mind is probably, "What's the difference between this Echo and that MsgBox?" There *is* a difference, although it's subtle.

## Command-Line Scripts

Most of the time, you'll likely use `WScript.exe` to execute your scripts, and when I refer to WSH I'll generally do so as a nickname for WScript. However, WSH consists of one other executable, `Cscript.exe`, which is used to execute scripts on a command line.

The difference with Cscript is that it doesn't provide any non-graphical means of collecting user input. In other words, although you can use a

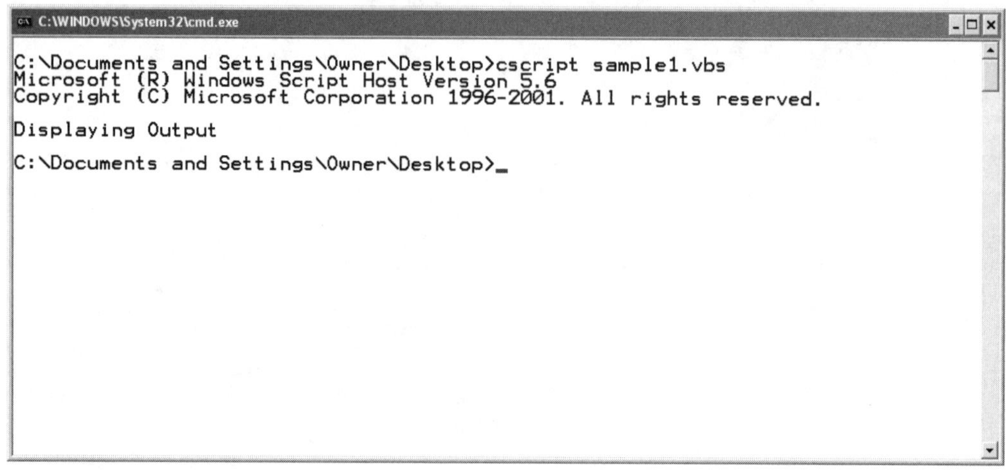


**Figure 2.5** Executing Sample1.vbs with Cscript.exe

Cscript script to display command-line output, you can't use it to get input from the command-line window. Try this and you'll see what I mean:

1. Open a command-line window.
2. Change to your Desktop folder.
3. Enter **Cscript sample1.vbs**.

You should see something like Figure 2.5: a basic command-line prompt, with "Displaying Output" shown in the command line. That's the work of `WScript.Echo`: When executed by `WScript.exe`, `Echo` creates a dialog box. When executed by `Cscript.exe`, `Echo` outputs to the command line. This allows you to create scripts that can be run graphically or from a command line. Scripts written with this technique will appear to be natively written for each environment.

Now try the same thing with Sample2.vbs. At first, you'll notice a command line like the one in Figure 2.6, simply displaying the output of `WScript.Echo` as in the previous example. However, when Cscript hits the `InputBox` function, it switches into graphical mode, as shown in Figure 2.7, just like WScript did. Finally, the `MsgBox` command also forces Cscript to display a dialog box, as shown in Figure 2.8 and exactly as WScript did—only `WScript.Echo` is *dual mode*, working differently in WScript or Cscript. Everything else defaults to a graphical mode of operation.

Why should you care about the differences? Someday, you may want to write scripts that can be scheduled for background execution using Task

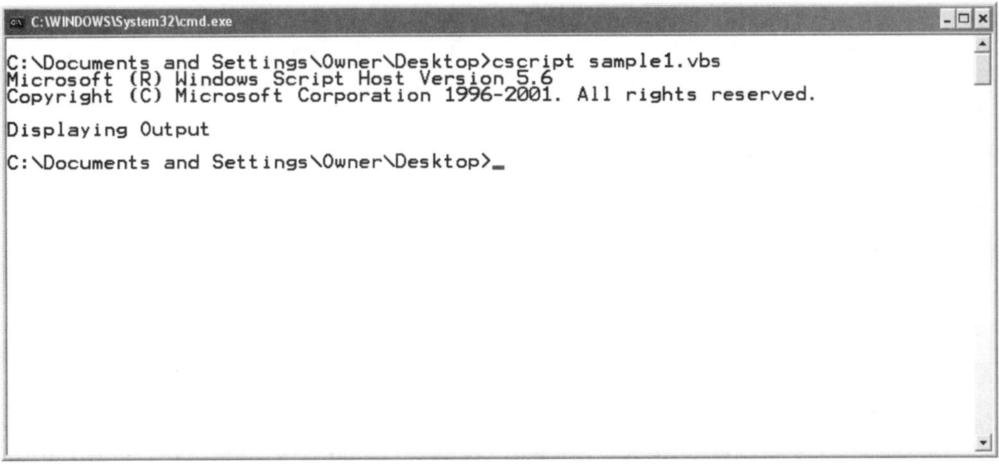


**Figure 2.6** Command-line output of WScript.echo

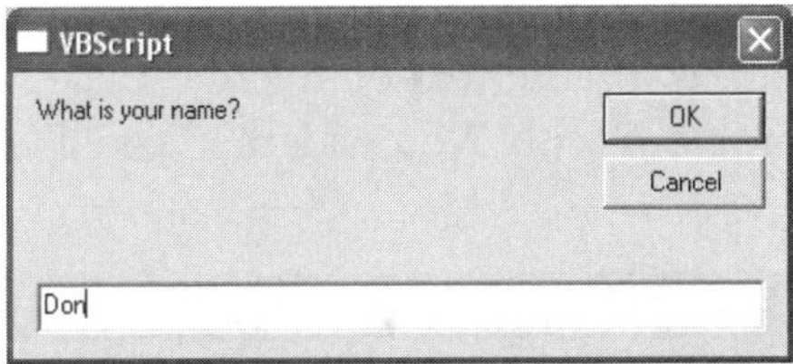


**Figure 2.7** Switching to GUI mode for InputBox

**Figure 2.8** MsgBox is also GUI-only

Scheduler or some other tool. It's always a good idea to have scripts display some kind of output so that you can see what they're doing while you debug them. If you use `Wscript.Echo` for that output, and run your scripts with WScript, you'll see each output message and have to click **OK** to have the script continue. When you go to schedule the script for background execution, you can use Cscript instead. Your output will still display (even though you won't see it), and the script won't wait for someone to click **OK**. Had you used `MsgBox`, Cscript would throw up a dialog box, and your script would stop running until someone clicked **OK.** Because the script would be running in the background as a scheduled task, nobody would ever be *able* to click **OK,** and the script would "hang" forever or until you killed Task Scheduler.

## Notepad and Script Editors

When it comes time to write your scripts, you'll probably take the path of many administrators before you and start with Notepad. It's free, easy to use, and did I mention that *it's free*?! But you'll probably come to a point where you realize that Notepad is making you work too hard, and it'll be time to look at some professional alternatives.

### Bare Bones: Notepad

Notepad, shown in Figure 2.9, is a basic text editor that makes a passable script editor. The biggest problem with Notepad that you'll notice right

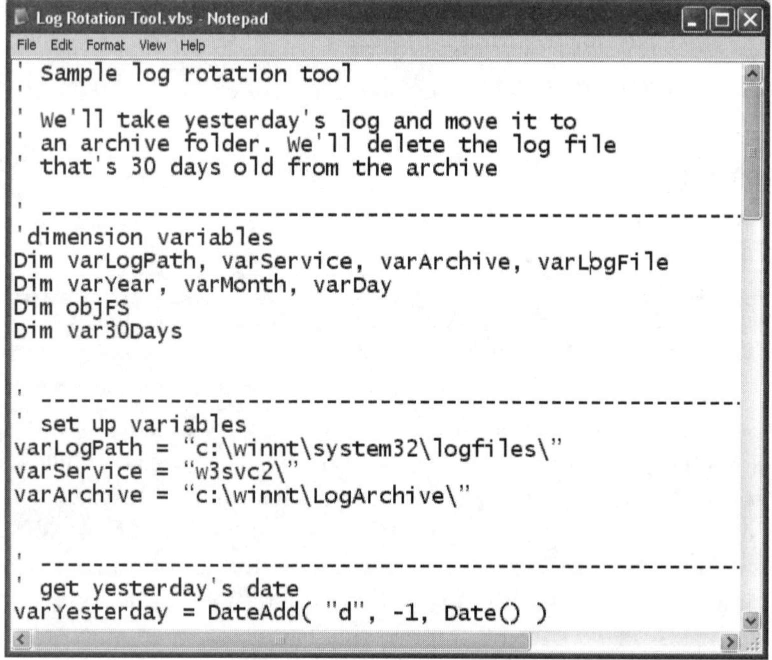


**Figure 2.9** Notepad as a script editor

away is a lack of line numbering. When you get a VBScript error, it'll refer to a specific line number. Notepad *does* have a "Go to line number" feature that lets you type in the offending line number and jump straight to it, but it isn't as satisfying as if Notepad displayed a line number on every line of text.

Notepad also lacks any kind of color-coding, which can make scripting *much* easier, especially for long scripts.

## A Step Up: Programmer's File Editor

Programmer's File Editor, or PFE, is a decent step up from Notepad. As shown in Figure 2.10, PFE can be configured to show line numbers on each line, making it easy to zip straight to the line of code that's causing errors.

PFE doesn't include any VBScript-specific functionality, however, such as color-coding of comment lines, strings, commands, and so forth. It also doesn't provide any kind of debugging integration, which is a nice thing to have for longer, more complex scripts.

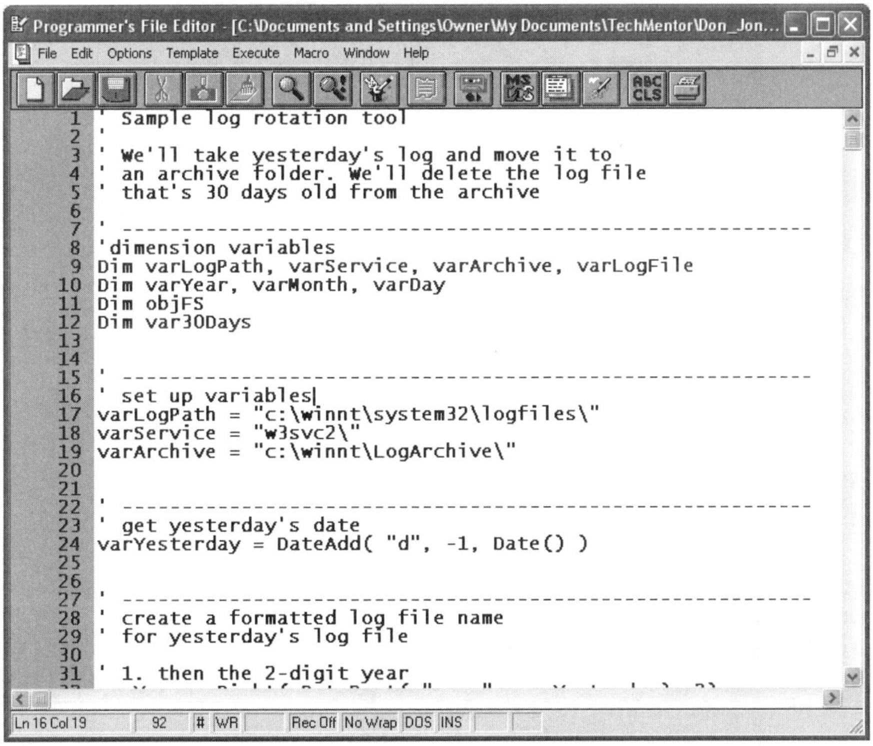
Programmer's File Editor - [C:\Documents and Settings\Owner\My Documents\TechMentor\Don_Jon...
File Edit Options Template Execute Macro Window Help
' Sample log rotation tool
'
' We'll take yesterday's log and move it to
' an archive folder. We'll delete the log file
' that's 30 days old from the archive
'
' ----------------------------------------------------------
'dimension variables
Dim varLogPath, varService, varArchive, varLogFile
Dim varYear, varMonth, varDay
Dim objFS
Dim var30Days
' ----------------------------------------------------------
' set up variables
varLogPath = "c:\winnt\system32\logfiles\"
varService = "w3svc2\"
varArchive = "c:\winnt\LogArchive\"
' ----------------------------------------------------------
' get yesterday's date
varYesterday = DateAdd( "d", -1, Date() )
' ----------------------------------------------------------
' create a formatted log file name
' for yesterday's log file
' 1. then the 2-digit year
Ln 16 Col 19 92 # WR Rec Off No Wrap DOS INS

**Figure 2.10** Programmer's File Editor

PFE is a free tool, although it's no longer under development for new versions. You can download the latest version, 1.01, from www.lancs.ac.uk/people/cpaap/pfe. It's compatible with all 32-bit Windows platforms, and there's even a version for Windows 3.1.

## Script-Specific: VBScript Editors

I have three VBScript-specific editors that I like to use. The first is Adersoft's VbsEdit (www.adersoft.com), shown in Figure 2.11. VbsEdit is currently in version 2.0 and costs $30 for a single-computer license. It provides a number of higher-end features, including:

- Color-coding of syntax, meaning comment lines, commands, and other types of script will show up in different colors.
- Line numbering.

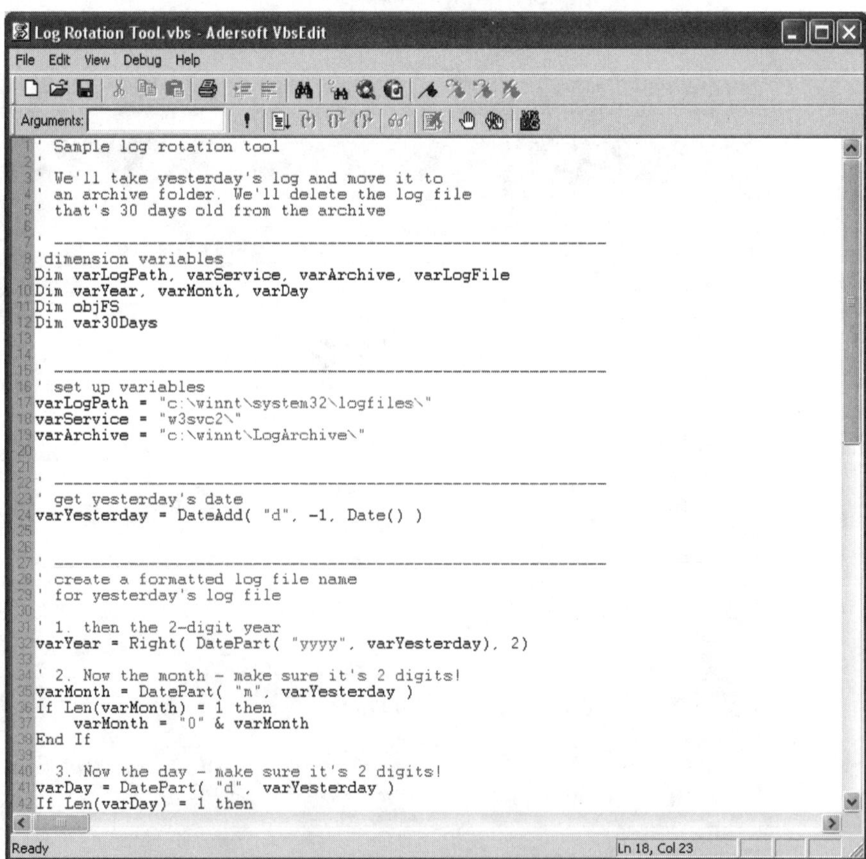


**Figure 2.11** VsbEdit

- Drag-and-drop editing, much like Microsoft Word.
- Auto-capitalization of VBScript commands. This doesn't improve your scripts, but it does make them nicer to read.

VbsEdit also includes a degree of IntelliSense-like functionality. For example, when working with objects, you can type the object's name and a period, and VbsEdit will display a list of properties and methods for that object. I haven't discussed objects in VBScript yet, but trust me when I say that this is a handy feature to have! (I'll get to objects in Chapter 5.)

Finally, VbsEdit has a built-in script debugger. This handy feature lets you run scripts one line at a time, checking variable values and seeing what's going on "under the hood." This is a great way to quickly debug scripts. VbsEdit even allows you to hover your mouse over a variable while the script is running, and it will pop up the value of that variable in a Tooltip. It's a great way to see what your script is doing as you try to track down bugs. Figure 2.12 shows VbsEdit's debugger.

My biggest complaint with VbsEdit—and it's a minor one—is that it doesn't include IntelliSense-like features for normal VBScript commands (you'll see those in PrimalScript, which I'll discuss in a bit). Also, VbsEdit uses its own script debugger, rather than integrating the Microsoft Script Debugger (more on that later in this chapter, too).

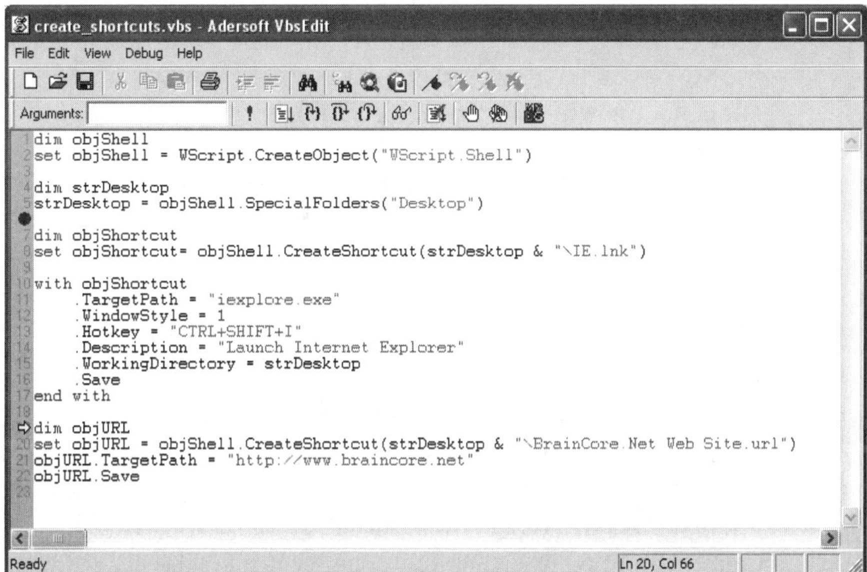


**Figure 2.12** VbsEdit's debugger

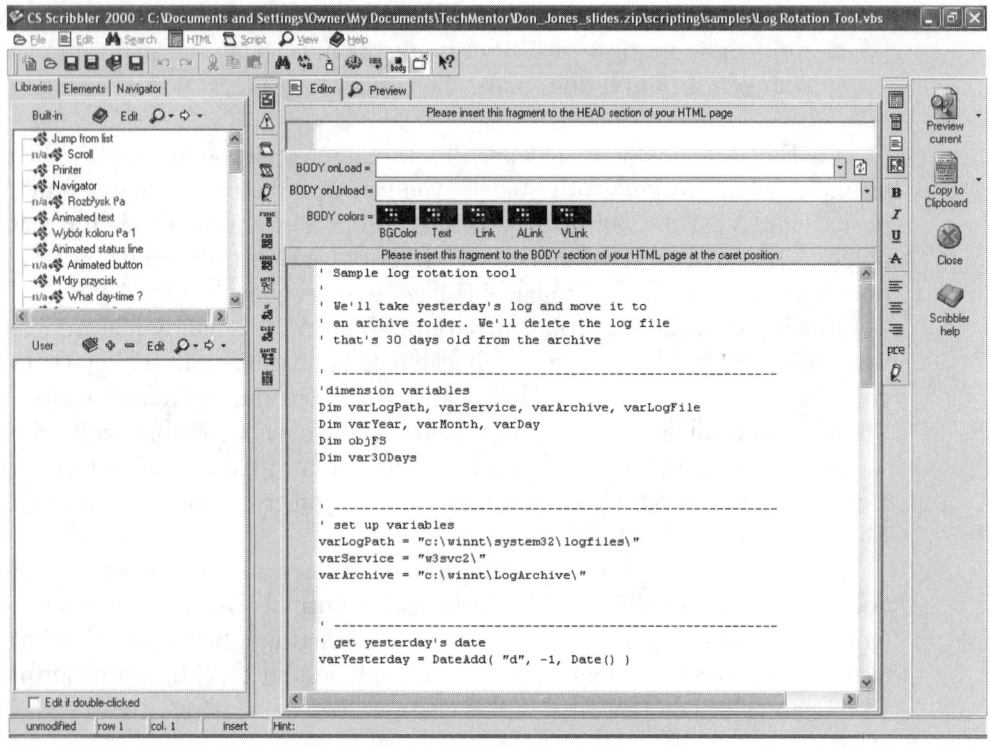


**Figure 2.13** Scribbler 2000

My next editing tool is Scribbler 2000 from Creamsoft (www.creamsoft.com). Shown in Figure 2.13, Scribbler is a solid VBScript editing tool with color-coding, drag-and-drop editing, built-in debugging, and more. Unfortunately, it's geared primarily for Web page scripting, and I find it a bit cumbersome to use in regular administrative scripts. If you plan to work with Web pages, though, you won't find a much better script editor, and Scribbler only costs $35. You can download a free evaluation from the company's Web site.

The "big gun" of VBScript editing is PrimalScript 2.2, which costs a hefty $149 for a single-computer license (www.sapien.com/products.htm). PrimalScript, shown in Figure 2.14, offers the usual VBScript editor frills, like color-coding, line numbering, and so forth. However, as shown in Figure 2.15, PrimalScript offers a true VBScript-specific clone of Microsoft's IntelliSense technology from Visual Studio. Notice in Figure 2.15 that there's a Tooltip displaying the proper syntax for the `DateAdd` statement I'm typing. This handy pop-up saves you from constant round-trips to the VBScript documentation, serving as a quick reminder of which parameters

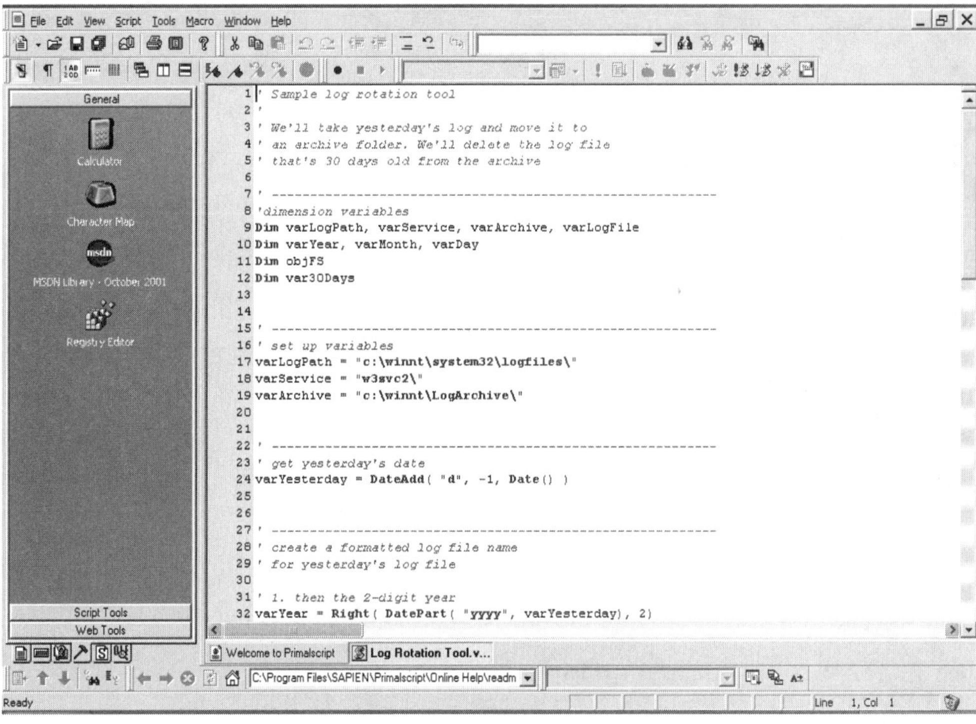


**Figure 2.14** PrimalScript

come in which order. You also get pop-up lists of object properties and methods, as in VbsEdit, automatic capitalization for prettier scripts, and so forth.

Finally, PrimalScript integrates the Microsoft Script Debugger, shown in Figure 2.16. This handy tool, which I'll cover in more detail later in this chapter, lets you step through script one line at a time, making it easier to pinpoint errors and correct coding issues.

---

**NOTE** PrimalScript also supports WinBatch, Ruby, ASP, HTML, PHP, JSP, and a bunch of other scripting languages—it's not VBScript only.

---

To my knowledge, PrimalScript is also the only VBScript editor that integrates script signing, which is a key function of secure scripting environments. By digitally signing scripts, you can instruct your client computers to execute only your scripts, based on their signed identity. (I'll cover script signing and other security topics in Chapter 28.)

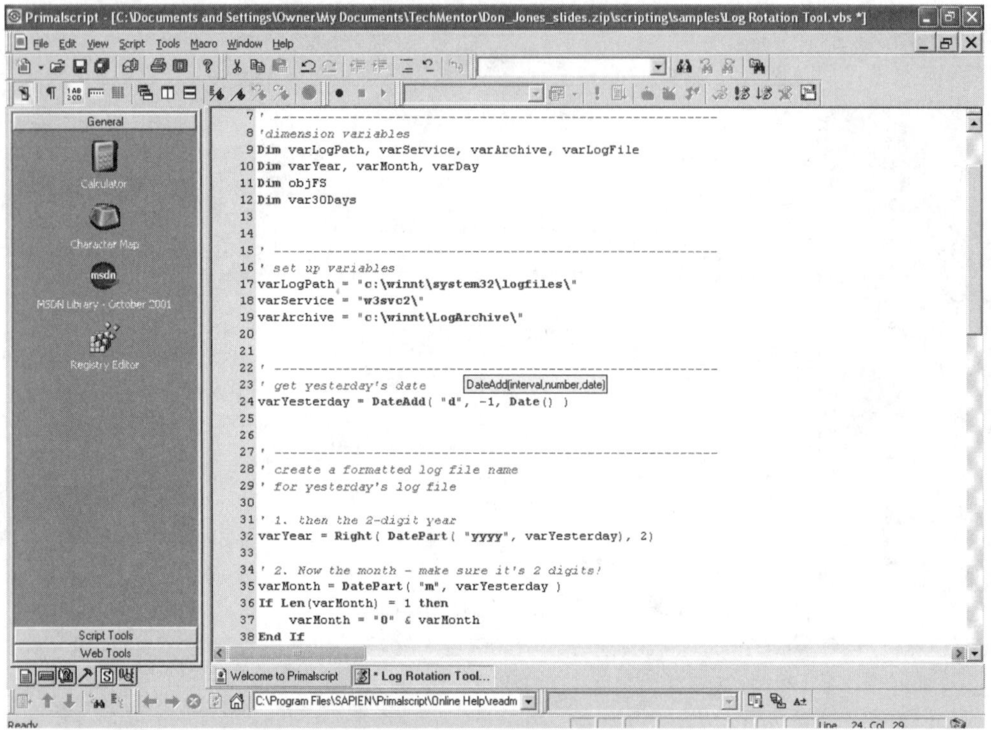


**Figure 2.15** PrimalScript's IntelliSense-like syntax help

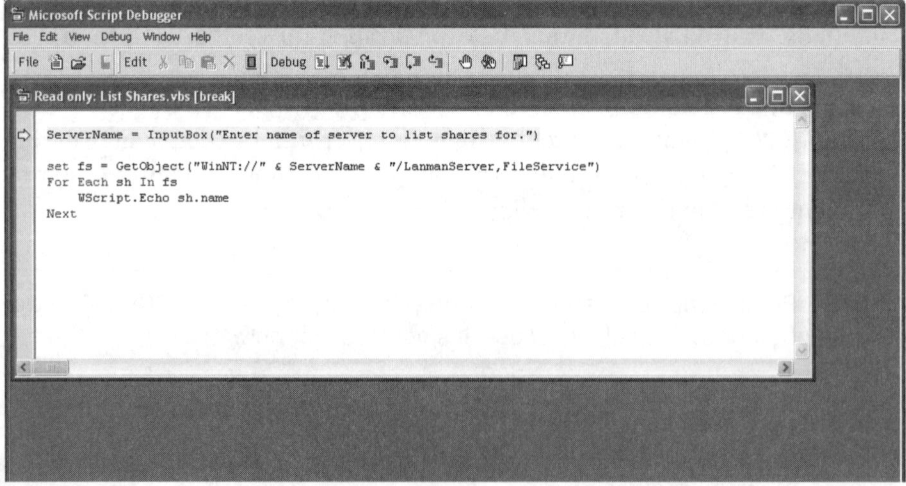


**Figure 2.16** PrimalScript launches the Microsoft Script Debugger with your script ready to go.

## Writing Your First Script

Because I don't expect you to plop down money to start scripting, I'm going to assume that you're either using Notepad or PFE as your script editor. I do highly recommend that you at least get PFE, because it's free and provides the all-important line numbering capability to your scripts. If you've decided to purchase another script editor, great! You shouldn't have any problems following along.

For your first script, I've selected a sample that will tell you which user or users, if any, have a particular file open through a shared folder on a file server. This can be a handy tool to have when you're trying to get to a file that's partially locked because someone else has it open. Listing 2.1 shows the complete script, which you can type into a text file and save as WhoHas.vbs.

**Listing 2.1** *WhoHas.vbs.* Displays the user or users who have a file open.

```
' first, get the server name we want to work with
varServer = InputBox ("Server name to check")

' get the local path of the file to check
varFile= InputBox _
 ("Full path and filename of the file on the " & _
 "server (use the local path as if you were at the " & _
 " server console)")

' bind to the server's file service
set objFS = GetObject("WinNT://" & varServer & "/
  lanmanserver,fileservice")

' scan through the open resources until we
' locate the file we want
varFoundNone = True

' use a FOR...EACH loop to walk through the
' open resources
For Each objRes in objFS.Resources

     ' does this resource match the one we're looking for?
     If objRes.Path = varFile then
```

*continues*

```
            ' we found the file - show who's got it
            varFoundNone = False
            WScript.Echo objRes.Path & " is opened by " & objRes.User
        End If
Next

' if we didn't find the file open, display a msg
if varFoundNone = True then
    WScript.Echo "Didn't find that file opened by anyone."
end if
```

**NOTE** You'll notice several lines that end in an underscore (_) character. The underscore is referred to as a *line continuation character,* meaning that the line of script is continued on the next line simply because it wouldn't all fit on the first line. When you type this script, you can type the underscore exactly as shown.

You shouldn't have to make any changes to this script to get it to run in your environment, especially if you're running it on a Windows 2000 or Windows XP computer (the script does use Active Directory Services Interface, or ADSI, which is on 2000 and XP by default).

**NOTE** Normally in this book, I'll follow each script with a detailed, line-by-line breakdown of what it does. Because this script is just meant to be an example of editing and debugging scripts, I'm going to forgo that explanation this time. I'll be using this script again later, though, so you'll still get that line-by-line explanation.

**TIP** Remember that all of the longer scripts in this book are also on the accompanying CD-ROM, so you don't need to type them from scratch. Each chapter has its own folder on the CD, and the script filenames match the listing numbers (2.1 in this case).

If you're using a script editor like PrimalScript or VbsEdit, take a moment to browse through the script. Notice how comment lines (those that begin with a single quote) appear in a different color, helping you to focus on them when you want an explanation of what the script is doing.

Also, notice the coloring for statements and commands, and for strings of text that appear in dialog boxes. Get used to how your script editor works and you'll become a much more efficient scripter.

## Running Your First Script

Double-clicking WhoHas.vbs should execute it in WScript. First, you'll be asked which server you want to connect to. Provide the server name, making sure you have administrative permissions on that server (the script will be using your user credentials to access the server). Next, provide the complete path and filename of the file you want to check.

For example, suppose a folder on the server, named D:\Shares\Sales, is shared as Sales. A user is accessing a file named \\Server\Sales\SalesGoals.doc, and you want to find out which user it is. You'd type **D:\Shares\Sales\SalesGoals.doc,** because that's the server-local path to the file.

When you click OK…whoops! There's an error on line 10 (or another line, depending on how you typed the script)! That's not good! Looks like you're ready to start debugging your first script.

## Debugging Your First Script

Microsoft offers a free script debugger from www.Microsoft.com/scripting. After you download and install the debugger, it will be available for the scripts that you write. In Figure 2.17, I've started the debugger, loaded WhoHas.vbs, and started execution. As you can see, the first line of code is highlighted, meaning the debugger is waiting to execute that code (it automatically skipped the very first line of text, which is just a comment line).

At this point, I can press F8 to execute *just* the highlighted line of text. Doing so displays an input box requesting the server name; after I provide that and click OK, the debugger jumps to the next line of text. A distinct disadvantage of the Microsoft Debugger is its lack of access to variable contents; in the VbsEdit debugger, I could hover my mouse over the `varServer` variable to verify that it contains whatever server name I had typed.

I can keep pressing F8 to execute each line of code, one at a time, until I run into the error again—as I do on line 10. Time to look at line 10 more carefully.

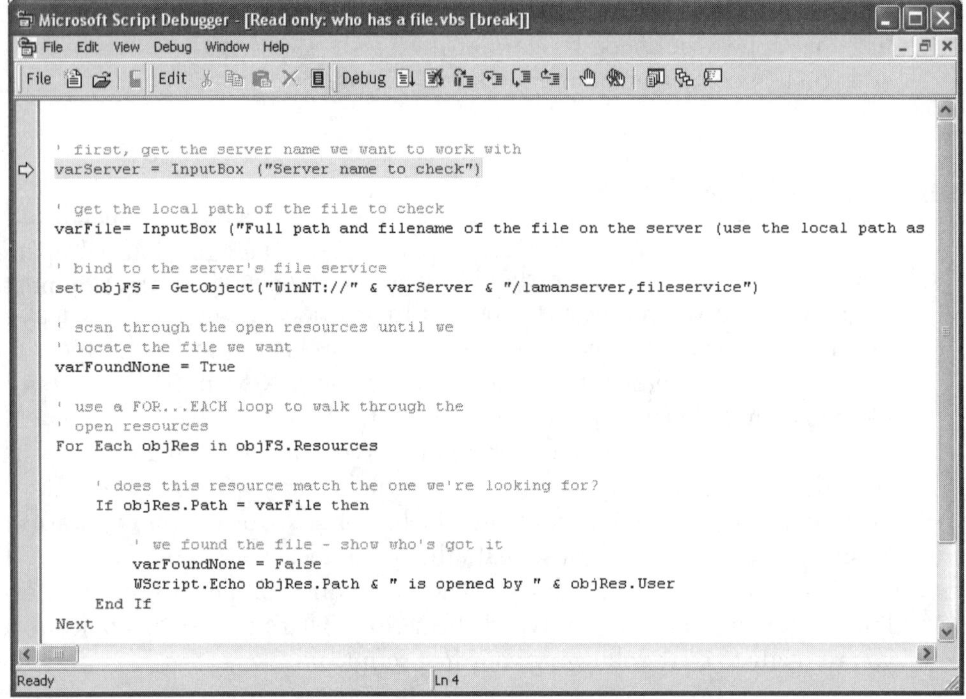


**Figure 2.17** Debugging WhoHas.vbs

The problem, in fact, is the word `lamanserver`. It should be `lanmanserver`, with an "n" after the initial "la." Correcting that lets the script continue normally.

Often times, the debugger is the best way to see what "path" VBScript is taking. For example, your script might be behaving unexpectedly because you entered an incorrect logical comparison, perhaps typing ">" instead of "<" in a numeric comparison. Those types of errors won't necessarily generate errors—at least, not ones you'd be able to track down easily—but using the debugger can let you "walk" through script one line at a time as it executes and spot the location where the script's logic begins to go wrong.

## Review

VBScript is easy to execute, because `WScript.exe` has been included with every major release of Windows since Windows 98. And, in Windows 2000 and later, WScript is even under Windows File Protection, ensuring that your users can't accidentally delete it. After you've taken precautions to ensure that only your scripts will execute (something I'll address in Chapter 28), you'll be ready to run!

Editing scripts can be a bit less satisfying. Windows doesn't come with any built-in tools specifically for editing scripts, and Notepad is a poor substitute. An advanced text editor like Programmer's File Editor makes things easier, and you can acquire some well-designed editors designed specifically for VBScript. Unfortunately, the most powerful script editors don't compare with the convenience and flexibility of professional software development tools like Visual Studio. On the other hand, your scripts probably won't ever be as complicated as most software development projects, so the extra convenience and flexibility isn't required.

### COMING UP

Now that you know everything you need to create and execute scripts, you're ready to start learning how they work. Chapter 3 will cover the various components of a script, and introduce some sample scripts for you to review. Chapter 4 will let you practice everything you've learned in Part I by designing a script from scratch.

CHAPTER 3

# The Components of a Script

**IN THIS CHAPTER**

When you started using Windows, you had to learn all kinds of new terms, like *minimize* and *mouse*. Scripting has a language all its own, too, and in this chapter, you'll learn the anatomy of a script and what some of those special terms mean.

Every good book has a structure. This book, for example, includes an introduction and some introductory chapters. Most of the book is taken up with explanatory chapters and examples. There's an appendix, an index, and a table of contents. All of these elements work together to make the book useful for a variety of purposes, including learning, referencing, and so forth.

Scripts have a structure, too. The main body of the script is a bit like its table of contents, organizing what the script will do. Functions and subroutines are the chapters of the book and perform the actual work. Finally, there are comments and documentation, which act as an index and help provide cross-references and meaning to the actual script code.

Do you really need to know these things to pump out a useful administrative script? Not at all. In fact, if your goal is to start programming as quickly as possible, skip ahead to the next chapter. However, understanding the structure of a good script can help make scripting easier, make your scripts more useful, and save you a lot of time and effort in the long run.

## A Typical VBScript

Listing 3.1 shows the example script I'll be using in this chapter. This is actually a sneak preview; you'll see this script again in various forms in the next chapter. For now, don't worry much about what the script does or how it works; instead, just focus on what it looks like.

**Listing 3.1** *LoginScript.vbs.* This is the sample I'll be using throughout this chapter.

```
'Display Message
MsgBox "Welcome to BrainCore.Net. You are now logged on."

'Map N: Drive
If IsMemberOf("Domain Users") Then
 MapDrive("N:","\\Server\Users")
End If

'Map R: Drive
If IsMemberOf("Research") Then
 MapDrive("R:","\\Server2\Research")
End If

'Map S: Drive
If IsMemberOf("Sales") Then
 MapDrive("S:","\\Server2\SalesDocs")
End If

'Get IP address
sIP = GetIP()

'Figure out 3rd octet
iFirstDot = InStr(0,sIP,".")
iSecondDot = InStr(iFirstDot+1,sIP,".")
iThirdDot = InStr(iSecondDot+1,sIP,".")
sThirdOctet = Mid(sIP, iSecondDot+1, _
 Len(sIP)-iThirdDot)

'Map printer based on octet
Select Case sThirdOctet
 Case "100"
  MapPrinter "\\NYDC\HPColor3"
 Case "110"
  MapPrinter "\\LADC\HP6"
 Case "120"
  MapPrinter "\\TXDC1\LaserJet"
End Select
```

```
'------------------------------------------
' FUNCTIONS
'------------------------------------------

Sub MapDrive(sLetter, sUNC)
 Set oNet = WScript.CreateObject("WScript.Network")
 oNet.MapNetworkDrive sLetter, sUNC)
End Sub

Function GetIP()
 Set myObj = GetObject("winmgmts:" & _
  "{impersonationLevel=impersonate}" & _
  "!//localhost".ExecQuery _
  ("select IPAddress from " & _
  "Win32_NetworkingAdapterConfiguration" & _
  " where IPEnabled=TRUE")

 'Go through the addresses
 For Each IPAddress in myObj
  If IPAddress.IPAddress(0) <> "0.0.0.0" Then
   LocalIP = IPAddress.IPAddress(0)
   Exit For
  End If
 Next
 GetIP = LocalIP
End Function

Sub MapPrinter(sUNC)
 Set oNet = WScript.CreateObject("WScript.Network")
 oNet.AddWindowsPrinterConnection sUNC
 oNet.SetDefaultPrinter sUNC
End Sub

Function IsMemberOf(sGroupName)
  Set oNetwork = CreateObject("WScript.Network")
  sDomain = oNetwork.UserDomain
  sUser = oNetwork.UserName
  bIsMember = False
  Set oUser = GetObject("WinNT://" & sDomain & "/" & _
   sUser & ",user")
  For Each oGroup In userObj.Groups
    If oGroup.Name = sGroupName Then
      bIsMember = True
      Exit For
    End If
```

*continues*

```
  Next
  IsMemberOf = bIsMember
End Function
```

Remember that this script isn't designed to run as-is (skip ahead to the next chapter to find out what it does and what needs to change to make it execute properly in your environment). Instead, it's just intended to represent the structure of a good script.

## Functions

*Functions* are one of the workhorses of any script. They perform operations of some kind, and return some kind of result back to the main script. For example, VBScript has a built-in function called `Date()` that simply returns the current date.

There are built-in functions and custom functions that you write. The only difference between them, of course, is that Microsoft wrote the built-in functions and you write your custom ones. The sample login script has a couple of custom functions.

```
Function GetIP()
 Set myObj = GetObject("winmgmts:" & _
  "{impersonationLevel=impersonate}" & _
  "!//localhost".ExecQuery _
  ("select IPAddress from " & _
  "Win32_NetworkingAdapterConfiguration" & _
  " where IPEnabled=TRUE")

 'Go through the addresses
 For Each IPAddress in myObj
  If IPAddress.IPAddress(0) <> "0.0.0.0" Then
   LocalIP = IPAddress.IPAddress(0)
   Exit For
  End If
 Next
 GetIP = LocalIP
End Function

Function IsMemberOf(sGroupName)
  Set oNetwork = CreateObject("WScript.Network")
```

```
  sDomain = oNetwork.UserDomain
  sUser = oNetwork.UserName
  bIsMember = False
  Set oUser = GetObject("WinNT://" & sDomain & "/" & _
   sUser & ",user")
  For Each oGroup In oUser.Groups
    If oGroup.Name = sGroupName Then
      bIsMember = True
      Exit For
    End If
  Next
  IsMemberOf = bIsMember
End Function
```

You'll notice that these all begin with the declaration `Function`, followed by the name of the function. They can include a list of input parameters, as the `IsMemberOf` function does. All of them return some information, too. Notice that the last line of each function sets the function name equal to some other variable; this action returns that other variable's value as the result of the function.

If this is not making sense, don't worry. For now, just make sure you can recognize a function at 30 feet by the keyword `Function`. I cover functions in more detail in Chapter 5, in the section, "What Are Functions?"

Why use functions? Well, in the case of intrinsic functions, they perform a very valuable service, providing information like the date and time, and allowing you to manipulate data. Custom functions do the same thing. Custom functions, however, can be a lot more useful in the end. Take the `IsMemberOf` function as an example. That function tells me if the current user is a member of a specific domain user group or not. It took me a couple of hours to figure out how to perform that little trick. In the future, though, I can just paste the function into whatever script I need, and I'll never have to spend those couple of hours again. Bundling the task into a function makes it easily portable between scripts, and allows me to easily reuse my hard work.

## Subroutines

The sample script has two custom subroutines, too. These are just like functions, except that they just do something; they don't return any result afterwards.

```
Sub MapDrive(sLetter, sUNC)
 Set oNet = WScript.CreateObject("WScript.Network")
 oNet.MapNetworkDrive sLetter, sUNC)
End Sub


Sub MapPrinter(sUNC)
 Set oNet = WScript.CreateObject("WScript.Network")
 oNet.AddWindowsPrinterConnection sUNC
 oNet.SetDefaultPrinter sUNC
End Sub
```

These subroutines are declared with the word `Sub`, followed by the name of the subroutine. Like a function, these two subroutines each accept some input parameters. Unlike a function, they never set their name to some value, which is why they don't return a value.

VBScript has intrinsic (built-in) subroutines, only they're called *statements*. A simple statement, like `Beep`, simply makes the computer beep.

Subroutines serve the same purpose as a function: Although mapping a drive or a printer obviously isn't difficult (taking only two or three lines of code), there's no reason I should have to type those lines of code over and over. Encapsulating the functionality into a subroutine means I can reuse the code repeatedly in one script, and easily paste it into other scripts, saving myself work.

## Main Script

The main script performs a good bit of work. Here it is in its entirety.

```
'Display Message
MsgBox "Welcome to BrainCore.Net. You are now logged on."

'Map N: Drive
If IsMemberOf("Domain Users") Then
 MapDrive("N:","\\Server\Users")
End If

'Map R: Drive
If IsMemberOf("Research") Then
 MapDrive("R:","\\Server2\Research")
End If
```

```
'Map S: Drive
If IsMemberOf("Sales") Then
 MapDrive("S:","\\Server2\SalesDocs")
End If

'Get IP address
sIP = GetIP()

'Figure out 3rd octet
iFirstDot = InStr(0,sIP,".")
iSecondDot = InStr(iFirstDot+1,sIP,".")
iThirdDot = InStr(iSecondDot+1,sIP,".")
sThirdOctet = Mid(sIP, iSecondDot+1, _
 Len(sIP)-iThirdDot)

'Map printer based on octet
Select Case sThirdOctet
 Case "100"
  MapPrinter "\\NYDC\HPColor3"
 Case "110"
  MapPrinter "\\LADC\HP6"
 Case "120"
  MapPrinter "\\TXDC1\LaserJet"
End Select
```

The main script does act as a sort of table of contents, organizing the flow of the overall script. For example, notice where the `MapDrive` and `MapPrinter` subroutines are used, and where the `IsMemberOf()` and `GetIP()` functions are used. The main script also utilizes some of VBScript's intrinsic functions, such as `InStr()` and `Mid()`. The main script acts as sort of a conductor, orchestrating the flow of the tasks that need to be completed, and calling on specialists—the functions and subroutines—to perform specialized tasks.

---

**TIP** You'll notice that the script uses subs and functions for some things, but uses in-line code for other things, like figuring out the third octet of an IP address. My general rule is to use functions and subs whenever I think the code will be useful elsewhere, or will be used more than once. Otherwise, I just use in-line code in the main script.

---

In the next few sections, I'll point out specific portions of the main script for you to pay attention to. Again, don't worry much about what these do or how they work; focus for now on the overall structure of the script and how the different pieces fit together. In the next chapter, you'll see how this script went together and what each line does.

## Using Custom Functions and Subroutines

Where does the main script call on custom functions and subroutines? I've boldfaced the custom bits in this version of the script.

```
'Display Message
MsgBox "Welcome to BrainCore.Net. You are now logged on."

'Map N: Drive
If IsMemberOf("Domain Users") Then
 MapDrive("N:","\\Server\Users")
End If

'Map S: Drive
If IsMemberOf("Research") Then
 MapDrive("R:","\\Server2\Research")
End If

'Map R: Drive
If IsMemberOf("Sales") Then
 MapDrive("S:","\\Server2\SalesDocs")
End If

'Get IP address
sIP = GetIP()

'Figure out 3rd octet
iFirstDot = InStr(0,sIP,".")
iSecondDot = InStr(iFirstDot+1,sIP,".")
iThirdDot = InStr(iSecondDot+1,sIP,".")
sThirdOctet = Mid(sIP, iSecondDot+1, _
 Len(sIP)-iThirdDot)

'Map printer based on octet
Select Case sThirdOctet
 Case "100"
  MapPrinter "\\NYDC\HPColor3"
```

```
 Case "110"
  MapPrinter "\\LADC\HP6"
 Case "120"
  MapPrinter "\\TXDC1\LaserJet"
End Select
```

You can see how using custom functions and subs saves a lot of typing and a lot of room. For example, without the custom function `IsMember()`, the script would have to look like this (this time, I've boldfaced the changes so they're easy to spot):

```
'Display Message
MsgBox "Welcome to BrainCore.Net. You are now logged on."

'Map N: Drive
Set oNetwork = CreateObject("WScript.Network")
sDomain = oNetwork.UserDomain
sUser = oNetwork.UserName
Set oUser = GetObject("WinNT://" & sDomain & "/" & _
 sUser & ",user")
For Each oGroup In oUser.Groups
  If oGroup.Name = "Domain Users" Then
    MapDrive("N:","\\Server\Users")
    Exit For
  End If
Next

'Map R: Drive
For Each oGroup In oUser.Groups
  If oGroup.Name = "Research" Then
    MapDrive("R:","\\Server2\ResearchDocs")
    Exit For
  End If
Next

'Map S: Drive
For Each oGroup In oUser.Groups
  If oGroup.Name = "Sales" Then
    MapDrive("S:","\\Server2\SalesDocs")
    Exit For
  End If
Next
```

*continues*

```
'Get IP address
sIP = GetIP()

'Figure out 3rd octet
iFirstDot = InStr(0,sIP,".")
iSecondDot = InStr(iFirstDot+1,sIP,".")
iThirdDot = InStr(iSecondDot+1,sIP,".")
sThirdOctet = Mid(sIP, iSecondDot+1, _
 Len(sIP)-iThirdDot)

'Map printer based on octet
Select Case sThirdOctet
 Case "100"
  MapPrinter "\\NYDC\HPColor3"
 Case "110"
  MapPrinter "\\LADC\HP6"
 Case "120"
  MapPrinter "\\TXDC1\LaserJet"
End Select
```

As you can see, the script is a lot easier to read when the repeated code is pulled into a custom function. Also, the function makes the script easier to maintain; if you find a bug, you only have to fix it in the function. If you haven't used functions, you have to go fix the bug everywhere you used the code. For example, suppose I'd used the wrong syntax for `For Each oGroup in oUser.Groups`. In the original script, I'd just have to fix it in the `IsMemberOf()` function. In the revised script, without the function, I'd have to make the fix three separate times.

## Using Intrinsic Functions and Statements

Where is the script using built-in functions and statements? I'll boldface them to call them out.

```
'Display Message
MsgBox "Welcome to BrainCore.Net. You are now logged on."

'Map N: Drive
If IsMemberOf("Domain Users") Then
 MapDrive("N:","\\Server\Users")
End If

'Map S: Drive
```

```
If IsMemberOf("Research") Then
 MapDrive("R:","\\Server2\Research")
End If

'Map R: Drive
If IsMemberOf("Sales") Then
 MapDrive("S:","\\Server2\SalesDocs")
End If

'Get IP address
sIP = GetIP()

'Figure out 3rd octet
iFirstDot = InStr(0,sIP,".")
iSecondDot = InStr(iFirstDot+1,sIP,".")
iThirdDot = InStr(iSecondDot+1,sIP,".")
sThirdOctet = Mid(sIP, iSecondDot+1, _
 Len(sIP)-iThirdDot)

'Map printer based on octet
Select Case sThirdOctet
 Case "100"
  MapPrinter "\\NYDC\HPColor3"
 Case "110"
  MapPrinter "\\LADC\HP6"
 Case "120"
  MapPrinter "\\TXDC1\LaserJet"
End Select
```

You can spot the built-in ones because they don't have a corresponding `Function` or `Sub` statement later in the script. If you're curious about what these do, check out the VBScript documentation, or flip through Chapters 8 and 10.

---

**NOTE** Notice that the intrinsic and custom functions and statements look identical. The only way to tell them apart is that the custom ones are defined somewhere in the script by the `Function` or `Sub` keywords. Right now, you just need to be adept at spotting the differences between the two.

For a custom function or sub, the only way to tell how it works is to read the corresponding `Function` or `Sub` block and figure out what's going on. For intrinsic functions and statements, you can look them up in the VBScript documentation to see how they work.

---

### Making Decisions in a Script

Sometimes, you need a script to do something different based on a set of circumstances. The sample script does this:

```
'Map printer based on octet
Select Case sThirdOctet
 Case "100"
  MapPrinter "\\NYDC\HPColor3"
 Case "110"
  MapPrinter "\\LADC\HP6"
 Case "120"
  MapPrinter "\\TXDC1\LaserJet"
End Select
```

The `Select...Case` construct is making a decision, mapping a different printer based on the third octet of the user's IP address. `Select...Case` is a special kind of intrinsic VBScript statement, one that helps your script to react to changing conditions automatically by building some kind of logic into the script. For more information on `Select...Case`, see "Conditional Execution" in Chapter 10.

## Comments and Documentation

Documenting your scripts is always a very good idea. After all, the script makes perfect sense now, but will you be able to figure out what it's doing a year, or even a couple of months, from now?

For example, examine the script in Listing 3.2. See if you can figure out what the various portions of the script are doing.

**Listing 3.2** *AddUsersFromXLS.vbs.* This script auto-creates users from an Excel spreadsheet.

```
Set oCN = CreateObject("ADODB.Connection")
oCN.Open "Excel"
Set oRS = oCN.Execute("SELECT * FROM [Sheet1$]")
Set oDomain = GetObject("WinNT://NT4PDC")
Set oFSO = CreateObject("Scripting.FileSystemObject")
```

```
Set oTS = oFSO.CreateTextFile("c:\passwords.txt",True)
sHomePath = "\\iridis1\c$\users\"
Do Until oRS.EOF
sUserID = oRS("UserID")
sFullName = oRS("FullName")
sDescription = oRS("Description")
sHomeDir = oRS("HomeDirectory")
sGroups = oRS("Groups")
sDialIn = oRS("DialIn")
sPassword = Left(sUserID,2) & DatePart("n",Time) & _
DatePart("y",Date) & DatePart("s",Time)
Set oUserAcct = oDomain.Create("user",sUserID)
oUserAcct.SetPassword sPassword
oUserAcct.FullName = sFullName
oUserAcct.Description = sDescription
oUserAcct.HomeDirectory = sHomeDir
If sDialIn = "Y" Then
oUserAcct.RasPermissions = 9
Else
oUserAcct.RasPermissions = 1
End If
oUserAcct.SetInfo
Set oUserAcct = GetObject("WinNT://NT4PDC/" & sUserID & ",user")
oTS.Write sUserID & "," & sPassword & vbCrLf
sGroupList = Split(sGroups, ",")
For iTemp = 0 To uBound(sGroupList)
Set oGroup = GetObject("WinNT://NT4PDC/" & _
sGroupList(iTemp) & ",group")
oGroup.Add oUserAcct.ADsPath
Set oGroup = Nothing
Next
Set oFolder = oFSO.CreateFolder(sHomePath & sUserID)
Set oUserAcct = Nothing
oRS.MoveNext
Loop
oRS.Close
oTS.Close
WScript.Echo "Passwords have been written to c:\passwords.txt."
```

It's a bit tough to follow, isn't it? Now look at Listing 3.3.

**Listing 3.3** *AddUsersFromXLS.vbs*. This script auto-creates users from an Excel spreadsheet.

```
' PART 1: Open up the Excel spreadsheet
' using ActiveX Data Objects
Dim oCN
Set oCN = CreateObject("ADODB.Connection")
oCN.Open "Excel"

Dim oRS
Set oRS = oCN.Execute("SELECT * FROM [Sheet1$]")


' PART 2: Get a reference to the
' Windows NT domain using ADSI
Dim oDomain
Set oDomain = GetObject("WinNT://NT4PDC")


' PART 3: Open an output text file
' to store users' initial passwords
Dim oFSO, oTS
Set oFSO = CreateObject("Scripting.FileSystemObject")
Set oTS = oFSO.CreateTextFile("c:\passwords.txt",True)


' PART 4: For each record in the recordset,
' add the user, set the correct user
' properties, and add the user to the
' appropriate groups

' create the necessary variables
Dim sUserID, sFullName, sDescription
Dim sHomeDir, sGroups, sDialIn
Dim sPassword, oUserAcct, oFolder
Dim sGroupList, iTemp, oGroup

' define the base path for the home
' directories to be created in
Dim sHomePath
sHomePath = "\\iridis1\c$\users\"

' now go through the recordset one
' row at a time
Do Until oRS.EOF
```

```
' get the user information from this row
sUserID = oRS("UserID")
sFullName = oRS("FullName")
sDescription = oRS("Description")
sHomeDir = oRS("HomeDirectory")
sGroups = oRS("Groups")
sDialIn = oRS("DialIn")

' make up a new password
sPassword = Left(sUserID,2) & DatePart("n",Time) & _
 DatePart("y",Date) & DatePart("s",Time)

' create the user account
Set oUserAcct = oDomain.Create("user",sUserID)

' set account properties
oUserAcct.SetPassword sPassword
oUserAcct.FullName = sFullName
oUserAcct.Description = sDescription
oUserAcct.HomeDirectory = sHomeDir

' set RAS permission
If sDialIn = "Y" Then
  oUserAcct.RasPermissions = 9
Else
  oUserAcct.RasPermissions = 1
End If

' save the account
oUserAcct.SetInfo

' get a reference to the new account
' this gets us a valid SID & other info
Set oUserAcct = GetObject("WinNT://NT4PDC/" & _
 sUserID & ",user")

' write password to file
oTS.Write sUserID & "," & sPassword & vbCrLf

' PART 4A: Add user account to groups
' use the Split function to turn the
' comma-separated list into an array
sGroupList = Split(sGroups, ",")
```

*continues*

```
    ' go through the array and add the user
    ' to each group
    For iTemp = 0 To uBound(sGroupList)

      ' get the group
      Set oGroup = GetObject("WinNT://NT4PDC/" & _
       sGroupList(iTemp) & ",group")

      ' add the user account
      oGroup.Add oUserAcct.ADsPath

      ' release the group
      Set oGroup = Nothing

    Next


    ' PART 4B: Create the user's Home Directory
    ' (append UserID to the Home Path variable)
    Set oFolder = oFSO.CreateFolder(sHomePath & sUserID)


    ' PART 5: All done!
    ' release the user account
    Set oUserAcct = Nothing

    ' move to the next row in the recordset
    oRS.MoveNext

Loop


' PART 6: Final clean up, close down
oTS.CloseoRS.Close
WScript.Echo "Passwords have been written to c:\passwords.txt."
```

The scripts in Listings 3.2 and 3.3 will execute and do the exact same thing, but the one in 3.3 is much, much easier to figure out. Here's why.

- Comment lines (those beginning with the `'` character) are included throughout, explaining what each section of the script is doing.

- The lines of code are indented, making it easy to see which blocks will be repeated in loops.
- White space in the form of blank lines is used to help break up the script and make different sections stand out more readily from one another.

As you can see from these examples, documentation and commenting isn't required, but it sure is nice. VBScript doesn't care about documentation and commenting, but you sure will if you ever have to work with a script that doesn't have it!

## Review

In this chapter, I tried to illustrate some of the different components of a good script. You've seen what functions, statements, and subroutines look like, how a main script ties them all together, and how comments and documentation make them easier to read and maintain in the future. Keep all these new concepts in mind as you move through the rest of the book. Try to spot intrinsic functions and custom ones, and watch for comment lines and other types of code documentation. Try to use these standards in your own scripts, and you'll find yourself becoming more efficient and more capable very quickly.

### COMING UP

You're almost ready to start learning VBScript, but you need to learn how to design your scripts first. In the next chapter, I'll show you my simple methodology for designing scripts that will let you write powerful administrative scripts without becoming a career programmer.

CHAPTER 4

# Designing a Script

**IN THIS CHAPTER**

Believe it or not, the toughest part about scripting isn't the language or programming objects or anything technology related. It's in how you design your scripts and get them to do what you want. I'll share tips and techniques that'll make scripting easier and more approachable.

Suppose you want to do a tune-up on your car, and you don't want to hire a mechanic to do the job for you. It's easy enough to run down to the hardware store and acquire the necessary tools, and you can even buy some books that explain how to use those tools. If you're like me, though, none of that will help you get the tune-up done. Where do you start? What should it look like? Which tools do you use, and when?

I've found that's how many administrators feel about scripting. Sure, the VBScript documentation is available, and there are plenty of examples on the Web. But where do you start when it comes time to write your own scripts? Much of this book will be focused on the tools, like VBScript and programming objects, that you'll need to do the job. In this chapter, I want to share some of the tips and techniques that I use to actually get started in designing a new script.

It'll be easier to see how my design process works with a meaningful example. Because login scripts are a popular administrative use of VBScript, I'll use a login script as an example. I want to write a login script that maps three network drives based on the users' group membership, and then maps a printer based on the user's DHCP-assigned IP address. That way, I can assign a printer that's local to wherever the user logged on. I also want to display a welcome message, and I want the script to run on Windows NT Workstation 4.0 (Service Pack 6a or later), Windows XP Professional (Service Pack 1 or later), and Windows 2000 Professional (Service Pack 3 or later).

## Creating a Task List

The first thing to do in the design process is to create a task list. This is essentially an English-language version of the script you plan to write. In the list, you must break down the various things you want the script to perform in as much detail as possible. I often go through several iterations of the task list, adding a bit more detail each time through. Listing 4.1 shows what my first pass might look like.

**Listing 4.1** *Login script task list.* Your first task list should just summarize what you want the script to do.

```
Login script task list

Display a logon welcome message.
Map the N: drive based on group membership.
Map the R: drive based on group membership.
Map the S: drive based on group membership.
Map a printer and make it the default. Base the printer selection on
  the user's physical location at the time.
```

**NOTE** Programmers call this kind of a task list *pseudocode,* because it sort of looks like programming code but isn't. It's a great way to lay out what a script is supposed to do without having to look up the exact VBScript syntax of every command. Plus, you can throw around phrases like, "I just finished pseudocoding that script, and boy was it tough," and you'll impress the software developers in your company.

After you've got your first task list completed, look at what detail might be missing. For example, "based on group membership" is vague. What specific parameters will be used to determine where the N: drive is mapped? Will the N: drive always be mapped, or will it be mapped only if the user is in one or more specific groups? Pretend you're explaining how the script will work to the least technical person you know, and add the level of detail they'd need to understand what the script should do. Listing 4.2 shows a second, more detailed attempt.

**Listing 4.2** *Login script task list II.* Adding detail makes the task list more useful.

```
Login script task list v2

Display a logon welcome message:
"Welcome to BrainCore.Net. You are now logged on."

Map the N: drive:
If the user is a member of the Domain Users group.
Map the drive to \\Server\Users.

Map the R: drive:
If the user is a member of the Research group.
Map the drive to \\Server2\ResearchDocs.

Map the S: drive:
If the user is a member of the Sales group.
Map the drive to \\Server2\SalesDocs.

Map a printer:
Examine the third octet of the user's IP address. If it is 100, map the
  printer \\NYDC\HPColor3. If the third octet is 110, map the printer
  to \\LADC2\HP6. If the third octet is 120, map the printer to \\
  TXDC1\LaserJet. Make the mapped printer the default on the user's
  system.
```

This new script provides much more in the way of detail. However, it's still lacking the feel of a procedure. For example, suppose you were going to manually perform the tasks in this script. How would you perform the drive-mapping task? You'd have to open the Domain Users group and see if the user's account was listed there. Rewrite the task list with that level of procedural detail, because that's what the computer executing the script will need to know. Look at Listing 4.3, which tries to make the task list even more detailed and procedural.

**Listing 4.3** *Login script task list III.* Making the tasks a procedure will help translate the list to a script later.

```
Login script task list v3

Display a logon welcome message:
```

```
"Welcome to BrainCore.Net. You are now logged on."
Wait until the user presses OK to dismiss the welcome message.

Map the N: drive:
Obtain a list of Domain Users group members. See if the user is in the
  list. If they are, map the drive to \\Server\Users.

Map the R: drive:
Obtain a list of Research group members. See if the user is in the
  list. If they are, map the drive to \\Server2\ResearchDocs.

Map the S: drive:
Obtain a list of Sales group members. See if the user is in the list.
  If they are, map the drive to \\Server2\SalesDocs.

Map a printer:
Get the user's IP address. Look at just the third octet. To find it,
  look for the last period in the IP address, and then the next-to-the-
  last period. The third octet is between the two periods. If the octet
  is 100, map to \\NYDC\HPColor3. If it's 110, map to \\LADC\HP6. If
  it's 120, map to \\TXDC1\LaserJet. Then make the mapped printer the
  default.
```

Now take one last pass through the list and think about the underlying technologies. For example, what information is really contained within a Windows domain user group? It's not a list of user names; it's a list of security identifiers, or SIDs. So, when you're checking group membership, you may need to get the user's SID and then check the groups' SID list. You don't necessarily need to modify your task list with this information, but make a note of it. That way when you start to write the script in VBScript, you'll remember what it is you really need the computer to do for you.

## Selecting the Appropriate Tools

Now comes what is truly the most difficult part of administrative scripting: selecting the right tools. You know what you want your script to do, and you know VBScript can do it (or you at least hope it can), so you just need to figure out *how* to make it work.

Software developers do this all the time. Typically, they know so much about the tools they have to work with, though, that they select the right ones without even thinking about it. As an administrator, I'm more likely to have to do some research first.

Looking at the task list, there are really six types of tasks I need the computer to perform:

1. Displaying a message
2. Mapping a drive
3. Checking group membership
4. Mapping a printer
5. Getting the local IP address
6. Getting the third octet from the IP address

I'll show you how I research each of these tasks to figure out how they can be accomplished.

---

**TIP** The Appendix of this book is a quick script reference. It's designed to list common administrative tasks and briefly describe what VBScript tools you can use to accomplish them. This reference should make it easier for you to figure out which tools to use when you write your own scripts.

---

## Displaying a Message

I always start my research in the VBScript documentation. You can find it online at www.microsoft.com/scripting, and there's even a downloadable version that you can use offline. You can also find the documentation in the MSDN Library. That's available online at http://msdn.microsoft.com/library, or you can receive it on CD or DVD as part of a yearly subscription. In either case, I find an offline version of the docs to be more convenient.

---

**TIP** At the very least, download the offline VBScript documentation. Go to www.microsoft.com/scripting and look for the appropriate link. The actual download URL changes from time to time, so you're better off starting at the main scripting page and locating the link.

---

When I need to search the VBScript documentation, I usually start with the alphabetical list of available functions and commands. That's just an easy way for me to scan through the docs and spot likely looking tools. In this case, down in the M section of the function list, I ran across MsgBox. Even if you know nothing about VBScript, MsgBox certainly sounds as if it displays a message box. Looking into the details of the function, I see that it does, in fact, display a dialog box with a message in it. I can specify the message, the title of the dialog box, and which buttons and icons appear on the dialog box. Sounds perfect for my welcome message.

There's no need at this point in the design process to actually start writing script. However, `MsgBox` appears to be a simple command.

```
'Display welcome message
MsgBox "Welcome to BrainCore.Net. You are now logged on."
```

Suppose you don't want to browse through the VBScript documentation (and you don't have this book handy). First, I definitely recommend the browsing method, because it exposes you to a lot of other functions and commands that might be useful later in life. Still, if that's just not your way of working, you can always fall back on my favorite search engine, Google.

Go up to www.google.com and enter a search phrase. Here are some tips.

- I always use "VBScript" as my first search term, because it narrows down Google's billions of Web pages to those that deal with VBScript.
- I always include "-browser" in the phrase. Doing so eliminates a lot of pages that talk about using VBScript in Dynamic HTML (DHTML) Web pages, which isn't what I'm usually looking for.
- Finally, include a term that describes what you're trying to do. In this case, "display message" should do the trick.

---

**TIP** Use quotes carefully in a search phrase. For example, if you type **display message,** you'll get hits that include both words, and hits that include just one of the two words. If you include **"display message"** in quotes, you'll only get hits that have the entire phrase "display message" in the page. That might not be helpful in this case; it's more likely the pages will contain something like "display a message" or "display the message." Using **display** and **message** outside of quotes will find these pages; using **"display message"** in quotes won't.

---

With the Google search phrase **vbscript display message –browser,** my first hit is a Web site on GeoCities that describes how to use the

VBScript `MsgBox` function. Farther down the first page of hits is a page entitled, "VBScript MsgBox Function," which could work, too.

Google's great for finding example scripts that do what you want, and I'll be using it a lot more as I try to figure out how to perform more complicated tasks.

I'll show you how to use the `MsgBox` function in more detail in Chapter 6, under "Displaying Messages."

## Mapping a Drive

Speaking of more complicated tasks, this one's a bit more difficult. There are plenty of command-line programs that can map a drive, including the easy-to-use `net` command, but that's cheating. I'm looking for a way to do it in VBScript.

Running through the VBScript documentation doesn't provide any help, either. I don't see any commands with "map" or "drive" anywhere in them. I do see something about a Drive object, but that seems to have something to do with accessing drives. I need to map it before that'll be possible.

Back to Google. Searching for **vbscript map drive –browser** doesn't return anything helpful in the first page of hits, so I'll need to be a little more creative. Searching for **vbscript "maps a drive" –browser** gets me a promising article in the first page of hits. Clicking on the first hit, I find myself at MyITForum.com (www.myitforum.com/articles/11/section.asp?w=2&au=lduncan). There's a list of articles here by Larry Duncan, and there are actually two that look useful: *How do I retrieve the IP Address using VBScript*, and *How can I map a drive using WSH?* WSH, VBScript, whatever. It's worth a look.

---

**TIP** The terms VBScript, ADSI, WSH, and WMI are interchangeable when you're looking through search results. They're all more or less a part of the larger world of administrative scripting.

---

Larry's article is actually a short snippet of VBScript code that uses just two lines of code. It uses the WScript.Network object, which seems to have a command called `MapNetworkDrive` associated with it. No need to go into more detail right now; this is the information I was looking for. I'll bookmark the URL for later reference and go on to the next task.

I cover the WScript.Network object, too; look in Chapter 11 under "The Network Object."

### Checking Group Membership

This task also seems complicated. This time, I'm not even going to bother with the VBScript docs, because I've been through them twice already and I don't remember seeing anything even remotely related to group membership. On to Google, where I search for **vbscript group membership –browser.** The first hit is entitled *Detecting Group Membership using VBScript.* Perfect!

The link takes me to www.sanx.org/tipShow.asp?articleRef=66. The article in question provides an example script. It's actually a complete function, where I just provide the name of a group, and the function tells me if the currently logged-on user is a member of that group or not. Great! Another bookmark in the browser, and I'll come back to the example when it's time to start writing the script.

### Mapping a Printer

This is a place where a little logic can save some time. I already discovered this WScript.Network thing, which maps drives. Surely, it also maps printers, right? Searching the MSDN Library for WScript.Network takes me to the documentation for that object, which does in fact include an `AddWindowsPrinterConnection`. I also find that it can set the default printer for the current user, which means it's exactly what I need. No need to perform any more complicated search than that, and I can review the documentation later to figure out how to use it. Right now, it's enough to know that it'll do what I need it to do.

### Getting the Local IP Address

I already found out how to do this, based on the list of Larry Duncan articles I ran across when looking for drive mapping techniques. Larry's article is at www.myitforum.com/articles/11/view.asp?id-3340, and it's a brief example of how to get the local IP address from within a script. At the very end of the script is the command `MsgBox Line`. I know that `MsgBox` displays a message, so it appears as if `Line` is a variable that contains the IP address I'm looking for. Keep in mind that I need to work with that IP address a little bit, so it's important for me to adapt Larry's script to my purposes.

Larry's script seems to be able to list all of the IP addresses associated with a computer. That's an important thing to understand! Remember that a computer usually has multiple network adapters. One of them might be a FireWire port, another might be a wireless network card, and still another might be an Ethernet card. Even if none of them is connected, they all have an IP address—even if it's 0.0.0.0.

This makes my task a bit more complicated. I was thinking I just had to pull out the IP address, but in fact, it looks like I have to pull *all* of the IP addresses, and then look for one that isn't 0.0.0.0. Looking again at Larry's example, it might be worth taking a quick guess at what my own IP address script might look like. Listing 4.4 shows an example. I don't know if this is perfect yet, but it's a guess.

---

**TIP** You'll see some code in the next few examples that won't make much sense. Remember: You're only on Chapter 4! I'm using this example because it's something you can use immediately in your environment. I promise you'll see these again in later chapters, where I'll also explain what each line of code is doing.

---

**Listing 4.4** *Retrieve IP Address.* I'll need to test this script later and figure out more about how it works so that I can make sure it'll work in my logon script.

```
Set myObj = GetObject("winmgmts:{impersonationLevel=" & _
 "impersonate}" & _
 "!//localhost".ExecQuery _
 ("select IPAddress from Win32_" & _
 "NetworkingAdapterConfiguration" & _
 " where IPEnabled=TRUE")

'Go through the addresses
For Each IPAddress in myObj
 If IPAddress.IPAddress(0) <> "0.0.0.0" Then
  LocalIP = IPAddress.IPAddress(0)
  Exit For
 End If
Next
MsgBox LocalIP
```

Larry's script was saving all of the IP addresses, so I just looked for the section of his script that seemed to be pulling the IP address out of the computer. I added an `If...Then` section to grab the first IP address that isn't 0.0.0.0. I'll try it later to see how it works.

I'm getting a little ahead of myself, but if you want to check out using `If...Then`, turn to Chapter 10 and look under "Conditional Execution." I cover variables in Chapter 5 under "What Are Variables?" and the rest of this script uses WMI, which I introduce in Chapter 17.

Anyway, it looks like I'll have a variable named `LocalIP` that contains my local IP address, which is exactly what I wanted.

## Getting the Third Octet from the IP Address

With my IP address in a variable, I need to figure out how to get just the third octet. Now, this seems like it could be harder than it looks. I can't just grab the ninth, tenth, and eleventh characters from the IP address, because in an address like "10.123.52.4," that wouldn't be right. What I need to do is what I put into my task list: Look for the location of the second and third periods, and then grab everything in between.

Back to the VBScript function list. It turns out there are two functions that might work: `InStr()`, which returns the specific location of a specific character, and `Mid()`, which grabs characters out of the middle of a string variable. These two look like they'll do the job, so I'm not going to worry too much about exactly how they work. I know I need to do something like this:

- Use `InStr()` to get the location of the first period. This way, I'll know that the *next* one is the second one.
- Use `InStr()` to get the location of the second period.
- Use `Instr()` to get the location of the third period.
- Use `Mid()` to grab everything in between the second and third periods.

## All Tasks Accounted For

It was a bit of work, but I think I know how to do everything I need my script to do. Hopefully, this helps you see how I go about figuring these things out; it's certainly not as easy as just sitting down and starting to type lines of VBScript! A little bit of up-front research is necessary, although it's not usually too hard. The Web, fortunately, is loaded with examples (as is this book), and you can usually find something that does what you want, or at least points you in the right direction.

## Creating Modules to Perform Tasks

After you've got your task list nailed down, and you've figured out how to perform each of the tasks in script, you can start designing the modules of the script. I often have to spend a lot of time figuring out how to do things like look up IP addresses or connect to domain controllers; after I've spent that time, I don't ever want to have to do it again. In other words, I want to *modularize* my scripts, so that difficult or commonly used tasks can be easily cut and pasted into future scripts.

VBScript provides a way for you to write your own functions and statements, making it easy to modularize your code. Most of the time, the tasks your script accomplishes—in this case, mapping drives, getting IP addresses, and so forth—can be easily written as functions and subroutines, which can be easily cut and pasted into future scripts.

For a quick overview of functions and statements, see "What Are Functions?" in Chapter 5. You can see how they fit into a script in "Functions" and "Subroutines" in Chapter 3. Finally, I provide more detail on modular script programming in Chapter 25.

Probably the best way to see how these tasks can be modularized is with an example of the completed login script.

### ➤➤ The Login Script

Listing 4.5 shows what the various functions for the logon script might look like, and also shows how the main script might be written to call on each of these functions.

---

**NOTE** Don't worry for now about how this script actually works. You'll be seeing all of these features again in later chapters, where I'll provide explanations that are more detailed. For now, just focus on how the various things are broken into modules that make them easier to reuse throughout the main script.

---

**Listing 4.5** *LoginScript.vbs.* This script includes a main script as well as functions, making a modular script.

```
'Display Message
MsgBox "Welcome to BrainCore.Net. You are now logged on."
```

*continues*

```
'Map N: Drive
If IsMemberOf("Domain Users") Then
 MapDrive("N:","\\Server\Users")
End If

'Map S: Drive
If IsMemberOf("Research") Then
 MapDrive("R:","\\Server2\Research")
End If

'Map R: Drive
If IsMemberOf("Sales") Then
 MapDrive("S:","\\Server2\SalesDocs")
End If

'Get IP address
sIP = GetIP()

'Figure out 3rd octet
iFirstDot = InStr(0,sIP,".")
iSecondDot = InStr(iFirstDot+1,sIP,".")
iThirdDot = InStr(iSecondDot+1,sIP,".")
sThirdOctet = Mid(sIP, iSecondDot+1, _
 Len(sIP)-iThirdDot)

'Map printer based on octet
Select Case sThirdOctet
 Case "100"
  MapPrinter "\\NYDC\HPColor3"
 Case "110"
  MapPrinter "\\LADC\HP6"
 Case "120"
  MapPrinter "\\TXDC1\LaserJet"
End Select

'---------------------------------------------
' FUNCTIONS
'---------------------------------------------

Sub MapDrive(sLetter, sUNC)
 Set oNet = WScript.CreateObject("WScript.Network")
 oNet.MapNetworkDrive sLetter, sUNC)
End Sub
```

```
Function GetIP()
 Set myObj = GetObject("winmgmts:{impersonationLevel=" & _
  "impersonate}" & _
  "!//localhost".ExecQuery _
  ("select IPAddress from " & _
  "Win32_NetworkingAdapterConfiguration" & _
  " where IPEnabled=TRUE")

 'Go through the addresses
 For Each IPAddress in myObj
  If IPAddress.IPAddress(0) <> "0.0.0.0" Then
   LocalIP = IPAddress.IPAddress(0)
   Exit For
  End If
 Next
 GetIP = LocalIP
End Function

Sub MapPrinter(sUNC)
 Set oNet = WScript.CreateObject("WScript.Network")
 oNet.AddWindowsPrinterConnection sUNC
 oNet.SetDefaultPrinter sUNC
End Sub

Function IsMemberOf(sGroupName)
  Set oNetwork = CreateObject("WScript.Network")
  sDomain = oNetwork.UserDomain
  sUser = oNetwork.UserName
  bIsMember = False
  Set oUser = GetObject("WinNT://" & sDomain & "/" & _
   sUser & ",user")
  For Each oGroup In oUser.Groups
    If oGroup.Name = sGroupName Then
      bIsMember = True
      Exit For
    End If
  Next
  IsMemberOf = bIsMember
End Function
```

Of course, you'll need to modify this script to suit your environment before you can use it. The universal naming conventions (UNCs), for example, will need to reflect ones that exist in your environment.

### ➤➤ The Login Script—Explained

I'll walk through this script line-by-line and explain what it does. This is the format I'll use for most longer examples in this book: Presenting the script in its entirety first, and then again with line-by-line explanations. Because I haven't yet covered most of the concepts this script is using, I'll provide cross-references where appropriate. That way, you can jump straight to more detailed explanations if you want.

The script starts off by using `MsgBox` to display a simple message. Notice the comment line, which begins with a single quotation mark. You should use comments to help describe what your script is doing; I'll be sure to do that in all the examples I show you.

For details on `MsgBox`, see "Displaying Messages" in Chapter 6.

```
'Display Message
MsgBox "Welcome to BrainCore.Net. You are now logged on."
```

Next, the script maps the three drives according to the user's group membership. Notice that each is using the `IsMemberOf()` function to check the group membership, and the `MapDrive` subroutine to actually map the drive. Both of these are modules I created; I'll cover how they work in a bit.

For details on `If…Then`, see "Conditional Execution" in Chapter 10.

```
'Map N: Drive
If IsMemberOf("Domain Users") Then
 MapDrive("N:","\\Server\Users")
End If

'Map S: Drive
If IsMemberOf("Research") Then
 MapDrive("R:","\\Server2\Research")
End If

'Map R: Drive
If IsMemberOf("Sales") Then
 MapDrive("S:","\\Server2\SalesDocs")
End If
```

Next, the script uses the custom `GetIP()` function to get the local IP address. Then, I use the `InStr()` and `Mid()` functions to pull out the third octet. `GetIP()` is a function I created, not one that's built into VBScript.

For details on `InStr()` and `Mid()`, see Chapter 8.

```
'Get IP address
sIP = GetIP()

'Figure out 3rd octet
iFirstDot = InStr(0,sIP,".")
iSecondDot = InStr(iFirstDot+1,sIP,".")
iThirdDot = InStr(iSecondDot+1,sIP,".")
sThirdOctet = Mid(sIP, iSecondDot+1, _
 Len(sIP)-iThirdDot)
```

Finally, I use the custom `MapPrinter` command to map a printer based on the third octet.

For details on `Select...Case`, see “Conditional Execution” in Chapter 10.

```
'Map printer based on octet
Select Case sThirdOctet
 Case "100"
  MapPrinter "\\NYDC\HPColor3"
 Case "110"
  MapPrinter "\\LADC\HP6"
 Case "120"
  MapPrinter "\\TXDC1\LaserJet"
End Select
```

Next come the parts of the script that actually do all of the work. First is the `MapDrive` routine, which simply maps a network drive.

For details on the Network object, see “The Network Object” in Chapter 11.

```
Sub MapDrive(sLetter, sUNC)
 Set oNet = WScript.CreateObject("WScript.Network")
 oNet.MapNetworkDrive sLetter, sUNC)
End Sub
```

Next, the `GetIP()` function retrieves the local IP address by using Windows Management Instrumentation (WMI).

For an introduction to WMI and lots of examples, turn to Chapter 17.

```
Function GetIP()
 Set myObj = GetObject("winmgmts:{impersonationLevel=" & _
  "impersonate}" & _
  "!//localhost".ExecQuery _
```

*continues*

```
  ("select IPAddress from " & _
  "Win32_NetworkingAdapterConfiguration" & _
  " where IPEnabled=TRUE")

 'Go through the addresses
 For Each IPAddress in myObj
  If IPAddress.IPAddress(0) <> "0.0.0.0" Then
   LocalIP = IPAddress.IPAddress(0)
   Exit For
  End If
 Next
 GetIP = LocalIP
End Function
```

`MapPrinter` works similarly to `MapDrive`, only it also sets the mapped printer to be the default.

```
Sub MapPrinter(sUNC)
 Set oNet = WScript.CreateObject("WScript.Network")
 oNet.AddWindowsPrinterConnection sUNC
 oNet.SetDefaultPrinter sUNC
End Sub
```

Finally, the `IsMemberOf()` function checks to see if the current user is a member of the specified user group.

```
Function IsMemberOf(sGroupName)
  Set oNetwork = CreateObject("WScript.Network")
  sDomain = oNetwork.UserDomain
  sUser = oNetwork.UserName
  bIsMember = False
  Set oUser = GetObject("WinNT://" & sDomain & "/" & _
   sUser & ",user")
  For Each oGroup In oUser.Groups
    If oGroup.Name = sGroupName Then
      bIsMember = True
      Exit For
    End If
  Next
  IsMemberOf = bIsMember
End Function
```

That's it! The new logon script is ready for testing and debugging.

## Validating User Input

This example logon script doesn't have any user input, but some of your scripts may. For example, you might write a script that asks for a server name, and then does some operation on that server. Any time you're asking for user input, you need to validate that input to make sure it's within the range that you expected.

For example, suppose you have a script that shuts down a remote server. You might have the script ask for the server name, and then ask for a shutdown delay in seconds. After accepting that input from the script's user (who might even be you), the script should check to make sure the server name was valid (perhaps it must start with two backslashes), and that the delay was within an acceptable range (maybe 5–30 seconds).

You can generally use `If…Then` constructs to validate user input. Why bother? Validation ensures that your scripts are working with proper input, and can help prevent the scripts from running into errors or performing unexpected actions.

Chapter 10 introduces `If…Then`, under "Conditional Execution."

If users provide incorrect or unexpected input, your script can display an error message and end, or even give users another chance to enter the necessary information.

---

**TIP** Plan to add user validation to all scripts that accept input from a user. The examples in this book don't always include input validation; I've deliberately left it out in many cases to help focus on what the script is supposed to accomplish. Scripts used in the real world, however, should always validate user input.

---

## Planning for Errors

Errors occur. There are actually a few different types of errors, with specific ways of dealing with each.

- Syntax errors. These are simple typos that you introduce when writing a script. You'll generally catch these when you test your scripts.
- Logic errors. These design flaws make the script behave unexpectedly or incorrectly. Again, these are usually your fault, and you'll find them as you test the script.

- Conditional errors. These errors occur because something in the script's operating environment was other than what you planned for when you wrote the script. For example, a domain controller might be unavailable, or a user may have typed a server name that doesn't exist.

Syntax and logic errors often crop up in scripting, and you'll find them as you test and debug your scripts. Conditional errors, however, are generally beyond your control. Your scripts should try to anticipate these errors, however, and handle them gracefully. For example, suppose you're using the WScript.Network object to map a network drive, and the server happens to be unavailable at the time. The basic script might look like this:

```
Set oNet = WScript.CreateObject("Wscript.Network")
oNet.MapNetworkDrive "S:", "\\Server2\SalesDocs"
```

If Server2 isn't available, the script will crash when executing the second line of code. That means the script will display an error message and won't execute anything else in the script. You can make the script a bit more resilient by anticipating the problem and adding *error-handling* code.

```
Set oNet = WScript.CreateObject("Wscript.Network")

On Error Resume Next
oNet.MapNetworkDrive "S:", "\\Server2\SalesDocs"
If Err <> 0 Then
 MsgBox "Server2 was unavailable; your S: drive was not mapped."
End If
On Error Goto 0
```

This modified script starts out by telling VBScript, "Look, if an error occurs, it's OK, I'll handle it. You just resume execution with the next line of script." That's done by `On Error Resume Next`.

After trying to map the drive, an `If…Then` construct checks the value of the special variable `Err`. If it's zero, the drive was mapped. If not, a friendlier error message is displayed to the user letting him know something went wrong. Finally, error checking is turned off with `On Error Goto 0`. From then on, errors will result in a VBScript error message and the script will stop executing.

`If...Then` is introduced under "Conditional Execution" in Chapter 10. Variables are covered under "What Are Variables?" in Chapter 5. I'll cover error handling in more detail throughout the book.

---

**NOTE** As you can see, error trapping and handling can add bulk to a script. To help keep the examples in this script focused on the task, I'll usually omit error handling. However, all scripts meant to run in the real world should include error handling wherever something might go wrong.

---

Error handling needs to be something you plan for in your initial script design. Listing 4.6 shows how you might make a note of possible conditional errors in your original task list.

**Listing 4.6** *Identifying possible errors.* Anticipating errors in your design will show you where to add error-handling code to your script.

```
Login script task list v3 with error notes

Display a logon welcome message:
"Welcome to BrainCore.Net. You are now logged on."
Wait until the user presses OK to dismiss the welcome message.
* Can't think of any potential errors here.

Map the N: drive:
Obtain a list of Domain Users group members. See if the user is in the
  list. If they are, map the drive to \\Server\Users.
* Server might be unavailable, need to handle this.

Map the R: drive:
Obtain a list of Research group members. See if the user is in the
  list. If they are, map the drive to \\Server2\ResearchDocs.
* Server might be unavailable, need to handle this.

Map the S: drive:
Obtain a list of Sales group members. See if the user is in the list.
  If they are, map the drive to \\Server2\SalesDocs.
* Server might be unavailable, need to handle this.

Map a printer:
Get the user's IP address. Look at just the third octet. To find it,
```

*continues*

```
look for the last period in the IP address, and then the next-to-the-
last period. The third octet is between the two periods. If the octet
is 100, map to \\NYDC\HPColor3. If it's 110, map to \\LADC\HP6. If
it's 120, map to \\TXDC1\LaserJet. Then make the mapped printer the
default.
* Printer or server might be unavailable. Need to handle this if
it occurs.
```

Anticipating errors and handling them within the script is definitely the mark of a careful, experienced scripter. Plan for errors in every script you write and you'll definitely be more appreciated by the folks who use your scripts.

## Creating Script Libraries

After you've created some useful functions, you can save them into a script library. That's nothing any fancier than a collection of useful scriptlets, which you can reuse in various scripts that you write. For example, you might pull out all of the functions and subroutines from the logon script you wrote, saving them into a separate file. That'll make it easier to reuse those useful bits of code later in the future.

By carefully modularizing your code, you'll quickly build a library of useful scripts, making it easier to write new scripts in the future.

## Review

In this chapter, I tried to provide you with a look at how I go about designing and writing scripts. I don't just sit down and start typing; instead, I create a list of tasks I want the script to accomplish, and then I try to do some research and find out exactly how to perform each of those tasks in a script. The VBScript documentation, Google, and other Web resources are useful for finding examples and information, and before long I usually find everything I need to know. Next, I try to modularize the script, so that I can reuse my hard-earned information in other scripts that I might write in the future.

If you approach script design and development with this methodical approach, you won't need to be an expert developer to write great scripts.

You can build on the work of those who came before you, and quickly start writing scripts that are useful in your environment.

**COMING UP**

You're ready to start learning VBScript, and your crash course begins in the next chapter. Don't worry; you're not going to be turned into a programmer! Instead, you'll be learning just enough VBScript to have some powerful tools at your disposal as you start scripting.

PART II

# VBScript Tutorial

CHAPTER 5

# Functions, Objects, Variables, and More

**IN THIS CHAPTER**

You've learned how to design a script, but you're not quite ready to write one. First, you have to learn the basics of VBScript, and this chapter begins your crash course.

Scripting is, of course, a form of computer programming, and computer programming is all about telling a computer what to do. Before you can start ordering the computer around, though, you need to learn to speak a language that it understands. VBScript is one such language, and in this chapter, I'll introduce you to the VBScript *syntax*, or language.

Almost all computer programming languages, including VBScript, have a few things in common.

- They have built-in commands that tell the computer to perform certain tasks or calculate certain kinds of information.
- They have a means for tracking temporary information, such as data entered by a user or collected during some calculation.
- Windows-based programming languages generally have a means for interacting with objects, because objects form the basis of Windows' functionality.

---

**NOTE** The capability to interact with objects is *not* the same thing as being an object-oriented programming language. Although the concepts and benefits of object-oriented programming are beyond the scope of this book, suffice to say that VBScript isn't object oriented, despite its capability to interact with objects created in other languages.

---

VBScript implements these common programming elements through variables, functions, and statements, and through an object interface.

- *Variables* act as storage areas for different types of data.
- *Functions* are VBScript's way of performing calculations or tasks and providing you with the results; *statements* simply perform tasks. You can even create your own functions and statements to customize VBScript's capabilities.
- VBScript includes a complete *object interface* based on Microsoft's Component Object Model, or COM.

In this chapter, you'll learn how to use each of these elements within scripts.

---

**NOTE** I've never liked programming books that provide short, useless snippets of script as examples, even as early in the book as you are right now. Most of the examples you'll see in this and subsequent chapters are fully functioning scripts that you can actually use in your environment. Of course, to make them fully functioning, they have to include some things that you won't learn about until later chapters. That's OK; I'll point out the parts of the scripts that are important for now, and as you read through the next few chapters in Part II, you'll learn more and more about how these scripts operate.

---

## What Are Variables?

Variables are temporary storage areas for data. You may even remember them from algebra: $x + 5 = 10$, solve for variable $x$. Of course, in those situations, $x$ wasn't really a variable, because it always equaled some fixed amount when you solved the equation. In scripting, variables can change their contents many times.

### ➤➤ Sample Script

Listing 5.1 shows a sample script. It's a fully functional script that will connect to a domain, locate any inactive user accounts, and disable them.

**NOTE** Once more, I'm showing you a script that uses some advanced features. This lets me show you functional, useful scripts rather than dumbed-down examples, but for now I'm just going to explain the bits that are important for this chapter. I promise you'll get to the rest later!

**Listing 5.1** *DisableUser.vbs.* We'll use this script as a running example throughout this chapter.

```
Dim sTheDate
Dim oUserObj
Dim oObject
Dim oGroupObj
Dim iFlags
Dim iDiff
Dim sResult
Dim sName
Const UF_ACCOUNTDISABLE = &H0002

' Constant for Log file path
 Const sLogFile = "C:\UserMgr1.txt"

' Point to Object containing users to check
Set oGroupObj = GetObject("WinNT://MYDOMAINCONTROLLER/Users")

On Error Resume Next
For Each oObject in oGroupObj.Members

  ' Find all User Objects Within Domain Users group
  ' (ignore machine accounts)
 If (oObject.Class = "User") And _
  (InStr(oObject.Name, "$") = 0) then Set oUserObj = _
  GetObject(oObject.ADsPath)

  ' get last login date
  sTheDate = UserObj.get("LastLogin")
  sTheDate = Left(sTheDate,8)
  sTheDate = CDate(sTheDate)

  ' find difference in week between then and now
  iDiff = DateDiff("ww", sTheDate, Now)
```

*continues*

```
' if 6 weeks or more then disable the account
  If iDiff >= 6 Then
   iFlags = UserObj.Get("UserFlags")
  End If

  ' if the account is not already disabled...
  If (iFlags And UF_ACCOUNTDISABLE) = 0 Then

   ' disable account
   oUserObj.Put "UserFlags", iFlags Or UF_ACCOUNTDISABLE
   oUserObj.SetInfo

   ' Get user name and write a log entry
   sName = oUserObj.Name
   sResult = Log(sName,iDiff)

  End If

 End If
Next

' Release object
Set oGroupObj = Nothing

Function Log(oUser,sDate)

' Create a FileSystemObject
 Dim oFS
 Set oFS = CreateObject("Scripting.FileSystemObject")

 ' Create a TextStream object
 Dim oTextStream
 Set oTextStream = objFS.OpenTextFile(sLogFile, 8, True)

 ' Write log entry
 oTextStream.WriteLine("Account:" & vbTab & oUser & vbTab & _
 "Inactive  for:" & vbTab & strdate & vbatb & "Weeks" & _
 vbtab & "Disabled on:" & vbTab & Date & vbTab & "at:" & _
 vbTab & Time)

 ' Close file
 oTextStream.Close
```

```
    ' Release objects
    Set oFS = Nothing
    Set oTextStream = Nothing

    Log = True

End Function
```

Before you can run this script, you'll need to make two important changes.

- Change `MYDOMAINCONTROLLER` to the name of an actual domain controller in your domain.
- Change `C:\UserMgr1.txt` to the path and filename of the log file that you want the script to create.

**NOTE** Note the use of the underscore (_) character at the end of some lines of text. Because the pages of this book are only so wide, I can't include very long lines of code. Instead, I break those lines up by using the underscore character. When you type this code, you can just skip right over the underscore and type the code as one long line. However, VBScript understands that the underscore is a *line continuation character,* so if you do type the underscore and keep the code on multiple lines, VBScript will understand perfectly. Try it both ways and see which one you like; I prefer to keep the underscore because it means I don't have to scroll to the right in my script editor to see the entire line of code.

This script logs in to the domain using the user credentials of whatever user runs the script; in order for it to work, of course, that user needs to be a member of the Domain Admins group. The script locates all users that haven't logged in for at least six weeks, disables their accounts, and writes an entry to the specified log file for your review.

**NOTE** There's a lot going on in this script that I won't be explaining right away. I'll be using this script, along with a couple of others, as a running example through the next few chapters. Eventually, I'll explain everything in it. In the meantime, though, feel free to use it both as a working tool in your environment and as a great example of administrative scripting.

## Declaring Variables

One of the first things you see in the DisableUsers script is the variable declarations.

```
Dim sTheDate
Dim oUserObj
Dim oObject
Dim oGroupObj
Dim iFlags
Dim iDiff
Dim sResult
Dim sName
Const UF_ACCOUNTDISABLE = &H0002
```

The `Dim` statements tell VBScript that you're defining, or declaring, a variable. Actually, `Dim` is short for *dimension,* a term that hearkens back to the early days of computing. Following each `Dim` statement is a variable name. Each of these statements tells VBScript to set aside room in memory for the variable, and to remember the variable's name.

Variable names must follow a few basic rules.

- They are not case-sensitive. For example, `sTheDate` and `sthedate` are treated the same.
- They must begin with a letter or an underscore (_) character.
- They may contain letters, underscores, and numbers.
- VBScript allows quite long variable names, but practically speaking they shouldn't be more than a dozen characters or so, or your script will become difficult for other people to read.

You may also notice the `Const` statement, which is short for *constant.* Constants are like variables in that they assign a meaningful name to an arbitrary value. In this case, the constant name `UF_ACCOUNTDISABLE` is a bit easier to remember than the hexadecimal value 02. However, unlike variables, constants—as their name implies—don't change. If you try to assign a different value to `UF_ACCOUNTDISABLE` during the course of the script, you'll receive an error message.

You need to understand that VBScript doesn't *require* you to define variables up front. In fact, you could delete every single `Dim` statement from this script and it would still work perfectly. So why bother?

One of the biggest causes of bugs in scripting is simple mistyping. For example, consider the following snippet of code from the DisableUsers script.

```
' get last login date
sTheDaet = UserObj.get("LastLogin")
sTheDate = Left(sTheDate,8)
sTheDate = CDate(sTheDate)
```

Notice anything peculiar? In the second line of code, I changed `sTheDate` to `sTheDaet`. Because VBScript doesn't require me to declare my variables up front, this line of code won't generate an error. Instead, VBScript will dynamically create a brand-new variable named `sTheDaet` on-the-fly. Of course, the third line of code assumes that the second line of code put some data into `sTheDate`, not `sTheDaet`, and so the third line of code won't work correctly. It still won't generate an error, but `sTheDate` will contain no data. Finally, the last line of code *will* generate an error—despite the fact that there's nothing wrong with the last line of code. The problem is all the way back in the second line of code where a simple typo created a new variable and introduced a serious logic error into the script.

Typos like this are easy to make and all too common. To help combat them, VBScript provides `Option Explicit`, a command you can add to the beginning of your script.

```
Option Explicit
Dim sTheDate
Dim oUserObj
Dim oObject
Dim oGroupObj
Dim iFlags
Dim iDiff
Dim sResult
Dim sName
Const UF_ACCOUNTDISABLE = &H0002
```

With `Option Explicit` in place, VBScript will *require* all variables to be declared before they can be used. Now suppose I were to rerun the script with the typo in the variable name.

```
' get last login date
  sTheDaet = UserObj.get("LastLogin")
  sTheDate = Left(sTheDate,8)
  sTheDate = CDate(sTheDate)
```

VBScript would generate an error on the second line of script, because I'm attempting to use a variable that hasn't yet been declared. That's exactly where I want VBScript to generate an error, too, because it's the line of script that actually contains the error.

---

**TIP** Always include `Option Explicit` in your scripts. For brevity, I won't always include the line in the sample scripts in this book, but it's a great way to avoid spending hours to track down a typo.

---

## Understanding Data Types

If you've worked with other programming languages, you may be familiar with the concept of *data types.* Simply put, there are different kinds of data in the world around us: numbers, letters, dates, huge numbers, pictures, and more. Most programming languages need to understand what kind of data a variable will contain, so that the language can treat the variable appropriately. For example, it wouldn't make sense to try to subtract the word Hello from a picture of a flower, and so most programming languages won't allow you to perform mathematical operations with anything but numeric variables. Languages that care about the type of data a variable will hold are called *strongly typed* languages.

VBScript, on the other hand, is *weakly typed.* You'll notice that none of the variable declarations include any hint as to the data type each variable would hold.

```
Dim sTheDate
Dim oUserObj
Dim oObject
Dim oGroupObj
Dim iFlags
Dim iDiff
Dim sResult
Dim sName
Const UF_ACCOUNTDISABLE = &H0002
```

There's no clue because VBScript only has one data type: variant. The variant data type can hold any kind of data, and that data can even change to a different type as your script runs. For example, the following snippet of code would be perfectly valid in VBScript.

```
Dim vData
vData = 1
vData = "Hello"
vData = Date()
```

You may think that this weakly typed stuff is great. After all, you can just pop any kind of data you like into a variable and VBScript won't care. In some ways, that's true; not having to worry about data types can be a time saver. On the other hand, as you'll see shortly, it can also be a real pain in the neck.

## Assigning Data to Variables

You've already seen several examples of how to assign data to a variable. Here's a section of the DisableUsers script, with the data assignment lines highlighted in boldface.

```
' get last login date
  sTheDate = UserObj.get("LastLogin")
  sTheDate = Left(sTheDate,8)
  sTheDate = CDate(sTheDate)

  ' find difference in week between then and now
  iDiff = DateDiff("ww", sTheDate, Now)
```

This actually looks a lot like the old algebra class, right? The variable name appears on the left side of the equal sign (=), which is referred to as the *assignment operator*. Whatever you want inserted into the variable appears on the right side of the assignment operator. In all four of these examples, the variable is being filled with the results of a function, which I'll cover later in this chapter.

The right side of the assignment operator can include any kind of operation that results in a single value. So all of the following commands are legal.

```
Dim vVariable
vVariable = 1
vVariable = 1 + 1
vVariable = "Hello"
vVariable = Date()
```

Variables can also be assigned to each other. This makes sense if you consider variables as simply a representation of a value; assigning one variable to another simply copies the value.

```
Dim vVar1
Dim vVar2
vVar1 = 1
vVar2 = 2
vVar1 = vVar1 + vVar2
```

After running this brief chunk of script, `vVar1` will contain the value 3.

## Data Coercion

As I've already mentioned, VBScript doesn't much care what kind of data you put into a variable. However, there are certain operations that only support certain data types, so you can run into trouble. For example, consider the following operations and see if you can predict their output.

```
Dim vVar1
Dim vVar2
Dim vVar3
vVar1 = 1
vVar2 = "1"
vVar3 = "2"

MsgBox vVar1 & vVar2
MsgBox vVar1 + vVar2
MsgBox vVar1 – vVar2
MsgBox vVar2 + vVar3
```

**NOTE** The `MsgBox` statement will display a small dialog box with the result of whatever operation you've given it. It's an easy way, in an example like this, to see how VBScript treats each operation.

If you type this script in and run it, you'll get four message boxes. They might not be what you expect! You should see an 11, a 2, a 0, and a 12. Can you guess why?

When you assign data to a variable, VBScript actually does care. It keeps track of what it *thinks* the data type is, based on what you gave it. For example, any number not included in quotes is definitely numeric data, without question. Anything in quotation marks is text, called a *string*. However, if the text is all numeric, VBScript acknowledges that it could be numeric data, not a string. Here's what happens.

- The first operation uses the concatenation operator (the ampersand). This operator is only used to tack one string onto another string. VBScript knows this, and so it *coerces*, or temporarily converts, `vVar1`—which was a numeric value—into a string so that the operation will work. The result is a 1 being tacked onto another 1, for a result of 11.
- The second operation seems to be adding a numeric value and a string. This doesn't make any sense, of course. However, in this case, VBScript can coerce the string data into a number, and it does so. The addition operation works smoothly from that point, with the result of 2.
- The third operation requires a similar coercion to complete the subtraction operation and arrive at the correct result of zero.
- The fourth operation is more interesting. Back before Microsoft added the ampersand as a concatenation operator, the plus (+) operator did double duty: For numbers, it was addition. For strings, it handled concatenation. Modern VBScript knows this, so when it sees two string values being "added" together, it concatenates them instead, giving you a result of 12.

Order isn't important to how VBScript tries to coerce data. For example, let's modify our sample script as follows:

```
Dim vVar1
Dim vVar2
Dim vVar3
vVar1 = 1
vVar2 = "1"
vVar3 = "2"

MsgBox vVar2 & vVar1
MsgBox vVar2 + vVar1
MsgBox vVar2 – vVar1
MsgBox vVar3 + vVar2
```

Rerun the script. Do you see any differences in the results? You shouldn't. VBScript prefers to use + as an addition operator, so it will try to do so when any of the involved values is numeric. However, in the last operation, where both values were set up as strings, VBScript gives in and performs concatenation.

What can you do to make sure VBScript treats your data the way you want?

- Keep track of the data types you put into variables. I do this with the first letter of the variable name: `s` tells me it's a string, `i` is for integers, `d` for dates, `b` for Boolean values (True or False), and so forth. You can use my naming scheme or make up your own.
- VBScript includes data conversion functions, which you'll learn about in Chapter 7. These functions can force data into a specific data type.
- Avoid using the ambiguous + operator for concatenation. Instead, use the dedicated ampersand (`&`) and save the + operator for addition.

## What Are Functions?

Functions are a way of performing a task and getting something back. For example, VBScript has a function named `Date()`, which simply looks up and provides the current date according to your computer's internal clock. Functions are used to perform special calculations, retrieve information, look up information, convert data types, manipulate data, and much more.

### Input Parameters

Functions may include one or more *input parameters,* which give the function something to work with and usually are a major part of the function's output. Not all functions need input, however. For example, the `Date()` function doesn't need any input parameters to function; it knows how to look up the date without any help from you.

Other functions may require multiple input parameters. For example, the `InStr()` function is used to locate a particular character within a string. Here's how it works.

```
Dim sVar
Dim iResult
```

```
sVar = "Hello!"
iResult = InStr(1, sVar, "l")
```

After running this short script, `iResult` will contain the value 3, meaning the `Instr()` function located the letter l at the third position within the variable `sVar`. `InStr()` requires three input parameters:

1. The character position where the search should start
2. The string in which to search
3. The string to search for

---

**NOTE** Of course, I haven't necessarily memorized `InStr()`'s input parameters. I looked them up in the VBScript documentation. After you use a function a few times in scripts, you'll remember its parameters without looking them up, but I don't use `InStr()` very often so I always refer to the documentation to see in which order the parameters should be.

---

Now that you know what a function looks like, refer to this section of the DisableUsers sample script and see if you can spot the functions (I've boldfaced them to make it easy).

```
' get last login date
  sTheDate = UserObj.get("LastLogin")
  sTheDate = Left(sTheDate,8)
  sTheDate = CDate(sTheDate)

  ' find difference in week between then and now
  iDiff = DateDiff("ww", sTheDate, Now)

  ' if 6 weeks or more then disable the account
  If iDiff >= 6 Then
   iFlags = UserObj.Get("UserFlags")
  End If

  ' if the account is not already disabled...
  If (iFlags And UF_ACCOUNTDISABLE) = 0 Then

   ' disable account
   oUserObj.Put "UserFlags", iFlags Or UF_ACCOUNTDISABLE
   oUserObj.SetInfo
```

*continues*

```
  ' Get user name and write a log entry
  sName = oUserObj.Name
  sResult = Log(sName,iDiff)

End If
```

---

**NOTE** I try to keep my scripts nice and pretty by capitalizing function names, but VBScript couldn't care less. `DateDiff()` and `datediff()` or even `DaTed-iFf()` are all the same as far as VBScript is concerned.

---

## Output Values

All functions return some kind of value to your script. The VBScript documentation can tell you what type of data that is (numeric, date, string, and so on), but you need to decide what to do with it. The most common action is to assign the result to a variable.

```
' get last login date
  sTheDate = UserObj.get("LastLogin")
  sTheDate = Left(sTheDate,8)
  sTheDate = CDate(sTheDate)
```

In this case, variable `sTheDate` is being used to hold the results of a function. In fact, the function is performing an operation with the old value of `sTheDate` and returning a new value to be stored into `sTheDate`, overwriting the old value.

The results of a function can also be fed as the input parameter to another function. For example, consider the following few lines of code.

```
Dim sVar1
sVar1 = "Transcription"
MsgBox Left(Right(sVar1, 9), 6)
```

The result will be a message box containing "script" and an OK button. Here's what's happening.

- VBScript executes functions from the inside out. In other words, it looks for the most deeply nested function and starts with that one, and then works its way out.

- The `Right()` function is executed first and returns the rightmost 9 characters of whatever is in `sVar1`. The result, of course, is "scrip-tion".
- The `Left()` function then takes the leftmost six characters of whatever the `Right()` function returned, resulting in "script".
- The `Left()` function's results are passed to the `MsgBox` statement, which displays the results.

Nesting functions can make your script difficult to read and troubleshoot, although VBScript itself doesn't mind. You can make your scripts easier to read by breaking each function out into its own line of code.

```
Dim sVar1
sVar1 = "Transcription"
sVar1 = Right(sVar1, 9)
sVar1 = Left(sVar1, 6)
MsgBox sVar1
```

This revised snippet takes a bit more reading, but it's clearer what the script is doing.

## Intrinsic versus Custom Functions

So far, the functions I've introduced have been *intrinsic* functions, which means they're built into VBScript. You can look them all up in the VBScript documentation to see how they work. However, you can build your own custom functions. For example, suppose you want a function that writes entries to a log file. That would be a useful function to have, and you could probably use it in any number of different scripts. In fact, the DisableUsers sample script contains a custom function that writes log file entries.

```
Function Log(oUser,sDate)

 ' Constant for Log file path
 Const sLogFile = "C:\UserMgr1.txt"

 ' Create a FileSystemObject
 Dim oFS
 Set oFS = CreateObject("Scripting.FileSystemObject")

 ' Create a TextStream object
 Dim oTextStream
```

*continues*

```
 Set oTextStream = objFS.OpenTextFile(sLogFile, 8, True)

 ' Write log entry
 oTextStream.WriteLine("Account:" & vbTab & oUser & vbTab & _
 "Inactive  for:" & vbTab & strdate & vbatb & "Weeks" & _
 vbtab & "Disabled on:" & vbTab & Date & vbTab & "at:" & _
 vbTab & Time)

 ' Close file
 oTextStream.Close

 ' Release objects
 Set oFS = Nothing
 Set oTextStream = Nothing

 Log = True

End Function
```

This function is defined by the `Function` statement, and all of the code within the function falls between `Function` and `End Function`. The `Function` statement has several important components:

- The `Function` statement itself
- The name of the function, in this case `Log`
- The function's input parameters, `oUser` and `sDate`

This function is called from within the main script just as if it were an intrinsic function.

```
' Get user name and write a log entry
   sName = oUserObj.Name
   sResult = Log(sName,iDiff)
```

The last line of code in the function is `Log = True`. This is a special line of code, because it uses the function's name on the left side of the assignment operator. This line of code tells VBScript that the function's return value will be True. In a custom function, you use this technique to return a value to whatever called your function—assign the return value to the function's name. You must generally do so in the last line of code before `End Function`.

However, this is really a *bad* example of how to write a custom function. It works perfectly, but it's doing a few things that you don't normally want a function to do.

- The function doesn't return a useful value. You can tell because the calling script doesn't do anything with the value; it just stores it in a variable. If the return value isn't useful, why have it at all? This function could have been written as a *subroutine,* which doesn't return a value. I'll be covering subroutines in the next section.
- The function is relying on data that was defined outside of itself. Specifically, the `sLogFile` variable was defined in the main part of the script, not the function. Generally, functions should be entirely self-contained, making them easier to transport from one script to another without modifications. Listing 5.2 shows a modified script that passes the log filename as an input parameter, because input parameters provide a legitimate way of getting information into a function.

**Listing 5.2** *DisableUser2.vbs.* This script has been modified to have a better-written function.

```
Dim sTheDate
Dim oUserObj
Dim oObject
Dim oGroupObj
Dim iFlags
Dim iDiff
Dim sResult
Dim sName
Const UF_ACCOUNTDISABLE = &H0002

' Point to Object containing users to check
Set oGroupObj = GetObject("WinNT://MYDOMAINCONTROLLER/Users")

On Error Resume Next
For Each oObject in oGroupObj.Members

 ' Find all User Objects Within Domain Users group
 ' (ignore machine accounts)
 If (oObject.Class = "User") And _
  (InStr(oObject.Name, "$") = 0) then Set oUserObj = _
  GetObject(oObject.ADsPath)
```

*continues*

```
   ' get last login date
   sTheDate = UserObj.get("LastLogin")
   sTheDate = Left(sTheDate,8)
   sTheDate = CDate(sTheDate)

   ' find difference in week between then and now
   iDiff = DateDiff("ww", sTheDate, Now)

   ' if 6 weeks or more then disable the account
   If iDiff >= 6 Then
    iFlags = UserObj.Get("UserFlags")
   End If

   ' if the account is not already disabled...
   If (iFlags And UF_ACCOUNTDISABLE) = 0 Then

    ' disable account
    oUserObj.Put "UserFlags", iFlags Or UF_ACCOUNTDISABLE
    oUserObj.SetInfo

    ' Get user name and write a log entry
    sName = oUserObj.Name
    sResult = Log(sName,iDiff,sLogFile)

   End If

 End If
Next

' Release object
Set oGroupObj = Nothing

Function Log(oUser,sDate,sLog)

 ' Constant for Log file path
 Const sLogFile = "C:\UserMgr1.txt"

 ' Create a FileSystemObject
 Dim oFS
 Set oFS = CreateObject("Scripting.FileSystemObject")

 ' Create a TextStream object
 Dim oTextStream
 Set oTextStream = objFS.OpenTextFile(sLog, 8, True)
```

```
 ' Write log entry
 oTextStream.WriteLine("Account:" & vbTab & oUser & vbTab & _
 "Inactive  for:" & vbTab & strdate & vbatb & "Weeks" & _
 vbtab & "Disabled on:" & vbTab & Date & vbTab & "at:" & _
 vbTab & Time)

 ' Close file
 oTextStream.Close

 ' Release objects
 Set oFS = Nothing
 Set oTextStream = Nothing

 Log = True

End Function
```

The boldfaced code indicates what's been changed. Now, the function is much more appropriate and will be easier to reuse in other scripts. It still isn't returning a useful value, so in the next section I'll show you how to convert it into a subroutine.

## What Are Statements and Subroutines?

Here's where VBScript's terminology gets a bit complicated, and for no good reason: Aside from the terms themselves, statements and subroutines are actually quite straightforward. A *statement* is an intrinsic command that accepts zero or more parameters and returns no value. A *subroutine* is simply a custom statement that you write yourself. Intrinsic and custom functions are both called functions; why custom statements are called subroutines (or *subs* for short) is a mystery from the depths of VBScript's past.

### Functions, without the Output

Statements (and subroutines) always perform some kind of task. Unlike a function, statements cannot return a value to your script, so they *just* perform a task. One of the simplest VBScript statements is `Beep`, which simply makes the computer beep. It takes no parameters, returns no value, and performs one task. Another simple statement, `End`, tells VBScript to stop running your script immediately. Pretty simple!

### ➤➤ A Custom Subroutine

You may want to create custom routines that perform a task but return no value. For example, suppose you're writing a script and you want your computer to beep a lot when it encounters some specific condition, such as an error or a full hard disk. You could just list multiple `Beep` statements in a series, but it would be more efficient to use a custom subroutine. You could program the subroutine to accept an input parameter describing how many times to beep. Listing 5.3 shows an example.

**Listing 5.3** *MultiBeep Subroutine.* This subroutine can be used to make the computer beep a specified number of times.

```
Sub MultiBeep(iTimes)
 Dim iTemp
 For iTemp = 1 To iTimes
  Beep
 Next
End Sub
```

You can use the MultiBeep subroutine from anywhere in the main portion of your script. For example, to make the computer beep five times, you'd use `MultiBeep(5)`.

### ➤➤ A Custom Subroutine—Explained

The MultiBeep subroutine actually uses several VBScript commands I haven't introduced yet, but I'll focus for now on the parts that define the subroutine. First, all subroutines include a `Sub` and an `End Sub` statement, in much the same way that custom functions use `Function` and `End Function`:

```
Sub MultiBeep(iTimes)
End Sub
```

As with a custom function, note that the parameters are defined in the `Sub` statement. In this case, the variable `iTimes` represents the number of times the computer should beep.

Everything else in the subroutine is your custom code.

```
Dim iTemp
For iTemp = 1 To iTimes
 Beep
Next
```

For now, don't worry about how this code works. You probably recognize the `Dim` statement as a variable declaration, and you've already learned what `Beep` does. I'll cover the `For...Next` construct in Chapter 10.

---

**TIP** Notice in Listing 5.3 that I indented the lines of script between `Sub` and `End Sub`. Indenting is a common programming practice that helps keep your code easier to read. The indent serves as a visual cue that the code is within some other routine or construct.

---

### Leading a Dual Life

A few of VBScript's built-in functions lead a double life as statements. The most common example is `MsgBox`. As a statement, it displays a message box, complete with whatever icons and buttons you like. When the user clicks one of those buttons, the message box goes away and your script continues.

However, `MsgBox()` can be a function, too. In this guise, it still displays the same type of message box, but it also returns a value indicating which button the user clicked. For example, this allows your script to ask Are-you-sure?-type messages with Yes and No buttons and act appropriately based on which button the user clicks.

There's only one real difference in the way you use `MsgBox` as a statement or a function. As a statement, there's no return value, so you can use `MsgBox` on a line of script by itself, as in `MsgBox "Hello!"`. However, as a function, `MsgBox()` returns a value, which you'll need to assign to a variable, as in `iResult = MsgBox("Are you sure?")`.

You'll see a lot more of `MsgBox`, both as a function and a statement, throughout this book and especially in Chapter 6.

## What Are Objects?

I've already made a big deal about how VBScript lets you access operating system functionality because VBScript is object based, and Windows exposes much of its functionality through objects. So you may be wondering, "What the heck is an object?"

Bear with me for the 10-second synopsis. You may have heard of COM or COM+, two versions of Microsoft's Component Object Model. The whole idea behind COM is that software developers can package their code in a way that makes it easily accessible to other applications. For example, suppose some poor developer spent a few years developing a cool way to interact with e-mail systems. If the developer wrote that code according to the rules of COM, every other developer—or scripter—would be able to take advantage of that e-mail interaction. In fact, a bunch of developers did exactly that! You may have heard of Microsoft's Mail Application Programming Interface, or MAPI. It's what Microsoft Outlook uses to access an Exchange Server, for example. MAPI is an example of COM in action; any programmer—including you—can use MAPI to access a mail server, because MAPI is written to the COM standard.

Therefore, an *object* is simply a piece of software that's written to the COM standard. VBScript can use most objects that are written to the COM standard; most of Windows' functionality is written to the COM standard, and that's what makes VBScript so powerful.

### Properties

Most software requires some kind of configuration to use it, and COM objects are no exception. You configure an object by setting its *properties*. Properties are simply a means of customizing an object's behavior. For example, an e-mail object might have properties for setting the mail server name, setting the user's name and password, and so forth.

Properties can also provide information to your script. A mail object might include a property that tells you how many new messages are available or how much space is left in the mailbox.

In your scripts, you'll generally use a variable name to represent an object. I use variable names that start with the letter `o`, so that I know the variable is really an object reference. To refer to an object's properties, simply list the property name after the object name. For example, suppose you have a mail object referenced by the variable `oMail`. To set the mail server name, you might use `oMail.ServerName = "mail.braincore.net"`. The period in between the object variable and the property name helps VBScript distinguish between the two.

### Methods

You already know that functions, statements, and subroutines exist in VBScript. Objects have functions, statements, and subroutines too, but they're called *methods*. Suppose your fictional mail object provided a statement named `GetMail`, which retrieved mail from the mail server. You could then simply include `oMail.GetMail` in your script to activate the statement and retrieve the mail.

Like functions and statements, some methods accept input parameters. For example, `oMail.GetMail(1)` might retrieve the first message in the mailbox. Other methods might work as functions `sMessage = oMail.GetMail(2)` might retrieve the second message and store the message body in the variable `sMessage`.

How do you know what methods an object supports? Check the documentation. Also, I'll introduce you to several useful objects in Chapters 11 and 12.

### Collections

Sometimes, programmers create objects that represent a hierarchy of real-world data. One common hierarchy that you're probably familiar with is the file system on a computer: It's a tree of folders and files. If you wanted to manipulate the file system in a script, you'd need an object that represented that hierarchy of folders and files.

COM provides a means for objects to represent hierarchies through *collections*. A collection is simply a special property that represents several other objects. Sound complicated? It's not! Consider a folder named Test, which contains two files: File1 and File2. Test also contains two subfolders, named Test1 and Test2. Test1 contains a file named FileA.

Now, suppose you've created a theoretical file management object and assigned it to variable `oFiles`. `oFiles` might have the following useful properties:

- A `Files` property that returns a collection of file objects.
- A `Subfolders` property that returns a collection of folder objects.
- Folder objects that have their own `Folders` and `Files` collections.
- File objects that have properties for `FileSize`, `FileName`, and so forth.

How would you find the size of the first file under Test? `oFile.Files(0).FileSize`. That starts with your `oFile` object reference, grabs the first file object in the `Files` collection (most collections start at zero, not one), and then gets that file's `FileSize` property. Notice the periods separating each portion of the object reference.

How would you get the size for `FileA`? `oFile.Subfolders(0).Files(0).FileSize`. You would start with your `oFile` object reference, move onto the first subfolder, grab the first file in that subfolder, and then get the file size.

---

**NOTE** This file management object isn't actually fictional—Windows includes one, called the FileSystemObject. I'll cover it in Chapter 12.

---

## A Sample Object

It may be easier to see what all of this object stuff is about with a nontechnical sample. Here, I'll break my usual policy of only including useful administrative samples in favor of clarity.

Suppose you're a biology major in college, and you're working with trees. You want to create a computer model of a tree so that you can simulate how it lives in various environmental conditions. You write the computer model to the COM specification, creating a Tree object. The object has the following properties.

- `Species`. This read/write property sets or retrieves the species of the simulated tree.
- `Age`. This read/write property sets or retrieves the age of the tree in years.
- `Environment`. This read/write property sets or retrieves the environment of the tree.
- `Disease`. This read-only property retrieves a True or False value, which indicates if the tree has a disease.

In addition, the Tree object has one method.

- `Grow`. This method accepts a parameter indicating how many months the tree should grow in the simulated environment.

Listing 5.4 shows a simulated script that uses the Tree object.

**Listing 5.4** *TreeObject model script.* Working with the fictional Tree object.

```
' Assumes the Tree object is referenced by
' variable oTree.

' set initial parameters
oTree.Species = "Oak"
oTree.Age = 12
oTree.Environment = "City"

' grow the tree
oTree.Grow(36)

' retrieve values
MsgBox "Tree is " & oTree.Species & ", " & _
 oTree.Age & " years old, in " & oTree.Environment
MsgBox "Tree is diseased: " & oTree.Disease
```

After running this script (if you could, which you can't), you'd get a message box saying "Tree is Oak, 15 years old, in City." A second message box would indicate whether the tree was healthy.

As you can see, the properties, collections, and methods of objects provide a straightforward way to access powerful features.

## Scripting with Objects

You've already seen a small version of how to work with objects in script, so it's time for a full example. This is actually a preview of Chapter 12 and uses the FileSystemObject I mentioned earlier.

### ➤➤ Listing Files

Listing 5.5 shows a brief sample script that displays the name of each file in the root of the C: drive.

**Listing 5.5** *RootFiles.* Filenames will be displayed in message boxes.

```
Dim oFSO, oFile, oFolder
Set oFSO = CreateObject("Scripting.FileSystemObject")
Set oFolder = oFSO.GetFolder("C:\")
```

*continues*

```
For Each oFile in oFolder.Files
 MsgBox oFile.Name
Next
```

### ➤➤ Listing Files—Explained

This script starts with a variable declaration. This might be a new type of declaration for you, because it declares three variables on one line. This functionally is the same as three separate `Dim` statements, just a bit shorter.

```
Dim oFSO, oFile, oFolder
' Same as:
' Dim oFSO
' Dim oFile
' Dim oFolder
```

Next, the script uses the `Set` statement and `CreateObject` function to create a reference to the FileSystemObject. `CreateObject` requires the class name of the object you want; you'll usually get that class name from the documentation for the object. Note that the `Set` command is required whenever you're assigning an object reference to a variable.

```
Set oFSO = CreateObject("Scripting.FileSystemObject")
Set oFolder = oFSO.GetFolder("C:\")
```

That second line of code uses the FileSystemObject's `GetFolder` method, which is actually a function. It accepts the name of a folder and returns a folder object that represents that folder. In this case, the object is assigned to the variable `oFolder`.

The next three lines of text loop through the folder's `Files` collection, one at a time. For each one, it displays the file's name in a message box.

```
For Each oFile in oFolder.Files
  MsgBox oFile.Name
Next
```

If you want to jump ahead and see what `For Each` is all about, you'll find it in the "For Each" section in Chapter 10.

## Review

You've started learning how VBScript works in this chapter. In fact, you've learned about the three main parts of any script: functions and subroutines (which you now know aren't really that different from one another), objects, and variables.

Variables act as temporary storage areas for your data and allow your scripts to change their behavior and manipulate data. VBScript's built-in functions and statements provide the actual functionality of the language, whereas your own functions and subroutines extend VBScript's power to perform custom tasks.

Finally, objects represent the functionality of the Windows operating system and its many features and capabilities. Objects have properties, which govern their behavior, and methods, which perform actions. Administrative scripting is all about using VBScript functions and statements to tie together operating system objects. For example, you might use a file system object to manipulate files and folders or use the WMI objects to manipulate the registry.

**COMING UP**

In the next chapter, you'll learn how VBScript accepts input and displays messages, enabling you to create interactive scripts. Chapters 7 through 9 show you how to manipulate the data that your scripts work with. If you're anxious to start working with objects, jump to Chapter 11, which introduces some of VBScript's own built-in objects.

CHAPTER 6

# Input and Output

**IN THIS CHAPTER**

Getting and displaying information is an essential function for most scripts. In this chapter, you'll learn the various ways that VBScript provides for this type of user interaction.

It's rare to need a script that doesn't involve some form of user interaction. At the very least, you might need to display some kind of completion message as an indication that your script has finished running. Sometimes, you'll need more complex interaction, such as the ability to ask Yes or No questions, get server names and other information, and so forth.

VBScript has very limited interactive capabilities. If you're expecting to create even simple dialog boxes like you've seen Visual Basic programmers do, forget about it: VBScript doesn't provide a dialog builder and doesn't provide any means for programmatically creating dialog boxes. If you need a custom user interface, you need to upgrade to a full-fledged programming environment like Visual Studio. VBScript's capabilities for interaction are limited to basic choices, simple messages, and one-line text input. However, in an administrative script, that's often all you'll need.

**NOTE** The script examples in this chapter won't be full administrative scripts. Instead, I'll provide snippets that you can easily cut and paste into your own scripts whenever you need to display a message, ask for user input, and so forth.

## Displaying Messages

VBScript displays messages using the Windows standard *message box*, which is a short dialog box that has a few display options to customize its behavior and appearance. VBScript exposes this functionality through the `MsgBox` statement and the `MsgBox()` function.

## The MsgBox Statement and Function

`MsgBox` is one of the few VBScript elements that can act as both a statement and a function. As a statement, `MsgBox` just displays a message box to your specifications. As a function, however, `MsgBox` can act as a form of user input, allowing simple Yes/No choices that can affect the behavior of your scripts.

The basic `MsgBox` statement accepts up to three parameters: a message, a numeric value designating which system icons or buttons should be displayed, and a message box title. It looks something like this:

```
MsgBox "The script has finished running.", _
 1, "Notice"
```

This command will display a message box that contains the text "The script has finished running." The box will include an OK button and a Cancel button, and the title of the box will contain "Notice." If you don't care about the title of the dialog or the buttons it displays, you can take a shortcut and just include your message.

```
MsgBox "The script has finished running." & _
 " Please check the server for the new user accounts."
```

The default message box title will be displayed, and the default button configuration—an OK button and a Cancel button with no icon—will be displayed.

Your scripts will look cooler, though, if you customize them a bit. For example, you might display an information icon on the message box, which helps cue the user that the message isn't an error or a question, but a simple informative message. You might also display just an OK button; a Cancel button doesn't really make sense because when the script is done, there's nothing left to cancel.

```
MsgBox "The script has finished running.", _
 64, "Thank you."
```

**TIP** When you include a system icon, Windows will play any associated event sounds when your dialog box is displayed. This feature makes your script seem much more professional and integrated with the operating system.

**Table 6.1** MsgBox display options

| Display | Value | Constant |
|---|---|---|
| OK button | 0 | `vbOKOnly` |
| OK and Cancel buttons | 1 | `vbOKCancel` |
| Abort, Retry, Ignore buttons | 2 | `vbAbortRetryIgnore` |
| Yes, No, and Cancel buttons | 3 | `vbYesNoCancel` |
| Yes and No buttons | 4 | `vbYesNo` |
| Retry and Cancel buttons | 5 | `vbRetryCancel` |
| Critical error icon | 16 | `vbCritical` |
| Question mark icon | 32 | `vbQuestion` |
| Exclamation mark icon | 48 | `vbExclamation` |
| Information ("i") icon | 64 | `vbInformation` |
| Make the first button the default | 0 | `vbDefaultButton1` |
| Make the second button the default | 256 | `vbDefaultButton2` |
| Make the third button the default | 512 | `vbDefaultButton3` |
| Make the fourth button the default | 768 | `vbDefaultButton4` |
| Application modal | 0 | `vbApplicationModal` |
| System modal | 4096 | `vbSystemModal` |

That middle parameter—the number 64, in this case—controls the icons and buttons that display on the dialog box. Table 6.1 shows the options you have available, along with their corresponding values.You can pick from four classes of options.

1. Buttons. Comprised of values 0 through 5, these control which buttons are displayed on the dialog box. You can only pick one from this set.
2. Icons. Values 16 through 64 control the icon that displays, and you can pick only one. An icon value of 0 displays no icon. You can choose only one of these options.
3. Defaults. Consisting of values 0, 256, 512, and 768, these options control which of the displayed buttons will be selected if the user

presses Enter, rather than clicking on a button. Choose only one of these options.

4. Modality. Values 0 or 4096 control how your message box affects the rest of Windows. The default, Application modal, means your script stops executing until the user clicks a button on the message box. Making the box system modal will display the box on top of all other applications, requiring the user to answer the dialog before doing anything else on Windows (note that not all versions of Windows support this functionality).

To come up with the appropriate value for the second `MsgBox` parameter, you just need to add up the values for each class of option that you want to display. For example, to display a message box that has a Yes and No button, a question mark icon, and has the No button as the default, you would add values 4, 32, and 256, for a total of 292: `MsgBox "Are you sure?", 292, "Delete file"` would be the VBScript command. Note that the message box will be application modal, because option value 4096 wasn't added in.

You're unlikely to remember all of these numeric values. I certainly never can. Fortunately, VBScript defines several *constants* to represent each value. Just use the constant in place of the value. For example, to display that same "Are you sure?" dialog box using constants:

```
MsgBox "Are you sure?", _
 vbYesNo + vbQuestion + vbDefaultButton2 + vbApplicationModal, _
 "Delete file"
```

That's *much* easier to remember with a little practice.

There's still a problem with this `MsgBox` statement, though. Remember from Chapter 5 that statements cannot return a value—only functions can do that. So how does this script know if the user clicked the Yes or No button? As written, it wouldn't. Instead, write the `MsgBox` as a function and assign the return value to a variable.

```
Dim vResult
vResult = MsgBox("Are you sure?", _
vbYesNo + vbQuestion + vbDefaultButton2 + vbApplicationModal, _
 "Delete file")

If vResult = 7 Then
 'put code here to handle
 'the user saying NO
End If
```

**Table 6.2** MsgBox return values

| User Clicked | Value | Constant |
|---|---|---|
| OK | 1 | vbOK |
| Cancel | 2 | vbCancel |
| Abort | 3 | vbAbort |
| Retry | 4 | vbRetry |
| Ignore | 5 | vbIgnore |
| Yes | 6 | vbYes |
| No | 7 | vbNo |

Notice that this example places the `MsgBox` parameters inside parentheses, like any other function. The result is stored in variable `vResult`. An `If…Then` construct examines the contents of `vResult` and ends the script if the variable contains a 7. The value 7 happens to be what `MsgBox()` returns if the user clicks the No button.

Fortunately, you don't have to remember that 7, either. VBScript also defines constants for the return values, as shown in Table 6.2.

To rewrite the example using the constants:

```
Dim vResult
vResult = MsgBox("Are you sure?", _
vbYesNo + vbQuestion + vbDefaultButton2 + vbApplicationModal, _
 "Delete file")

If vResult = vbNo Then
 'put code here to handle
 'the user saying NO
End If
```

**NOTE** If your dialog box displays a Cancel button, you can press the Esc (Escape) key on your keyboard. Doing so is the same as clicking the Cancel button and VBScript will return `vbCancel`.

You can take one more shortcut. You don't have to first assign the `MsgBox()` return value to a variable; you can use `MsgBox()` as part of the `If…Then` construct's logical evaluation.

```
If MsgBox("Are you sure?", _
vbYesNo + vbQuestion + vbDefaultButton2 + vbApplicationModal, _
 "Delete file") = vbNo Then
End If
```

This is a much more compact piece of script, keeps your script nice and easy to read, and performs the same as the previous, longer example.

## More Complex Messages

MsgBox doesn't limit you to a line or two of text. Try running the following script snippet.

```
MsgBox "This is a warning message. " & _
 vbCrLf & vbCrLf & _
 "You have chosen to delete this user or group " & _
 "the domain:" & vbCrLf & vbCrLf & _
 vbTab & "JohnDoe" & vbCrLf & vbCrLf & _
 "Are you sure this is what you want to do?", _
 vbYesNo + vbExclamation + vbDefaultButton2, _
 "Delete user"
```

---

**TIP** I'm using a lot of underscore characters in this example to make a very long statement spread across several lines of text. That's a requirement when printing scripts in a book like this, but you should consider using this technique even in a script editor like Notepad or PrimalScript. You'll find that you don't have to do as much horizontal scrolling, making your scripts easier to edit.

---

You should see something like the dialog box in Figure 6.1

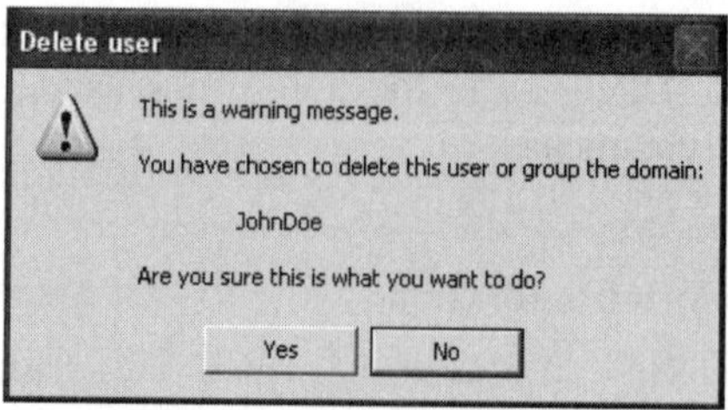


**Figure 6.1** Complex message box

I've used two powerful VBScript constants in this example: `vbCrLf` and `vbTab`. `vbCrLf` inserts a carriage return and linefeed character, forcing `MsgBox` to begin a new line of text. Putting two `vbCrLfs` in a row puts a blank line in between, helping to emphasize the message. `vbTab` inserts a tab character, indenting the first line of a paragraph. I used it in this example to make the user account name stand out a bit from the rest of the message. Using these constants, you can create simply formatted messages that have more impact and convey more information than a simple line or two of text can.

## MsgBox Best Practices

You should get into the habit of following Windows user interface conventions when using `MsgBox`. To begin, select the appropriate icons for your message boxes.

- Always use an icon. They help visually cue users as to the importance and nature of your message.
- Use the information icon to display non-error, non-warning messages that don't require a choice, such as a message that the script has finished running.
- Use the question mark icon whenever you're asking for a decision that doesn't have potentially devastating consequences. For example, you might use this icon when you're asking if the user wants to create a new user home directory in addition to the user's domain account.
- Use the exclamation mark icon to warn the user of a condition that has occurred when the condition won't stop the script from running. For example, if a script tries to connect to a server to create a home directory but is unsuccessful, an exclamation mark is appropriate if the script continues to create the user's domain account and perform other tasks. Also, use the exclamation mark when asking the user to make a potentially dangerous choice, such as confirming a user account deletion.
- Use the critical icon when the script will stop running due to some condition it encountered.

You should also select buttons that are appropriate to the task. For example, don't ask a Yes/No question and then display Abort, Retry, and Ignore buttons. The buttons don't provide answers that correspond to the question you asked.

Finally, always set the default button to be the least dangerous choice. If you're asking whether or not to delete a user account, make the No button the default. That way, if the user accidentally hits Enter without thoroughly reading your warning, nothing bad will occur.

## Go Generic with WScript.Echo

In Chapter 2, I introduced you to WScript and Cscript, the Windows and command-line scripting hosts. `MsgBox` will work from within either one, although it will always pop up with a graphical message box, even when running under Cscript.

If you're writing scripts intended entirely for the command line and Cscript, you can use another technique to produce output: `WScript.Echo`. Despite its name, this command can be used within either graphical WScript or command-line Cscript scripts. When used in a WScript script, `WScript.Echo` displays a graphical message box. When used under Cscript, it outputs text to the command line.

---

**NOTE** Echo is actually a method of the built-in WScript object. For more information on objects and methods, read Chapter 5. I'll cover more of the built-in scripting objects in Chapter 11.

---

`WScript.Echo` is easy enough to use.

```
WScript.Echo "Hello, world! " & _
"It's nice to see you."
```

Under WScript, you'll see a message box like the one in Figure 6.2. Notice that you cannot control the icons, buttons, or title of this message box as you can with the `MsgBox` statement or function; `WScript.Echo` is much more simplistic.

**Figure 6.2** WScript.Echo executed within WScript.exe

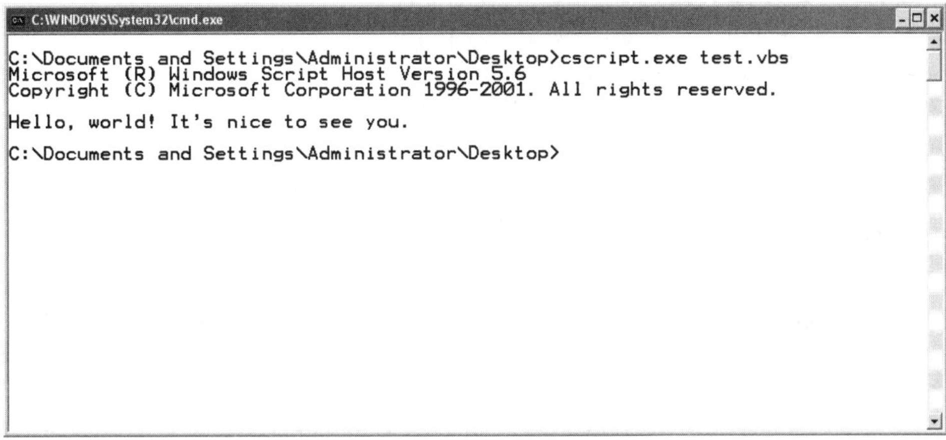


**Figure 6.3** WScript.Echo executed within Cscript.exe

Execute the exact same script in Cscript and you'll see something like Figure 6.3. `WScript.Echo` doesn't provide any means for collecting input, as the `MsgBox()` function does; its entire purpose is to display messages. Because it functions in both a graphical and command-line environment, it's ideal for scripts that need to run in either environment. It's also the only easy way to create command-line output for Cscript scripts.

## Asking for Input

Although the `MsgBox()` function provides a way to collect simple Yes/No style input, you may need to collect more complex input, such as server names, user names, or other data. VBScript provides a way for users to input this type of string information.

### Graphical Input

The `InputBox()` function displays a graphical input box with a title, a short message, a one-line text input box, and an **OK** and **Cancel** button. Whatever the user types is returned as the result of the function; if the user clicks **Cancel** or presses **Esc** on his keyboard, the function returns -1. Figure 6.4 shows what this quick sample looks like.

```
Dim vInput
vInput = InputBox("Enter a server name","Server")
MsgBox "You entered " & vInput
```

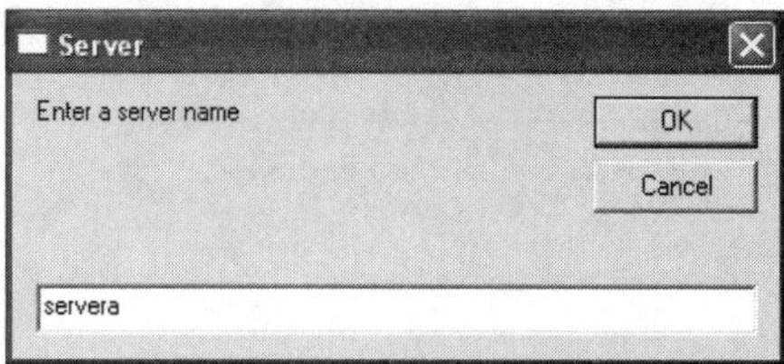


**Figure 6.4** Collecting text input by using InputBox()

You should always test to see if the user clicked **Cancel** or pressed **Esc**.

```
Dim vInput
vInput = InputBox("Enter a server name","Server")
If vInput = -1 Or vInput = "" Then
 MsgBox "You cancelled."
Else
 MsgBox "You entered " & vInput
End If
```

This type of check prevents your script from trying, for example, to connect to a server named `\\-1` when the user cancels the input box.

You can expand `InputBox()` slightly to provide a default entry. Users can accept your default by simply clicking **OK** or pressing **Enter** when the input box is displayed, or they can type their own input instead of your default. Here's how.

```
Dim vInput, vDefault
vDefault = "\\ServerA"
vInput = InputBox("Enter a server name","Server",vDefault)
If vInput = -1 Then
 MsgBox "You cancelled."
ElseIf vInput = vDefault Then
 MsgBox "You selected the default, ServerA."
Else
 MsgBox "You entered " & vInput
End If
```

Your default entry simply becomes the third parameter of the `InputBox()` function. It will be shown in the input box and selected, allowing users to simply start typing if they want to enter their own input rather than accept your default.

### Command-Line Input

Asking for input from a command-line script is a bit more complex. Unfortunately, there's no command-line version of the `InputBox()` function to make things simple. Instead, you have to deal with something called `StdIn`, which is the system's standard input stream, representing text typed by the user. For example:

```
WScript.Echo "Type something, and then press Enter, to continue."
Dim vInput
vInput = ""
Do While Not WScript.StdIn.AtEndOfLine
 Input = Input & WScript.StdIn.Read(1)
Loop
WScript.Echo "You typed " & Input
```

This script collects one character at a time from `StdIn` until the user presses Enter. At that point, `StdIn`'s `AtEndOfLine` property is set to True, and the loop terminates. Note that this script will *only* work under Cscript; WScript doesn't supply access to `StdIn` when you're running a graphical environment script. Figure 6.5 shows what this example looks like from the command line. If you try to run this script from within WScript, you'll receive an error message on the fourth line of code saying, "The handle is invalid."

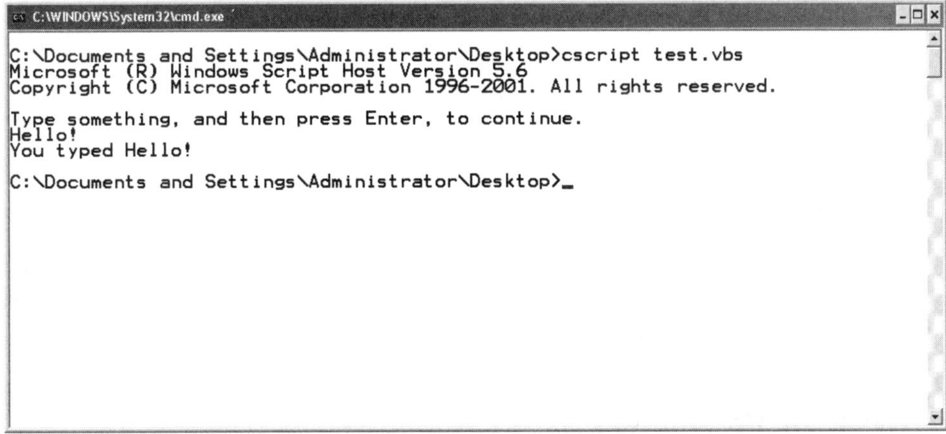


**Figure 6.5** Collecting text input from the command line

If you'd like to learn more about `StdIn` and command-line text input, refer to the Windows Script Host documentation at http://msdn.microsoft.com/scripting.

## Command-Line Parameters as Input

Many of the administrative utilities you use every day are command-line utilities, such as `ipconfig`, `ping`, and `tracert`. These utilities can all perform different tasks, or different variations of a task, through the use of command-line parameters. For example, `ipconfig /all` displays IP configuration settings, whereas `ipconfig /renew` refreshes your computer's DHCP address. You also can write scripts that accept command-line parameters, giving you the ability to create flexible command-line utilities of your own.

---

**NOTE** Command-line scripts usually execute under `Cscript.exe`, giving them the capability to produce command-line output. Keep in mind that you'll need to use `WScript.Echo` rather than `MsgBox` to produce the command-line output.

---

### Running Command-Line Scripts

Because none of the script file extensions—VBS, VB, SCR, and so forth—are recognized as executable by the Windows command-line processor, you'll need to execute `Cscript.exe` directly. Tell Cscript which script file you want to execute, and then tack on any of the script's command-line parameters, followed by any Cscript parameters. For example:

```
Cscript.exe MyScript.vbs /option:yes /value:4 //B
```

This would execute the VBScript MyScript.vbs, passing it a parameter named `option` and one named "value," and telling Cscript to suppress any script error messages (see the sidebar, "Power Cscript.exe," later in this chapter for more on Cscript parameters).

### Parsing Parameters

The scripting engine includes a built-in parameter-parsing object named `WshNamed`, which is designed to help your script accept named command-line parameters. Note that this object is also available to graphical scripts executing under WScript, although it's less common to see those scripts using command-line parameters. `WshNamed` is part of the WshArguments object, which provides top-level access to all command-line arguments passed to the script. I introduced you to objects in VBScript in "What Are Objects?" in Chapter 5.

Suppose you're writing a script that will display basic information about a remote computer. You want the script to accept a command-line parameter named `Computer` that will provide the computer name to check. You'll execute the script with something like the following:

```
Cscript.exe GetInfo.vbs /computer:server1
```

You want the script to run from the command line, so you'll display the output by using `WScript.Echo` instead of the `MsgBox` statement.

## ➤➤ Getting Remote Machine Information

Listing 6.1 shows what your script might look like.

**Listing 6.1** *GetInfo.vbs.* This script will retrieve basic information about a remote computer.

```
'Create an arguments object
Dim oArgs
Set oArgs = WScript.Arguments

'Get the named arguments
Dim oNamed
Set oNamed = oArgs.Named

'Get the computer name argument
Dim sComputer
sComputer = oNamed("computer")

'Connect to the remote computer by using WMI
Dim oSystem
Set oSystem = GetObject("winmgmts:{impersonationLevel=" & _
 "impersonate}!//" & sComputer & "/root/cimv2:" & _
 "Win32_ComputerSystem=" & Chr(34) & sComputer & _
 Chr(34))
```

*continues*

```
'Display information
WScript.Echo oSystem.Caption
WScript.Echo oSystem.PrimaryOwnerName
WScript.Echo oSystem.Domain
WScript.Echo oSystem.SystemType
```

Because this script uses a command-line parameter, or argument, to figure out which computer to connect to, you shouldn't have to make any changes to use it in your environment.

## ➤➤ Getting Remote Machine Information—Explained

The script starts by getting a reference to the built-in Arguments object. Notice that you don't need to use `CreateObject` for this because the object is always loaded when the scripting engine is running.

```
'Create an arguments object
Dim oArgs
Set oArgs = WScript.Arguments
```

Next, the script gets the Named object, which is an array of named command-line parameters.

```
'Get the named arguments
Dim oNamed
Set oNamed = oArgs.Named
```

With access to the Named object, the script can retrieve the value assigned to the "Computer" named argument. This value is stored in a variable named `sComputer`.

```
'Get the computer named argument
Dim sComputer
sComputer = oNamed("computer")
```

Now the script uses WMI to connect to the designated computer. Notice the use of `Chr(34)` in this section of the script. This function inserts a quotation mark, which is required around the computer name in the WMI query.

```
'Connect to the remote computer by using WMI
Dim oSystem
Set oSystem = GetObject("winmgmts:{impersonationLevel=" & _
 "impersonate}!//" & sComputer & "/root/cimv2:" & _
 "Win32_ComputerSystem=" & Chr(34) & sComputer & _
 Chr(34))
```

For more information on scripting with WMI, start with Chapter 17. For more information on the `Chr()` function, turn to Chapter 8.

Finally, the script uses the retrieved WMI object to display some information about the computer.

```
'Display information
WScript.Echo oSystem.Caption
WScript.Echo oSystem.PrimaryOwnerName
WScript.Echo oSystem.Domain
WScript.Echo oSystem.SystemType
```

Figure 6.6 shows the type of output you should expect at the command line.

Note that I could have chosen not to use the Named object to retrieve the command-line argument in this script. After all, there's only one argument; I could have just as easily used `WScript.Arguments(0)` to retrieve the first argument. However, I prefer to always use the Named object to access command-line parameters. There are a number of reasons for doing so.

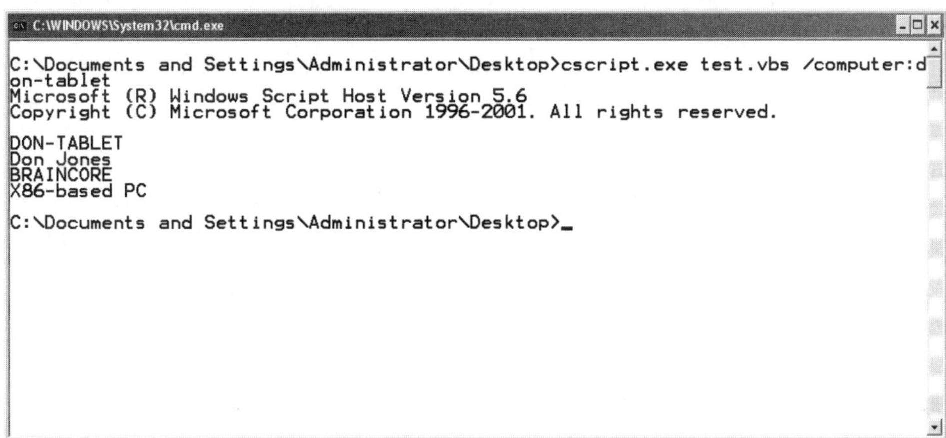


**Figure 6.6** Running a script with command-line parameters

- If an unexpected parameter is included, your script won't accidentally mistake it for a legitimate parameter.
- If your script has multiple parameters, accessing them through Named allows the user to include them in any order, as they can with most Windows command-line utilities.
- Named parameters are easier to work with when maintaining your script. For example, it's easier to tell what `Wscript.Arguments.Named("computer")` is doing than to try to figure out what `WScript.Arguments(0)` stands for.

### Power Cscript.exe

`Cscript.exe` accepts a number of command-line parameters of its own. To distinguish these from your script's own parameters, Cscript's parameters start with two slashes (//) instead of the usual one. You can see a list of available parameters by running Cscript from a command line with no parameters or script name; some of the most useful parameters are

- `//B`. This suppresses script errors and prompts, making your scripts more suitable for use within a batch file or as Task Scheduler jobs.
- `//H:Cscript`. This changes the default scripting engine to Cscript, so that when you double-click a VBS file, a command-line window opens and Cscript executes the file instead of WScript. `//H:WScript` puts things back to normal.
- `//S`. Saves your command-line options as the defaults for the current user account.

You can use these and other commands to customize your scripting environment. For example, if you find that most of your scripts are of the command-line variety, set Cscript to be the default scripting engine.

## Review

Scripts can be made more general-purpose when they're capable of collecting input and customizing their behavior based upon that input. You can have scripts connect to different servers, create user accounts, delete files, and perform hundreds of other actions when you're able to collect and evaluate user input when the script is run.

Using `MsgBox` allows you to display messages, even those with some basic formatting. You can also ask for simple Yes/No decisions from the user by using `MsgBox()` as a function. `WScript.Echo` provides text-output capabilities that work within a graphical WScript or command-line Cscript environment.

`InputBox()` allows you to collect text input from a graphical script, and you can use `WScript.StdIn` to collect text input within a command-line script. You can also use script command-line parameters to create scripts that work just like Windows' built-in command-line tools, complete with named parameters that customize the script's behavior.

**COMING UP**

In the next chapter, you'll start learning how to manipulate data in VBScript. I'll start with numeric data in Chapter 7, move on to string data in Chapter 8, and finish up with other types of data in Chapter 9.

CHAPTER 7

# Manipulating Numbers

**IN THIS CHAPTER**

Most scripts involve math and numbers, and learning how to work with them is important. Other types of data manipulation, including strings and dates, build upon basic number manipulation, too, making this a core skill. Fortunately, VBScript makes numeric data easy to work with.

Incredibly, I almost became a professional software developer. It's what I wanted to do in high school, and my school even offered a two-year vocational course for programmers. I never pursued it, though, because I'm horrible with higher math. In school, everyone tells you that programmers have to really know their math. That's not true, of course. With VBScript in particular, you'll find that manipulating numeric data and performing even complex calculations is easy. Even better, you probably won't need more than basic math skills for administrative scripting.

## Numbers in VBScript

VBScript considers any unquoted, non-date value to be a number. Issuing the statement `MyVariable = 5`, for example, will assign the numeric value 5 to the variable `MyVariable`. The one catch in VBScript is that there are actually different types of numbers.

- Any whole number—that is, a number with no decimal portion—is called an *integer*. The numbers 5, -6, 43,233, and -42 are all integers. VBScript integers can be anything from -32,768 to 32,767.
- VBScript also supports *long integers*, which are just big integers. They can be anything from -2,147,483,648 to 2,147,483,647.
- Numbers with a fractional value can be either *singles* or *doubles*. The only difference between them is in how large they can be. A single

can be any numeric value from -3.4028235E+38 to -1.401298E-45, or from 3.4028235E+38 to 1.3401298E-45. In other words, a really big number. Sometimes, however, you may need an even larger number, which is where doubles come in. A double can be truly huge—as big as 1.79769313486231570E+308. I have no idea what you'd call a number like that other than humongous.

- VBScript also supports a *currency* number type. This has a maximum precision of four decimal places and has the added capability to properly recognize and format currencies based on the system's locale settings. That means you can properly display thousandths separators and decimal places according to the system configuration.

Now, as I mentioned in Chapter 5, you don't usually have to worry much about these different types of numbers, because VBScript does it for you. Variables in VBScript can hold any kind of data; if you try to put the number 64,555 into a variable, VBScript will just invisibly make the variable into a long integer. If you add .3 to it, VBScript will convert it into a single. The only time you'll need to worry about data types is if you want to perform some specialized function, like a currency operation, and then you'll need to explicitly convert the variable into the appropriate type—something I'll cover later in this chapter.

## Basic Arithmetic

You use VBScript's mathematical *operators* for most basic math. VBScript's operators should look pretty familiar and self-explanatory:

- Addition: +
- Subtraction: -
- Multiplication: *
- Division: /
- Order of evaluation: ( )
- Exponentiation: ^ (usually located in the 6 key on your keyboard)

Normally, you just assign the results of such an operation to a variable or a statement like `MsgBox`, as in the following examples.

```
myVar = 1 + 2
MsgBox myVar
myVar = myVar + (myVar * .03)
```

```
MsgBox myVar
myVar = myVar^2
MsgBox myVar
```

VBScript evaluates expressions from left to right, performing exponentiation first, then multiplication and division, then addition and subtraction. Anything in parentheses is evaluated first, starting at the innermost level of nested parentheses. To put that in context, consider these similar-looking expressions, which all generate a different result due to the order of evaluation.

```
myVar = 1 * 2 + 1
MsgBox myVar
myVar = 1 + 1 * 2
MsgBox myVar
myVar = (1 + 1) * 2
MsgBox myVar
myVar = ((1 + (1 * 2))
MsgBox myVar
```

You might be wondering why all this math stuff should be important to you. After all, you're trying to administer services, not launch space shuttles. You might not use *lots* of math in your scripts, but you're likely to use some. For example, suppose you want to write a quick function that generates unique passwords for users. You could use the function when creating new user accounts or when resetting user accounts. Listing 7.1 shows what the function might look like.

### ➤➤ Making Up a Password

You can include this function in another script, and then call it. This function takes a user name or another unique string and generates a unique password to go with it. The password generated is based partially upon the current system time, so it'll be different even for the same user if you use it multiple times.

**Listing 7.1** *MakePW.vbs.* This script is intended to be included within another script.

```
Function MakePW(sUserName)
 Dim vTemp, vPasswd, vLetter, vValue
```

*continues*

```
 For vTemp = 1 To Len(sUserName)
  vLetter = Mid(sUserName, vTemp, 1)
  vValue = Asc(vLetter) * vTemp
  vValue = vValue - DatePart("n",Now)
  vPasswd = vPasswd & CStr(vValue)
 Next
 MakePW = Right(vPasswd, 8)
End Function
```

The script can be used as-is within your other scripts. You might call it by using a statement like `sNewPassword = MakePW("JohnD")`.

## ➤➤ Making Up a Password—Explained

In Chapter 4, I introduced the concept of functions and subroutines as a means of modularizing your code. I explained them further in Chapter 5. `MakePW` is a custom function that encapsulates a certain piece of functionality. It's declared with the initial `Function` statement, and I've followed the function declaration with some variable declarations.

```
Function MakePW(sUserName)
 Dim vTemp, vPasswd, vLetter, vValue
```

Next, I use a `For…Next` loop. It will execute the loop contents once for each letter in the user name.

For more details on `For…Next`, skip ahead to "Loops" in Chapter 10.

```
 For vTemp = 1 To Len(sUserName)

 Next
```

Within the loop, several functions are used, including some mathematical operations. First, I use the `Mid()` function to extract the current letter of the user's name. Then, I use the `Asc()` function to convert that letter to its ASCII value (65 for A, 66 for B, and so forth). I multiply the ASCII value by the value of `vTemp`, which helps to obfuscate the password-generation scheme.

Next, I get the seconds from the system clock by using the `DatePart()` function and contract that from the value. This provides a pseudorandomness to the password. Finally, I convert the value to a string and append it to a variable named **vPasswd**.

```
vLetter = Mid(sUserName, vTemp, 1)
vValue = Asc(vLetter) * vTemp
vValue = vValue – DatePart("n",Now)
vPasswd = vPasswd & CStr(vValue)
```

Finally, I assign the rightmost eight characters of **vPasswd** to the function's name. This returns the rightmost characters to whatever called the function, completing the function's task.

```
 MakePW = Right(vPasswd, 8)
End Function
```

This isn't the most amazing password ever created, and it's all numbers with no letters or symbols, but it provides a useful example of how math functions can be used within an administrative script.

## Advanced Arithmetic

If you're getting heavy-duty with the math in a script, you may need to take advantage of some of VBScript's advanced math functions. These include

- `Atn()`: Arctangent
- `Cos()`: Cosine
- `Sin()`: Sine
- `Tan()`: Tangent
- `Log()`: Logarithm
- `Sqr()`: Square root
- `Exp()`: Returns *e* (the base of natural logarithm) raised to a power
- `Randomize`: Randomizes the system's random number generator
- `Rnd()`: Generates a random number

This random number business in particular deserves some explanation, because you may think that'd be a much better way to come up with values for a password. It can be, provided you thoroughly understand how randomness works inside a computer.

First, never forget that computers are giant calculating devices. There's nothing remotely random about anything that goes on inside a computer. As a result, no computer can generate a truly random number without special hardware that's designed to do so.

The `Rnd()` function returns a value less than 1, but greater than or equal to zero. You can pass a parameter to `Rnd()` to control its behavior.

- A number less than zero, such as `Rnd(-2)`, will return the exact same number every time, using the number you supply as the seed. This isn't random at all.
- A number greater than zero, such as `Rnd(2)`, will return the next "random" number in the computer's sequence.
- Zero, or `Rnd(0)`, will return the most recently generated random number again and again.

VBScript's random number generator uses a *seed* as its initial value, and then calculates pseudorandom numbers from there. Given the same seed, VBScript will always calculate the same sequence of random numbers every time, because they're not random: They're derived from a mathematical formula.

That's where `Randomize` comes in. This statement seeds the random-number generator, either with a number you supply—guaranteeing a repeatable sequence of "random" numbers—or with a value from the system's timer. Because the system timer has a millisecond resolution, the odds are good that you'll get a unique "random number" sequence every time.

For example, try the following short script.

```
Randomize 5
For t = 1 to 10
 MsgBox Int((6 * Rnd()) + 1)
Next
```

Run this script on a couple of different computers a couple of different times, and you'll likely get the exact same results every time. Not exactly random, is it? Now, try this modified script.

```
Randomize
For t = 1 to 10
 MsgBox Int((6 * Rnd()) + 1)
Next
```

The difference here is that the generator is seeded from the system timer, which will virtually guarantee unique—if not necessarily random—results. Using the timer generally creates "random enough" sequences of numbers.

### ➤➤ Making a Better Password

Listing 7.2 revises the password-generating function to generate random sequences of uppercase letters.

**Listing 7.2** *MakePW.vbs.* Revised example uses Rnd() and Randomize for better-looking passwords.

```
Function MakePW()
 Dim vPasswd, vTemp, vValue
 Randomize
 For vTemp = 1 to 8
  vValue = Int((26 * Rnd()) + 64)
  vPasswd = vPasswd & Chr(vValue)
 Next vTemp
 MakePW = vPasswd
End Function
```

This example generates a pseudorandom, eight-character password comprised of uppercase letters.

### ➤➤ Making a Better Password—Explained

This example begins much like the previous one, with function and variable declarations.

```
Function MakePW()
 Dim vPasswd, vTemp, vValue
```

The `Randomize` statement seeds the generator from the system timer, and then begins a `For...Next` loop that will run eight times.

```
 Randomize
 For vTemp = 1 to 8
```

First, I calculate a random value from 65 to 91. These are the ASCII values for uppercase A through Z. Remember that the `Rnd()` function returns a fractional number from zero to less than one; I'm multiplying that by 26, which will give me a result between 1 and 26. I'm adding 64 to the result to get the result in the 65 to 91 range. Finally, I'm using the `Int()` function to convert the result to a whole number by truncating the decimal portion.

Last, I convert the numeric value to the appropriate ASCII character and append it to the password I'm building.

```
  vValue = Int((26 * Rnd()) + 64)
  vPasswd = vPasswd & Chr(vValue)
```

Finally, I wrap up the loop and end the function.

```
 Next vTemp
 MakePW = vPasswd
End Function
```

There you have it: a "random enough" password.

## Boolean Math

Boolean math is a special kind of logical math. If you know how to subnet TCP/IP addresses, you already know Boolean math, although you may not realize it. First, here are the basic Boolean operators that VBScript supports:

- `NOT`: Reverses a value from 0 to 1 (or False to True) or vice versa.
- `AND`: Returns a True if both values are True.
- `OR`: Returns a True if either value is True.
- `XOR`: Returns a True if one, but not both, values are True.

In VBScript, the value zero represents False; all other values represent True. Internally, VBScript generally uses -1 to represent True. To demonstrate Boolean math, try the following examples:

```
'Not
MsgBox NOT True
```

```
MsgBox NOT False

'And
MsgBox True AND False
MsgBox True AND True

'Or
MsgBox True OR False
MsgBox True OR True

'Xor
MsgBox True XOR False
MsgBox True XOR True
```

You should get the following results in message boxes:

- False (the opposite of True)
- True (the opposite of False)
- False (both values aren't True)
- True (both values are True)
- True (at least one value is True)
- True (at least one value is True)
- True (only one value is True)
- False (both values are True)

So who cares? You'll primarily deal with Boolean math like this in the form of setting flags. For example, Windows domains (Active Directory and NT) store a user flags value, which controls several things, like whether the user account is locked out, expired, disabled, and so forth. The flags are stored as a single byte of information, and each bit in the flag has a different meaning. For example:

- Bit 1, with a value of 1, indicates if the account is locked out.
- Bit 2, with a value of 2, indicates if the account has expired.
- Bit 3, with a value of 4, indicates if the account is disabled.
- Bit 4, with a value of 8, indicates if the password needs to be changed.
- Bit 5, with a value of 16, indicates if the user can change his password.

All bytes have bits, and all bits have a value. In the number 5, for example, bits 1 and 3 are turned on. Their combined values (1 + 4) create the value of 5. To test to see if a value is on or not, you can use the AND operator:

```
'Assume variable vFlag has a flag byte in it
If vFlag AND 1 Then
 MsgBox "Account locked out"
End If

If vFlag AND 2 Then
 MsgBox "Account expired"
End If

If vFlag AND 4 Then
 MsgBox "Account disabled"
End If

If vFlag AND 8 Then
 MsgBox "User must change pw"
End If

If vFlag AND 16 Then
 MsgBox "User cannot change pw"
End If
```

To set these values yourself, you would use the OR operator.

```
'Assume variable vFlag already has a flag byte in it

'Turn on account disabled
vFlag = vFlag OR 4

'Force password change
vFlag = vFlag OR 8
```

You'll use this type of math a lot when dealing with ADSI. I introduce ADSI in Chapter 14, and start working with user accounts in Chapter 16. If this business of using Boolean operators to set values seems confusing, you're right; it is. Consider the OR operator, which is the one you'll use the most to set values.

Imagine that vFlag in the preceding example starts out with a value of zero. If you were to expand that out into binary, you'd get eight bits, all set to zero.

```
00000000
```

Using the code `vFlag = vFlag OR 4` tries to combine whatever is in `vFlag` and the number 4. The number 4, written in binary, looks like this:

```
00000100
```

The first zero in that chain represents the value 128, the second represents 64, then 32, then 16, then 8, then 4, then 2, and then 1. So, the bit representing 4 is set to one, making the total value of the byte four.

The `OR` operator compares all the bits in `vFlag` with all the bits in 4.

```
00000000
00000100
```

`OR` always accepts two values and returns a 1 whenever either value contains a 1. So `OR`'s output in this case would be

```
00000100
```

which means it simply returned a bit set to 1 whenever it encountered a 1 in either of the input values. Translating that to decimal, the result of `0 OR 4` is 4.

---

**TIP** You can use Windows Calculator in Scientific mode to convert decimal numbers to binary—definitely a quicker way to do the conversion than doing it manually!

---

Following the example along, `vFlag` will now contain 4. The second operation is `vFlag = vFlag OR 8`. Let's convert both `vFlag` and 8 to binary to see how the `OR` operator will handle them.

```
00000100
00001000
```

That's `vFlag`—which currently contains 4—on the top, and 8 on the bottom. `OR` will return a 1 whenever it encounters a 1 in *either* input, so the output will be

```
00001100
```

Windows Calculator tells me that that converts to 12 in decimal, so `vFlag` will not contain the value 12. But it's not really the number 12 that's important. In this case, `vFlag` is being used to represent user account settings, so each bit is really a little switch. The first switch, when turned on, disables the account. The second requires the user to change his password. By using the `OR` operator, you can flip each switch independently.

What if you want to turn a switch off, re-enabling a user account? Use the `AND` operator. Suppose that `vFlag` contains 12.

```
00001100
```

You want to flip off the switch that's represented by the value 4. You can't use `OR`, because `OR` can only turn bits on. Instead, you use `AND`: `vFlag = vFlag AND 8`. That's because `AND` will return a 1 only when both inputs are set to 1. If either input is set to 0, `AND` will return 0. Breaking down 8 into binary reveals the following.

```
00001000
```

Notice that the bit representing the value 4 is set to 0. So when `AND` compares `vFlag` and 251, you get the following.

```
00001100
00001000
```

Only one bit has a mismatch between the two, so the output will be

```
00001000
```

thus turning off the switch representing account disabled.

---

**NOTE** These Boolean operators also play a role in logical comparisons. For example, `If v = 1 OR v = 2` is a comparison that will result in True if variable `v` contains either 1 or 2. Similarly, the comparison `If v=1 And v = 2` would never be true, because `v` cannot contain both 1 and 2 at the same time.

---

## Converting Numeric Data Types

As I mentioned earlier, VBScript happily converts data types for you when necessary. This process is called *coercion,* and it happens entirely behind the scenes as needed. There are times, however, when you want VBScript to handle data in a particular fashion. In those cases, you'll need to explicitly convert the data type.

For example, in Listing 7.2, you saw how I used the `Rnd()` function to generate a pseudorandom number. This number is a fraction, but I wanted a whole number, and so I used the `Int()` function to convert it to an integer. Other numeric conversion functions include

- `Abs()`: Returns the absolute value of a number, removing the positive or negative
- `CBool()`: Converts a value to either True or False
- `CCur()`: Converts a value to Currency
- `CDbl()`: Converts a value to a Double
- `CSng()`: Converts a value to a Single
- `CInt()` and `Int()`: Converts a value to an integer
- `CLng()`: Converts a value to a long integer

You'll often use these functions to convert user input to a specific data type. For example, if you have an input box that accepts the number of servers to shut down, you want to make sure that's a whole number, and not some fractional number, because a fraction wouldn't make sense. You might use something like this.

```
Dim vInput
vInput = InputBox("Shut down how many servers?")
If CInt(vInput) = vInput Then
 'Shut them down
Else
 MsgBox "You didn't type a whole number."
End If
```

In this case, I used `CInt()` to force `vInput` to be an integer, and then compared the result to the original value in `vInput`. If the two were the same, the original input was an integer and the script continues. If not, the script displays an error message and ends.

---

**TIP** *Never* assume that some piece of data is a particular type. If the operation you are performing demands a specific type of data, you should explicitly convert your data to the proper type first. Doing so will help prevent runtime errors when unexpected conditions occur.

---

## Converting Other Data Types to Numeric Data

You can also convert some non-numeric data into numeric data. For example, suppose you have the following in a script.

```
Dim vValue
vValue = InputBox("Enter a number of servers")
```

At this point, you've no idea what `vValue` contains. You can try to convert it to a number, though. Consider the following examples.

- If `vValue` contains "5 servers", `CInt(vValue)` would return 5, because the character 5 can be interpreted as an integer.
- If `vValue` contains "five", `CInt(vValue)` would return zero, because there are no numbers that can be converted to an integer.
- If `vValue` contains "5.2 servers", `CInt(vValue)` would return 5, because 5.2 can be interpreted as a number and the integer portion of that number is 5.

You can use any of the numeric conversion functions I've already covered to convert non-numeric data into numeric data. If `vValue` contains "five or 6 servers", `CInt(vValue)` would return zero, because the first characters cannot be interpreted as a number.

## Review

VBScript's numeric and mathematical functions can be useful in a variety of situations. You can use basic math operators to perform simple math, and more advanced functions are available for complex geometric and algebraic operations. Boolean math plays a key role in logical comparisons, and

VBScript provides a number of functions to convert numeric data into specific forms. You can also convert non-numeric data, such as strings, to numeric data in order to work with it.

### COMING UP

In the next chapter, you'll build on your number manipulation skills to manipulate string data. Then, you'll move on to date and time data, Boolean data, and more. In fact, by the end of Chapter 9, you'll have mastered more than two-thirds of VBScript's functions!

CHAPTER 8

# Manipulating Strings

**IN THIS CHAPTER**

It's a rare script that doesn't involve some sort of string data, such as user names, server names, and so forth. Working with string data is a key requirement. Fortunately, VBScript makes it easy, and almost fun, to perform even the most complex string operations. You'll learn to change strings, pull strings out of the middle of other strings, and much more.

Computer names, group names, user names, queries—strings are all around us in the world of administrative scripting. Learning to manipulate those strings is a key skill. You'll find yourself building file paths, working with server names, creating WMI queries, and much more. In fact, string manipulation is such a fundamental VBScript skill that you'll need to master it to some degree before you can start writing effective scripts.

## Strings in VBScript

As you learned in Chapter 5, VBScript can store any type of data in a variable. *String data* is anything VBScript cannot interpret as another data type, such as a number or a date. Strings are simply any combination of letters, numbers, spaces, symbols, punctuation, and so forth. Often times, VBScript might interpret data as different types. For example, `5/7/2003` could be treated as a date or as a string, because it qualifies as both. In those instances, VBScript will *coerce* the data into one type or the other, depending on what you're trying to do with the data. Coercion is an important concept, especially when dealing with strings. For more information, refer to "What Are Variables?" in Chapter 5.

In your scripts, you'll always include strings within double quotation marks, which is how you let VBScript know to treat data as a string. For example, all of the following are acceptable ways to assign string data to a variable.

```
Var = "Hello"
Var = ""Hello""
Var = "Hello, there"
Var = vSomeOtherStringVariable
```

The second example is worth special attention. Notice that two sets of double quotes were used: This method will cause the variable `Var` to contain a seven-character string that begins and ends with quotes. Use this technique of doubling-up on quote marks whenever you need to assign the quote character itself as a part of the string.

VBScript refers to any portion of a string as a *substring*. Given the string `Hello`, one possible substring would be `ell` and another would be `ello`. The substring `ello` has its own substrings, including `llo` and `ell`. VBScript provides a number of functions for working with substrings. For example, you might write a script that accepts a computer name. The user might type just the name, such as `Server1`, or he might include a UNC-style name, such as `\\Server1`. Using VBScript's substring functions, you can get just the substring you want.

A large number of VBScript's intrinsic functions are devoted to string manipulation, and I'll cover most of them in this chapter. As a quick reference, here's each one, in alphabetical order, along with a quick description of what each does.

- `Asc()`. Returns the ASCII code for any single character.
- `Chr()`. Given an ASCII code, returns the corresponding character.
- `CStr()`. Converts a variable to a string.
- `Escape()`. Encodes a string for proper transmission as part of an Internet URL, so that strings such as "Hello world" become "Hello%20world."
- `FormatCurrency()`. Accepts a currency value and returns a properly formatted string. For example, formats 45.67 as $45.67.
- `FormatDateTime()`. Returns a properly formatted date or time string. For example, formats 4/5/2003 as April 5, 2003.
- `FormatNumber()`. Returns a formatted number. For example, formats 1055774 as 1,055,774.00.
- `FormatPercent()`. Returns a formatted percentage. For example, formats .67 as 67%.
- `InStr()`. Returns the position at which a specified substring can be found within a specified string.
- `InStrRev()`. Same as `InStr()`, but starts its search at the end of the specified string rather than the beginning.

- `LCase()`. Returns a string converted to lowercase.
- `Left()`. Returns the specified leftmost characters of a specified string.
- `Len()`. Returns the length of a string.
- `LTrim()`. Trims spaces from the left end of a string.
- `Mid()`. Returns a substring from a specified string, starting with the specified beginning character and continuing for the specified length.
- `Replace()`. Replaces all instances of the specified substring with the specified replacement substring.
- `Right()`. Returns the specified rightmost characters of a specified string.
- `RTrim()`. Trims spaces from the right end of a string.
- `Space()`. Returns a string containing the specified number of spaces.
- `StrComp()`. Compares two strings and returns an appropriate value.
- `StrReverse()`. Reverses the specified string's characters, so that "Hello" would become "olleH."
- `Trim()`. Trims spaces from both ends of a string.
- `UCase()`. Returns a string with all characters converted to uppercase.
- `Unescape()`. Decodes a string encoded with the `Escape()` function.

You should realize that none of these functions change the contents of a string variable. For example, `Var1 = Trim(Var2)` does not change the contents of `Var2`. Instead, it trims all spaces from the left and right ends of `Var2`'s contents, and assigns the result to `Var1`. If you want to change the contents of a variable, you can use something like `Var1 = Trim(Var1)`. Internally, VBScript creates a new string to hold the result of the `Trim()` function, and then assigns that result back to the `Var1` variable. This behind-the-scenes assignment is what actually changes the contents of `Var1`, not the `Trim()` function.

## Working with Substrings

As I mentioned, string manipulation is often valuable when dealing with user input. For example, suppose you have a script that will work with a server, and you want the user to enter the server name in an input box. You might start with something like this.

```
Function GetServer()
 Dim sServer
 sServer = InputBox("Work with what server?")
 GetServer = sServer
End Function
```

---

**NOTE** There doesn't seem much point in making this a special function at present, but bear with me. By the way, don't bother typing in these scriptlets yet—I'll be building on this example throughout the chapter.

---

The problem is that the user could type nearly anything. If this is a script that only you will be using, you can probably be sloppy and leave it as-is, knowing that you'll always type the right thing. However, if a junior administrator or technician will use the script, you should program some intelligence into it.

As an example, suppose the administrator typed a UNC-style name, such as `\\Server1`. If your script is expecting a simple name like `Server1`, the extra characters could cause problems. You can build your function to manipulate the string.

```
Function GetServer()
 Dim sServer
 sServer = InputBox("Work with what server?")

 'trim backslashes
 Do While Left(sServer,1) = "\"
  sServer = Right(sServer, Len(sServer) - 1)
 Loop

 'return result
 GetServer = sServer
End Function
```

In this new example, a `Do...Loop` construct is used to examine the left-most character of `sServer`. As long as the leftmost character is a backslash, the loop will set `sServer` equal to `sServer`'s rightmost characters. This is done with the `Right()` function, which accepts `sServer` as its input string, and then accepts the current length of `sServer` (via the `Len()` function), minus one, as the number of characters to pull. The result is that all but the leftmost character—which is known to be a backslash at this point—is saved. The loop repeats until the leftmost character is no longer a backslash.

I haven't covered Do...Loop yet, but if you want to read up on it quickly, skip ahead to "Loops" in Chapter 10.

Suppose your company's server naming convention always starts with a few letters, then a hyphen, and then finishes up with numbers. Perhaps the letters indicate which office the server is located in, and you want to pull that information out so that a user account (or something else) can be created in the appropriate Active Directory organizational unit (OU). No problem.

```
Function GetOffice(sServerName)

 'find the hyphen
 Dim iHyphen
 iHyphen = InStr(1, sServerName, "-")

 'get just the part before the hyphen
 Dim sOffice
 sOffice = Left(sServerName, iHyphen - 1)

 'return result
 GetOffice = sOffice
End Function
```

In this function, I've used the `InStr()` function to locate the first occurrence of a hyphen within `sServerName`. Suppose the server name in this case is PHL-77432; the hyphen is at location 4, so variable `iHyphen` will now contain a 4.

Next, I used `Left()` to grab the leftmost characters before the hyphen. In this case, I only want the leftmost three characters, so the `Left()` function is asked to return `iHyphen - 1`, which in this example evaluates to the leftmost three characters.

Notice the `1`, the first input parameter to `InStr()`. That tells `InStr()` to start searching at the first character of `sServerName`. Suppose your server names look something like WIN-7745-PHL and you want to get the office code (PHL). In that case, you need to find the first hyphen, and then start looking *after* it for the second hyphen.

```
Function GetOffice(sServerName)

 'find the first hyphen
 Dim iHyphen1
 iHyphen1 = InStr(1, sServerName, "-")

 'find the second hyphen
 Dim iHyphen2
 iHyphen2 = InStr(iHyphen1, sServerName, "-")

 'get just the part after the 2nd hyphen
 Dim sOffice
 sOffice = Right(sServerName, Len(sServerName) - iHyphen2)

 'return result
 GetOffice = sOffice
End Function
```

First, this script locates the first hyphen by having `InStr()` start at the beginning of `sServerName`. Then, the script locates the second hyphen by having `InStr()` start at the *location after the first hyphen.* Finally, the script uses the `Right()` function to get everything after the second hyphen. This is done by taking the length of `sServerName` (which is 12 in this example) and subtracting the character location of the second hyphen (which is 9), giving us the rightmost three characters we want.

You could do this same task with a bit less code by using `InStrRev()`.

```
Function GetOffice(sServerName)

'find the second hyphen
 Dim iHyphen2
 iHyphen2 = InStrRev(sServerName, "-")

 'get just the part after the 2nd hyphen
 Dim sOffice
 sOffice = Right(sServerName, Len(sServerName) - iHyphen2)submit.x:
 41submit.y: 8

 'return result
 GetOffice = sOffice
End Function
```

In this example, `InStrRev()` would return 4, because the second hyphen is four characters from the end of WIN-7745-PHL. The `Right()`

function is told to subtract one from that value, giving us the rightmost three characters we want.

---

**TIP** Playing with substrings and the associated calculations can be a bit of fun, like working out a puzzle. I find it's often easier to think of an example string and write it down on paper in large letters. I then number each letter with its character position. Doing so makes it easier to work out the math of the `Left()`, `Right()`, `InStr()`, and `InStrRev()` functions.

---

But wait, there's one more substring function! `Mid()` makes it possible to pull substrings from the middle of other strings. For example, suppose you need to pull the second three characters from a string such as "492NYCFILES." You could use `Left()` to get the leftmost three characters, and then use `Right()` to get the rightmost three characters from that. Or, you could just use `Mid("492NYCFILES",4,3)` to start at the fourth character and pull three characters. If all of your server names were formatted that way, you might rewrite the `GetOffice()` function as follows:

```
Function GetOffice(sServerName)
 Dim sOffice
 sOffice = Mid(sServerName, 4, 3)
 GetOffice = sOffice
End Function
```

## Concatenating Strings

You've already learned about string concatenation, but let's look at it again. It's an important technique that you'll use repeatedly in your scripts.

For example, suppose you need to display a long, complicated message inside a message box. You could write a single `MsgBox` statement on a *very* long line of code, but that's harder to do and will make it tougher to maintain the script in the future. Instead, it's often easier to use string concatenation and line-continuation characters.

```
Dim sMessage
sMessage = "The server name you typed is invalid." & _
 vbCrLf & _
 vbCrLf & "Remember that all server names must : & _
 be seven characters " & _
 "long. The first three characters " & _
```

*continues*

```
 must be the server's internal " & _
 "serial number. The second three characters " & _
 must be the three-" & _
 "character code for the office in which the " & _
 server is located. " & _
 "Finally, the last four characters indicate " & _
 the server's function:" & _
 vbCrLf & vbCrLf & "FILES = File Server" & _
 vbCrLf & vbCrLf & _
 "DOMC = Domain Controller" & vbCrLf & vbCrLf & _
 "SQLS = SQL Server" & vbCrLf & vbCrLf & _
 "Please try again."
MsgBox sMsg
```

I can't even show you the alternative in this book—there's no way for me to spread a single line of code across multiple pages!

String concatenation is also useful when you're working with variables. For example, suppose you need to generate some kind of unique password for new users. The following function might be used in a script that creates new user accounts.

```
Function MakePassword(sUserName)
 Dim sPassword
 sPassword = Left(sUserName,1)
 sPassword = sPassword & UCase(Right(sUserName,1))
 sPassword = sPassword & DatePart("n",Now)
 sPassword = sPassword & UCase(Mid(sUserName, 3, 2)
 MakePassword = sPassword
End Function
```

This function uses concatenation—and several other functions—to make up a reasonably complex password that can be assigned to new user accounts. String concatenation is used to append the results from each function to the gradually growing password, with a final password that's about seven characters long. I'll cover the `DatePart()` function in the next chapter, and I'll cover the `UCase()` function in the next section of this chapter.

---

**NOTE** Remember that in Chapter 5 I explained how you could use both `&` and + for string concatenation. I mention it because you may see example scripts on the Web that use +; because + can also be used for addition, you should never use it for string concatenation. Always use `&`, which VBScript knows can only be used for concatenation.

---

## Changing Strings

VBScript includes a wide array of functions designed to change strings. I'll start with `LCase()` and `UCase()`, which change a variable to lower- or uppercase letters, respectively. Try running the following scriptlet to see how these functions work.

```
Dim sInput
sInput = InputBox("Enter a string to try.")

MsgBox "All upper: " & UCase(sInput)
MsgBox "All lower: " & LCase(sInput)
```

These functions can be very useful when dealing with case-sensitive strings, such as passwords, WMI queries, and so forth. Using these functions, you can ensure that the case of the strings is exactly what you need for whatever you're doing.

Combining these functions with the substring functions lets you perform some very powerful tricks. For example, the following function will accept a full user name, such as "john doe," and convert it to the proper name case, where the first letters of each name are capitalized, no matter how you capitalize the input.

```
Dim sUserName

'get the user name
sUserName = InputBox("Enter user name")

'does it contain a space?
If InStr(1, sUserName, " ") = 0 Then

 'no – error message!
 MsgBox "Name must contain a space."

Else

 'display the name case version
 MsgBox "Proper case is " & NameCase(sUserName)

End If
```

*continues*

```
Function NameCase(sName)

 'lowercase everything
 sName = LCase(sName)

 'locate the space position
 Dim iPos
 iPos = InStr(1, sName, " ")

 'build the output
 sName = UCase(Left(sName,1)) & _
  Mid(sName, 2, iPos-2) & " " & _
  UCase(Mid(sName, iPos + 1, 1)) & _
  Right(sName, Len(sName)-iPos-1)

 NameCase = sName

End Function
```

Try walking through the `NameCase()` function to see if you can figure out how it works. It's just using substring functions to pull out the first character of the first name, then the rest of the first name, then the first character of the last name, and then the rest of the last name. The first character of each name is run through `UCase()` to ensure it's uppercased properly.

Another very cool string-changing function is `Replace()`. With it, you can replace any occurrence of one substring with another substring, all without affecting the other contents of the main string. Sound complicated? It's not! Just check out this example.

```
Dim sMsg
sMsg = "Hello, %1%. Today is %2%."

Dim sName
sName = InputBox("What is your name?")

sMsg = Replace(sMsg, "%1%", sName)
sMsg = Replace(sMsg, "%2%", Date)

MsgBox sMsg
```

`Replace()` can be incredibly useful in administrative scripts. For now, concentrate on learning how it works—you'll see plenty of examples of its usefulness through this book.

## Formatting Strings

VBScript provides several functions designed to format strings—and other data types—into specially formatted strings. For example, suppose you have a function that calculates the total up time for a server, and you want to display that information as a percentage. The following script is an example of how VBScript lets you format the output.

```
Dim iUpHours, iDownHours
iUpHours = InputBox("How many hours has the server " & _
 been up?" & _
 " Fractional numbers are OK.")
iDownHours = InputBox("How many hours has the server " & _
 been down?" & _
 " Fractional numbers are OK.")

Dim sResult
sResult = CalcDownPerc(iUpHours, iDownHours)
MsgBox "The server has been down for " & _
 sResult & " of the " & _
 "time it has been up."

Function CalcDownPerc(iUpHours, iDownHours)
 Dim iPerc
 iPerc = iDownHours / iUpHours

 Dim sDisplay
 sDisplay = FormatPercent(iPerc, 4)

 CalcDownPerc = sDisplay
End Function
```

In this example, `FormatPercent()` is used to format the contents of variable `iPerc` so that the result has four digits after the decimal place, and the result may have a leading zero before the decimal depending upon the computer's locale settings.

Another popular formatting function is `FormatDateTime()`. In the next example, suppose that variable `dLastLogon` contains a user's last logon date.

```
Dim sDate
sDate = FormatDateTime(dLastLogon, vbShortDate)
```

This example will display the date in the computer's short date format, which in the U.S. looks like 5/26/2003. Other formats include

- `vbGeneralDate`. This can display a date, a time, or both. Dates are formatted using the short date format, and times are displayed as a long time. If both parts are included, both parts are displayed.
- `vbLongDate`. This displays a date using the computer's long date format, such as "Monday, May 26, 2003."
- `vbShortDate`. This displays a date using the computer's short date format, such as "5/26/2003."
- `vbLongTime`. This displays a time using the computer's long time format, such as "8:53 A.M."
- `vbShortTime`. This displays a time using the computer's short time format. This is generally a 24-hour format, such as "13:26" rather than "1:26 P.M."

---

**NOTE** As you'll learn in the next chapter, VBScript stores date and time information in an internal serial number format, so that a date and time together might look something like 857387.5784893. A date by itself might be stored as 859340.0, whereas a time might look like 0.589738. *All* date and time variables contain both a date and time component, so it's best to use `FormatDateTime()` to display just the portion you want.

---

VBScript also includes `FormatNumber()` and `FormatCurrency()` functions. You can learn more about these in the VBScript documentation if you need them; I find that they have pretty limited application in common administrative scripts.

## Converting Other Data Types to String Data

First, keep in mind that the formatting functions I introduced you to in the previous section will return a string value. So, if you use something like this:

```
Dim iNumber, sString
iNumber = 5
sString = FormatPercent(iNumber, 2)
MsgBox sString
```

variable `sString` will contain a string value, because that's what `FormatPercent()` returns. Technically, the formatting functions are a sort of specialized string conversion function, too.

```
Dim dDate, sString
```

VBScript does provide a general string conversion function: `CStr()`. This function simply takes any type of data—numeric, date/time, currency, or whatever—and converts it to a string. The function works by taking each character of the input data and appending it to an output string. So the number 5 will become "5," the number -2 will become "-2," and so forth. Dates and times are converted to their short display format. For example, try running this.

```
dDate = Date()
sString = CStr(dDate)
MsgBox sString
```

The result should be a short formatted date, such as "5/26/2003."

---

**NOTE** If your computer is displaying short dates with a two-digit year, you probably have an outdated version of the Windows Script Host or an incredibly old operating system. All newer versions of Windows and the Windows Script Host display four-digit years to help eliminate future recurrences of the infamous "Y2K bug."

---

## Review

Believe it or not, you've probably covered half of VBScript's functions in this chapter. That alone should help you realize how important string manipulation is, and may explain the spinning feeling in your head right now! Don't worry—string manipulation, like everything else involved in scripting, becomes easier with practice.

For now, keep in mind the basic functions for working with substrings, such as `Right()`, `Left()`, `Mid()`, and `InStr()`. String concatenation using the `&` operator is also important, as is the ability to change strings with functions like `Replace()`. Finally, string conversion functions—especially

`CStr()`—can help make your scripts less error-prone, while enabling you to work with a broad variety of data.

Your string manipulation skills will serve you well in other areas of VBScript, such as date and time manipulation, Active Directory querying, Windows Management Instrumentation, and more.

## COMING UP

In the next chapter, I'll explore other types of data, such as dates and times, bytes, and a couple of others, that you might find in your scripts. Then, in Chapter 10, I'll look at adding logic to your scripts with control-of-flow statements.

CHAPTER 9

# Manipulating Other Types of Data

**IN THIS CHAPTER**

Dates and times, arrays, bytes, and more—all data types you may run across from time to time, especially when you're writing more complex scripts that involve Windows Management Instrumentation. I'll explain how each of these data types works, and how you can work with them in VBScript.

In the prior two chapters, you learned a lot of about string and numeric data. In this chapter, I'll cover everything else—the lesser-used data types that are nonetheless so important to VBScript. You'll find yourself using these data types most frequently in complex scripts. For example, I'll begin with date and time data, which you'll use frequently in many Windows Management Instrumentation (WMI) scripts. I'll also cover byte data, which is a lot less common in administrative scripts, but worth knowing about in case you need it. Finally, I'll cover arrays, which aren't really a data type at all. They're a special type of variable capable of holding multiple values, and you'll use them in many of the scripts you write.

## Working with Dates and Times

Dates and times allow your scripts to interact more precisely with the real world. You can copy or move files based on their "last changed" date, delete users based on the last time they logged on, and so forth. Next to strings and numbers, dates and times are the third most common data type that you'll use in your scripts.

## Dates and Times in VBScript

VBScript stores dates and times in a serial number format that looks like a large decimal number. The serial number counts the number of milliseconds that have elapsed since January 1, 100 C.E., and can represent dates and times up to December 31, 9999. The integer portion of a date serial number—the portion before the decimal point—is used to represent days (and thus, months and years), whereas the fractional portion—the part after the decimal point—represents milliseconds (and seconds, minutes, and hours).

VBScript includes a number of functions for working with dates and times. For example, the `DatePart()` function analyzes a date and returns just the specified part of it. `DatePart("yyyy", Date())`, for example, returns the year portion of the current date. `DatePart()` accepts a number of different strings, which tell it which portion of the date you're interested in.

- "`yyyy`" returns the year.
- "`q`" returns the quarter of the year.
- "`m`" returns the month.
- "`y`" returns the Julian date, which is the number of days that have elapsed since the beginning of the year.
- "`d`" returns the day as a number.
- "`w`" returns the weekday, such as "`Monday`."
- "`ww`" returns the week of the year.
- "`h`" returns the hour.
- "`n`" returns the minute. Don't confuse this with "`m`," which actually returns the month.
- "`s`" returns the second.

The second parameter of `DatePart()` can be anything VBScript recognizes as a date or time, including string variables that contain date or time information, such as "1/1/2004" or "10:26 P.M."

## Getting the Date or Time

VBScript has a number of functions that return the current date or time, or portions thereof.

- `Date()` returns the current date.
- `Day()` returns the current day, numbered 1 to 31.

- `Now()` returns the current date and time.
- `Month()` returns the current month, numbered 1 to 12.
- `Year()` returns the current year.
- `Weekday()` returns the current day of the week, numbered 1 to 7.
- `Time()` returns the current system clock time.
- `Hour()` returns the current hour, numbered 0 to 23.
- `Minute()` returns the current minute of the system clock.
- `Second()` returns the current second of the system clock.

There are a couple of additional functions used to turn numeric date data, such as month or day numbers, into strings.

- `MonthName()` returns the name of the month. For example, `MonthName(1)` returns "January." `MonthName(1,True)` returns "Jan," the abbreviated form of the month name.
- `WeekdayName()` returns the name of a day of the week. `WeekdayName(2)` returns "Monday," whereas `WeekdayName(2,True)` returns the abbreviated "Mon." Sunday is the default first day of the week.

## Converting Date and Time Data

You can convert data to a date or time by using the `CDate()` function. For example, `CDate("1/1/2004")` will convert the string value "1/1/2004", which looks like a date, into the corresponding date serial number. It's difficult to get VBScript to display the internal serial number, and an example like the following simply displays something that looks like a normal date.

```
dDate = CDate("1/1/2004")
MsgBox dDate
MsgBox Date()
```

When VBScript executes the `MsgBox` statements, it redisplays the dates in whatever format your computer is configured to use based on its region settings.

You can also generate date or time data from individual date or time components, by using the `DateSerial()` and `TimeSerial()` functions. For example, `DateSerial(2004, 5, 12)` will return the date 5/12/2004. Similarly, `TimeSerial(5, 23)` will return 5:23 A.M.

### Working with Past and Future Dates

VBScript provides the `DateAdd()` function, which allows you to perform math with dates and times. `DateAdd()` requires three parameters: an *interval,* a number, and a starting date or time. Intervals can be the following:

- "yyyy" for the year.
- "q" for the quarter of the year
- "m" for the month
- "y" for the Julian date, which is the number of days that have elapsed since the beginning of the year
- "d" for the day as a number
- "w" for the weekday, such as "Monday"
- "ww" for the week of the year
- "h" for the hour
- "n" for the minute
- "s" for the second

For example, `DateAdd("yyyy", 1, "1/1/2004")` will return 1/1/2005, which is the starting date plus one year. You can use `DateAdd()` to subtract by specifying a negative number: `DateAdd("m", -1, "1/1/2004")` will return 12/1/2003, removing one month from the starting date. The function is leap-year-aware, meaning that `DateAdd("yyyy", 1, "2/29/2000")` will *not* return 2/29/2001, because 2001 is not a leap year. The function will instead return 3/1/2001, which is 365 days after the starting date.

`DateDiff()` is a similar function that returns the difference between two dates. It accepts the same interval parameters as `DateAdd()`, and accepts two dates for comparison. `DateDiff("d", "12/31/2002", "12/31/2003")` will return 365, because that's the number of days between the two dates. If the first date specified is later than the second, the number returned will be negative.

## Working with Arrays

An *array* is a collection of values assigned to a single variable. Normal variables can hold just one value. For example:

```
Dim sMonths
sMonths = "January"
```

In this example, `sMonths` could be changed to contain "February," but doing so would eliminate "January" from the variable's contents. With an array, however, a single variable can contain multiple values. For example:

```
Dim sMonths(12)
sMonths(1) = "January"
sMonths(2) = "February"
sMonths(3) = "March"
sMonths(4) = "April"
sMonths(5) = "May"
sMonths(6) = "June"
sMonths(7) = "July"
sMonths(8) = "August"
sMonths(9) = "September"
sMonths(10) = "October"
sMonths(11) = "November"
sMonths(12) = "December"
```

This capability to assign multiple values to a single variable can come in handy in a number of scripting situations.

## Arrays in VBScript

VBScript supports *multidimensional arrays*. For example, suppose you declare a variable using `Dim sData(5,4)`. This creates a two-dimensional variable. The first dimension can hold six data *elements*, whereas the second dimension can hold five. Note that elements always begin numbering at zero. I sometimes find it easier to imagine a two-dimensional array as a table of elements. The columns represent one dimension, whereas the rows represent another dimension.

| sData | 0 | 1 | 2 | 3 | 4 |
|---|---|---|---|---|---|
| 0 | Harold | Todd | Lura | Ben | Mary |
| 1 | Cyndi | David | Deb | Amy | Barb |
| 2 | Liza | Judy | Tina | Bette | Will |
| 3 | Martha | Doug | Peter | Derek | Jeremy |
| 4 | Don | Chris | Joe | Hector | Maria |
| 5 | Tom | Mary | Jill | Ruth | Bill |

I might decide that the first dimension (the columns) represents different job positions at my company, such as Sales, Marketing, Human Resources, MIS, and Operations. I might decide that the second dimension represents individuals within each role. Therefore, `sData(2,4)` would contain "Joe," the fourth person in the MIS department; `sData(0,1)` would contain "Cyndi," the second person in the Marketing department; and so forth.

Three-dimensional arrays can be pictured as a cube, with each dimension of the cube (X, Y, and Z) representing a dimension of the array. Four-dimensional and larger arrays are a bit more difficult to imagine, but you get the idea; and fortunately, arrays larger than two dimensions are rare in administrative scripts.

Arrays are not actually a data type in and of themselves; they can, in fact, be any type of data I've shown you in this book: strings, numbers, bytes, dates and times, and so forth.

## Creating and Manipulating Arrays

You can declare *static* arrays by using the `Dim` keyword, as I've already done in a couple of examples. You can declare a *dynamic* array by using the `Dim` keyword and by leaving one dimension of the array unspecified. For example, to declare a dynamic, single-dimension array, simply use `Dim sVariable()`. Notice that you still need to include the parentheses; these tell VBScript that you're declaring an array, but declining to specifically size it for now.

When you decide to size the array, you do so by using the `ReDim` statement. For example:

```
Dim sArray()
ReDim sArray(4)
```

This example will create a new array, and then size it to have five elements numbered zero to four. Note that `ReDim()` will *remove* any data in the array when resizing it. If you already have data in an array and want to keep it, add the `Preserve` keyword, as follows:

```
Dim sArray()
ReDim sArray(2)
sArray(0) = "One"
sArray(1) = "Two"
sArray(2) = "Three"
ReDim Preserve sArray(3)
sArray(3) = "Four"
```

The result of this example is an array of four elements, each containing string data. `ReDim` is pretty powerful.

- You can use it to change the number of dimensions. For example, a one-dimensional array named `sArray` with four elements can be resized using `ReDim sArray(4,2)`. Doing so adds a new dimension of three elements. However, you cannot use the `Preserve` keyword when changing the number of dimensions.
- When you use the `Preserve` keyword, you can only resize the *last* dimension. For example, if you have a two-dimensional array named `sArray`, and already have four elements in each dimension, using `ReDim Preserve sArray(8,4)` would generate an error because you're trying to resize the *first* dimension in conjunction with the `Preserve` keyword.
- You can resize an array to make it smaller. When you do, any data contained in the truncated portion of the array is lost.

You can also create arrays from an existing value. For example, suppose you have a script that's reading an IIS log file. Normally, those files are comma-delimited values. You might read an entire line of data into a variable named `sLog`, and that variable might contain something like, "12-12-2003,12:43,index.html,400" or something similar. If you want to get just the name of the Web page from that line of the log, you *could* use some heavy-duty string manipulation to find the third comma, pull out the Web page name, and so forth. However, because there's a comma delimiting each piece of data, it may be easier to convert the data to an array.

```
'sLog contains log file line
Dim sLogData()
sLogData = Split(sLog, ",")

MsgBox "Web page is " & sLogData(2)
```

The magic lies in the `Split()` function. This function accepts a variable, such as `sLog`, and a delimiter character, such as the comma. `Split()` returns an array, with one element for each piece of data separated by a comma. In my example, `sLogData` would contain four elements, numbered from zero to three. The third element, number two, contains "index.html," which is what I was after in the first place.

The opposite of `Split()` is `Join()`. This function accepts a one-dimensional array and a delimiter character, and returns a single delimited string. For example, using my `sMonths` array from the first part of this section:

```
Dim sMonths(12)
sMonths(1) = "January"
sMonths(2) = "February"
sMonths(3) = "March"
sMonths(4) = "April"
sMonths(5) = "May"
sMonths(6) = "June"
sMonths(7) = "July"
sMonths(8) = "August"
sMonths(9) = "September"
sMonths(10) = "October"
sMonths(11) = "November"
sMonths(12) = "December"

Dim sMonthList
sMonthList = Join(sMonths, ",")
```

`sMonthList` will contain "January,February,March,April,May,June,July, August,September,October,November,December". Notice that there are no spaces inserted between the month names; only the specified delimiter—in this example, a comma—is inserted between the list elements.

## Working with Array Data

You can use numeric variables to represent array elements when accessing arrays. For example, the following example works fine.

```
Dim sMonths(12)
sMonths(1) = "January"
sMonths(2) = "February"
sMonths(3) = "March"
sMonths(4) = "April"
sMonths(5) = "May"
sMonths(6) = "June"
sMonths(7) = "July"
sMonths(8) = "August"
sMonths(9) = "September"
sMonths(10) = "October"
```

```
sMonths(11) = "November"
sMonths(12) = "December"

iMonth = InputBox("Enter a number from 1-12")
MsgBox "You selected " & sMonths(iMonth)
```

The last line of this example uses the variable `iMonth` to dynamically access a given element in the array `sMonths`.

---

**NOTE** You'll see a number of examples of arrays in administrative scripts later in this book. For now, just know what an array looks like, and remember that it's a collection of values assigned to a single variable name. It will all come together for you later on; so if you don't see a clear use for arrays yet, don't worry. You will!

---

One last trick is the `IsArray()` function. This function accepts a variable, and returns True or False depending on whether the variable is an array.

## Working with Bytes

A *byte* variable can contain a single byte of data—that is, a number from 0 to 255. Doesn't sound very useful, does it? Bytes aren't often used alone, though; they're often used in arrays, where a single byte array can represent a stream of binary data. For example, files on a computer's hard drive are a simple one-dimensional array of bytes. A file that's 1KB in length has 1,024 elements in its array, and can be contained with a byte array in an administrative script.

### Bytes in VBScript

Your most frequent use for byte variables will be to pass data to WMI functions that require a byte array. You'll usually work with bytes in the form of an array, where the data inside the array represents a file or some other binary data. Still, bytes are reasonably rare in administrative scripts, which is why I won't bore you with a long example. You'll see one or two examples elsewhere in this book that use bytes; I'll call your attention to them and explain them in a bit more detail at that time.

### Converting Byte Data

The `CByte()` function converts data to a byte. Generally, only numeric data in the range of 0 to 255 can be successfully converted to a byte.

```
Dim iDouble, bByte
iDouble = 104.76
bByte = CByte(iDouble)
```

In this example, `bByte` now contains the value 105, which is the closest whole number to what `iDouble` contains.

## Review

Dates, times, bytes, and arrays are used less often, but are important types of data in VBScript. Although you may not have an immediate need for them in your administrative scripts, keep them in mind. When you do run into them in the future, or when you see them in the example scripts I'll present throughout this book, you can refer back to this chapter to learn more about them or to refresh your memory.

Bytes, dates, and times use conversion and manipulation functions very similar to those you've learned to use with string and numeric data. Date and time data can also be used with the unique calculation functions `DateAdd()` and `DateDiff()`. Arrays, however, aren't really a data type at all; they're a way to collect multiple values into a single variable. Arrays can be strings, numbers, dates, times, or bytes. You can create and manipulate arrays with functions like `Join()`, `Split()`, and `ReDim`.

**COMING UP**

Now it's time to add some intelligence to your scripts, teaching them how to react to changing conditions and to change their behavior based on your input. In the next chapter, I'll introduce you to control-of-flow statements and constructs, and, you'll be nearly finished with your VBScript tutorial. After a quick overview of the built-in scripting objects and the file system objects, I'll show you how to pull everything together in your first script.

CHAPTER 10

# Controlling the Flow of Execution

**IN THIS CHAPTER**

You've learned almost everything you need to know to write great scripts. The last step in your VBScript crash course is to add complexity and logic to your scripts by using control-of-flow constructs.

At this point, you should know enough VBScript to write some useful administrative scripts. In fact, the previous few chapters contained some great example scripts that you should be able to put right to use, in addition to using them as reference examples.

What you lack at this point, and what I'll cover in this chapter, is a way to make your scripts automatically respond to certain conditions, and execute different lines of script accordingly. For example, suppose you need to write a script that tells you which user has a particular file open on a file server. Your script must be able to iterate through all of the open resources on a server to find the one you're interested in, and then iterate through the list of users that have the resource open, displaying that information to you. Such a script would require certain lines of code to be repeated over and over, while requiring other lines of code to be executed only if certain conditions are true (such as if the current server resource is the one you're interested in).

VBScript includes control-of-flow statements that give your scripts the necessary logical-evaluation capabilities. In this chapter, you'll learn how they work, and see some examples of how to use them in your scripts.

## Conditional Execution

Many administrative scripts that you write will execute some simple, straightforward task that doesn't require any decisions. Other scripts, however, will be more complex, and will require your scripts to evaluate conditions and values and make a decision about what to do. VBScript conditional execution statements make this possible, giving your scripts a form of intelligence and decision-making capabilities.

### If...Then

The most common conditional execution statement is the `If...Then` construct. It's referred to as a construct because it involves more than a single statement or more than even a single line of code. Here's a very simple example.

```
Dim iMyNumber
iMyNumber = InputBox("Enter a number from 1-100")

If iMyNumber < 1 Or iMyNumber > 100 Then
 MsgBox "I said 1 to 100!"
Else
 MsgBox "Thank you!"
End If
```

The script declares a variable named `iMyNumber`, and then uses `InputBox()` to retrieve user input. Next, the script uses an `If...Then` construct to evaluate the input. Here's how it works.

- First, VBScript evaluates the two logical expressions in the `If` statement. Does `iMyNumber` contain a number that is less than one? Does it contain a number that is more than 100? If either of these two conditions are true, VBScript will execute the code following the `Then` statement. VBScript will accept either of these two conditions because they're connected with an `Or` statement, which means either one of them being true is acceptable.
- If neither of the `If` conditions are true, VBScript looks for an alternate execution path, which it finds after the `Else` statement. VBScript executes that code instead of the code following `Then`.
- Conditional execution stops whenever another portion of the `If...Then` construct is reached.

### Boolean Operators

`And` and `Or` are examples of *Boolean operators*. These operators are similar to mathematical operators, except that instead of resolving a value, these resolve a logical condition and return a True or False value.

For example, suppose you have a variable named `iNumber`, which contains the value 4. The logical condition `iNumber > 1 And iNumber < 100` would evaluate to True, because both subconditions evaluate to True. Similarly, the logical condition `iNumber > 1 Or iNumber < 0` would also evaluate to True, because one of the two subconditions evaluates to True.

On the other hand, `iNumber > 1 And iNumber > 100` would evaluate to False, because only one of the two subconditions evaluates to True. The rules regarding `And` and `Or` are pretty simple: With `And`, both conditions must be true in order for the overall evaluation to be true. With `Or`, either or both conditions must be true in order for the overall expression to be evaluated as true.

You can get complex with Boolean operators, and you can group them with parentheses to control the order of evaluation. Consider this monster example: `(iNumber > 10 Or iNumber < 5) And (iNumber <> 5 And iNumber <> 10)`. How will this evaluate?

First, VBScript looks at the deepest level of parentheses and evaluates them left to right for True or False. The first expression is `iNumber > 10 Or iNumber < 5`. Because `iNumber` is less than five, this expression evaluates as True. VBScript now looks at `iNumber <>5 And iNumber <> 10`. This expression is also True, because `iNumber` is neither 5 nor 10. Now, VBScript evaluates the last expression, which comes down to `True And True`. The result of this is True, so the overall expression's result is True.

What would this evaluate to if `iNumber` contained ten? It would be False. The first expression in parentheses is False, because `iNumber` is neither greater than ten nor less than five. The second expression is also False, because `iNumber` does equal ten. The final result becomes `False And False`, which is False.

Let's walk through what happens if you run this script and enter the number 2 in the input box.

1. VBScript evaluates the `If` conditions and discovers that `iMyNumber` is neither less than one nor more than 100. VBScript looks for an alternative, which it finds in the `Else` statement.
2. VBScript executes all code following the `Else` statement, displaying a message box reading "Thank you!"

3. VBScript encounters the `End If` statement, meaning the `If...Then` construct is complete. VBScript begins executing any code that follows `End If`.

Now, let's look at what happens if you enter 101 in the input box instead.

1. VBScript evaluates the `If` conditions. The first condition isn't true, but the second one is. Because the conditions are connected by an `Or` statement (as opposed to an `And` statement, which would require them both to be true), VBScript resolves the overall `If` statement as true, and begins executing everything that follows `Then`.
2. VBScript displays a message box that reads, "I said 1 to 100!"
3. VBScript encounters the `Else` statement. This tells VBScript that the current block of code is complete, and it looks for the `End If` statement.
4. VBScript locates `End If` and begins executing any code that follows it.

---

**TIP** In the next example, I slightly indented the lines of code within each section of the `If...Then` construct. This indenting makes it easier to visually spot which code will execute in either condition.

---

### *Nesting If...Then*

`If...Then` constructs can be nested as well, meaning you can place them one within the other. Let's extend the sample script to be a bit more complex.

```
Dim iMyNumber
iMyNumber = InputBox("Enter a number from 1-100")

If iMyNumber < 1 Or iMyNumber > 100 Then
 If iMyNumber > 10000 Then
  MsgBox "You're not being serious!"
 End If
 MsgBox "I said 1 to 100!"
Else
 MsgBox "Thank you!"
End If
```

I didn't change anything after the `Else` statement, but I did add another `If…Then` construct after the `Then` statement. Here's what will happen if you run this script and enter 20,000 in the input box.

1. VBScript will evaluate the `If` conditions and find that `iMyNumber` is indeed greater than 100, forcing execution of the code following `Then`.
2. VBScript will evaluate the second `If…Then` construct. Because it's true, VBScript will display a message box that reads, "You're not being serious!"
3. VBScript will continue to execute the original `Then` code, displaying a message box that reads, "I said 1 to 100!"
4. Finally, VBScript will hit the `Else` statement, telling it to jump right to `End If`.

---

**TIP** Note the indenting in the following sample. All of the code within each construct is indented. When you start nesting constructs, indenting can help make sure you're matching up `If` and `End If` statements correctly.

---

Also, notice that the second `If…Then` construct doesn't include an `Else` statement. `Else` is always optional, and you don't have to include it. The only required statements are `If`, `Then`, and `End If`.

### *If…Then…Else…ElseIf*

What if you want to evaluate multiple, different, possible values in a single `If…Then` construct? You can, using `ElseIf`. I'll revise the last sample to show you how it works.

```
Dim iMyNumber
iMyNumber = InputBox("Enter a number from 1-100")

If iMyNumber < 1 Then
 MsgBox "That isn't more than 1"
ElseIf iMyNumber > 100 Then
 MsgBox "That isn't less than 100"
Else
 MsgBox "Thank you!"
End If
```

Here's how VBScripts treats that code.

1. The first `If` expression is evaluated. If it's true, VBScript executes everything following `Then`.
2. If the first `If` expression is false, VBScript evaluates the `ElseIf` expression. If that's true, it executes whatever follows `Then`.
3. If the `ElseIf` expression is false, VBScript executes whatever is after `Else`.

You can stack up any number of `ElseIf` statements to evaluate various conditions. Listing 10.1 is an over-the-top example to give you the idea.

**Listing 10.1** *ElseIf.vbs*. Using ElseIf.

```
Dim iMyNumber
iMyNumber = InputBox("Enter a number from 1-100")

If iMyNumber = 1 Then
 MsgBox "1 is a good number."
ElseIf iMyNumber > 1 And iMyNumber < 50
 MsgBox "2 to 49: Numbers of indecision"
ElseIf iMyNumber = 50
 MsgBox "Heading right for the middle, huh?"
ElseIf iMyNumber > 50 And iMyNumber < 99
 MsgBox "51 to 99: You like the upper half"
ElseIf iMyNumber = 99
 MsgBox "99 is just short of 100"
ElseIf iMyNumber = 100
 MsgBox "You went all the way!"
Else
 MsgBox "You didn't enter 1 to 100!"
End If
```

Perhaps not an overly exciting example, but this definitely shows how `ElseIf` can allow your scripts to react to very specific conditions and execute different lines of code for each.

## Select...Case

If you've mastered the use of `ElseIf`, you'll really appreciate the `Select...Case` construct. Listing 10.2 shows how it works.

**Listing 10.2** *SelectCase.vbs.* Using Select...Case.

```
Dim iMyNumber
iMyNumber = InputBox("Enter a number from 1-5")

Select Case iMyNumber
 Case 1
  MsgBox "1 is a good number."
 Case 2, 3, 4
  MsgBox "2 to 4: Numbers of indecision"
 Case 5
  MsgBox "Heading for the end, huh?"
 Case Else
  MsgBox "What part of 1-5 did you not understand?"
End Select
```

Notice that this script isn't exactly the same as Listing 10.1. While `If...ElseIf...End If` constructs can evaluate ranges `(iMyNumber > 1 And iMyNumber < 50)`, VBScript's `Select...Case` can't. What follows the `Case` statement must be a single value or a list of values, as shown in Listing 10.2, without any operators.

If none of the `Case` expressions evaluate to True, VBScript executes whatever it finds with `Case Else`. As with the `Else` statement in an `If...Then` construct, `Case Else` is optional. If you omit it and none of your `Case` expressions are True, VBScript will just start executing whatever code follows `End Select`.

## Loops

There will be times when you want VBScript to repeat the same task over and over. Perhaps you're having it evaluate a number of different files, or perhaps you simply want to make the computer beep a lot and annoy the person in the cube next to yours! Regardless of your motives, VBScript provides statements that make repetitive execution easy, and gives you full control over how many repetitions VBScript performs.

### Do While...Loop and Do...Loop While

The `Do While...Loop` construct is used to execute a given section of code so long as a specified logical condition is true. Here's one way in which `Do While...Loop` can be used.

```
Dim iNumber
Do
 iNumber = InputBox("Please enter a number.")
Loop While Not IsNumeric(iNumber)
MsgBox "Thank you!"
```

This short script is an excellent example of collecting and validating user input. It starts by declaring a variable, `iNumber`. Next, VBScript enters the `Do` loop. Notice that there are no logical conditions specified with `Do`; it's on a line by itself, meaning VBScript will always execute the code within the loop.

Within the loop, VBScript uses an input box to collect user input, and assigns that input to the variable `iNumber`. The `Loop` statement contains the logic of the `Do While...Loop` construct: `Not IsNumeric(iNumber)`. `IsNumeric()` is a function that evaluates a variable and returns True if the contents are numeric, and False otherwise. The `Not` Boolean operator tells VBScript to reverse the output of `IsNumeric`. So, if `iNumber` contains a number, the result of `Not IsNumeric(iNumber)` will be False, the opposite of what `IsNumeric(iNumber)` would return.

The `Loop While` statement tells VBScript to return to the `Do` statement whenever the logical expression is True. In this case, the logical expression will be True only if `iNumber` doesn't contain a numeric value. In other words, VBScript will continue asking for input repeatedly until that input is numeric.

When the input is finally numeric, VBScript stops executing the loop and responds with a message box reading, "Thank you!" and the script ends.

When you include a logical expression with `Loop`, VBScript always executes the code within the loop at least once. That's because VBScript executes code in the order in which it finds it, so it doesn't get to the `Loop` until it has already executed the code within the loop at least once. There may, however, be times when you don't want the script in the loop executed at all, unless a certain condition is true to begin with. For example, suppose you've written a script that opens a text file of unknown length. The file itself is represented by an object name oFile, and that object has an `EndOfFile` property that will be True when the end of the file is reached. You can use the `Read` method of the oFile object to read data from the file. In that case, you might use a section of script like this one to read through the entire file.

```
' assumes oFile is some kind of file object
' that is opened for reading
Dim sData
Do While Not oFile.EndOfFile
 sData = oFile.Read
 MsgBox sData
Loop
```

In this chunk of script, the logical condition is included with `Do`. Again, the Boolean `Not` operator is used to flip the output of the `EndOfFile` property. Therefore, the loop will continue to execute so long as `EndOfFile` is False.

---

**NOTE** Another way to enter this logic would be `Do While oFile.EndOfFile = False`.

---

This loop does not necessarily execute at all. If oFile represents an empty file, `EndOfFile` will be True at the beginning of the loop. VBScript will evaluate this and skip the `Do While...Loop` construct completely, executing whatever code follows the `Loop` statement.

---

**NOTE** You can include `While` and a logical expression with either `Do` or `Loop`, but not both.

---

### Do Until...Loop and Do...Loop Until

The `While` statement in a `Do...Loop` construct tells VBScript to continue executing the loop so long as the specified condition is true. `Until` does exactly the opposite, executing the loop only until the specified condition becomes true. For example, you could rewrite the file reading sample as follows:

```
' assumes oFile is some kind of file object
' that is opened for reading
Dim sData
Do Until oFile.EndOfFile
 sData = oFile.Read
 MsgBox sData
Loop
```

In this case, the script will execute the same. VBScript simply performs the script until `oFile.EndOfFile` is True.

---

**NOTE** The logical condition in this example could be written `Do Until oFile.EndOfFile = True`. However, you don't have to specify the `= True` part, because VBScript assumes it. If you don't specify some logical comparison using an equal sign, VBScript assumes that you meant to include `= True`.

---

Like `While`, `Until` can be included with either the `Do` or `Loop` statement. When you add it to the `Loop`, VBScript always executes the loop at least once, and then evaluates your `Until` expression to see if the loop should be executed again. When you include `Until` with `Do`, the loop only executes if the `Until` expression is False to begin with.

### For...Next

Sometimes, you just need to execute a script a fixed number of times. For example, suppose you just want to make the computer beep eight times. Using a `Do...Loop` construct, you could write code like this.

```
Dim iCount
iCount = 1
Do Until iCount = 9
 Beep
 iCount = iCount + 1
Loop
```

This loop executes exactly eight times. However, it's quite a bit of code just to count from 1 to 8, and VBScript offers an easier way: `For...Next`. You can rewrite the preceding script as follows:

```
Dim iCount
For iCount = 1 To 8
 Beep
Next
```

When VBScript hits the `For` statement, it sets the specified variable (`iCount`) to the first specified value (1). Then, VBScript executes the loop's contents. When it reaches `Next`, VBScript increments the variable (`iCount`) by one and returns to the `For` statement for another go-round. When the value of `iCount` exceeds the specified range (greater than eight in this example), the loop stops executing and VBScript continues with whatever code follows `Next`.

`Next` increments the variable value by one by default, but you can control that. The following sample makes VBScript display the even numbers from 2 to 10.

```
Dim iCount
For iCount = 2 To 10 Step 2
 MsgBox iCount
Next
```

The `Step` statement tells VBScript to increment `iCount` by 2, rather than 1, each time it hits `Next`. You can specify a negative number to make `Step` go backward.

```
Dim iCount
For iCount = 10 to 1 Step -1
 MsgBox iCount
Next
MsgBox "Blast off!"
```

This sample will count down from 10 to 1 and then display "Blast off!"

## For Each...Next

I've already introduced you to some objects that include collections, such as the `FileSystemObject` (which I'll discuss in full detail in Chapter 12). The tricky part about a collection of objects is that you may not know how many objects to expect in the collection. `For Each...Next` provides a useful way to work with each object in the collection, one at a time, without knowing exactly how many objects there are in the collection. Here's an example.

```
' Assume oRoot represents the root folder of C:\
' and has a Subfolders property that is a
' collection of folder objects that represent
' the subfolders of C:\
Dim oSubfolder
For Each oSubfolder In oRoot.Subfolders
 If oFolder.Name = "WINDOWS" Then
  MsgBox "Found the Windows folder!"
 End If
Next
```

VBScript goes through each object in the `Subfolders` collection, one at a time. For each object in the collection, VBScript assigns the object to the object reference variable oFolder and then executes the contents of the loop. WhenVBScript reaches `Next`, it sets oFolder to refer to the next object in the collection and executes the loop again. When VBScript finally reaches the end of the collection, it stops executing the loop and starts executing whatever code follows `Next`.

You'll see a lot more of `For Each...Next` in Chapter 12, which deals more fully with the FileSystemObject.

If you'd like a non-technical example, consider that Tree object I introduced in Chapter 5. Suppose the Tree object has a `Leaves` collection. Each object in the `Leaves` collection is a Leaf, and each Leaf object includes a `Color` property that retrieves that leaf's current color. You could use `For Each...Next` to count the number of yellow leaves.

```
Dim iYellowLeaves, oLeaf
' assumes oTree is a reference to the
' Tree object
For Each oLeaf in oTree.Leaves
 If oLeaf.Color = "Yellow" Then
  iYellowLeaves = iYellowLeaves + 1
 End If
Next

MsgBox "There are " & iYellowLeaves & _
 " yellow leaves on the tree."
```

Without knowing how many Leaf objects there are, `For Each...Next` efficiently steps through the collection one leaf at a time.

## Exiting Loops

Suppose you don't always want a loop to finish executing. For example, take that file-reading script that I used in the `Do While...Loop` section earlier in this chapter. Suppose that what I really want to do is read through the file either until I reach the end of the file or until some calculation made on the file's contents is true. For example, suppose that the file contains a series of numbers, and I don't want to read any more data if the sum of those numbers exceeds 1000. Here's how I could do it.

```
' that is opened for reading' assumes oFile is some kind of file object
Dim iData, iSum
Do Until oFile.EndOfFile
 iData = oFile.Read
 iSum = iSum + iData
 If iSum > 1000 Then
  Exit Loop
 End If
Loop
```

The key here is `Exit Loop`. If the value of `iSum` ever exceeds 1000, VBScript immediately exits the loop whether the `Until` condition was ever true. You can do the same thing in a `For...Next` loop.

```
Dim iCount, sInput
For iCount = 1 To 100
 sInput = "What's the password?"
 If sInput = "Sesame" Then
  Exit For
 End If
Next
```

In this example, VBScript will continue to ask "What's the password?" until you either type "Sesame" or until you've made 100 wrong guesses. The `Exit For` statement forces VBScript to exit the loop and begin executing whatever code it finds after the `Next` statement.

## Putting It All Together

With all of these loops and conditional execution constructs under your belt, you're probably ready to see them in action!

### ➤➤ Who Has a File?

Listing 10.3 is a sample script that shows you which user or users has a particular file open on a file server.

**Listing 10.3** *WhoHasFile.vbs.* Shows who has a particular file open.

```
' first, get the server name we want to work with
varServer = InputBox ("Server name to check")

' get the local path of the file to check
varFile= InputBox ("Full path and filename of the file" & _
 " on the server (use the local path as if you were" & _
 " at the server console)")

' bind to the server's file service
set objFS = GetObject("WinNT://" & varServer & _ "/
  lanmanserver,fileservice")

' scan through the open resources until we
' locate the file we want
varFoundNone = True

' use a FOR...EACH loop to walk through the
' open resources
For Each objRes in objFS.Resources

     ' does this resource match the one we're looking for?
     If objRes.Path = varFile then
          ' we found the file - show who's got it
          varFoundNone = False
          WScript.Echo objRes.Path & " is opened by " & objRes.User
     End If
Next

' if we didn't find the file open, display a msg
if varFoundNone = True then
```

```
    WScript.Echo "Didn't find that file opened by anyone."
end if
```

Because this script uses an input box to get the server name, you can run it without modification in your environment. Of course, you need to be a Domain Admin or a member of the server's Server Operators group for the script to run; those groups have the permissions necessary to retrieve the information the script requires.

### ➤➤ Who Has a File—Explained

The first lines of code simply get the file server's name, and the complete path and filename of the file that you want to check. This file path must start with a drive letter, and cannot be a UNC.

```
' first, get the server name we want to work with
varServer = InputBox ("Server name to check")

' get the local path of the file to check
varFile= InputBox ("Full path and filename of the file" & _
 " on the server (use the local path as if you were" & _
 " at the server console)")
```

The next line of code uses Active Directory Services Interface (ADSI) to connect to the server's file server service. Note that ADSI will work fine even against NT file servers, because it's using the WinNT provider.

```
' bind to the server's file service
set objFS = GetObject("WinNT://" & varServer & _ "/
  lanmanserver,fileservice")
```

If you want to jump ahead and read more about ADSI, head for Chapters 14, 15, and 16.

Next, the script sets a variable to False, meaning it hasn't yet found the file that you're interested in.

```
' scan through the open resources until we
' locate the file we want
varFoundNone = True
```

The script uses a `For...Next` loop to look at each resource opened by the file server service. This is kind of an important concept: When users connect to a file server, the users themselves don't open files. Instead, the file server service (called the Server service in Windows) opens the files on behalf of the user. The file service maintains a collection named `Resources` that lists each opened file.

```
' use a FOR...EACH loop to walk through the
' open resources
For Each objRes in objFS.Resources

     ' does this resource match the one we're looking for?
     If objRes.Path = varFile then
          ' we found the file - show who's got it
          varFoundNone = False
          WScript.Echo objRes.Path & " is opened by " & objRes.User
     End If
Next
```

Within the `For...Next` construct, an `If...Then` construct determines if the current file resource is the one you're interested in.

```
' use a FOR...EACH loop to walk through the
' open resources
For Each objRes in objFS.Resources

     ' does this resource match the one we're looking for?
     If objRes.Path = varFile then
          ' we found the file - show who's got it
          varFoundNone = False
          WScript.Echo objRes.Path & " is opened by " & objRes.User
     End If
Next
```

In other words, does the `Path` property of the current resource equal the value you provided for the file path and name? If so, the code within the `If...Then` construct is executed. The variable is set to false, indicating that the script did locate the file you were interested in. The script also displays a message box indicating the user name that has opened the resource. If more than one user has the file open, VBScript continues scanning and displays each user name as it goes through this loop.

```
' use a FOR...EACH loop to walk through the
' open resources
For Each objRes in objFS.Resources

     ' does this resource match the one we're looking for?
     If objRes.Path = varFile then
          ' we found the file - show who's got it
          varFoundNone = False
          WScript.Echo objRes.Path & " is opened by " &
  objRes.User
     End If
Next
```

Finally, the script winds up with a brief message if the file wasn't found. This is only polite; if you don't include this last bit, the script might not appear to be doing anything if the file wasn't found.

```
' if we didn't find the file open, display a msg
if varFoundNone = True then
     WScript.Echo "Didn't find that file opened by anyone."
end if
```

**NOTE** You may notice the use of `WScript.Echo` to display messages. This is functionally the same as the `MsgBox` statement, and you'll learn more about the WScript object in Chapter 11.

As you can see, `For...Next` and `If...Then` are powerful tools in this complex and highly useful administrative script.

## Review

In this chapter, you've learned to write scripts that can evaluate various criteria and change the execution of the script accordingly. You can use the `If...Then` construct to evaluate logical conditions and execute different sections of script depending on those conditions. `Select...Case` is a sort of super `If...Then` construct, allowing your script to evaluate a number of possible conditions and execute script code accordingly.

You also learned how to write loops, such as `Do...Loop` and `For...Next`. These constructs allow your script to execute specific lines of code over and over, while evaluating logical criteria to determine when the repetitive execution should stop. Finally, you learned how to use `For Each...Next` to iterate through a collection of objects, making it easier to work with collections.

That's about all there is to VBScript! You've already learned about functions, statements, objects, and variables (in Chapter 5), which provide the basis of VBScript's operations. You also learned how to collect user input and display messages (in Chapter 6), which provides your script with interactivity. Chapters 7, 8, and 9 covered how to manipulate various types of data within your script. With all of that under your belt, you're ready to start "gluing together" various operating system objects and writing truly functional administrative scripts.

**COMING UP**

Incredibly, you have finished learning VBScript. Now, you can start learning about the various objects that provide access to key operating system features. You'll begin with the built-in scripting objects in the next chapter, and move on to the FileSystemObject in Chapter 12.

CHAPTER 11

# Built-in Scripting Objects

**IN THIS CHAPTER**

You've now seen most of the VBScript language, so it's time to start working with those "objects" that you've heard so much about. I'll begin with the objects that are built into the scripting engine itself, and you'll find that they're quite useful in a number of situations.

I've already described how VBScript's real value is as a sort of electronic "glue," which you can use to piece together the many objects of the Windows operating system. Windows Management Instrumentation (WMI) and Active Directory Services Interface (ADSI) are good examples of operating system functionality that you can access by using VBScript. The Windows Script Host (WSH) even has its own built-in object library, and these objects allow you to perform some powerful tasks.

In this chapter, you'll learn to use the WSH Network object, which provides access to the computer's network environment; the Shell object, which allows you to manipulate Explorer and other shell-related information; and the Shortcut object, which allows you to work with Explorer shortcuts and Internet links.

All of these objects can be used in a wide variety of situations, but I think you'll find them more useful in logon scripts. The Network object, for example, allows you to map network drives and printers, which is perhaps the most common job of a logon script.

Chapter 29 contains additional logon script examples for both NT and Active Directory domains, and includes some suggestions for using logoff scripts.

## The WScript Object

All of these objects are accessed through the top-level WScript object. You've already seen WScript in use in Chapter 6, where I showed you how

`WScript.Echo` can be used to produce both command-line output and message boxes, depending on whether you are using `Cscript.exe` or `WScript.exe` to execute your script. The WScript object is the only one your scripts get free, meaning you don't have to explicitly create a reference to it. WScript is always available when you're running a script in WSH.

In addition to `Echo`, the WScript object has new methods and properties that may be useful to you in your scripts. For example, you can execute the `WScript.Sleep` method, passing a specific number of milliseconds, to have your script pause its execution.

```
'Pause for 5 seconds
WScript.Sleep 300000
```

You can have your scripts immediately stop execution and exit, if you want.

```
If varInput = "" Then
 WScript.Quit
End If
```

In this example, the script will immediately exit if variable `varInput` is empty. You can also ensure that your scripts have a timeout. By default, WSH will continue executing your scripts forever; you may, however, want to automatically have your scripts end if they don't complete within, say, 30 seconds. That way, a script that has the chance of entering some endless loop, or trying to connect to a remote computer that isn't available, will eventually stop running. To do so, simply set a timeout value.

```
'Specify a timeout in seconds
WScript.Timeout = 30
```

Most importantly, the WScript top-level object provides access to important child objects that you'll need to use in many of your scripts.

## The Network Object

The WScript.Network object provides access to drive and printer mapping functions, as well as access to network information, such as the current user and domain names. You must explicitly create an instance of the Network object in order to use it.

```
'Create reference
Dim oNetwork
Set oNetwork = CreateObject("WScript.Network")
```

When created, you can use the object in your scripts.

## Overview

The Network object is designed primarily for use in logon scripts, where you'll need to map both drives and printers. Obviously, it has uses elsewhere, but logon scripts demonstrate its usefulness. The **Network** object provides three functions.

1. Working with network drives, including mapping and unmapping them, as well as enumerating them.
2. Working with network printers, including mapping and unmapping them, as well as enumerating them.
3. Providing access to the network environment's information, such as the current user and domain names.

---

**NOTE** All of the examples in this section assume that you've created a variable named `oNetwork` and set it to be a reference to the WScript.Network object.

---

By the way, if you're in a rush to get to WMI, you should know that it's not the be-all and end-all of scripting. In fact, most of the functionality offered by the Network object, particularly mapping network drives, isn't possible through WMI.

## Methods and Properties

The MapNetworkDrive object has several different methods for working with drives and printers, and three properties for obtaining network environment information.

### *MapNetworkDrive*

You'll most often see drives mapped using a simplified version of the `MapNetworkDrive` method.

```
'map a drive
oNetwork.MapNetworkDrive "Z:", "\\Server1\public"
```

However, the method offers other parameters that give you more flexibility and functionality.

- Local name. This is a required parameter (such as "`Z:`") and allows you to specify the local drive name for the new mapping.
- Remote name. This is a required parameter (such as "`\\server1\public`") and allows you to specify the UNC of the shared folder you want to map to.
- Update profile. This is an optional parameter and can be either True or False. If True, the user's profile is updated with the new drive mapping. The default is False.
- User name. This is an optional parameter and allows you to specify an alternate user name for authenticating to the remote server.
- Password. Another optional parameter, allowing you to specify an alternate password for authenticating to the remote server.

An example of the full method might look like this.

```
oNetwork.MapNetworkDrive "Z:", "\\Server1\public", _
 False, "DonJ", "Pa55word!"
```

---

**NOTE** It's a very poor security practice to include passwords in a script, because the passwords can be easily read by almost anyone. Only use the parameters for alternate credentials if you plan to use the script for only your own purposes, and if the script is secured so that only you have access to it.

---

### *RemoveNetworkDrive*

As its name implies, the `RemoveNetworkDrive` method disconnects a network drive. You must pass one parameter, which is the drive letter to disconnect. Two optional parameters allow you to specify if the drive should be disconnected even if files are in use, and whether the user's profile should be updated to indicate that the drive is no longer mapped. If you set that last parameter to False (which is the default if you omit the parameter), and the user's profile contains the drive mapping, the drive mapping will be restored the next time the user logs on.

Here's what the method looks like in action.

```
oNetwork.RemoveNetworkDrive "Z:", _
 False, True
```

This method can generate errors if the drive you try to remove isn't a network drive (if, for example, you try to unmap the C: drive), or if there are files on the network drive opened by the client and you don't specify True for the second parameter.

### *EnumNetworkDrives*

This method allows your script to list information about connected network drives. Here's an example.

```
Set oDrives = oNetwork.EnumNetworkDrives
For x = 0 to oDrives.Count – 1 Step 2
 WScript.Echo oDrives.Item(x) & ": " & oDrives.Item(x+1)
Next
```

The `EnumNetworkDrives` method returns a collection, and the items in the collection are paired. The first item (displayed with `WScript.Echo-oDrives.Item(x)` in the example) is the drive's name, such as "`Z:`". The second item (`oDrives.Item(x+1)`) is the drive's UNC, which is the network location that the drive is connected to.

### *AddWindowsPrinterConnection*

Windows-based printers do not require the use of a printer port; the printers simply show up as icons in the Printers (or Printers & Faxes) folder, and Windows applications can then print to them. Adding a connection to a network printer is as easy as using the `AddWindowsPrinterConnection` method.

```
oNetwork.AddWindowsPrinterConnection _
 "\\Server1\LaserJet"
```

The parameter you provide specifies the UNC for the network printer. For NT-based operating systems, including Windows 2000 and Windows XP, that's all you need to provide. In Windows 9x operating systems, however, you also need to specify the name of the printer driver that supports the printer, and that printer driver must already be installed on the client.

```
oNetwork.AddWindowsPrinterConnection _
 "\\Server1\LaserJet", "HP LaserJet 5n"
```

Printer connections made using this method cannot be used by older MS-DOS applications (if you still have any), because MS-DOS applications are designed to print to a local printer port.

### *AddPrinterConnection*

This method is similar to `AddWindowsPrinterConnection`, except that it captures a local printer port (generally LPT1 or LPT2) and makes the printer available to MS-DOS applications. The syntax is also similar.

```
oNetwork.AddPrinterConnection _
 "LPT1:", "\\Server1\LaserJet"
```

It's rare to see this method in use, because so few companies have any old MS-DOS applications that they're using to print. Still, if you need it, it's available.

### *EnumPrinterConnections*

This method works very similarly to the `EnumNetworkDrives` method described earlier. Here's an example of it in use.

```
Set oPrinters = oNetwork.EnumPrinterConnections
For x = 0 to oPrinters.Count – 1
 WScript.Echo oPrinters.Item(x) & ": " & oPrinters.Item(x+1)
Next
```

For MS-DOS printer connections, you'll see the printer's captured port (`oPrinters.Item(x)`) and the printer's name (`oPrinters.Item(x+1)`). However, for Windows printer connections, you'll see the printer's local name, which might look like "HP083828288867," instead of a port name. You'll see the printer's UNC for the second item.

### *SetDefaultPrinter*

You can force any connected printer to be the default by using the `SetDefaultPrinter` method. Simply specify the printer's UNC to make it the default.

```
oNetwork.SetDefaultPrinter( _
 "\\Server1\LaserJet")
```

There's no way, however, to discern the *current* default printer. Therefore, if you change the user's default printer, you won't easily be able to set it back to whatever the user had previously selected as the default.

### *RemovePrinterConnection*

Like removing a network drive, you can remove printer connections. You must specify the printer name to disconnect, and you can specify options to force the disconnect and to update the user's profile. If you don't force a disconnect and the printer is being used by the client, you'll receive an error. Here's how to use the `RemovePrinterConnection` method.

```
oNetwork.RemovePrinterConnection _
 "\\server1\LaserJet", True, True
```

### *ComputerName, UserDomain, and UserName*

These properties expose information about the current network environment.

```
Dim sComputer, sDomain, sUser
sComputer = oNetwork.ComputerName
sDomain = oNetwork.UserDomain
sUser = oNetwork.UserName
```

There are some caveats. First, as I'll discuss in more detail in Chapter 29, the `UserName` and `UserDomain` properties aren't populated on Windows 9x machines until after the logon process is complete, and scripts can begin executing before that occurs. Also, there's no way to retrieve the domain name of the *computer*, and if your environment contains multiple domains with trusts, you cannot assume that the user's logon domain is the same as the computer's.

## Practical Application

Obviously, the most practical application for the Network object is in logon scripts. Listing 11.1 shows a short logon script example that uses the Network object.

**Listing 11.1** *Logon.vbs.* Using the Network object in a logon script.

```
dim objNetwork
set objNetwork = WScript.CreateObject("WScript.Network")

' let's display a welcome message
dim strDomain, strUser
strDomain = objNetwork.UserDomain
strUser = objNetwork.UserName
msgbox "Welcome to the " & strDomain & ", " & strUser & "!"

'we'll map the Z: drive to a network location
objNetwork.MapNetworkDrive "Z:", "\\Server\Share"

'let's connect to a network printer - we'll capture LPT2:
objNetwork.AddPrinterConnection "LPT2", "\\Server\Print1"

'connect a second printer without capturing a printer port
objNetwork.AddWindowsPrinterConnection "\\server\print2", _
 "Lexmark Optra S 1650"

'let's make that the default printer
objNetwork.SetDefaultPrinter "\\Server\Print2"
```

You should be able to easily follow what the script is doing by referring to the method and property descriptions I've provided. This script simply displays a personalized welcome message, maps a network drive, captures a printer port to a network printer, and adds a Windows printer connection as the default printer.

## The Shell Object

The Shell object must be explicitly created and assigned to a variable, just like the Network object. In this section, I'll assume that your scripts already contain the following code.

```
'Create shell object
Set oShell = CreateObject("WScript.Shell")
```

### Overview

You can use the Shell object to execute external applications, work with special folders and shortcuts, manipulate environment variables, write to the event log, read and write to the registry, create timed dialog boxes, and even send keystrokes to another application. Shell is sort of the catchall of the WSH, containing a number of useful functions.

### Methods and Properties

The Shell object's methods and properties provide access to its functionality. Many of these methods and properties are complementary, so I'll discuss them together in the following sections.

#### *Run and Exec*

*Scripting can't do it all.* That's an important thing to remember. I always set myself a research time limit: If I can't figure out how to do something in script within 30 minutes of searching on the Web, I'll do it whatever way I already know how. If that means launching an external command line, so be it. A good example is setting NTFS permissions on files and folders. You can absolutely do that from within WMI, but it's a thankless, complicated task. I've taken the pain to figure it out a few times, but it's almost always easier to just launch `Cacls.exe` with the appropriate parameters, so that's what I usually do, using `Run` and `Exec`.

Both methods launch new applications in separate processes. With `Run`, that process is completely detached from your script, and your script will have no access to it. Most of the time, that's fine. With `Exec`, your script has access to the new process' input and output streams, meaning you can read the output of command-line utilities or other applications into your script, and then do something else based on what happened.

Here's how you can use `Run` to launch the `DIR` command.

```
Call oShell.Run("cmd /c dir " & _
 "/a")
```

Notice that you have to launch the command-line processor, CMD, first; you can tell it to run `DIR` for you. This is an interesting technique, but not useful, as your script has no way to get at the `DIR` results. You could have `DIR` redirect its output to a text file, and then read in the text file…but what a pain. There's an easier way.

```
Dim oExecObject, sDir
Set oExecObject = oShell.Exec("cmd /c dir /a")
Do While Not oExecObject.StdOut.AtEndOfStream
 sDir = sDir & oExecObject.StdOut.Readline()
Loop
WScript.Echo sDir
```

In this example, the `Exec` method is used, which returns an execution object. That object actually represents the process space of the command window that's running `DIR` for you. That process has a standard input (`StdIn`) and standard output (`StdOut`) property, which you can utilize. In this example, the script is reading the `StdOut` property line-by-line until there are no more lines to read. Then, the script displays the results. You could, of course, read the results into an array and allow the user to select a specified folder, or whatever you want to do with the output.

You might be wondering why `Run` is even included if `Exec` is so useful. Here's why: With `Run`, you can control the type of window the new process occupies. Simply include a second parameter to `Run` with one of the following numbers:

- 0: Hidden window
- 1: Normal window with focus
- 2: Minimized window with focus
- 3: Maximized window with focus
- 4: Display window in its default size, without focus
- 5: Activate the window
- 6: Minimize the window and give focus to the next window up in the Z-order
- 7: Minimized window without focus
- 8: Default size without focus
- 9: Display the window with focus

The *focus*, of course, refers to the active window. Specifying 7, for example, launches the new application in a minimized window while leaving the current window active. This is nice for running background processes that you don't necessarily want the script's user to see.

`Run` accepts a third optional parameter, True or False, that decides whether your script will pause and wait for the launched application to finish and quit or launch the application and then continue execution right away. Try this.

```
Call oShell.Run("notepad.exe",,True)
MsgBox "Wow, that took a long time"
```

You'll notice the two serial commas in the `Run` statement. That's because I didn't want to specify a window style, which is the second parameter. This script executes Notepad, and then continues by displaying a message only after you close Notepad.

### *SpecialFolders*

There may be times when you want to create a shortcut in, or copy a file to, one of Windows' "special" folders, such as My Documents or the Desktop. The `SpecialFolders` method allows you to figure out the actual path of these special folders so that you can utilize them. Here's how.

```
Dim sPath
sPath = oShell.SpecialFolders("name")
```

Simply replace *`name`* with one of the following:

- `AllUsersDesktop`
- `AllUsersStartMenu`
- `AllUsersPrograms`
- `AllUsersStartup`
- `Desktop`
- `Favorites`
- `Fonts`
- `MyDocuments`
- `NetHood`
- `PrintHood`
- `Recent`
- `SendTo`

- StartMenu
- Startup
- Templates

### *CreateShortcut*

The CreateShortcut method is a quick and dirty way to create shortcuts; the CreateShortcut method returns a Shortcut object, which I'll discuss later in this chapter. The basic syntax looks like this.

```
Dim oShortcut
Set oShortcut = oShell.CreateShortcut(path)
```

After the shortcut is created, you use the properties of the Shortcut object to set its target, shortcut keys, and so forth.

### *Environment*

Environment variables are a useful way to access critical system information, such as the path of the Windows folder. The Environment object provides access to this information and allows you to manipulate it. There are actually different categories of environment variables: Computer-specific variables and user-specific variables are the two main ones you'll work with. The user-specific variables are stored in a space named "User," whereas computer-specific variables are stored in "System."

Some variables exist in both locations. For example, "PATH" exists both in the "User" and "System" spaces. Why should you care? Because you can also *modify* these variables. If you modify the "System" space, you're changing the entire computer, even after the current user logs off. If you just want to change an environment variable for your script, use the special "Process" space, which only exists until your script stops running.

Here's how you can retrieve an environment variable.

```
'get the system space
Dim oEnv
Set oEnv = oShell.Environment("System")

'get the PATH
WScript.Echo oEnv("PATH")
```

You can modify them using a similar technique.

```
'get the system space
Dim oEnv
Set oEnv = oShell.Environment("System")

'get the PATH
oEnv("PATH") = "new path"
```

### *ExpandEnvironmentStrings*

Environment variables can sometimes contain expandable strings, such as "%systemroot%". You can use `ExpandEnvironmentStrings` to expand these into their full values.

```
Dim oEnv
Set oEnv = oShell.Environment("System")
WScript.Echo oShell.ExpandEnvironmentStrings("%TEMP%")
```

### *LogEvent*

Need to log an event to the Windows Event log? No problem.

```
oShell.LogEvent 0, "Success!"
oShell.LogEvent 2, "Warning!"
```

The second parameter is a simple string and will be logged in the event itself. All events are logged to the Application log. The first parameter specifies the type of event:

- 0: Success
- 1: Error
- 2: Warning
- 3: Informational
- 8: Audit Success
- 16: Audit Failure

### *RegRead, RegWrite, and RegDelete*

Working with the registry is easy using the Shell object. Obviously, the usual caveats and warnings about editing the registry apply: You're messing with the heart and soul of Windows here, so exercise caution.

To read information from the registry:

```
sVariable = oShell.RegRead( _To read information from the registry:
 "HKLM\SOFTWARE\Microsoft\Windows NT\" & _
 "CurrentVersion\CurrentVersion")
```

You must provide the complete path to the value you're interested in. Shortcut HKEY_LOCAL_MACHINE by using HKLM; HKEY_ CURRENT_ USER becomes HKCU, and so forth. To create or modify a value, you'll need to know the path, the data for the value, and the data type.

```
oShell.RegWrite( _
 "HKLM\SOFTWARE\Company\Key\Value", "Data", "REG_SZ")
```

Data types are

- REG_SZ for strings
- REG_DWORD for numbers
- REG_BINARY for byte data
- REG_EXPAND_SZ for expandable strings
- REG_MULTI_SZ for string arrays

If you try to modify a value that doesn't exist, Windows will create it for you. Deleting a key simply requires you to know its name.

```
oShell.RegDelete( _
 "HKCU\SOFTWARE\Test")
```

### AppActivate

Your scripts not only can launch external applications using `Run` and `Exec`, but can also activate already running applications. You just need to know the window title, or a portion of it.

```
oShell.AppActivate _
 "Notepad"
```

After the application is active and has the system focus, you can send keystrokes to it using `SendKeys`.

### *SendKeys*

Try this script.

```
oShell.Run "Notepad.exe"
Wscript.Sleep 5000
oShell.AppActivate "Notepad"
oShell.SendKeys "Ghost writing is fun."
```

---

**TIP** Notice the `Sleep` command. This gives Notepad time to launch before the script activates it and starts sending keystrokes to it.

---

`SendKeys` allows you to send keystrokes to other applications. This is a wonderful way to control applications that don't provide any other means of doing so; effectively, you're writing your own old-style macros to control the application's functions. You can even send special keys by using the following strings along with `SendKeys`:

- `{BS}` Backspace
- `{BREAK}` Break
- `{CAPSLOCK}` Caps lock
- `{DEL}` Delete
- `{DOWN}` Down arrow
- `{END}` End
- `{ENTER}` Enter
- `{ESC}` Escape
- `{HELP}` Help
- `{HOME}` Home
- `{INS}` Insert
- `{LEFT}` Left arrow
- `{NUMLOCK}` Num lock
- `{PGDN}` Page down
- `{PGUP}` Page up
- `{PRTSC}` Print screen
- `{RIGHT}` Right arrow
- `{SCROLLLOCK}` Scroll lock
- `{TAB}` Tab
- `{UP}` Up arrow
- + Shift key, as in +P for Shift+P
- ^ Control key, as in ^P for Ctrl+P
- % ALT key, as in %P for Alt+P

Notice that the special keys must be enclosed in curly brackets (braces) as shown, except for Shift, Alt, and Control key combinations.

### *Popup*

You've already seen the `MsgBox` statement and used it to display dialog boxes; the `Popup` method displays similar boxes, but puts a time limit and a default response on them. To display a five-second notification:

```
oShell.Popup _
 "Everything is complete", 5
```

You can use the same values as the `MsgBox` statement, which I covered in Chapter 6, to display icons and buttons. For example, to display a critical error with Yes and No buttons, and to make it time out and accept the default:

```
oShell.Popup _
 "Severe error. Continue?", 5, 16 + 4
```

## The Shortcut Object

Shortcut objects are created by using the Shell object's `CreateShortcut` method. This method only specifies the final location for the shortcut; it doesn't allow you to specify the shortcut's own properties. To do that, you modify the properties of the Shortcut object, and then call the Shortcut object's `Save` method to save your changes.

### Methods and Properties

The Shortcut object offers the following properties.

- `Arguments`. These are any command-line arguments that should be passed when the shortcut is launched.
- `Description`. A description of the shortcut.
- `FullName`. This is a read-only property and returns the full name of the target application.
- `HotKey`. The hot key that can be used to launch the shortcut from the keyboard. You can use any letter, number, or function key (F1 to F12). You can also specify Control, Alt, or Shift keys, such as Alt+F9.

- `IconLocation`. The name of an icon file, along with an index to a specific icon, that should be used for the shortcut.
- `TargetPath`. The complete path and filename to the target application. UNCs are acceptable.
- `WindowStyle`. Specifies the starting window style for the shortcut when launched.
- `WorkingDirectory`. Sets the working directory for the application launched by the shortcut.

You can create two types of shortcuts:

1. *Standard* shortcuts have an LNK filename extension and generally point to applications on the local computer or network.
2. *Internet* shortcuts have a URL filename extension and point to Web sites.

You'll see examples of both in Listing 11.2.

## Practical Application

Listing 11.2 shows an example script that creates both a normal application shortcut and a URL shortcut.

**Listing 11.2** *Shortcuts.vbs.* Creates shortcuts on the user's desktop.

```
' this sample creates two shortcuts on the current user's desktop
' shows how to use the Shell interface from within Script.

'first, we need to create an instance of the shell object
dim objShell
set objShell = WScript.CreateObject("WScript.Shell")

'next, we need to get the path to the special Desktop folder
dim strDesktop
strDesktop = objShell.SpecialFolders("Desktop")

'now, we can create shortcuts on the desktop

'let's do Internet Explorer
dim objShortcut
set objShortcut= objShell.CreateShortcut(strDesktop & "\IE.lnk")
```

*continues*

```
with objShortcut
     .TargetPath = "iexplore.exe"
     .WindowStyle = 1
     .Hotkey = "CTRL+SHIFT+I"
     .Description = "Launch Internet Explorer"
     .WorkingDirectory = strDesktop
     .Save
end with

'let's create a link to my home page
dim objURL
set objURL = objShell.CreateShortcut(strDesktop & _
 "\BrainCore Website.url")
objURL.TargetPath = "http://www.braincore.net"
objURL.Save
```

I briefly introduced you to the `With...End With` construct earlier. Here, it's used so that I don't have to keep retyping `objShortcut` over and over. Each of the lines following the `With` statement begins with a period, and so VBScript assumes I'm talking about `objShortcut`, the object mentioned in the `With` statement.

## Review

In this chapter, you've seen how the built-in WScript, Network, Shell, and Shortcut objects work. With these, you'll be able to write effective logon scripts, utility scripts, and much more. Perhaps more importantly, you've seen examples of how VBScript can be used to call on objects that are provided by the Windows operating system. Throughout the rest of this book, you'll be building on that skill to utilize more complex and powerful objects, including ADSI and WMI, to accomplish even the most difficult administrative tasks.

**COMING UP**

I'll continue working with objects in the next chapter by introducing you to the FileSystemObject. Then, in Chapter 13, I'll show you how to put together everything you've learned so far: You'll design, write, test, and debug an entire script, all from scratch.

CHAPTER 12

# Working with the File System

**IN THIS CHAPTER**

Manipulating files and folders is one of the most common things an administrative script needs to do. Windows provides the script-friendly FileSystemObject to make it easy for administrative scripts to access the file system on your computer.

You'd be surprised how often you might need to access a computer's file system from within an administrative script. For example, a script that adds new users to the domain might need to read those names from a script, or might need to write out new passwords into a file. A script designed to query TCP/IP addresses from workstation computers will need to write that information somewhere—why not a text file? File system access is almost a prerequisite for any number of useful scripts, even ones that don't have a basic goal of manipulating files or folders. Fortunately, the Windows scripting library includes the FileSystemObject, or FSO, which provides easy access to the drives, files, and folders on your computer.

## The FileSystemObject Library

The FSO is actually an *object library*, which simply means that it's made up of bunches of other objects. These other objects represent things like files and folders on your computer. As with any other object—or library—you start working with the FSO in a script by declaring a variable and creating an instance of the object.

```
Dim oFSO
Set oFSO = WScript.CreateObject("Scripting.FileSystemObject")
```

---

**TIP** Where do I get these object names? Generally, from their documentation. In the case of the FSO, the MSDN Library contains complete documentation under its Platform SDK section. If you're using the Library, either from CD, DVD, or http://msdn.Microsoft.com/library, look under Platform SDK first. Then look under Tools and Scripting, expanding each section as you go. Alternatively, open the index and simply type **FileSystemObject** to jump straight to an overview.

---

One look at the FSO's documentation and you may wonder what you've gotten yourself into. The FSO contains an almost bewildering number of properties, objects, and methods for you to work with. Don't let this bounty of options overwhelm you! The FSO only has four basic objects that you'll work with.

- A Drive object represents a drive on your system. Drives can include removable drives, fixed drives, mapped network drives, and so forth.
- A Folder object represents a folder in the file system.
- A File object represents—you guessed it—a file.
- A TextStream object represents a stream of text, which is a fancy way of describing a text file. More precisely, a TextStream allows you to pull (or stream) text in and out of a file, providing a handy way to work with the contents of text files.

All of the FSO's other methods, properties, and objects are designed for working with these four basic objects. I'll cover each of these objects in their own section, along with their associated properties and methods.

---

**TIP** One of the things you often have to worry about with objects is whether the objects will be available on every machine that you want to run your script on. With the FSO, that's not a problem: It's implemented in Scrrun.dll, the Scripting Runtime, which is present on all Windows 2000 and later computers, Windows Me, and generally on Windows 98. In fact, on Windows 2000 and later, the file is under Windows File Protection and cannot easily be removed.

---

## Working with Drives

Drive objects represent the logical drives attached to your system, including network drives, CD-ROM drives, and so forth. Drives also provide an entry point into each drive's file system, starting with the root folder of the file system hierarchy. Because the Drive object represents one of the simplest aspects of the file system, it's one of the simplest objects in the FSO.

The method you'll use most with drives is `GetDrive`, which returns a Drive object given a specific drive letter. For example, to obtain a Drive object that represents your C: drive:

```
Dim oDriveC, oFSO
Set oFSO = WScript.CreateObject("Scripting.FileSystemObject")
Set oDriveC = oFSO.GetDrive("C:")
```

You can also use the FSO's root-level `Drives` collection to iterate through all of the drives attached to your system.

```
Dim oFSO, oDrive
Set oFSO = WScript.CreateObject("Scripting.FileSystemObject")
For Each oDrive In oFSO.Drives
 MsgBox "Drive " & oDrive.DriveLetter & _
  " has a capacity of " & oDrive.TotalSize & " bytes " & _
  " and is drive type " & oDrive.DriveType
Next
```

## Working with Drive Objects

The previous example illustrates the use of some of the Drive object's properties. The full list includes the following.

- `AvailableSpace` and `FreeSpace` return the number of bytes available on the disk. `FreeSpace` returns the amount of free space on the drive; `AvailableSpace` returns the amount available to the user running the script. File quotas and other concerns can result in a difference between these two properties.
- `DriveLetter` returns the drive's logical letter. Note that not all drives must have a drive letter, especially in Windows 2000 or later, although most of the time they will.
- `DriveType` tells you what kind of drive you're looking at. This property returns a number corresponding to a specific drive type.
- `FileSystem` tells you what kind of file system the drive uses. This is a string, such as FAT, NTFS, or CDFS (used for optical media like CDs and DVDs).

- `IsReady` returns a True or False. This is mainly useful for network and removable drives, and allows you to see if they're ready (connected or with a disk inserted) before trying to use them.
- `Path` returns the drive letter and the root folder; for example, "C:\".
- `RootFolder` returns a Folder object representing the root folder of the file system.
- `SerialNumber` returns the drive's volume serial number.
- `ShareName` gives you the share name (UNC) for network drives, such as "\\Server1\Share." For non-network drives, this property returns an empty string.
- `TotalSize` is the total size of the drive in bytes. To figure the size in kilobytes, divide by a thousand; to find megabytes, divide by one million; for gigabytes, divide by a billion.
- `VolumeName` gives you the name of the drive's logical volume.

---

**NOTE** The term *drive* can be confusing. In Windows, and therefore in the FSO, a *drive* is a logical entity. More than one drive can live on a *disk,* with the disk being the physical device. The terms *drive* and *volume* are more or less interchangeable as far as the FSO is concerned.

---

When working with the `DriveType` property, the following values correspond to specific drive types.

- 0: Unknown. This is rare, although some weird devices like tape backup drives hooked into a parallel port can show up this way.
- 1: Removable. This applies to any removable media drive, such as a floppy or Zip disk, but not to optical media drives.
- 2: Fixed. This is used for all hard drives, and for some devices that aren't recognized as removable, like older FireWire drives.
- 3: Network. This is used for all mapped network drives.
- 4: CD-ROM. This is used for all optical media drives, including DVD-ROMs.
- 5: RAM Disk. This is rare, as most of us don't use RAM disks anymore. Note that USB "pen" drives show up as either type 1 or 2, not as RAM disks.

The base FSO object has a couple of other interesting methods for working with drives, including `DriveExists,` which accepts a drive letter and returns a True or False indicating whether the drive exists. This is useful for checking to see if a drive exists before trying to work with it. Note that `GetDrive` returns an error if the drive you specify doesn't exist, so using `DriveExists` first is always a good idea.

Listing 12.1 shows an example of how the FSO's Drive object can be used to iterate through available drives and set the volume name for all fixed drives to "Fixed."

**Listing 12.1** *NameDrives.vbs.* Changes the volume name for fixed drives to "Fixed."

```
Dim oFSO, oDrive
Set oFSO = WScript.CreateObject("Scripting.FileSystemObject")
For Each oDrive In oFSO.Drives
 If oDrive.Type = 2 Then
  If oDrive.VolumeName <> "Fixed" Then
   oDrive.VolumeName = "Fixed"
  End If
 End If
Next
MsgBox "Finished!"
```

This script illustrates an important concept, which is that some Drive properties are writable and others aren't. For example, you can change the `VolumeName` property, which changes the actual name of a drive. However, you cannot change the `TotalSize` property. Although it might be nice to have a script expand the size of your drives, it just isn't possible!

Another important concept is the `RootFolder` property. Unlike the other properties, which return a value of some kind, `RootFolder` returns a completely new Folder object, which represents the root folder of the drive.

## Working with Folders

Folders offer up a bit more complexity. First, the FSO itself offers more methods for manipulating specific folders.

- `CopyFolder` copies a folder.
- `CreateFolder` creates a new folder.

- `DeleteFolder` removes a folder permanently. Note that the deleted folder doesn't ever make it to the Recycle Bin, and there's no "Are you sure?" prompt.
- `FolderExists`, like `DriveExists`, returns a True or False indicating whether the specified folder exists.
- `GetFolder` accepts a complete folder path and, if the folder exists, returns a Folder object that represents the folder.
- `GetParentFolderName` accepts a complete folder path and returns the name of its parent folder. For example, `GetParentFolderName("C:\Windows\System32")` would return `"C:\Windows"`.
- `GetSpecialFolder` returns the complete path to special operating system folders. For example, `GetSpecialFolder(0)` returns the path for the Windows folder. Use 1 for the System32 folder, and use 2 for the system's temporary files folder.
- `MoveFolder` moves a file a folder.

The following example illustrates a few of these base functions.

```
Dim oFSO
Set oFSO = WScript.CreateObject("Scripting.FileSystemObject")

Dim oFolder
If oFSO.FolderExists("C:\MyFolder") Then
 Set oFolder = oFSO.GetFolder("C:\MyFolder")
Else
 oFSO.CreateFolder "C:\MyFolder")
 Set oFolder = oFSO.GetFolder(C:\MyFolder")
End If

MsgBox oFSO.GetParentFolderName(oFolder.Path)
```

This example creates a folder named C:\MyFolder, and then displays its parent folder, which of course is just C:\.

## Working with Folder Objects

Although the FSO's base methods are useful for manipulating folders, folders themselves have a number of useful methods and properties that allow a more granular level of control. For example, Folder objects have four methods.

- `Copy` copies the folder. You just specify the destination for the copy. This method provides the same functionality as the FSO's `CopyFolder` method.
- `Delete` mimics the FSO's `DeleteFolder` method. However, because you're using the folder's method directly, you don't have to specify which folder to delete.
- `Move` mimics the FSO's `MoveFolder` method.
- `CreateTextFile` returns a TextStream object and creates a new text file in the folder. I'll cover this functionality in the next section.

To illustrate these methods, I'll expand on the last example.

```
Dim oFSO
Set oFSO = WScript.CreateObject("Scripting.FileSystemObject")

Dim oFolder
If oFSO.FolderExists("C:\MyFolder") Then
 Set oFolder = oFSO.GetFolder("C:\MyFolder")
Else
 oFSO.CreateFolder "C:\MyFolder")
 Set oFolder = oFSO.GetFolder(C:\MyFolder")
End If

oFolder.Copy "C:\MyOtherFolder"
oFolder.Delete
```

The result is a single folder named C:\MyOtherFolder. The operations of creating the new C:\MyFolder folder, copying it, and deleting it all occur almost instantly.

Folder objects support a number of useful properties, as well:

- `Attributes`
- `DateCreated`
- `DateLastAccessed`
- `DateLastModified`
- `Drive`
- `Files`
- `IsRootFolder`
- `Name`
- `ParentFolder`

- Path
- ShortName
- ShortPath
- Size
- SubFolders
- Type

Some of these properties are straightforward. For example, you can probably figure out what type of information the `DateLastModified` property will return, and you can guess what the `Path` property will display. A few of these properties, however, deserve further explanation.

The `Type` property in particular is interesting. To see what it returns, try the example in Listing 12.2 (which will work for files and folders, both of which have a `Type` property). Try specifying the Recycle Bin or other special folders to see what you get.

**Listing 12.2** *Types.vbs.* Shows the type of a file or folder.

```
Dim oFSO, oF
Set oFSO = WScript.CreateObject("Scripting.FileSystemObject")

Dim sPath
sPath = InputBox("Enter the path to a file or folder.")

If oFSO.FolderExists(sPath) Then
 Set oF = oFSO.GetFolder(sPath)
ElseIf oFSO.FileExists(sPath) Then
 Set oF = oFSO.GetFile(sPath)
Else
 MsgBox "Can't find what you typed."
 WScript.Exit
End If

MsgBox oF.Type
```

## Folder Attributes

The `Attributes` property returns specific attributes of the folder, such as whether it is read only or compressed. These attributes are numeric, and because a folder can have many different attributes at once—such as both compressed and hidden—you have to manipulate the `Attributes` property a bit to figure out what's what.

The possible values are

- Normal: 0
- Read-only: 1
- Hidden: 2
- System: 4
- Volume: 8
- Directory: 16
- Archive: 32
- Alias: 1024
- Compressed: 2048

To figure out which attributes are turned on, you have to perform some Boolean math. Because you're a systems administrator, I'm going to assume that you don't really care for a detailed explanation of what Boolean math is or does, but that you probably just prefer to see an example of it in action. Listing 12.3 is just that.

**Listing 12.3** *CheckFolder.vbs.* Checks the attributes of a specified folder

```
Dim oFSO, sFolder, oFolder
Set oFSO = WScript.CreateObject("Scripting.FileSystemObject")
sFolder = InputBox("Full path of folder to check?")

Set oFolder = oFSO.GetFolder(sFolder)

Dim sMsg

If oFolder.Attributes AND 0 Then
 sMsg = sMsg & "Folder is normal" & vbCrLf
End If

If oFolder.Attributes AND 1 Then
 sMsg = sMsg & "Folder is Read only" & vbCrLf
End If

If oFolder.Attributes AND 2 Then
 sMsg = sMsg & "Folder is Hidden" & vbCrLf
End If

If oFolder.Attributes AND 4 Then
 sMsg = sMsg & "Folder is a system folder" & vbCrLf
```

continues

```
End If

If oFolder.Attributes AND 8 Then
 sMsg = sMsg & "Folder is really a volume" & vbCrLf
End If

If oFolder.Attributes AND 16 Then
 sMsg = sMsg & "Folder is a directory" & vbCrLf
End If

If oFolder.Attributes AND 32 Then
 sMsg = sMsg & "Folder has changed since the last backup" & vbCrLf
End If

If oFolder.Attributes AND 1024 Then
 sMsg = sMsg & "Folder is a shortcut" & vbCrLf
End If

If oFolder.Attributes AND 2048 Then
 sMsg = sMsg & "Folder is compressed" & vbCrLf
End If

MsgBox sMsg
```

By using the Boolean `AND` operator to compare the `Attributes` property to the predefined values, you can figure out which attributes are turned on and which ones aren't. This script builds up a message in variable `sMsg`, which contains the status of the various attribute flags.

Some of these attributes can be changed. You can use the `Attributes` property to alter the read-only status, the hidden status, the system status, and the archive status. You cannot change any of the other attributes. To set an attribute, use the `AND` operator again.

```
'Set the Read-Only status to be true
oFolder.Attributes = oFolder.Attributes AND 1

'Now try turning on compression:
oFolder.Attributes = oFolder.Attributes AND 2048
```

The last line of code causes an error, because the compression attribute is read-only within scripting, and cannot be changed by the FSO.

## Properties That Are Objects

Some of a Folder object's properties are actually references to other objects.

- The `Drive` property returns a Drive object that represents the drive that contains the folder.
- The `Files` property returns a collection of File objects, representing the files within the folder. I'll cover File objects in the next section.
- The `ParentFolder` property returns a Folder object that represents the folder's parent folder. If the folder is the root folder, you cannot use `ParentFolder` because the root doesn't have a parent. Use the `IsRootFolder` property, which returns True or False, to figure out if the folder is the root or not.
- The `SubFolders` property returns a collection of Folder objects, representing the folders contained within the folder.

The `SubFolders` property provides access to an object hierarchy that represents the folder hierarchy of the file system. Figure 12.1 illustrates the relationship between a Drive object (in this case, a network drive), its `RootFolder` property (which returns a Folder object), and that folder's `SubFolders` property (which returns a collection of Folder objects).

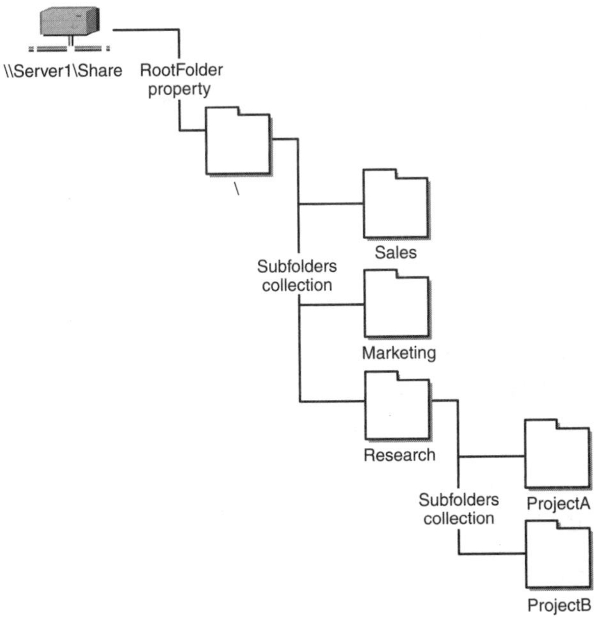


**Figure 12.1** The hierarchy of Drive and Folder objects in the FSO

## Working with Files

Files, of course, are the most granular object you can work with inside the FSO, and they're relatively uncomplicated. As with Drive and Folder objects, the FSO itself has some useful methods for working with files:

- `CopyFile`
- `DeleteFile`
- `FileExists`
- `GetFile`
- `MoveFile`

These all work similarly to their Folder object counterparts, allowing you to obtain a reference to a file (`GetFile`), check for a file's existence (`FileExists`), and copy, delete, and move files. You can also create files, which is a process I'll cover a bit later in this chapter.

### Working with File Objects

File objects themselves have a few methods.

- `Copy` copies a file.
- `Delete` removes a file without warning and without using the Recycle Bin.
- `Move` moves a file.
- `OpenAsTextStream` opens a file for reading (which I'll cover in the next section).

Properties of the File object include

- `Attributes`
- `DateCreated`
- `DateLastAccessed`
- `DateLastModified`
- `Drive`
- `Name`
- `ParentFolder`
- `Path`
- `ShortName`
- `Size`
- `Type`

These all work identically to their Folder object property counterparts, which I covered in the previous section. The `Type` property can return different values for a file; use Listing 12.2 with different files to see what you get back. For example, for a file with a TXT filename extension, you should get something like "Text Document" from the `Type` property.

## ➤➤ File Properties and Methods

Listing 12.4 shows an example of the File object's properties and methods in use.

**Listing 12.4** *FileProperties.vbs.* This script uses both File and Folder objects to demonstrate various properties and methods.

```
Dim oFSO, oFolder, oFile, oNewFolder
Set oFSO = WScript.CreateObject("Scripting.FileSystemObject")

Dim sPath
sPath = InputBox("Provide starting folder path")

If oFSO.FolderExists(sPath) Then

 Set oNewFolder = _
  oFSO.CreateFolder(oFSO.BuildPath(sPath,"Copies"))

 For Each oFile in oFolder.Files
  oFile.Copy oNewFolder.Path
  MsgBox "File " & Name & " last changed on " & _
   oFile.DateLastModified & " and of type " & _
   oFile.Type & ". It is contained in folder " & _
   oFile.ParentFolder.Path & " and uses the short " & _
   " filename " & oFile.ShortName & "."
 Next
End If

MsgBox "All Done!"
```

This script is ready to execute as-is on any system.

### ➤➤ File Properties and Methods—Explained

This is a straightforward script. It starts by setting up some variables and creating an FSO.

```
Dim oFSO, oFolder, oFile, oNewFolder
Set oFSO = WScript.CreateObject("Scripting.FileSystemObject")
```

Next, the script asks you to provide a starting path. An `If...Then` construct is used to perform the rest of the script's work only if the folder you provide actually exists.

```
Dim sPath
sPath = InputBox("Provide starting folder path")

If oFSO.FolderExists(sPath) Then
```

Next, the script uses the FSO's `CreateFolder` method to create a new folder. This method actually returns a Folder object referencing the new folder. Notice the `BuildPath` method, which is used to create an appropriate path string including the correct backslashes. I'll cover `BuildPath` in more detail later in this chapter.

```
Set oNewFolder = _
 oFSO.CreateFolder(oFSO.BuildPath(sPath,"Copies"))
```

Next, the script uses a `For Each...Next` construct to loop through each file in the folder that you specified. For each one, it copies the file into the newly created folder, using the `Copy` method of the file. Finally, it uses several of the File object's properties to display information about the file.

```
For Each oFile in oFolder.Files
 oFile.Copy oNewFolder.Path
  oFile.DateLastModified & " and of type " & _  MsgBox "File " & Name
 & " last changed on " & _
  oFile.Type & ". It is contained in folder " & _
  oFile.ParentFolder.Path & " and uses the short " & _
  " filename " & oFile.ShortName & "."
```

Notice in particular the use of the `ParentFolder` property. This property actually represents a Folder object, with all of the properties and methods—including the `Path` property—of any Folder object.

`oFile.ParentFolder.Path` is using the `Path` property of a Folder object—specifically, the folder that contains the file referenced by oFile.

The script finishes up by closing loops and constructs and displaying a message.

```
 Next
End If

MsgBox "All Done!"
```

This example should help you see how various properties and methods of the File object can be used, particularly those properties that are actually object references, such as `ParentFolder`.

## Reading and Writing Text Files

The FSO provides basic functionality for reading from, and writing to, text files. If you think of a text file as one long string of characters, you'll have an idea of how the FSO views text files. In fact, that long string of characters is what the FSO calls a *TextStream*. TextStream objects are how you get text into and out of text files.

The FSO has two basic methods for creating a TextStream: `CreateTextFile` and `OpenTextFile`. Both methods require you to provide a filename, and allow you to specify optional parameters, such as whether to overwrite any existing file when creating a new one. Here's an example.

```
Dim oFSO, oTS
Set oFSO = WScript.CreateObject("Scripting.FileSystemObject")
Set oTS = oFSO.CreateTextFile("c:\test.txt")
oTS.WriteLine "Hello, World!"
MsgBox "All Done!"
oTS.Close
```

As you can see, the result of the `CreateTextFile` method is a TextStream, which is assigned via the `Set` command to variable `oTS`. TextStream objects have some properties and methods all their own. First, the methods:

- `Write` writes one or more characters to the file.
- `WriteLine` writes one or more characters and follows them with a carriage return/linefeed combination, thus ending the line as you would in Notepad when you press Enter.

- `Close` closes the TextStream.
- `Read` reads a specified number of characters from a TextStream.
- `ReadLine` reads an entire line of characters—up to a carriage return/linefeed.
- `ReadAll` reads the entire TextStream.

One useful property of a TextStream is `AtEndOfStream`, which is set to True when you've read all the way through a text file and reached its end.

Files must be opened either for reading, writing, or appending. When a file is opened for reading, you can only use the `Read`, `ReadLine`, and `ReadAll` methods; similarly, when the file is opened for writing or appending, you can only use `Write` or `WriteLine`. Of course, you can always use `Close`.

---

**NOTE** Appending a file simply opens it and begins writing to the end of the file, while leaving the previous contents intact. This can be useful for writing messages to an ongoing log file.

---

Another way to open a file is to use the `OpenAsTextStream` method of a File object that represents the file. This technique also returns a TextStream object. The `OpenAsTextStream` method allows you to specify how you want the file opened—for reading, writing, or appending.

## ➤➤ Reading and Writing Files

Listing 12.5 is a robust example script that demonstrates how to read and write text files from within a script. I'll use these same techniques at the end of the chapter, when I'll show you how to create a script that scans IIS log files for Active Server Pages errors.

**Listing 12.5** *FileWork.vbs.* This script creates a file, writes text to it, and then reads the text back in again.

```
Dim sFileName, oFSO, oTS, sText
Set oFSO = WScript.CreateObject("Scripting.FileSystemObject")

sFileName = InputBox("Enter the full path and " & _
 "name of a file to be created.")

If oFSO.FileExists(sFileName) Then
 If MsgBox("This file exists. OK to overwrite?", _
```

```
   "Are you sure?" & _
   4 + 32) <> 6 Then
   MsgBox "Script aborted."
   WScript.Exit
  Else
   Set oTS = oFSO.CreateTextFile(sFileName,True)
  End If
End If

oTS.WriteLine "Script log file:"
oTS.WriteLine "Started " & Now()
oTS.WriteLine "Finished" & Now()
oTS.Close

MsgBox "Finished making file. Feel free to edit it," & _
 " and click OK to continue."

Set oTS = oFSO.OpenTextFile(sFileName)
sText = oTS.ReadAll
oTS.Close

MsgBox "Your file contains: " & vbCrLf & vbCrLf & _
 sText
```

This script is ready to run on any system.

## ➤➤ Reading and Writing Files—Explained

This is a straightforward script, and it's a good review of VBScript in general because it combines some important elements that you've already learned. It starts by declaring some variables and creating a new FSO.

```
Dim sFileName, oFSO, oTS, sText
Set oFSO = WScript.CreateObject("Scripting.FileSystemObject")
```

Next, it uses an input box to get a filename.

```
sFileName = InputBox("Enter the full " & _

 "path and name of a file " & _
 "to be created.")
```

Next, the script checks to see if the file exists. If it does, it uses a message box to ask permission to overwrite the file. Notice that this is a more complete version of `MsgBox()` than I usually use in examples. This version provides a title for the message box and specifies that it should contain a question mark icon and Yes and No buttons (4 is the question mark, 32 is Yes/No). I had to look those values up in the VBScript documentation. Finally, `MsgBox` is being used as a function—if the user clicks Yes, the function will return a 6 (also from the documentation), so this code checks to see if a 6 was returned.

```
If oFSO.FileExists(sFileName) Then
 If MsgBox("This file exists. OK to overwrite?", _
  "Are you sure?" & _
  4 + 32) <> 6 Then
  MsgBox "Script aborted."
  End
```

If the user clicks Yes, the script creates a new text file. Notice the `True`, which tells `CreateTextFile` to overwrite any existing file, if there is one.

```
 Else
  Set oTS = oFSO.CreateTextFile(sFileName,True)
 End If
End If
```

The script uses the `WriteLine` method to add some text to the file before closing it.

```
oTS.WriteLine "Script log file:"
oTS.WriteLine "Started " & Now()
oTS.WriteLine "Finished" & Now()
oTS.Close
```

Finally, the script displays a message. If you want, open the text file and edit it—that'll prove that the script is reading back the text file in the next step.

```
MsgBox "Finished making file. Feel free to edit it," & _
 " and click OK to continue."
```

In the next step, I reuse the same variable to reference a new TextStream, this time reopening the same file by using `OpenTextFile`. I use `ReadAll` to load the entire file into a variable, and then close the TextStream. I finish by displaying the contents of the file in a message box.

```
Set oTS = oFSO.OpenTextFile(sFileName)
sText = oTS.ReadAll
oTS.Close

MsgBox "Your file contains: " & vbCrLf & vbCrLf & _
 sText
```

This example is a good reference for you to use when you start working with text files in your own scripts.

## Other FSO Methods and Properties

The base FSO object offers a few other useful methods and properties that you may need from time to time.

The first is the `BuildPath` function. It accepts components of a file or folder path and appends them together. Normally, you could do that with the simple `&` concatenation operator, but `BuildPath` actually worries about getting backslashes in the right place. So, consider this example:

```
Dim sFolder, sFile
sFolder = "C:\Windows"
sFile = "MyFile.exe"

Dim oFSO
Set oFSO = WScript.CreateObject("Scripting.FileSystemObject")
MsgBox sFolder & sFile
MsgBox oFSO.BuildPath(sFolder,sFile)
```

The first message box displays "C:\WindowsMyFile.exe", which isn't right—it is missing the backslash in the middle. The second message box, which uses `BuildPath`, displays the correct "C:\Windows\MyFile.exe" because the `BuildPath` function figured out that a backslash was necessary.

While working with paths, you may also have a need to get the absolute or base path name, and the FSO's `GetAbsolutePathName` and `GetBaseName` methods will do it for you. Here's an example.

```
Dim oFSO, sPath1, sPath2
Set oFSO = WScript.CreateObject("Scripting.FileSystemObject")
sPath1 = "C:\Windows\System32\Scrrun.dll"
sPath2 = "..\My Documents\Files"

MsgBox oFSO.GetAbsolutePathName(sPath1)
MsgBox oFSO.GetAbsolutePathName(sPath2)

MsgBox oFSO.GetBaseName(sPath1)
MsgBox oFSO.GetBaseName(sPath2)
```

The result of this is four message boxes.

- "C:\Windows\System32\Scrrun.dll": There's no difference between the input and output, because the input in this case is already a complete, unambiguous path.
- "C:\Documents and Settings\Administrator\My Documents\Files": This is an example output you might see. The difference is that the path has been resolved into a complete, final path starting at the root of the drive.
- "Scrrun": This is the base name of the last component in the input, without any file extension.
- "Files": Again, this is the base name of the last component, although in this case it's a folder instead of a file.

Finally, there's `GetTempName`. If you need to create a temporary file or folder, especially within the system's temporary files folder, it's important that you use a filename that other applications won't already be using. `GetTempName` simply makes up a filename that is unique, allowing you to create your temp file with confidence.

## Creating a Log File Scanner

### ➤➤ The Log File Scanner

Listing 12.6 shows the complete log file scanner.

**Listing 12.6** *ScanLog.vbs.* Scans for "500" errors in an IIS log file.

```
' Scan a log file from a webserver for
' occurrences of " - 500" which indicates an
' internal server error
```

```
' get the log file
Dim varLogFile
varLogFile = InputBox ("Enter the complete " & _
 "path and filename " & _
 "of log file to scan.")

' create filesystemobject
Dim oFSO
Set oFSO = WScript.CreateObject("Scripting.FileSystemObject")

' open file into a TextStream object
Dim oTS
Set oTS = oFSO.OpenTextFile (varLogFile)

Dim oTSOut
Set oTSOut = oFSO.CreateTextFile ("c:\errors.htm")


' begin reading each line in the textstream
dim varLine, varFoundNone
varFoundNone = true
Do Until oTS.AtEndOfStream
 varLine = oTS.ReadLine

 ' contains a 500 error?
 If instr(1, varLine, " - 500 ") <> 0 Then
  WScript.Echo varLine
  oTSOut.WriteLine "<b>" & varline & "</b>"
  varFoundNone = False
 End If
Loop

' close the textstream
oTS.Close
oTSOut.Close

' found any?
If varFoundNone = True Then
 WScript.Echo "Didn't find any errors."
Else
 WScript.Echo "Found Error. You need to fix them."
End If
```

Before you can start using this script, you simply need to figure out where IIS stores its log files. Normally, it's in %systemroot%\LogFiles with a subfolder (such as W3Svc) for each virtual Web server that you've created.

### ➤➤ The Log File Scanner—Explained

The script starts simply enough, by using an input box to ask for the complete path and filename of the log file to scan. This actually is a limitation of the script in its current form; in the next section, I'll enhance it to scan through every log file in a given folder, further automating the error-checking process.

```
' Scan a log file from a webserver for
' occurrences of " - 500" which indicates an
' internal server error

' get the log file
Dim varLogFile
varLogFile = InputBox ("Enter the complete path and filename " & _
 "of log file to scan.")
```

Next, the script creates an FSO to work with.

```
' create filesystemobject
Dim oFSO
Set oFSO = WScript.CreateObject("Scripting.FileSystemObject")
```

Because the script has to read a text file, it needs to create a TextStream object. As you've already seen, the way to do this is to simply declare a variable, and then use one of the FSO methods that returns a TextStream. In this case, because the script just needs to read an existing file, it's using the `OpenTextFile` method.

```
' open file into a TextStream object
Dim oTS
Set oTS = oFSO.OpenTextFile (varLogFile)
```

The script is going to need to log any errors it finds, so it creates a second TextStream object. This one represents a new file, and the TextStream is obtained from the FSO's `CreateTextFile` method.

```
Dim oTSOut
Set oTSOut = oFSO.CreateTextFile ("c:\errors.htm")
```

Now the script needs to loop through the contents of the log file, which is opened for reading. I've created a variable, `varFoundNone`, and set it to the Boolean value of False. I'm using that variable to figure out if I've found any errors so that I can give an appropriate message at the end of the script. To loop through the log file, the script utilizes the `AtEndOfStream` property of the TextStream object. This property is automatically set to True when the script reaches the end of the file.

```
' begin reading each line in the textstream
dim varLine, varFoundNone
varFoundNone = true
Do Until oTS.AtEndOfStream
```

Next, the script reads a line of text from the file. The `ReadLine` method actually pulls an entire string of text and stores it in `varLine`. At the same time, `ReadLine` moves a pointer in the file to the next line, which is where the next `ReadLine` operation begins. This internal pointer is used to set the `AtEndOfStream` property to True when the end of the file is reached.

After reading the line of text, the script needs to see if it contains an ASP application error. Remember, each line of an IIS log file represents one logged message. If that line contains " – 500", it's an application error. To check, the script uses the `InStr()` function, telling the function to start looking for " – 500" at the first character of the line. `InStr()`returns a number indicating the character position where " – 500" was found. I don't really care about that; what's important is that `InStr()`returns a zero if it doesn't find " – 500" within the string.

```
varLine = oTS.ReadLine

' contains a 500 error?
If instr(1, varLine, " - 500 ") <> 0 Then
```

If there's no error in the line, the script skips down to the `Loop` and goes back to read the next line from the file. However, if `InStr()` finds the string, the script outputs the line of text using the `WScript.Echo` command. It also writes the line of text to the output file, prefixing it with `<b>` and suffixing it with `</b>` which are the HTML tags for boldfacing.

```
  WScript.Echo varLine
  oTSOut.WriteLine "<b>" & varline & "</b>"
  varFoundNone = False
 End If
Loop
```

Also notice that my tracking variable gets set to False when an error is found. At the end of the script, this lets me know that I did, in fact, find an error.

---

**NOTE** The `WScript.Echo` command behaves differently depending on how you run the script. If you used `WScript.exe` (or just double-clicked on the VBS file, which does the same thing), the script displays a message box for each error line found in the log file. However, if you use `Cscript.exe` to execute the script from a command line, the errors will be written as command-line messages, and you won't be prompted to click OK for each one.

---

After the script reaches the end of the file, it can start wrapping up. The first step is to close both of the TextStreams that are open.

```
' close the textstream
oTS.Close
oTSOut.Close
```

Finally, the script needs to display an appropriate ending message. This is especially important because otherwise there's no clear indication that the script finished running, especially if no errors were found.

```
' found any?
If varFoundNone = True Then
 WScript.Echo "Didn't find any errors."
Else
 WScript.Echo "Found Error. You need to fix them."
End If
```

---

**TIP** Why did I choose to add the HTML tags in the output file? Just for fun, mainly. In theory, I could have written the file to a Web server, allowing my company's Web application developers to easily access the file to review their application's errors. You can omit the <b> and </b> tags, and just e-mail the completed text file.

---

As I've already mentioned, the script is lacking in one significant way, which I'll fix in the next section.

## ➤➤ The Enhanced Log File Scanner

As you know, IIS stores multiple log files in its log file folder. The odds that you're going to find the time to scan each new log file every day are slim, so it'd be nice if this script just asked for a folder and then scanned automatically through each log file it found there. Listing 12.7 does exactly that. The changes from the original log file scanner are shown in boldface.

**Listing 12.7** *ScanLog2.vbs.* Scans for "500" errors in an IIS log file.

```
' Scan a log file from a webserver for
' occurrences of " - 500" which indicates an
' internal server error

' get the log file
Dim varLogPath
varLogPath = InputBox ("Enter the " & _
 "complete path and logs folder.")

' create filesystemobject
Dim oFSO
Set oFSO = WScript.CreateObject("Scripting.FileSystemObject")

Dim oTSOut
Set oTSOut = oFSO.CreateTextFile ("c:\errors.htm")

' Loop through each file in the folder
Dim oFile, varFoundNone
varFoundNone = true
For Each oFile In oFSO.GetFolder("varLogPath").Files

 'Is this a log file?
 If Lcase(Right(oFile.Name,3)) = "log" Then

  'Open the log file
  Dim oTS
  oTS = oFSO.OpenTextFile(oFSO.BuildPath(oFile.Path, _
   oFile.Name))
```

*continues*

```
   ' begin reading each line in the textstream
   dim varLine
   Do Until oTS.AtEndOfStream
    varLine = oTS.ReadLine

    ' contains a 500 error?
    If instr(1, varLine, " - 500 ") <> 0 Then
     WScript.Echo varLine
     oTSOut.WriteLine "<b>" & varline & "</b>"
     varFoundNone = False
    End If
   Loop

   ' close the input textstream
   oTS.Close

  End If

Next

' close the output textstream
oTSOut.Close

' found any?
If varFoundNone = True Then
 WScript.Echo "Didn't find any errors."
Else
 WScript.Echo "Found Error. You need to fix them."
End If
```

This new script will run as-is on just about any system, provided you've given it the path to a folder that contains log files.

### ➤➤ The Enhanced Log File Scanner—Explained

This enhanced script starts much like the previous one, but asks only for a folder name. The beauty of the way the FSO treats folder names is that it doesn't matter whether the user includes a trailing backslash; the script works fine either way.

```
' Scan a log file from a webserver for
' occurrences of " - 500" which indicates an
' internal server error
```

```
' get the log file
Dim varLogPath
varLogPath = InputBox ("Enter the complete path and logs
  folder.")
```

Another minor change is that only the output TextStream is opened at this point. Because the script is working with multiple files, it needs to open each one, one at a time, as it encounters them.

```
' create filesystemobject
Dim oFSO
Set oFSO = WScript.CreateObject("Scripting.FileSystemObject")

Dim oTSOut
Set oTSOut = oFSO.CreateTextFile ("c:\errors.htm")
```

Finally, the first big change. I've declared a variable to represent a file object, and I'm using a `For Each...Next` construct to loop through a collection of objects. Here's how it works: The FSO's `GetFolder` method returns a Folder object; specifically, it's returning the folder specified by the user from the earlier `InputBox()` function. The Folder object has a property called `Files`, which is a collection of File objects. The construct loops through each file in the collection. Each time through the loop, variable `oFile` will be set to a different file.

```
' Loop through each file in the folder
Dim oFile, varFoundNone
varFoundNone = true
For Each oFile In oFSO.GetFolder("varLogPath").Files
```

I cannot be assured that every file in the specified folder will be a log file, so I've used an `If...Then` construct. If the rightmost three characters of the filename are "log", I'll allow the script to work with the file and scan for errors. Otherwise, I'll skip the file. Notice the use of the `Lcase()` function to force the filename into lowercase characters. This ensures that files with a log or LOG filename extension will be scanned.

```
 'Is this a log file?
 If Lcase(Right(oFile.Name,3)) = "log" Then
```

Now I'm ready to open the log file—the current one, that is—into a TextStream. I'm still using the `OpenTextFile` method, along with the `Path` property of the File object. The `Path` property provides a complete path, including the filename, for the file.

```
'Open the log file
Dim oTS
oTS = oFSO.OpenTextFile(oFile.Path)
```

Most of the rest of the script is the same: Read each line of the file, scan for the error text, and output a message if an error is found.

```
dim varLine
' begin reading each line in the textstream
  Do Until oTS.AtEndOfStream
   varLine = oTS.ReadLine

   ' contains a 500 error?
   If instr(1, varLine, " - 500 ") <> 0 Then
    WScript.Echo varLine
    oTSOut.WriteLine "<b>" & varline & "</b>"
    varFoundNone = False
   End If
  Loop
```

Notice that I've had to rearrange the file closing statements. In this case, I'm finished reading the current input file, so I can close it before looping back up—via the `Next` statement—to open the next file in the folder.

```
  ' close the input textstream
  oTS.Close

 End If

Next
```

Finally, I can close the output text file and finish up as I did before.

```
' close the output textstream
oTSOut.Close
```

```
' found any?
If varFoundNone = True Then
 WScript.Echo "Didn't find any errors."
Else
 WScript.Echo "Found Error. You need to fix them."
End If
```

The new script is a much more efficient administrative tool, because it can be run whenever you like and always scans through every log file you have.

---

**TIP** You could enhance this script to scan for other types of errors, such as the common errors that occur when a user tries to access a file that doesn't exist, or when users try to access a file that they're not authorized for.

---

## Review

In this chapter, you learned about the scripting FileSystemObject, which can be used to manipulate the files and folders on a computer. You learned about the object's flexible object hierarchy, which emulates the hierarchy of files and folders on your computer. You saw an example script of how the FileSystemObject can be used to move and copy files, delete them, and even open and read through existing text files. The FileSystemObject is flexible enough to earn a place in many of your scripts, and you'll see it in many of the example scripts in upcoming chapters.

**COMING UP**

You have finished learning VBScript, and you're ready to pull together everything you have learned up to now. In the next chapter, you'll design, build, and test a script designed to automate the process of archiving and rotating IIS log files. In Chapter 14, you'll begin working with advanced scripting topics, including Active Directory.

CHAPTER 13

# Putting It All Together: Your First Script

**IN THIS CHAPTER**

You've learned how to use VBScript and several operating system objects; in this chapter, you'll bring together everything you know to design, write, and test an IIS log file rotation tool.

You've already learned just about all the VBScript commands, statements, and functions that you'll need to write administrative scripts. You've learned about some of the built-in scripting objects, and you've had a chance to work with the Windows FileSystemObject. Altogether, that's plenty of information and experience to start writing useful administrative scripts!

In this chapter, you'll design and write a tool that rotates IIS log files. As you probably know, IIS can create a log file for each Web site it operates, and by default, it starts a new log file each day. Your rotation tool will copy the previous day's completed log file to an archival folder for long-term storage. At the same time, the script will delete the oldest log file, keeping a rolling thirty days' worth of log files in the archival folder.

---

**NOTE** To keep things interesting, I'm going to introduce a couple of *logic errors* into the scripts in this chapter. These scripts should run more or less without error, but they'll have unexpected results due to the way they're written. If you spot the logic errors as you read, great! If not, don't worry—that's what the debugging section of this chapter is for!

---

## Designing the Script

Before you fire up Notepad or your favorite script editor, you need to sit down and figure out exactly what your script will do. This is the best way to answer the question "Where do I start?", which is the most common question you'll have when you start writing your own administrative scripts. By following a specific script design process like the one I'm about to show you, you'll always know exactly where to start, and the script itself will come much easier when you start programming.

Whenever I design a script, I use a three-step process.

1. Gather facts.

   This step lets me document what I know about my environment that will affect the script. I'm simply writing down the various things that my script will need to know, or that I'll need to consider as I write the script. This may include details about how Windows works, specific business requirements, and so forth.

2. Define tasks.

   This step lets me define the specific tasks my script will accomplish. I get detailed here, focusing on each tiny step I'd have to perform if I were manually performing what I want my script to do.

3. Outline the script.

   This step rolls up what I know and what I want to do into a sort of plain-English version of the script. I list each step I think the script will need to take, along with any related information. This becomes the basis for the script I'll write, and scripting itself becomes a simple matter of translating English into VBScript.

In the next three sections, I'll go through this design process with the IIS log rotation tool that you'll be helping me develop in this chapter. If you'd like to practice, take a few moments and walk through the process yourself before reading my results in the following sections.

### Gathering Facts

What do you know about IIS and log files? You need to capture the information that your script will need to operate, such as log file locations, names, and so forth. After giving it some thought, I come up with the following list.

- Filenames. IIS log files use a file naming format that's based upon the date. Each log filename starts with the letters "ex," followed by a two-digit year, a two-digit month, and a two-digit day. The log file uses the filename extension .log.
- Files are stored in C:\Winnt\System32\LogFiles by default, at least on a Windows 2000 system. Windows Server 2003 uses C:\Windows\System32\LogFiles.
- I can store my archived files anywhere I want, so I'll create a folder named C:\Winnt\LogArchive. I'm assuming a Windows 2000 Server computer; for Windows Server 2003, I'd probably use C:\Windows\LogArchive instead.
- IIS closes each log file at the end of the day and opens a new one. I probably shouldn't try to move the log file that's currently opened by IIS; I should just go for *yesterday's* log file, instead.
- Under the main LogFiles folder, IIS creates a subfolder for each Web site. The first one is named W3Svc, the second is W3Svc2, and so forth. For now, I'll concentrate on the first Web site, which uses W3Svc.

That seems to be all the facts I can think of about log files, so now it's time to figure out exactly what the script needs to do.

## Defining Tasks

Scripts can use a graphical user interface, so when I start defining the tasks I need to complete I try to think about how I'd do the task from the Windows command line, instead of through the user interface. For example, when I think about how to perform the log rotation task myself, I come up with the following steps.

1. Locate the folder that contains the log files.
2. Locate the folder that contains the archived files.
3. Figure out the name of yesterday's log file.
4. Move yesterday's log file into the archive folder.
5. Figure out the name of the log file from 30 days ago.
6. Delete the 30-day-old log file.

It's a simple list of steps, because it's not a complicated task. Note that working from the command line forces me to consider steps like figuring out the filename, which I wouldn't have to do if I was using Explorer. In

Explorer, I could just look at the filenames because they would be listed for me. Because scripts cannot "look" at things, the command line more closely represents the way the script itself will need to function.

With the basic steps out of the way, I can start outlining my script.

## Outlining the Script

The script outline should be a detailed, English explanation of what the script will do, in a systematic fashion. Use your task list as a starting point for the outline. For the log rotation tool, I come up with the following outline. Note that some of these tasks actually get broken down into subtasks.

1. Define the location of the log files.
2. Define the location of the archived files.
3. Figure out yesterday's date.**
4. Figure out the name of yesterday's log file.*
5. Move yesterday's log file into the archive folder.
6. Figure out the date from 30 days ago.**
7. Figure out the name of the log file from 30 days ago.*
8. Delete the 30-day-old log file.

Notice the two steps with an asterisk (*). These are pretty much the same thing: Given a date, give out a matching file log name. This subtask can be broken down as follows.

1. Start with "ex" as the filename.
2. Append the last two digits of the year.
3. Append a two-digit month.
4. Append a two-digit day.
5. Append ".log".

The steps in the main outline with two asterisks also seem to be related, because they're both somehow calculating a date in the past. I don't readily know how to do a few of these steps in VBScript, such as how to figure out the exact date from 30 days ago. But I'm sure there's a way, so I'll worry about that later. If VBScript doesn't provide an easy way to do it, I can always break it down into a subtask.

## Writing Functions and Subroutines

Generally, any kind of subtask you've identified is a great candidate for a function or subroutine, because subtasks get used more than once. You'll need to carefully examine your subtasks and decide which ones should be written as functions or subroutines. I have a general rule that I use: If a subtask involves more than one line of VBScript to accomplish, I write it as a function or subroutine. If I can do it in one line of VBScript code, I don't bother with a separate function or subroutine.

If you need a quick refresher of functions and subroutines, flip back to "What Are Functions?" in Chapter 5.

### Identifying Candidate Modules

In this log rotation tool, I've already identified two potential modules (functions or subroutines): The date calculation and the log filename bit. A quick read through the VBScript documentation leads me to the `DateAdd` function, which can be used to calculate past or future dates. That seems to cover the date calculation subtask, so I don't think I'll need to write a function for that. I do see several `Format` commands that will help format a log filename, but none of them seem to do everything that I need in one line of code (at least, not one reasonably short line of code); I'll write the filename formatter as its own module.

### Writing the Filename Formatting Function

Before writing a function, I need to consider a couple of facts. One fact is that the function is designed to encapsulate some subtask. Therefore, the function is going to need some kind of input to work on, and it's going to give me back some result that my script needs. Defining that input and output is critical. I want the function to be generic enough to be reusable, but specific enough to be useful.

#### *Defining Function Input*

In the case of the filename formatter, I know that the filename is always going to start with "ex," so I don't need that information in the input. The filename will always end in .log, so I don't need that in the input, either. What changes from filename to filename is the date information, so that seems like a logical piece of information for the function's input.

### Defining Function Output

I want this function to take a date—its input—and create a fully formatted log filename. The output is obvious: a fully formatted log filename.

### Writing the Function

Writing the actual function code requires a bit more task definition. You need to really break the task of formatting a filename down into small pieces. This can be a tough process, because the human brain does so many things for you without conscious thought. Think about what a three-year old would have to do to accomplish this task: Remember, all they have to work with at the beginning is a date.

You might come up with a task list like this.

1. Start with a blank piece of paper.
2. Write "ex" on the piece of paper.
3. On a separate piece of paper, write down the date you were given.
4. Erase everything but the year.
5. From the year, erase everything but the last two digits.
6. Write those last two digits after the "ex" on the first piece of paper.
7. On a new piece of paper, write down the date again.
8. Erase everything but the month.
9. If the month is only one digit long, add a zero to the front of it.
10. Copy the two-digit month to the first sheet of paper, after the two-digit year.
11. On a new piece of paper, write down the date one more time.
12. Erase everything but the day.
13. If the day is only one digit long, add a zero to the front of it.
14. Copy the two-digit day to the first sheet of paper, after the two-digit month.
15. On the first sheet of paper, add ".log" to what's already there.
16. Return the contents of the first sheet of paper.

Now, that's a lot of detail! All you need to do is translate that into VBScript. First, figure out which VBScript functions seem to line up with each step in the task, and eliminate any redundant tasks.

1. Declare a variable.
2. Place "ex" into the variable.
3. Declare a new variable to hold the year portion of the date.

4. Use the `DatePart` command to extract the year.
5. Use the `Right` command to take the last two digits of the year.
6. Append the two-digit year to the variable.
7. Declare a new variable to hold the month portion of the date.
8. Use the `DatePart` command to extract the month.
9. Use the `Len` command to figure out if the month is one digit; if it is, add a zero to the front.
10. Append the month to the variable.
11. Declare a new variable to hold the day portion of the date.
12. Use the `DatePart` command to extract the day.
13. Use the `Len` command to figure out if the day is one digit; if it is, add a zero to the front.
14. Append the day to the variable.
15. Append ".log" to the variable.
16. Return the variable.

Now you're ready to put the translated task list into an actual script.

### ➤➤ The FormatLogFileName Function

Listing 13.1 shows the function in VBScript.

**Listing 13.1** *FormatLogFileName Function.* Accepts a date and returns an appropriate log filename.

```
Function FormatLogFileName(dDate)

 Dim sFileName
 sFileName = "ex"

 Dim sYear
 sYear = DatePart("yyyy",dDate)
 sYear = Right(sYear,2)
 sFileName = sFileName & sYear

 Dim sMonth
 sMonth = DatePart("m",dDate)
 If Len(sMonth) = 1 Then
  sMonth = "0" & sMonth
 End If
 sFileName = sFileName & sMonth
```

*continues*

```
 Dim sDay
 sDay = DatePart("d",dDate)
 If Len(sDay) = 1 Then
  sDay = "0" & sDay
 End If
 sFileName = sFileName & sDay

 sFileName = ".log" & sFileName

 FormatLogFileName = sFileName

End Function
```

Now, that's the complete script for the function, and it's ready to be plugged into the main script.

## ➤➤ The FormatLogFileName Function—Explained

This function simply extracts various parts of a specific date, appends them together, and returns the results. I start with a function declaration, which gives the function its name and defines its input. This function will receive a date, which will be stored in a variable named `dDate`.

```
Function FormatLogFileName(dDate)
End Function
```

Next, I declare a variable to store the filename, and put "ex" in that variable.

```
 Dim sFileName
 sFileName = "ex"
```

Then, I declare a new variable for the year. The `DatePart` function extracts the four-digit year from `dDate`, which was passed as input to the function. Then, the `Right` function grabs just the last two digits of that four-digit year. Finally, I tack those two digits onto the filename using the ampersand (`&`) operator.

```
 Dim sYear
 sYear = DatePart("yyyy",dDate)
 sYear = Right(sYear,2)
 sFileName = sFileName & sYear
```

I use a similar set of steps for the month. Obviously, the `DatePart` command gets a slightly different parameter, so that it pulls the month out. This time, I'm not guaranteed of a two-character result.

```
Dim sMonth
sMonth = DatePart("m",dDate)
```

I compensate by using the `Len` function to see if `sMonth` is only one character long. If it is, I use the ampersand operator again to prepend a zero to the month, and then add the result to the filename I'm building.

```
If Len(sMonth) = 1 Then
 sMonth = "0" & sMonth
End If
sFileName = sFileName & sMonth
```

I perform the exact same set of steps again for the day portion of the date. Notice the difference in the `DatePart` command to pull the day, rather than the month or year. You can check out `DatePart`'s other possibilities in the VBScript documentation.

```
Dim sDay
sDay = DatePart("d",dDate)
If Len(sDay) = 1 Then
 sDay = "0" & sDay
End If
sFileName = sFileName & sDay
```

Finally, I add the last part of the filename, ".log", to the variable I'm building. As the last step, I set the name of the function itself equal to the variable that contains the filename. This tells VBScript to pass back the completed filename as the result of the function.

```
sFileName = ".log" & sFileName

FormatLogFileName = sFileName
```

That's all there is to it. Now I have a completed function that rolls up an otherwise reasonably complicated task into a single command. Effectively, I have my own custom `FormatLogFileName` command, which I can use in the main part of my script.

### Variable Names

This isn't the first time you've seen me name variables with a prefix letter like s or d. There's a good reason for this.

First, keep in mind that VBScript doesn't really care what type of data I put into a variable. Data types are all pretty much the same to VBScript. However, VBScript will get upset if I try to perform certain operations with certain data types. For example, if I store "Hello" into variable `Var1`, and store "Mom" in variable `Var2`, and then ask VBScript to calculate Var1 * Var2, I'll get an error because VBScript can't multiply two strings.

One purpose of my variable names, then, is to remind me what I've put into them. I use d when the variable contains data I intend to treat as a date, s for strings, i for integers, and so forth.

Another purpose is to avoid overlapping with VBScript reserved words. VBScript doesn't allow variable names to duplicate any of VBScript's built-in names or functions. For example, the VBScript `Date()` function returns the current system date. Because that's a built-in function, I'm not allowed to name a variable `Date`, because VBScript wouldn't be able to tell the difference between the built-in function and my variable. By using a name prefix like d, however, I can create a meaningful variable name like `dDate` without conflicting with VBScript's reserved words.

## Writing the Main Script

Now you're ready to fire up your script editor and write the main portion of the script. Any functions or subroutines you've written—including the `FormatLogFileName` function—will need to be copied and pasted into the first pat of the script.

**NOTE** You can add the function to the script at the end, if you want. It's strictly a matter of personal preference.

### ➤➤ Log Rotation Script

With the supporting functions out of the way, you can start concentrating on the main script. Refer back to your original task list and translate it to VBScript; you might come up with something like Listing 13.2.

**Listing 13.2** *Log Rotation.vbs.* This is the first-pass script and contains all the important program logic.

```
' Sample log rotation tool
'
' We'll take yesterday's log and move it to
' an archive folder. We'll delete the log file
' that's 30 days old from the archive

' ----------------------------------------------------------
'declare variables
Dim sLogPath, sService, sArchive, sLogFile
Dim oFSO
Dim d30Days, dYesterday


' ----------------------------------------------------------
' set up variables for folder locations
sLogPath = "c:\winnt\system32\logfiles\"
sService = "w3svc2\"
sArchive = "c:\winnt\LogArchive\"


' ----------------------------------------------------------
' get yesterday's date
dYesterday = DateAdd( "d", -1, Date() )


' ----------------------------------------------------------
' create a formatted log filename
' for yesterday's log file
sLogFile = FormatLogFileName(dYesterday)


' ----------------------------------------------------------
' Create a file system object
Set oFSO = WScript.CreateObject("Scripting.FileSystemObject")
```

*continues*

```
' -----------------------------------------------------------
' Move the file to the archive path
oFSO.MoveFile sLogPath & sService & sLogFile, _
  sArchive & sLogFile


' -----------------------------------------------------------
' get date for 30 days ago
d30Days = DateAdd( "d", -30, Date() )


' -----------------------------------------------------------
' create a formatted log filename
' for 30-day-ago log file
sLogFile = FormatLogFileName(d30Days)


' -----------------------------------------------------------
' Delete the file from the archive path
oFSO.DeleteFile sArchive & sLogFile
```

Obviously, this didn't include the `FormatLogFileName` function. Be sure to copy that into the first part of the file before you try to do anything with it. Before you can use this script, you'll need to check a few things.

- Make sure the folders specified all exist. For example, if you're on Windows Server 2003, you'll need to change "Winnt" to "Windows" in many cases.
- Make sure you add the `FormatLogFileName` function to the beginning of the script, or you'll get an error message.

## ➤➤ Log Rotation Script—Explained

One thing you'll notice about my scripts is that I like to use lots of comment lines. These allow me to document what the script is doing; if I have to make changes or figure out what the script is up to a year later, the comment lines help me remember what I was thinking when I originally wrote the script. I even use comment lines with lots of hyphens to create little separators, breaking the script into logical sections.

The first few lines in any script should explain what it does.

```
' Sample log rotation tool
'
' We'll take yesterday's log and move it to
' an archive folder. We'll delete the log file
' that's 30 days old from the archive
```

Next, I usually declare the variables I intend to use in the script.

```
' ----------------------------------------------------------
'declare variables
Dim sLogPath, sService, sArchive, sLogFile
Dim oFSO
Dim d30Days, dYesterday
```

The first thing in my task list is to define folder locations, and so that's what I do next. Notice that I've actually defined the log file folder path in two parts: the main path and the service. This will make it easier to modify the script to accommodate other Web sites later, if I want.

```
' ----------------------------------------------------------
' set up variables for folder locations
sLogPath = "c:\winnt\system32\logfiles\"
sService = "w3svc\"
sArchive = "c:\winnt\LogArchive\"
```

Now, I use VBScript's `Date()` and `DateAdd()` functions to figure out yesterday's date. VBScript doesn't have a "DateSubtract" function; instead, just add a negative number. Adding a negative is the same as subtracting.

```
' ----------------------------------------------------------
' get yesterday's date
dYesterday = DateAdd( "d", -1, Date() )
```

Now, I'll use that handy `FormatLogFileName` function to figure out the filename of yesterday's log file.

```
' ----------------------------------------------------------
' create a formatted log filename
' for yesterday's log file
sLogFile = FormatLogFileName(dYesterday)
```

Next, I create a reference to the FileSystemObject, which will let me manipulate the log files. I'm storing the reference in a variable named `oFSO`;

the "o" prefix tells me that this variable contains an object reference, and not some kind of data. I also have to remember to use the `Set` command, because I'm assigning an object reference to the variable, and not just data.

```
' ------------------------------------------------------------
' Create a file system object
Set oFSO = WScript.CreateObject("Scripting.FileSystemObject")
```

One of the FileSystemObject's handy methods is `MoveFile`. It accepts two parameters: the file to move and where to move it. This accomplishes the task of moving the log file into the archive folder.

```
' ------------------------------------------------------------
' Move the file to the archive path
oFSO.MoveFile sLogPath & sService & sLogFile, _
  sArchive & sLogFile
```

Having accomplished the first major task, I'm ready to delete the oldest log file. I'll need to figure out what date it was 30 days ago, which means using `DateAdd()` to add a negative 30 days to today's date.

```
' ------------------------------------------------------------
' get date for 30 days ago
d30Days = DateAdd( "d", -30, Date() )
```

Now I can use `FormatLogFileName` again to get the filename from 30 days ago.

```
' ------------------------------------------------------------
' create a formatted log filename
' for 30-day-ago log file
sLogFile = FormatLogFileName(d30Days)
```

Finally, use the FileSystemObject's `DeleteFile` command to delete the old log file.

```
' ------------------------------------------------------------
' Delete the file from the archive path
oFSO.DeleteFile sArchive & sLogFile
```

If everything's working well, this script should be ready to run.

### Identifying Potential Errors

Re-reading the script, I can think of a few things that might go wrong. For starters, the archive folder might not exist. Also, the log file I'm trying to move might not exist if something was wrong with IIS. In addition, it's possible that someone already deleted the old log file, meaning it won't exist when I try to delete it in the script. Any of these obvious conditions could cause an error that would make my script quit running.

How can I avoid these errors?

- Make sure the archive folder exists and, if it doesn't, create it.
- Make sure files exist before moving or deleting them.

Anticipating what can go wrong allows you to add code to your script to handle potential errors gracefully.

### ➤➤ Modified Log Rotation Script

Listing 13.3 presents a modified log rotation script with some error-handling built in.

**Listing 13.3** *LogRotation2.vbs.* This version of the script checks for files and folders rather than assuming they exist.

```
' Sample log rotation tool
'
' We'll take yesterday's log and move it to
' an archive folder. We'll delete the log file
' that's 30 days old from the archive

' ------------------------------------------------------------
'declare variables
Dim sLogPath, sService, sArchive, sLogFile
Dim oFSO
Dim d30Days, dYesterday


' ------------------------------------------------------------
' set up variables for folder locations
sLogPath = "c:\winnt\system32\logfiles\"
sService = "w3svc2\"
sArchive = "c:\winnt\LogArchive\"
```

*continues*

```
' -------------------------------------------------------------
' get yesterday's date
dYesterday = DateAdd( "d", -1, Date() )


' -------------------------------------------------------------
' create a formatted log filename
' for yesterday's log file
sLogFile = FormatLogFileName(dYesterday)


' -------------------------------------------------------------
' Create a file system object
Set oFSO = WScript.CreateObject("Scripting.FileSystemObject")


' -------------------------------------------------------------
' make sure files and folders exist
' first the archive folder
If Not oFSO.FolderExists(sArchive) Then
 oFSO.CreateFolder(sArchvie)
End If


' -------------------------------------------------------------
' Move the file to the archive path
If oFSO.FileExists(sLogPath & sService & sLogFile) Then
 oFSO.MoveFile sLogPath & sService & sLogFile, _
   sArchive & sLogFile
End If


' -------------------------------------------------------------
' get date for 30 days ago
d30Days = DateAdd( "d", -30, Date() )


' -------------------------------------------------------------
' create a formatted log filename
' for 30-day-ago log file
sLogFile = FormatLogFileName(d30Days)


' -------------------------------------------------------------
```

```
' Delete the file from the archive path
If oFSO.FileExists(sArchive & sLogFile) Then
     oFSO.DeleteFile sArchive & sLogFile
End If
```

Can you spot what's changed in the script?

### ➤➤ Modified Log Rotation Script—Explained

There are just three major changes to the script. First, I'm using the FileSystemObject's `FolderExists()` method to ensure that the archive folder exists. If it doesn't, I use the `CreateFolder()` method to create the folder, automatically handling the problem before it becomes a problem.

```
' ----------------------------------------------------------
' make sure files and folders exist
' first the archive folder
If Not oFSO.FolderExists(sArchive) Then
 oFSO.CreateFolder(sArchvie)
End If
```

I also modified the code that moves the log file. Now, it's in an `If…Then` construct that uses the FileSystemObject's `FileExists()` method to only perform the move if the file exists to begin with.

```
' ----------------------------------------------------------
' Move the file to the archive path
If oFSO.FileExists(sLogPath & sService & sLogFile) Then
 oFSO.MoveFile sLogPath & sService & sLogFile, _
   sArchive & sLogFile
End If
```

Similarly, I modified the line of code that deletes the old log file to only do so if that file already exists.

```
' ----------------------------------------------------------
' Delete the file from the archive path
If oFSO.FileExists(sArchive & sLogFile) Then
     oFSO.DeleteFile sArchive & sLogFile
End If
```

Now, the script is prepared to handle these anticipated potential problems. Again, be sure to paste in the `FormatLogFileName` function before attempting to execute this script!

## Testing the Script

You're ready to test your script. Just to make sure you're on the same page, Listing 13.4 lists the entire log rotation script, including the `FormatLogFileName` function.

**Listing 13.4** *LogRotation3.vbs.* Here's the entire script, ready to run.

```
' Sample log rotation tool
'
' We'll take yesterday's log and move it to
' an archive folder. We'll delete the log file
' that's 30 days old from the archive

Function FormatLogFileName(dDate)

 Dim sFileName
 sFileName = "ex"

 Dim sYear
 sYear = DatePart("yyyy",dDate)
 sYear = Right(sYear,2)
 sFileName = sFileName & sYear

 Dim sMonth
 sMonth = DatePart("m",dDate)
 If Len(sMonth) = 1 Then
  sMonth = "0" & sMonth
 End If
 sFileName = sFileName & sMonth

 Dim sDay
 sDay = DatePart("d",dDate)
 If Len(sDay) = 1 Then
  sDay = "0" & sDay
 End If
 sFileName = sFileName & sDay
```

```
 sFileName = ".log" & sFileName

 FormatLogFileName = sFileName

End Function

' ------------------------------------------------------------
'declare variables
Dim sLogPath, sService, sArchive, sLogFile
Dim oFSO
Dim d30Days, dYesterday


' ------------------------------------------------------------
' set up variables for folder locations
sLogPath = "c:\winnt\system32\logfiles\"
sService = "w3svc2\"
sArchive = "c:\winnt\LogArchive\"

' ------------------------------------------------------------
' get yesterday's date
dYesterday = DateAdd( "d", -1, Date() )


' ------------------------------------------------------------
' create a formatted log filename
' for yesterday's log file
sLogFile = FormatLogFileName(dYesterday)


' ------------------------------------------------------------
' Create a file system object
Set oFSO = WScript.CreateObject("Scripting.FileSystemObject")


' ------------------------------------------------------------
' make sure files and folders exist
' first the archive folder
If Not oFSO.FolderExists(sArchive) Then
 oFSO.CreateFolder(sArchvie)
End If


' ------------------------------------------------------------
```

continues

```
' Move the file to the archive path
If oFSO.FileExists(sLogPath & sService & sLogFile) Then
 oFSO.MoveFile sLogPath & sService & sLogFile, _
   sArchive & sLogFile
End If


' ------------------------------------------------------------
' get date for 30 days ago
d30Days = DateAdd( "d", -30, Date() )


' ------------------------------------------------------------
' create a formatted log filename
' for 30-day-ago log file
sLogFile = FormatLogFileName(d30Days)


' ------------------------------------------------------------
' Delete the file from the archive path
If oFSO.FileExists(sArchive & sLogFile) Then
     oFSO.DeleteFile sArchive & sLogFile
End If
```

Save the script to a .VBS file and double-click to execute it. To make sure it has something to do, make sure you have a log file in the appropriate folder with yesterday's date.

## Analyzing the Results

What happens when you run the script? If you type it carefully, or copy it from this book's accompanying CD-ROM, either it doesn't do anything or it gives you an error. That's because the code contains two logic errors.

Logic errors are especially difficult to track down, because VBScript doesn't usually complain about them. As far as VBScript is concerned, everything is just fine. You're the one with the problem, because your script runs, but doesn't do what you want it to do.

There are a couple of ways to catch these errors. Because the errors aren't ones that VBScript cares about, you can't rely on the Script Debugger or other fancy tools. The easiest way to track down the problem is to add debug code.

### Adding Debug Code

Debug code is usually as straightforward as a bunch of `MsgBox` statements that tell you what your script is doing. For example:

```
sLogFile = FormatLogFileName(d30Days)
MsgBox sLogFile
```

The boldfaced line of code tells you what the `FormatLogFileName` function did, by displaying its results. You can use that to double-check what's going on in your code, and find out where things are going wrong.

#### ➤➤ Log Rotation Script with Debug Code

Listing 13.5 shows the complete log rotation script with debug code added. I've highlighted the debug code in bold so that you can spot it more easily.

**Listing 13.5** *LogRotation4.vbs.* I've added MsgBox statements as a debugging aid.

```
' Sample log rotation tool
'
' We'll take yesterday's log and move it to
' an archive folder. We'll delete the log file
' that's 30 days old from the archive

Function FormatLogFileName(dDate)

 Dim sFileName
 sFileName = "ex"

 Dim sYear
 sYear = DatePart("yyyy",dDate)
 sYear = Right(sYear,2)
 sFileName = sFileName & sYear

 Dim sMonth
 sMonth = DatePart("m",dDate)
 If Len(sMonth) = 1 Then
  sMonth = "0" & sMonth
 End If
 sFileName = sFileName & sMonth
```

*continues*

```
 Dim sDay
 sDay = DatePart("d",dDate)
 If Len(sDay) = 1 Then
  sDay = "0" & sDay
 End If
 sFileName = sFileName & sDay

 sFileName = ".log" & sFileName

 FormatLogFileName = sFileName

End Function

' ------------------------------------------------------------
'declare variables
Dim sLogPath, sService, sArchive, sLogFile
Dim oFSO
Dim d30Days, dYesterday


' ------------------------------------------------------------
' set up variables for folder locations
sLogPath = "c:\winnt\system32\logfiles\"
sService = "w3svc2\"
sArchive = "c:\winnt\LogArchive\"

' ------------------------------------------------------------
' get yesterday's date
dYesterday = DateAdd( "d", -1, Date() )
MsgBox "Yesterday was " & dYesterday


' ------------------------------------------------------------
' create a formatted log filename
' for yesterday's log file
sLogFile = FormatLogFileName(dYesterday)
MsgBox "Yesterday's log filename is " & sLogFile


' ------------------------------------------------------------
' Create a file system object
Set oFSO = WScript.CreateObject("Scripting.FileSystemObject")
```

```
' ----------------------------------------------------------
' make sure files and folders exist
' first the archive folder
If Not oFSO.FolderExists(sArchive) Then
 oFSO.CreateFolder(sArchvie)
 MsgBox "Created Folder"
Else
 MsgBox "Didn't Create Folder"
End If


' ----------------------------------------------------------
' Move the file to the archive path
If oFSO.FileExists(sLogPath & sService & sLogFile) Then
 oFSO.MoveFile sLogPath & sService & sLogFile, _
   sArchive & sLogFile
 MsgBox "Moved File"
Else
 MsgBox "Didn't Move File"
End If


' ----------------------------------------------------------
' get date for 30 days ago
d30Days = DateAdd( "d", -30, Date() )
MsgBox "30 days ago was " & d30Days


' ----------------------------------------------------------
' create a formatted log filename
' for 30-day-ago log file
sLogFile = FormatLogFileName(d30Days)
MsgBox "Log file from 30 days ago was " & sLogFile


' ----------------------------------------------------------
' Delete the file from the archive path
If oFSO.FileExists(sArchive & sLogFile) Then
     oFSO.DeleteFile sArchive & sLogFile
 MsgBox "Deleted file."
Else
 MsgBox "Didn't delete file."
End If
```

Run the script again and see what happens. Are you surprised by the results?

### ➤➤ Log Rotation Script with Debug Code—Explained

Some of the code I added displays the results of operations by tacking a variable onto the `MsgBox` statement, like this one.

```
' ------------------------------------------------------------
' create a formatted log filename
' for 30-day-ago log file
sLogFile = FormatLogFileName(d30Days)
MsgBox "Log file from 30 days ago was " & sLogFile
```

Other sections of code added an `If…Then` construct. This ensures some kind of feedback on the script's progress, no matter how the `If…Then` condition turned out.

```
' ------------------------------------------------------------
' Delete the file from the archive path
If oFSO.FileExists(sArchive & sLogFile) Then
     oFSO.DeleteFile sArchive & sLogFile
 MsgBox "Deleted file."
Else
 MsgBox "Didn't delete file."
End If
```

## Modifying the Script

If you're getting the same results I am, you've probably spotted the logic errors. Here's the first one, in the `FormatLogFileName` function.

```
Dim sDay
 sDay = DatePart("d",dDate)
 If Len(sDay) = 1 Then
  sDay = "0" & sDay
 End If
 sFileName = sFileName & sDay

 sFileName = ".log" & sFileName

 FormatLogFileName = sFileName

End Function
```

The problem is in boldface, and the code is actually backward. It's prepending ".log" to the filename that's been built, rather than appending it. The result is that every filename coming out of the function is wrong. You would have noticed this with the debug version of the script because the messages, "Didn't move file" and "Didn't delete file" were displayed. You saw those messages because no file with the incorrect filename existed. Correct this line of code to read

```
sFileName = sFileName & sDay

 sFileName = sFileName & ".log"

 FormatLogFileName = sFileName
```

The next error is a simple typo.

```
' ----------------------------------------------------------
' make sure files and folders exist
' first the archive folder
If Not oFSO.FolderExists(sArchive) Then
 oFSO.CreateFolder(sArchvie)
 MsgBox "Created Folder"
Else
 MsgBox "Didn't Create Folder"
End If
```

The result of this code is to see if the archive folder exists, If it doesn't, VBScript attempts to create the folder…except that the wrong variable name is listed. The variable given, `sArchive`, is empty, and so VBScript tries to create an empty folder. Depending upon how your system is configured, you might have received an error message on this line of code. Correct it to read

```
' ----------------------------------------------------------
' make sure files and folders exist
' first the archive folder
If Not oFSO.FolderExists(sArchive) Then
 oFSO.CreateFolder(sArchive)
 MsgBox "Created Folder"
Else
 MsgBox "Didn't Create Folder"
End If
```

By the way, this problem could have been caught earlier if you'd included `Option Explicit` as the first line of your script. With that option, VBScript requires you to declare all variables; when it spotted the undeclared `sArchvie` variable, it would have given an immediate error.

You can refresh your memory on Option Explicit by referring to "Declaring Variables" in Chapter 5.

## Completing the Script

Listing 13.6 shows the completed, corrected script, with debug code removed. It's ready to use! Note that I've added the `Option Explicit` statement to help catch any other variable name typos.

**Listing 13.6** *LogRotation5.vbs.* Here's the entire script, ready to run.

```
Option Explicit
' Sample log rotation tool
'
' We'll take yesterday's log and move it to
' an archive folder. We'll delete the log file
' that's 30 days old from the archive

Function FormatLogFileName(dDate)

 Dim sFileName
 sFileName = "ex"

 Dim sYear
 sYear = DatePart("yyyy",dDate)
 sYear = Right(sYear,2)
 sFileName = sFileName & sYear

 Dim sMonth
 sMonth = DatePart("m",dDate)
 If Len(sMonth) = 1 Then
  sMonth = "0" & sMonth
 End If
 sFileName = sFileName & sMonth

 Dim sDay
 sDay = DatePart("d",dDate)
 If Len(sDay) = 1 Then
  sDay = "0" & sDay
 End If
```

```
 sFileName = sFileName & sDay

 sFileName = sFileName & ".log"

 FormatLogFileName = sFileName

End Function

' -----------------------------------------------------------
'declare variables
Dim sLogPath, sService, sArchive, sLogFile
Dim oFSO
Dim d30Days, dYesterday


' -----------------------------------------------------------
' set up variables for folder locations
sLogPath = "c:\winnt\system32\logfiles\"
sService = "w3svc2\"
sArchive = "c:\winnt\LogArchive\"

' -----------------------------------------------------------
' get yesterday's date
dYesterday = DateAdd( "d", -1, Date() )


' -----------------------------------------------------------
' create a formatted log filename
' for yesterday's log file
sLogFile = FormatLogFileName(dYesterday)


' -----------------------------------------------------------
' Create a file system object
Set oFSO = WScript.CreateObject("Scripting.FileSystemObject")


' -----------------------------------------------------------
' make sure files and folders exist
' first the archive folder
If Not oFSO.FolderExists(sArchive) Then
 oFSO.CreateFolder(sArchive)
End If
```

*continues*

```
' ----------------------------------------------------------
' Move the file to the archive path
If oFSO.FileExists(sLogPath & sService & sLogFile) Then
 oFSO.MoveFile sLogPath & sService & sLogFile, _
   sArchive & sLogFile
End If


' ----------------------------------------------------------
' get date for 30 days ago
d30Days = DateAdd( "d", -30, Date() )


' ----------------------------------------------------------
' create a formatted log filename
' for 30-day-ago log file
sLogFile = FormatLogFileName(d30Days)


' ----------------------------------------------------------
' Delete the file from the archive path
If oFSO.FileExists(sArchive & sLogFile) Then
     oFSO.DeleteFile sArchive & sLogFile
End If
```

### Polishing Your Script

You can make this script more effective with a little work. For example, as written, the script only works with the first Web site on the server, which uses the W3CSvc folder. You could modify the script to work with multiple folders by including a `For…Next` construct or some other kind of loop.

Also, the script requires that you remember to run it each day for the best effect. However, you could use the Windows Task Scheduler to automatically run the script each morning at 1 A.M. or some other convenient time. You simply tell Task Scheduler to run `Wscript.exe` *`scriptname`*, where *`scriptname`* is the complete path and filename to your log rotation script.

You could even write the script to run against multiple Web servers. That way, it could execute from a single central server and rotate the log files for an entire Web farm. The beauty of scripting is that you're in complete control, so you can have the script do anything you like to suit your environment and meet your particular administrative needs.

## Review

In this chapter, you combined what you've learned about script design, VBScript basics, and the Windows FileSystemObject to create a completely functional tool for rotating IIS log files. I deliberately designed some errors into the first revision of the script to walk you through the debugging process, and I showed you some great tips for easily debugging scripts even without the Microsoft Script Debugger or other fancy tools.

You practiced a couple of key tasks in this chapter. The design process is very important, as it helps you gather facts about what your script needs to accomplish and figure out how to break those tasks down into scriptable steps. The debugging process is also very important, and you'll find that the techniques you practiced in this chapter will come in handy as you start developing your own administrative scripts.

**COMING UP**

You've finished with your VBScript crash course. If you'd like to start using advanced administration technologies like Active Directory Services Interface and Windows Management Instrumentation, head on to Chapter 14. If you want to start working on a Web-based administrative script, turn to Chapter 21. Finally, if you'd like to move on to advanced scripting concepts like security, start with Chapter 25.

PART III

# Windows Management Instrumentation and Active Directory Services Interface

CHAPTER 14

# Working with ADSI Providers

**IN THIS CHAPTER**

ADSI is *the* way to manipulate domain and local users, groups, and other domain objects. I'll show you how ADSI's collection of providers make a number of different directories—including NT and AD—easily accessible from within your scripts.

## Using ADSI Objects

ADSI, the Active Directory Services Interface, is an object library very similar in nature to the FileSystemObject and WScript objects I covered in Chapters 11 and 12. ADSI is a bit more complicated than the objects you've worked with so far, mainly because the information ADSI deals with is inherently more complicated.

For example, with the FileSystemObject, you learned to use `CreateObject` to have VBScript load the object's DLL into memory and provide a reference to your script. For example:

```
Dim oFSO
Set oFSO = CreateObject("Scripting.FileSystemObject")
```

That's not quite how you'll use ADSI, though. For example, to have ADSI change password policy in a domain named BRAINCORE, you'd use the following code.

```
Set objDomain = GetObject("WinNT://BRAINCORE")

objDomain.Put "MinPasswordLength", 8
objDomain.Put "MinPasswordAge", 10
objDomain.Put "MaxPasswordAge", 45
objDomain.Put "MaxBadPasswordsAllowed", 3
objDomain.Put "PasswordHistoryLength", 8
objDomain.Put "AutoUnlockInterval", 30000
objDomain.Put "LockoutObservationInterval", 30000
objDomain.SetInfo
```

Notice that the `GetObject` statement is used, rather than `CreateObject`. I like to remember the difference by telling myself that I'm not trying to *create* a domain, just *get* to an existing one. Another important part of that statement is `WinNT://`, which tells ADSI which *provider* to use. The two main providers you'll work with are WinNT: and LDAP.

---

**NOTE** ADSI provider names are case-sensitive, so be sure you're using WinNT and not winnt or some other derivation.

---

The WinNT provider can connect to any NT-compatible domain, including AD. Obviously, the provider cannot work with advanced AD functionality like organizational units (OUs), which don't exist in NT domains. The WinNT provider can also connect to the local SAM and other services on member and standalone computers. The LDAP provider can connect to any LDAP-compatible directory, such as the Exchange 5.5 directory or Active Directory. Both providers can be used to obtain a reference to an entire domain, an OU (in AD), users, groups, and much, much more. You'll even find areas of functionality that overlap with Windows Management Instrumentation (WMI); that's because ADSI is a bit older, and when WMI came on the scene, it started taking over. In fact, it's possible that someday ADSI will fade away entirely and that WMI will become the single means of accessing management information. For now, though, there's plenty that ADSI can do that WMI cannot.

Another important part of the `GetObject` statement is the `ADsPath`, which tells the provider what to connect to. In this example, the path was a simple domain name; it could also be a path like "//BRAINCORE/Donj,user", which would connect to a user object named DonJ in the domain named BRAINCORE.

The object reference created by `GetObject`—in this case, the variable `objDomain`—has several basic methods:

- `Create`. Creates a new object, provided the reference object is a container of some kind, like a domain or OU.
- `Get`. Retrieves a specified attribute.
- `Put`. Writes a specified attribute.
- `SetInfo`. Saves changes made by `Put`.
- `Delete`. Deletes an object, provided the reference object is a container of some kind.

These methods usually accept one or more parameters. In the example, the `Put` method requires the name of an attribute to change, along with a new value for the attribute. Obviously, the available attribute names depend on what type of directory you're working with; ADSI itself doesn't care, because it's designed to access *any* directory service. In the remainder of this chapter, I'll introduce you to what each of the two main providers can help you accomplish.

## Using the WinNT Provider

With Active Directory several years old, and now available in its second version (Wind2003), why would you bother using the WinNT provider? *Ease of use.* Although the WinNT provider is definitely less functional than the LDAP provider is, it's easier to use, and there are certain functions that you cannot easily do with the LDAP provider, such as connecting to a file server service. You can do some of those things with WMI, but again…ease of use. There are just some things, as you'll see, that the WinNT provider makes easy. For example, in Chapter 10, I showed you how the WinNT provider can be used to connect to a file server and find out which users have a particular file open.

Here's an example of how the WinNT provider can be used to connect to a file server and list its available shares.

```
ServerName = InputBox("Enter name of server " & _
 "to list shares for.")

set fs = GetObject("WinNT://" & ServerName & _
 "/LanmanServer,FileService")
For Each sh In fs
     'do something with the share
Next
```

You can do the same thing in WMI.

```
'get server name
strComputer = InputBox("Server name?")

'connect to WMI
Set objWMIService = GetObject("winmgmts:" & _
 "\\" & strComputer & "\root\cimv2")

'retrieve the list of shares
Set colShares = objWMIService.ExecQuery _
 ("SELECT * FROM Win32_Share WHERE " & _
 "Type = 0")

'for each share returned...
For Each objShare In colShares
 'do something with the share
Next
```

The ADSI method is obviously easier. Notice something about how the ADSI call is written.

```
set fs = GetObject("WinNT://" & ServerName & _
 "/LanmanServer,FileService")
```

The first part, as I noted earlier, is the provider: `WinNT`. Next is the server name, which in this case is provided in a string variable. Next is the name of the object you want to connect to, a comma, and the type of object that is. The comma and type are optional. For example, the following would usually work fine.

```
set fs = GetObject("WinNT://" & ServerName & _
 "/LanmanServer")
```

This method lets ADSI pick the object based solely on its name. If you have a user or group named LanmanServer, ADSI might pick one of those, which is why I usually specify the object type. Doing so restricts ADSI's options to the type of object I'm expecting. Connecting to a user object would be similar.

```
set fs = GetObject("WinNT://" & ServerName & _
 "/DonJ,user")
```

Or a group:

```
set fs = GetObject("WinNT://" & ServerName & _
 "/Guests,group")
```

What do you specify for the server name? If you want a domain user or group, specify either the domain name or the name of a domain controller. If you want a local user or group, or a service, specify a server name. Keep in mind that all of these techniques will work perfectly with NT, 2000, XP, and 2003 computers in either an NT domain or an AD domain.

## Examples

Here's an example of how to start a service by using the WinNT provider.

```
Set objService = GetObject("WinNT://Server1/browser")
objService.Start
Set objService = Nothing
```

Obviously, you can change the service name to anything valid on the computer. You can stop the service by using the `Stop` method instead of `Start`.

Here's an example of how to output all members of a group to a text file. This example uses the FileSystemObject to create the text file and the WinNT provider to access the group membership list.

```
Dim oGroup
  Dim sGroupName
  Dim sGroupDomain
  Dim oMember
  Dim oTS
  Dim oFSO

  const ForReading = 1
  const ForWriting = 2
  const ForAppending = 8
  Const TristateFalse = 0

  sGroupDomain = "DomainName"
  sGroupName = InputBox ("Group name?")
```

*continues*

```
 Set oFSO = CreateObject ("Scripting.FileSystemObject")
 Set oTS = oFSO.OpenTextFile ("C:\Scripts\" & _
GroupName & " members.txt")

Set oGroup = GetObject("WinNT://" & GroupDomain & "/" & _
 GroupName & ",group")

 For Each oMember in oGroup.Members
  oTS.WriteLine oMember.Name
 Next

WScript.Echo "Complete"
```

The following script connects to a domain, iterates through each object, and for the user objects it finds, outputs the total size of the user's home directory.

```
Dim oDomain, oFolder
Dim oFSO, oTS, oUser

Set oFSO = CreateObject("Scripting.FileSystemObject")
Set oTS = oFSO.CreateTextFile("c:\homedirs.txt")
Set oDomain = GetObject("WinNT://DOMAIN")

For Each oUser in oDomain
 If oUser.Class = "User" Then
  Set oFolder = oFSO.GetFolder(oUser.HomeDirectory)
  oTS.WriteLine( _
   oFolder.Name & "," & oUser.HomeDirectory & "," & _
    oFolder.Size)
 End IF
 Set oFolder = Nothing
Next
```

You can see in each of these examples how the WinNT provider makes the task a bit easier by providing ready access to the necessary information.

## Using the LDAP Provider

The ADSI LDAP provider looks superficially similar to the WinNT provider, but uses LDAP-style naming conventions to name specific objects. A typical LDAP connection might look like this:

```
Dim objDomain
Set objDomain = GetObject("LDAP://dc=braincore,dc-net")
```

Notice that the `LDAP` provider is specified, and then an LDAP naming path is listed. In this case, `objDomain` will become a reference to the `braincore.net` domain. Perhaps the most confusing part of these LDAP paths is figuring out which components to use.

- Use `DC` when specifying any portion of a domain name. Always list the domain name components in their regular order. For example, a domain named east.braincore.net would have an LDAP path of "dc=east,dc=braincore,dc=net". DC stands for *domain component*, not domain controller; this type of LDAP path will force ADSI to find a domain controller following Windows' normal rules for doing so.
- Use `OU` when specifying an organizational unit. For example, to connect to the Sales OU in the braincore.net domain, specify "ou=sales,dc=braincore,dc=net". Notice that the domain name components are still required, so that ADSI can locate the domain that contains the OU.
- Use `CN` when specifying a *common name,* such as a user, group, or *any of the built-in AD containers.* Remember that the Users, Computers, and Built-in containers aren't technically OUs, and so they can't be accessed with the `OU` component. To connect to the Users container, use "cn=Users,dc=braincore,dc=net". To connect to a specific user, you can just specify the user and domain name: "cn=Donj,dc=braincore,dc=net". You don't need to specify the OU, because AD won't normally allow two users in the same domain to have the same name.

---

**NOTE** It doesn't hurt to specify the OU containing a user or group; in fact, with some LDAP directories, it's required. Even though you don't have to, try to get into the habit of using *fully qualified domain names,* such as "cn=DonJ,ou=Sales,dc=braincore,dc=net".

---

After you've bound to an object, you can work with its properties. For example, suppose I want to modify the description of a particular user group. The following code will do it.

```
Dim objGroup
Set objGroup = GetObject( _
 "cn=Sales,ou=EastSales,dc=domain,dc=com")
objGroup.Put "description", "Eastern Sales representatives"
objGroup.SetInfo
```

The `Put` method allows me to specify a property to modify (in this case, the description of the group), and a new value. I have to call `SetInfo` to actually save the change. This is a straightforward technique with single-value properties like `description`; many AD properties, however, are *multi-valued.* For example, the `otherTelephone` property can contain multiple telephone numbers. Here's how you might modify them.

```
Dim objUser
Set objUser = GetObject("cn=DonJ,ou=Sales,dc=braincore,dc=net")
objUser.PutEx 3, "otherTelephone", Array("555-1212")
objUser.SetInfo
```

The `PutEx` method accepts three parameters. The last two should look familiar: They're the property name and the value you're adding. The first parameter tells `PutEx` what you're doing.

- 1: Clear all values
- 2: Update all entries
- 3: Append an entry
- 4: Delete an entry

You can make these a bit easier to work with by specifying constants. For example:

```
Const MVP_CLEAR = 1
Const MVP_UPDATE = 2
Const MVP_APPEND = 3
Const MVP_DELETE = 4

Dim objUser
Set objUser = GetObject("cn=DonJ,ou=Sales,dc=braincore,dc=net")
objUser.PutEx MVP_APPEND, "otherTelephone", Array("555-1212")
objUser.SetInfo
```

Whenever you're modifying a multivalued property more than once in a script, be sure to call `SetInfo` after each modification. Otherwise, ADSI will lose track of what you're doing, and only the last change will be saved back to the directory.

---

**NOTE** Most of the examples in Chapters 15 and 16 will use ADSI's LDAP provider.

---

## Other Providers

ADSI doesn't stop with LDAP and WinNT. Here are some of the other providers that you can work with.

- GC. This provider allows you to work with the Global Catalog on AD domain controllers that host a replica of the Global Catalog. It works similarly to the LDAP provider, but uses the TCP ports assigned to access the Global Catalog.
- OLE DB. This provider allows you to perform search operations on AD by using Microsoft's OLE DB database interface.
- IIS. Provides access to the IIS metabase, which contains all of IIS' configuration information.
- NDS. This provides connects to Novell NetWare Directory Services. Note that later versions of NDS also support LDAP queries, meaning you can use the more generic LDAP provider for some operations.
- NWCOMPAT. Connects to Novell NetWare Bindery directories, found in NetWare 3.x and later.

Because most of your administrative tasks will involve the LDAP and WinNT providers, I'm not going to provide coverage or examples of how to use these other ADSI providers. However, you can access the ADSI documentation online at msdn.microsoft.com/library to learn more about them, if necessary.

## Review

With this brief introduction to ADSI out of the way, you're ready to start managing domains, users, and groups by writing scripts that incorporate ADSI. You've learned how to write ADSI scripts that utilize both the

WinNT and LDAP ADSI providers, and you've learned a bit about how the two providers function. Remember that the WinNT provider is *not* limited just to NT domains; it works fine in AD domains, and also provides a way to work with the local SAM and services on standalone and member computers, including NT-based client computers.

**COMING UP**

Ready to start ADSI scripting? In the next chapter, you'll learn how to work with domains, including creating OUs and other objects at the domain level. In Chapter 16, you'll learn how to manipulate users and groups in a domain, using both the LDAP and WinNT providers.

CHAPTER 15

# Manipulating Domains

**IN THIS CHAPTER**

You'll learn to work with OUs, domain settings, domain information, and other domain-related items. These items are the basis for ADSI domain management, and I'll provide plenty of examples to help get you started.

Working with domains via ADSI is often easier if you start at the top level. In the last chapter, you learned how to use both the WinNT and LDAP ADSI providers to get an object reference to the domain.

```
Dim objNTDomain, objADDomain
objNTDomain = GetObject("WinNT://DOMAIN")
objADDomain = GetObject("LDAP://dc=domain,dc=com")
```

After you have a reference to the domain, you can start working with its properties. That'll be the focus of the first part of this chapter; toward the end of this chapter, I'll show you how to work with the main domain-level objects, organizational units (OUs), by using the LDAP provider.

Obviously, you need to make sure you have ADSI running on your computer in order to use it. ADSI comes with Windows 2000 and Windows XP, as well as Windows Server 2003. It's available for, but not included with, Windows NT, Windows 95, Windows 98, and Windows Me. To install ADSI, simply install the Microsoft Directory Services client on these older operating systems. You can also visit the ADSI link located at www.microsoft.com/windows/reskits/webresources.

## Querying Domain Information

Querying domain information by using the LDAP provider is easy. Connect to the domain and simply use the `Get` method, along with the desired attribute name.

```
Dim objDomain
objDomain = GetObject("LDAP://dc=domain,dc=com")
WScript.Echo objDomain.Get("minPwdAge")
```

Of course, you need to know the attribute names that you want to query. Some of the interesting domain LDAP attributes include

- `pwdHistoryLength`. The number of old passwords the domain remembers for each user.
- `minPwdLength`. The minimum number of characters per user password.
- `minPwdAge`. The minimum number of days a user must keep his password.
- `maxPwdAge`. Maximum number of days a user may keep his password.
- `lockoutThreshold`. The number of tries you have to guess a password before the account is locked out.
- `lockoutDuration`. How long a password is left locked out.
- `lockOutObservationWindow`. The time window during which the `lockoutThreshold` number of wrong password attempts will cause an account lockout.
- `forceLogoff`. Forces account logoff when account restriction time expires.

You can explore more of the domain's attributes by examining the `domain` and `domainPolicy` classes in the AD schema; I'll describe how to view the attributes associated with a class later in this chapter.

Querying this information by using the WinNT provider is remarkably similar, although the attributes' names do change somewhat. Here's an example.

```
Dim objDomain
objDomain = GetObject("WinNT://DOMAIN")
WScript.Echo objDomain.Get("MinPasswordAge")
```

As you can see, the syntax is virtually identical, with the ADSI connection string and the attribute name being the only differences.

If you're an advanced Active Directory (AD) user, you can also work directly with the domain's root object, configuration partition, and schema partition. To do so, simply connect directly to the appropriate object.

```
Dim objRoot, objConfig, objSchema, objRootDomain

'get the forest root domain:
Set objRoot = GetObject("LDAP://rootDSE")
Set objRootDomain = GetObject("LDAP://" & _
 objRoot.Get("rootDomainNamingContext"))

'get the configuration partition
Set objConfig = GetObject("LDAP://" & _
 objRoot.Get("configurationNamingContext"))

'get the schema partition
Set objSchema = GetObject("LDAP://" & _
 objRoot.Get("schemaNamingContect"))
```

I'm not going to cover scripting operations that modify the configuration or schema partitions; doing so is pretty dangerous stuff, and it's not the sort of thing you do so frequently that you're likely to need to automate it.

## Changing Domain Settings

In the last chapter, I showed you an example of how you can use the WinNT provider to modify a domain's password and lockout policies. Here it is again.

```
' first bind to the domain
set objDomain = GetObject("WinNT://MyDomain")

objDomain.Put "MinPasswordLength", 8
objDomain.Put "MinPasswordAge", 10
objDomain.Put "MaxPasswordAge", 45
objDomain.Put "PasswordHistoryLength", 8
objDomain.Put "LockoutObservationInterval", 30000
objDomain.SetInfo
```

This same syntax works pretty well for LDAP connections to a domain, although as I noted in the previous section the attribute names are different. Here's an LDAP version of the same example.

```
' first bind to the domain
set objDomain = GetObject("LDAP://dc=domain,dc=com")

objDomain.Put "minPwdLength", 8
objDomain.Put "minPwdAge", 10
objDomain.Put "maxPwdAge", 45
objDomain.Put "pwdHistoryLength", 8
objDomain.Put "lockoutObservationWindow", 30000
objDomain.SetInfo
```

As you can see, the basic syntax is to use the `Put` method, the appropriate attribute name, and the new value, and then to call the `SetInfo` method when you're finished. `SetInfo` copies the changes back to the directory, committing the changes.

## Working with OUs

You'll likely do four basic things with an OU. By the way, some of these operations also apply to the built-in, OU-like containers: Users, Computers, and Built-In. Keep in mind that these are *not* proper OUs and cannot be accessed in quite the same way as I described in the previous chapter. In the next four sections, I'll demonstrate how to use ADSI to create, modify, query, and delete an OU.

**NOTE** Because OUs don't exist in NT domains, all of these examples will only use the LDAP provider that works with Active Directory in its native mode.

### Creating an OU

Creating an OU is simple enough. First, you need to obtain a reference to the parent of the new OU, and then use that object's `Create` method to create a new OU. To create a new top-level OU named Sales:

```
Dim objDomain, objNewOU
Set objDomain = GetObject("LDAP://dc=domain,dc=com")
Set objNewOU = objDomain.Create("organizationalUnit", "ou=Sales")
objNewOU.SetInfo
```

**Classes and Attributes**

As you're working with AD, it's important to understand the system of classes and attributes that the AD schema uses for its organization. An *attribute* is some discrete piece of information, such as a name or description. A *class* is simply a collection of attributes that describes some real-world object. For example, a `user` is a class that includes attributes such as `name`, `description`, `address`, and so forth. A `group` is another class, which includes such attributes as `name`, `description`, and `members`.

AD does not allow multiple attributes to use the same name. So, when you see two classes with the same attributes (such as `description`), both classes are actually using the same attribute definition from the AD schema. This sort of re-use makes AD very efficient.

An *instance* is a copy of a class with its attributes' values filled in. For example, DonJ might be the name of a particular user. The user object you see in the AD GUI is an instance of the `user` class.

Notice that the `Create` method returns a reference to the newly created object, and I still have to call that object's `SetInfo` method to save the changes into the directory. I could also modify properties of the new OU prior to calling `SetInfo`. Let me extend this example and create both a top-level Sales OU and a child OU named West under that.

```
Dim objDomain, objNewOU
Set objDomain = GetObject("LDAP://dc=domain,dc=com")
Set objNewOU = objDomain.Create("organizationalUnit", _
 "ou=Sales")
objNewOU.SetInfo

Dim objChildOU
Set objChildOU = objNewOU.Create("organizationalUnit, "ou=West")
objChildOU.SetInfo
```

The child OU is created by using the `Create` method of its parent. If you want to create a child OU under an existing OU, you must obtain a reference to that existing OU first, not the domain.

```
Dim objParent, objNewOU
Set objParent = GetObject("LDAP://ou=Sales,dc=domain,dc=com")
Set objNewOU = objParent.Create("organizationalUnit", "ou=East")
objNewOU.SetInfo
```

Notice that the `GetObject` call is now focusing on a specific OU, meaning the new OU will be created under that specific OU.

### Modifying an OU

Need to modify the attributes of an OU? No problem. Simply obtain a reference to it, use its `Put` method to change one or more attributes, and use `SetInfo` to save your changes.

```
Dim objOU
Set objOU = GetObject("LDAP://ou=Sales,dc=domain,dc=com")
objOU.Put "description", "Sales"
objOU.SetInfo
```

The trick to working with the `Put` method is that you have to know the name of the attributes that are available to you. One way to see them all is to look right in AD's schema. To do so:

1. You need to register the AD Schema console the first time you do this. Open a command-line window and run **regsvr32 schmmgmt.dll**.
2. Run **MMC** from the Start, Run option, or the command-line window, to open a blank Microsoft Management Console window.
3. Select **Add/Remove Snap-ins** from the **File** menu.
4. Click **Add.**
5. Double-click **Active Directory Schema**.
6. Click **Close**, and then **OK**.
7. You might want to save this new console for future use.
8. Expand the schema tree in the console, and open the Classes folder.
9. Locate **organizationalUnit** in the list, and select it. All of the associated attributes will be displayed in the right-hand pane of the window, as shown in Figure 15.1.

Many of the optional attributes—the ones shown in the console with `Optional` as their type—may not make sense. For example, why would an

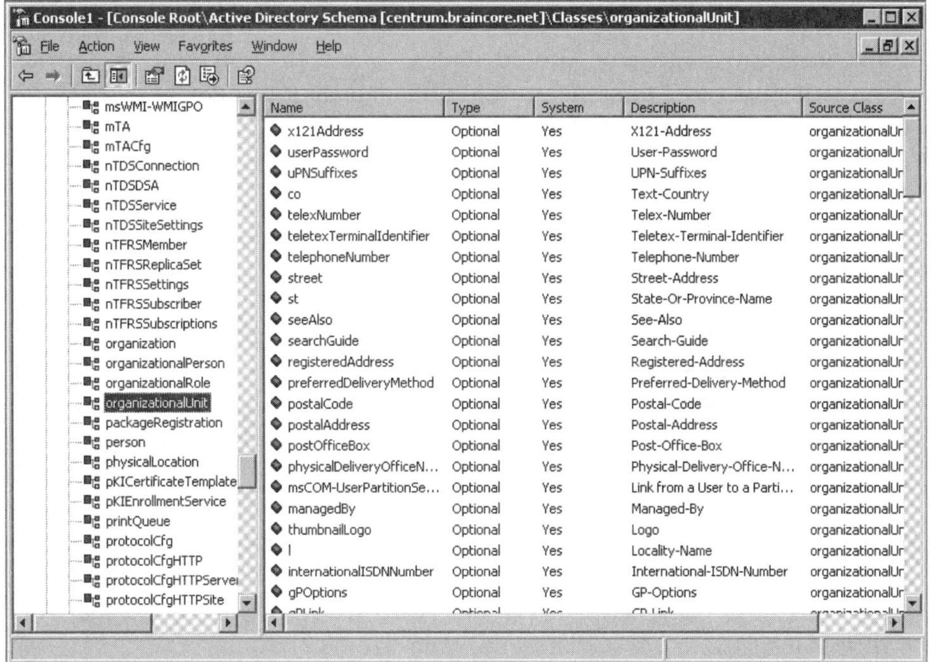


**Figure 15.1** Exploring classes and attributes in the Schema console

OU need an associated PO box? Some of these attributes aren't even shown in the AD tools' user interface. Others, however, such as `description`, are definitely useful.

---

**TIP** You can use the console to find the correct attribute names for other classes, too, such as users and groups. You'll want to remember that as you read the next chapter.

---

Using `Put` requires you to know the correct attribute name, including the correct capitalization, and the value that you want to put into that attribute.

---

**NOTE** Most OU attributes, such as `description`, only accept a single value. There are AD attributes, however, that are designed to hold an array of values. For more information on working with multivalued attributes, refer to Chapter 14.

---

## Querying an OU

If you just want to read the attributes of an OU, you can use the **Get** method. Just get a reference to the OU, and then use **Get** to retrieve the attributes you're interested in.

```
Dim objOU
Set objOU = GetObject("LDAP://ou=Sales,dc=domain,dc=com")
WScript.Echo objOU.Get("description")
```

As with **Put**, you need to know the name of the attribute you're after. You should also understand about how ADSI works under the hood. When you call either **Get** or **GetEx**, both methods actually call a behind-the-scenes method called **GetInfo**. This method's job is to go out to AD and physically load the attributes and their values into a cache on the client. You can also call **GetInfo** directly, forcing ADSI to load attributes and their values from AD into your client's local attribute cache. Your scripts actually work with this cache. For example, if you suspect that someone else will be modifying AD info while your script is running, **GetInfo** will help ensure that your script's local cache has the latest AD data. Here's how.

```
Dim objOU
Set objOU = GetObject("LDAP://ou=Sales,dc=domain,dc=com")
objOU.GetInfo
```

Note that the **Put** method also works with the local cache; **SetInfo** writes the local cache back to AD. If you use **Put** to change an attribute, and then call **GetInfo**, your changes will be lost when the cache is refreshed. Always make sure you call **SetInfo** first to save the cache back to AD.

## Deleting an OU

Deleting an object is perhaps the easiest operation: Connect to the object's parent and call its **Delete** method. Note that there's no "Are you sure?" confirmation, no possibility of undoing the deletion, and unless you have a backup, no way to reverse the operation. Here's how to do it.

```
Dim objOU
Set objOU = GetObject("LDAP:// dc=domain,dc=com")
objOU.Delete "organizationalUnit", "ou=HR"
```

In the case of an OU, *every object in the OU will also be deleted,* including users, groups, and child OUs. So, use this capability with extreme caution! Note that you do have to connect to the object's parent, just as if you were creating a new object; you cannot connect to the object itself and call `Delete` with no parameters.

## Putting It All Together

One potential use for domain- and OU-manipulation scripts is to configure a test or pilot domain that resembles your production domain. By using a script, you can install a domain controller in a lab, and then quickly recreate aspects of your production environment, such as OU structure and user accounts.

### ➤➤ Preload Domain

Listing 15.1 shows a script that preloads a domain with a specific OU structure. Just for fun, I've thrown in a couple of new methods that copy and move OUs around within the domain. See if you can figure out how they work before you read the line-by-line explanation.

**Listing 15.1** *PreLoad.vbs.* Preloads a specific OU configuration into a domain via LDAP.

```
'bind to domain
Dim oDomain
Set oDomain = GetObject("LDAP://dc=domain,dc=com")

'Create top-level OUs
Dim oSales, oHR, oMIS
Set oSales = oDomain.Create("organizationalUnit", "Sales")
Set oHR = oDomain.Create("organizationalUnit", "HR")
Set oMIS = oDomain.Create("organizationalUnit", "MIS")
oDomain.SetInfo

'set descriptions
oSales.Put "description", "Sales OU"
oHR.Put "description", "HR OU"
oMIS.Put "description", "MIS OU"
```

*continues*

```
'save
oSales.SetInfo
oHR.SetInfo
oMIS.SetInfo

'create child OUs for Sales
Dim oChild
Set oChild = oSales.Create("organizationalUnit", "Widgets")
oChild.SetInfo
Set oChild = oSales.Create("organizationalUnit", "Wodgets")
oChild.SetInfo
Set oChild = oSales.Create("organizationalUnit", "Worm Gears")
oChild.SetInfo

'create child OUs for HR
Set oChild = oSales.Create("organizationalUnit", "Recruiting")
oChild.SetInfo
Set oChild = oSales.Create("organizationalUnit", "Counseling")
oChild.SetInfo

'create child OUs for MIS
Set oChild = oSales.Create("organizationalUnit", "Engineering")
oChild.SetInfo
Set oChild = oSales.Create("organizationalUnit", "Desktop")
oChild.SetInfo
Set oChild = oSales.Create("organizationalUnit", _
 "Configuration")
oChild.SetInfo

'set domain-wide password policy
oDomain.Put "minPwdLength", 10
oDomain.Put "maxPwdAge", 30
oDomain.Put "minPwdAge", 2
oDomain.SetInfo

'display contents of Users
Dim sContents, oUsers, oObject
Set oUsers = GetObject("LDAP://cn=Users,dc=domain,dc=com")
For Each oObject In oUsers
 sContents = sContents & oObject.Name & ", "
Next
WScript.Echo "Users contains: " & sContents

'create another top-level OU
```

```
Dim oOU
Set oOU = oDomain.Create("organizationalUnit", "Management")
oDomain.SetInfo

'move the top-level OU into Sales
oSales.MoveHere "LDAP://ou=Management,dc=domain,dc=com"

'create a management OU in HR, too
Dim oCopy
oCopy = oHR.Create("organizationalUnit", "Management")
oCopy.SetInfo

'now we're going to copy the Sales Management OU
'attributes to the HR Management OU
Dim oTemplate, aAttributes, sAttribute, sValue

'use the Sales OU as a reference
Set oTemplate = GetObject( _
 "LDAP://ou=Management,ou=Sales,dc=domain,dc=com")
aAttributes = Array("description", "location")

'copy each attribute from the source to the target
For Each sAttribute In aAttributes
 sValue = oTemplate.Get(sAttribute)
 oCopy.Put sAttribute, sValue
Next

'save the information
oCopy.SetInfo
```

Before you run this script, you obviously need to modify the LDAP connection strings to point to a domain in your environment. Of course, I highly recommend the use of a test domain, not your production domain!

### ➤➤ Preload Domain—Explained

This script begins by binding to the domain itself.

```
'bind to domain
Dim oDomain
Set oDomain = GetObject("LDAP://dc=domain,dc=com")
```

Then, the script creates three top-level OUs: Sales, HR, and MIS. These are each referenced by their own object variables.

```
'Create top-level OUs
Dim oSales, oHR, oMIS
Set oSales = oDomain.Create("organizationalUnit", "Sales")
Set oHR = oDomain.Create("organizationalUnit", "HR")
Set oMIS = oDomain.Create("organizationalUnit", "MIS")
oDomain.SetInfo
```

The script then sets a description for each new OU.

```
'set descriptions
oSales.Put "description", "Sales OU"
oHR.Put "description", "HR OU"
oMIS.Put "description", "MIS OU"
```

Next, I save the information using the `SetInfo` method of each new OU.

```
'save
oSales.SetInfo
oHR.SetInfo
oMIS.SetInfo
```

Now, I create three child OUs under the Sales OU. After creating each, I save it, so that I can reuse the oChild object.

```
'create child OUs for Sales
Dim oChild
Set oChild = oSales.Create("organizationalUnit", "Widgets")
oChild.SetInfo
Set oChild = oSales.Create("organizationalUnit", "Wodgets")
oChild.SetInfo
Set oChild = oSales.Create("organizationalUnit", "Worm Gears")
oChild.SetInfo
```

Now the script creates two child OUs for HR, and three more under MIS. Again, notice the use of `SetInfo` after each call to `Create`.

```
'create child OUs for HR
Set oChild = oSales.Create("organizationalUnit", "Recruiting")
oChild.SetInfo
```

```
Set oChild = oSales.Create("organizationalUnit", "Counseling")
oChild.SetInfo

'create child OUs for MIS
Set oChild = oSales.Create("organizationalUnit", "Engineering")
oChild.SetInfo
Set oChild = oSales.Create("organizationalUnit", "Desktop")
oChild.SetInfo
Set oChild = oSales.Create("organizationalUnit", _
 "Configuration")
oChild.SetInfo
```

Now I return to the top-level domain object to set a few domain-wide password policy attributes. I've used `Put` to set each one, and then called `SetInfo` to save the new configuration.

```
'set domain-wide password policy
oDomain.Put "minPwdLength", 10
oDomain.Put "maxPwdAge", 30
oDomain.Put "minPwdAge", 2
oDomain.SetInfo
```

Just for fun, I have the script iterate through each object in the built-in `Users` container. Remember: Although it looks like an OU, it isn't one, so it has to be accessed by using the `CN` component, not the `OU` component. The result should be a comma-separated list of the object names in the container.

```
'display contents of Users
Dim sContents, oUsers, oObject
Set oUsers = GetObject("LDAP://cn=Users,dc=domain,dc=com")
For Each oObject In oUsers
 sContents = sContents & oObject.Name & ", "
Next
WScript.Echo "Users contains: " & sContents
```

Next, I create another top-level OU.

```
'create another top-level OU
Dim oOU
Set oOU = oDomain.Create("organizationalUnit", "Management")
oDomain.SetInfo
```

The script now moves the new OU to be a child OU of Sales. I could have created the OU directly under Sales, but that wouldn't have shown off the `MoveHere` method. Notice how this works: I use the `MoveHere` method of the *parent object*, specifying the LDAP string of the object to be moved. There's no need to call `SetInfo` in this case.

```
'move the top-level OU into Sales
oSales.MoveHere "LDAP://ou=Management,dc=domain,dc=com"
```

Now I want to copy the Sales/Management OU into HR, so that there will also be an HR/Management OU. I want the attributes of both OUs to be the same. I have to start by creating the new child OU under HR.

```
'create a management OU in HR, too
Dim oCopy
oCopy = oHR.Create("organizationalUnit", "Management")
oCopy.SetInfo
```

I need a reference to my template object, which is the Management OU that already exists under the Sales OU.

```
'now we're going to copy the Sales Management OU
'attributes to the HR Management OU
Dim oTemplate, aAttributes, sAttribute, sValue

'use the Sales OU as a reference
Set oTemplate = GetObject( _
 "LDAP://ou=Management,ou=Sales,dc=domain,dc=com")
aAttributes = Array("description", "location")
```

Next, I can use a `For Each...Next` loop to copy each attribute from Sales/Management to HR/Management.

```
'copy each attribute from the source to the target
For Each sAttribute In aAttributes
 sValue = oTemplate.Get(sAttribute)
 oCopy.Put sAttribute, sValue
Next
```

When the attributes are copied, a call to `SetInfo` saves the changes.

```
'save the information
oCopy.SetInfo
```

Using this type of script to quickly load a domain is a valuable trick, and can save you many hours in the test lab. Unlike a backup, which always restores the same thing, this script can be easily tweaked to set up different test environments, or to reflect changes in your production domain.

## Review

ADSI makes it easy to connect to and manipulate domains. You've seen how to query and modify domain-level attributes, and how to create, modify, query, and delete domain-level objects, such as OUs. These techniques can be applied not only to OUs, but also to users and groups, as you'll see in the next chapter. Having the ability to easily manipulate domain and OU information from script can allow you to restructure domains, automate bulk domain configuration tasks, and much more.

**COMING UP**

In the next chapter, I'll dive a bit deeper into ADSI and show you how to create, modify, and delete users and groups. I'll also show you tricks for querying ADSI, such as determining whether a user is a member of a particular group.

CHAPTER 16

# Manipulating Users and Groups

**IN THIS CHAPTER**

With domains and OUs under your belt, you're ready to start writing scripts that manipulate and query the users and groups in your domains. I'll focus on using the LDAP provider for domain operations, and the WinNT provider for working with computers' local SAMs.

User and group maintenance is probably one of the top administrative tasks that you wanted to automate when you picked up this book. You may be interested primarily in domain user and group management, or local computer user and group management, or possibly both. Remember that the WinNT ADSI provider can be used both in NT domains and, for limited operations, in Active Directory (AD) domains. The WinNT provider also gives you access to the SAM on standalone and member servers and NT-based client computers, such as Windows XP machines. The LDAP provider is AD's native provider, and gives you the best access to AD's capabilities, including the ability to work with OUs.

In an AD domain, the WinNT provider gives you a flat view of the domain: All users are in a single space, not separated into containers and OUs. With the LDAP provider, however, you need to remain aware of your domain's OU structure, and you need to become accustomed to fully qualified domain names (FQDNs) that describe users and groups not only by their name, but also by their position within the domain's OU hierarchy.

## Creating Users and Groups

Creating users and groups is probably one of the most frequently automated tasks for administrators, or at least the task they'd most *like* to automate.

Scripting makes it easy, whether you're using the WinNT provider or the LDAP provider.

### The WinNT Way

With the WinNT provider, you start by obtaining a connection to the domain itself. Because all users and groups exist at the top level of the domain, you don't need to connect to a specific OU. Note that you can also use this technique to create local user and group accounts, by simply connecting directly to a non-domain controller instead of connecting to a domain.

---

**TIP** If you want to create a user or group on a specific domain controller, thus making it available immediately on that domain controller without waiting for replication to occur, connect to the domain controller by name rather than connecting to the domain. Domain controllers don't technically have local accounts, so when you attempt to create new local accounts on a domain controller, you're really creating domain accounts.

---

After you are connected, simply use the `Create` method—much as I did with OUs in the previous chapter—to create the user account. Here's an example.

```
Dim oDomain, oUser
Set oDomain = GetObject("WinNT://DOMAIN")
Set oUser = oDomain.Create("user","DonJ")
```

Not much to it. You need to call `SetInfo` to save the new user, but first you probably want to set some of the user's attributes. Here's an extended example.

```
Dim oDomain, oUser
Set oDomain = GetObject("WinNT://DOMAIN")
Set oUser = oDomain.Create("user","DonJ")

oUser.SetPassword "pa55w0rd!"
oUser.FullName = "Don Jones"
oUser.Description = "Author"
oUser.HomeDirectory = "\\server1\donj"
oUser.RasPermissions = 9
oUser.SetInfo
```

The WinNT provider helpfully exposes these attributes as properties of the user object, meaning you don't have to use raw attribute names like you do with the LDAP provider (which I'll cover next).

Creating a group requires a similar process.

```
Dim oDomain, oGroup
Set oDomain = GetObject("WinNT://DOMAIN")
Set oGroup = oDomain.Create("group","HelpDesk")
oGroup.SetInfo
```

Again, not much to it. Later in this chapter, I'll show you how to manipulate the group's membership list.

### The LDAP Way

Creating groups and users with the LDAP provider is very similar, although because the LDAP provider is a bit more generic than the WinNT provider is, you have to provide a bit more detail in the way of attribute names. Also, because LDAP recognizes AD OUs, you need to connect to the parent object—either an OU or a container—that you want the new user or group to live in. If you just connect to the domain, the new object will be created in the domain's default container, which is generally the Users container. Here's an example.

```
Dim oUser, oGroup, oDomain

'Connect to the MIS OU
Set oDomain = GetObject("LDAP://ou=MIS,dc=domain,dc=com")

'Create a user
Set oUser = oDomain.Create("user", "cn=DonJ")
oUser.Put "sAMAccountName", "donj"
oUser.SetInfo

'create a group
Set oGroup = oDomain.Create("group", "cn=HelpDesk")
oGroup.Put "sAMAccountName", "HelpDesk"
oGroup.SetInfo
```

The overall layout is very similar to the WinNT way of doing things. However, when you create a new object, you must specify its canonical name (CN), such as `cn=DonJ`. You must also provide a value for one of the user class' mandatory attributes, sAMAccountName. Generally, that should be the same as the CN, without the cn= part. Finally, you call SetInfo to save everything.

## Querying User Information

Reading user information (or group information, for that matter) requires the use of the Get method, as well as the name of the attribute you want to read. In the previous chapter, I showed you how to use the AD Schema console to browse a class for its available attributes; you can use the same technique on the user and group classes to see what attributes they support. To query information, simply connect to the object in question and use Get to retrieve the attribute values that you need.

```
Dim oUser
Set oUser = GetObject("LDAP://cn=DonJ,ou=MIS,dc=domain,dc=com")
WScript.Echo oUser.Get("name")
WScript.Echo oUser.Get("description")
WScript.Echo oUser.Get("sAMAccountName")
```

That's easy enough. Using the WinNT provider, you can directly access many attributes that are exposed as regular properties.

```
Dim oUser
Set oUser = GetObject("WinNT://DOMAIN/DonJ")
WScript.Echo oUser.Name
WScript.Echo oUser.Description
```

One thing to be careful of with the WinNT provider is that it grabs the first object it finds matching your query. For example, if I have a user *and* a group named DonJ, the preceding example might bind to the user or the group. You can force the object type by specifying it.

```
Dim oUser
Set oUser = GetObject("WinNT://DOMAIN/DonJ,user")
WScript.Echo oUser.Name
WScript.Echo oUser.Description
```

You can also use Get with the WinNT provider, making its syntax parallel to the LDAP provider. Keep in mind that user objects have a number of multivalued attributes, as I mentioned in Chapter 14. Reading those requires a slightly different technique.

```
Dim oUser
Set oUser = GetObject("LDAP://cn=DonJ,ou=MIS,dc=domain,dc=com")

Dim sURL
For Each sURL in objUser.GetEX("url")
 WScript.Echo sURL
Next
```

In this case, I'm working with the "url" attribute of a user object, which can actually contain multiple URLs. The `GetEx` method retrieves them all into a collection, which I iterate through by using a `For Each...Next` collection.

## Changing User Settings

Using the LDAP provider, you can use `Put` to change user and group attributes.

```
Dim oUser
Set oUser = GetObject("LDAP://cn=DonJ,ou=MIS,dc=domain,dc=com")
oUser.Put "description", "Author"
oUser.SetInfo
```

Keep in mind that users in particular offer a number of multivalued attributes. I discussed how to work with those in Chapter 14. Here's quick refresher.

```
Const MVP_CLEAR = 1
Const MVP_UPDATE = 2
Const MVP_APPEND = 3
Const MVP_DELETE = 4

Dim objUser
Set objUser = GetObject("cn=DonJ,ou=Sales,dc=braincore,dc=net")
objUser.PutEx MVP_APPEND, "otherTelephone", Array("555-1212")
objUser.SetInfo
```

This example appends another telephone number to a user's `otherTelephone` multivalued attribute. You can also clear the attribute completely, delete entries, or change a particular entry. The following example adds a new telephone number, and then deletes it.

```
Const MVP_CLEAR = 1
Const MVP_UPDATE = 2
Const MVP_APPEND = 3
Const MVP_DELETE = 4

Dim objUser
Set objUser = GetObject("cn=DonJ,ou=Sales,dc=braincore,dc=net")
objUser.PutEx MVP_APPEND, "otherTelephone", Array("555-1212")
objUser.SetInfo

objUser.PutEx MVP_DELETE, "otherTelephone", Array("555-1212")
objUser.SetInfo
```

The `PutEx` method accepts the operation type (clear, update, append, or delete), the attribute you want to change, and the value you want to update, append, or delete. In the case of a clear operation, you don't need to provide a new value; the attribute is simply cleared out completely.

If you're using the WinNT provider, either you can set properties directly or you can use `Put`, just like the LDAP provider.

## Working with Groups

You'll want to do two primary things with groups: modify their membership and check their membership. The former can be useful in scripts that bulk-add new users to the domain; the latter is invaluable in logon scripts. Let's take checking group membership first. The basic trick is to get a reference to a group, and then scan through its members until you find a particular user (or not). This is best implemented as a function, which can be easily reused in different scripts. The function is in Listing 16.1.

**Listing 16.1** *CheckGroupMembership.vbs.* This function checks to see if a specified user belongs to a specified group.

```
Function IsMember(sUser, sGroup)
 Dim oGroup, bIsMember, oMember
 bIsMember = False
 Set oGroup = GetObject("LDAP://" & sGroup)
 For Each oMember in oGroup.GetEx("member")
  If oMember.Name = sUser Then
   bIsMember = True
   Exit For
  End If
 Next
 IsMember = bIsMember
End Function
```

You need to pass FQDNs to this function. For example, to see if user DonJ, located in the MIS OU, is a member of the HelpDesk group, also located in the MIS OU, you'd do something like this.

```
If IsMember( _
 "cn=DonJ,ou=MIS,dc=domain,dc=com", _
 "cn=HelpDesk,ou=MIS,dc=domain,dc=com") Then
 WScript.Echo "He's a member!"
Else
 WScript.Echo "He's not a member!"
End If
```

Notice that the function uses the `GetEx` method to retrieve the group object's `member` attribute, which is a multivalued attribute. Each entry in the attribute is the FQDN of a user that belongs to the group. The benefit of a function like this is that it can check for users from different domains belonging to, for example, a Universal security group, because you're using the FQDN of the user, which includes his home domain.

Given this example on how to *read* the group's membership list, you probably have a good idea of how to *modify* that list. Suppose you have a group named HelpDesk in the MIS OU. You want to add a user named DonJ, also from the MIS OU, and delete a user named GregM from the Sales OU. Here's how.

```
Dim oGroup
Set oGroup = GetObject("LDAP://cn=HelpDesk,ou=MIS,dc=" & _
 "domain,dc=com")

'PutEx constants
Const MVP_CLEAR = 1
Const MVP_UPDATE = 2
Const MVP_APPEND = 3
Const MVP_DELETE = 4

'add user
oGroup.PutEx MVP_APPEND, "member", "cn=DonJ,ou=MIS,dc=" & _
 "domain,dc=com"
oGroup.SetInfo

'delete user
oGroup.PutEx MVP_DELETE, "member", "cn-GregM,ou=Sales,dc=" & _
 "domain,dc=com"
oGroup.SetInfo
```

What if you want to do this with an NT domain or a local SAM? Using the WinNT provider is slightly different. First, you need to connect to the user account to obtain its security identifier (SID), and then you can add that to the group.

```
Dim oUser, oGroup
Set oUser = GetObject("WinNT://DOMAIN/DonJ,user")
Set oGroup = GetObject("WinNT://DOMAIN/HelpDesk,group")

oGroup.Add oUser.ADsPath
```

Here again, you see how the WinNT provider can make things a tiny bit easier, because it's designed specifically for dealing with users, groups, and other stuff like that. The LDAP provider, on the other hand, provides more flexibility because it's designed as a generic LDAP provider. That means future changes to AD won't require a new LDAP provider.

## Putting It All Together

In the previous chapter, I demonstrated a script that sets up a domain with some OUs, designed to model a production environment in a test lab. But what's a domain without users?

### ➤➤ Preload Domain II

Listing 16.2 shows a script that utilizes everything I've covered in this chapter. It's designed to be added to the end of Listing 15.1 for a complete domain preloading script. This script creates a couple of thousand users accounts, some groups, and distributes users into the groups.

**Listing 16.2** *PreloadDomain2.vbs.* Creating dummy user and group accounts for a domain in a test environment.

```
'create 10,000 user accounts
'seriously - don't run this in a
'production domain!

'connect to the root
Dim oRoot
Set oRoot = GetObject("LDAP://rootDES")

'connect to the Users container
Dim oContainer
Set oContainer = GetObject("LDAP://cn=Users," & _
 oRoot.Get("defaultNamingContext")

'create 10,000 users
Dim iUser, oUser
For iUser = 1 To 10000
 Set oUser = oContainer.Create("user", _
  "DummyUser" & CStr(iUser)
 oUser.SetInfo
Next

'create 1,000 groups
Dim iGroup, oGroup
For iGroup = 1 To 1000
 Set oGroup = oContainer.Create("group", _
  "DummyGroup" & CStr(iGroup)
 oGroup.SetInfo
Next

'go through the users and place
'1,000 of them in each group
Dim iLastUser
iLastUser = 1
For iGroup = 1 To 1000
```

*continues*

```
 'get the group
 Set oGroup = GetObject("LDAP://cn=DummyGroup" & _
  CStr(iGroup) & ",dc=domain,dc=com")

 'go through users
 For iUser = iLastUser To iLastUser + 999
  oGroup.PutEx 3, "member", _
   "cn=DummyUser" & CStr(iUser) & _
    ",dc=domain,dc=com"
 Next

 iLastUser = iUser

Next
```

Please, please, please note: Don't run this in a production domain. It's intended only for use in a test lab, and it will create 10,000 users and 1,000 groups—definitely a rough burden to place on a production domain that isn't expecting it!

### ➤➤ Preload Domain II—Explained

This script starts by connecting to the root domain.

```
'create 10,000 user accounts
'seriously - don't run this in a
'production domain!

'connect to the root
Dim oRoot
Set oRoot = GetObject("LDAP://rootDSE")
```

Next, it gets a reference to the Users container, which is where the new users and groups will be placed.

```
'connect to the Users container
Dim oContainer
Set oContainer = GetObject("LDAP://cn=Users," & _
 oRoot.Get("defaultNamingContext")
```

Now the script creates 10,000 users, named DummyUser1, DummyUser2, and so forth. Note that they'll all have empty passwords, meaning your domain policies will need to be set to allow a minimum password length of zero. That's *not* the default in Windows Server 2003 domains.

```
'create 10,000 users
Dim iUser, oUser
For iUser = 1 To 10000
 Set oUser = oContainer.Create("user", _
  "DummyUser" & CStr(iUser)
 oUser.SetInfo
Next
```

Next, the script creates 1,000 user groups, named DummyGroup1, DummyGroup2, and so forth.

```
'create 1,000 groups
Dim iGroup, oGroup
For iGroup = 1 To 1000
 Set oGroup = oContainer.Create("group", _
  "DummyGroup" & CStr(iGroup)
 oGroup.SetInfo
Next
```

The script next runs through each of the 1,000 groups. I'm using a variable named `iLastUser` to keep track of the last user I worked with.

```
'go through the users and place
'1,000 of them in each group
Dim iLastUser
iLastUser = 1
For iGroup = 1 To 1000
```

For each group, I get an LDAP reference to the group itself.

```
 'get the group
 Set oGroup = GetObject("LDAP://cn=DummyGroup" & _
  CStr(iGroup) & ",dc=domain,dc=com")
```

Then, I go through 1,000 users. I preloaded `iLastUser` with 1, so the first pass will be 1 to 999. After the last `Next`, `iUser` will equal 1,000, so the second loop will be 1,000 to 1,999. I add each user's FQDN to the member property of the group.

```
 'go through users
 For iUser = iLastUser To iLastUser + 999
  oGroup.PutEx 3, "member", _
   "cn=DummyUser" & CStr(iUser) & _
    ",dc=domain,dc=com"
 Next

 iLastUser = iUser

Next
```

That's a neat way to quickly load a bunch of data into a domain, so that you can do load testing, application testing, backup and restore testing, or whatever else you need to do. You've seen examples of how to use both the LDAP and WinNT providers to work with users and groups, and you'll continue to see more examples throughout this book. In fact, Chapter 30 contains additional ready-to-run example scripts that focus entirely on Windows and domain administration, and Chapter 20 allows you to combine your knowledge of ADSI and WMI—which is coming up next—to design, write, test, and debug a complete Windows and domain management script.

## Review

Working with users and groups is relatively easy from within ADSI. Remember that you can use the WinNT provider to access not only Windows NT domains, but also Active Directory domains, standalone computers, domain member computers, and so forth. Native Active Directory access is provided through the LDAP provider, which also provides access to other LDAP-based directories, such as Exchange 5.x. Some of the most useful scripts you'll develop will use ADSI to manage local user accounts, such as service accounts and built-in accounts like Administrator.

**COMING UP**

You're ready to start working with Windows Management Instrumentation (WMI), Microsoft's way of providing you with almost total administrative control of your computers through scripts. WMI builds upon the object-based scripting you've been using for files and directory services, and provides a nearly unlimited range of administrative possibilities.

CHAPTER 17

# Understanding WMI

**IN THIS CHAPTER**

You've no doubt heard about Windows Management Instrumentation and how it's the holy grail of systems administration. You may have even looked into it and realized how complicated it appears to be! WMI is a powerful tool, but I'll show you that it's not as complicated as it appears.

Whenever I speak at conferences, I'm nearly always asked about Windows Management Instrumentation, or WMI. WMI first caught on in Windows 2000 (although it's partially supported in Windows NT 4.0), and administrators have been hearing about how wonderful a tool it is for managing systems, especially through scripting. Unfortunately, WMI is also one of the most complex-looking technologies to have come out of Redmond in a long time, and many administrators are justifiably concerned about having to spend the rest of their lives understanding it. In this chapter and the two that follow, however, I'm going to show you that WMI isn't as complicated as it looks. In fact, I'll even provide you with some code templates that you can modify to query or set almost any kind of management information from a Windows computer.

## The WMI Hierarchy

One of the most complicated parts of WMI is the sheer number of acronyms that come with it: DMTF, CIM, Win32, and so forth. First, bear in mind that you don't really need to remember any of them to use WMI effectively. However, it can be helpful to understand what they all mean, because they help WMI make more sense.

The DMTF is the Desktop Management Task Force. It's an industry group primarily concerned with making desktop computers (they do care about servers, too) easier to manage. Microsoft pays close attention to the DMTF and is a contributing member. One of the things that the DMTF realized is that every hardware, software, and operating system vendor has different names for the same things. Windows, for example, has logical disks, partitions, volumes, and so forth; Novell NetWare uses these terms for slightly different things. To clear up the confusion, the DMTF created the Common Information Model, or CIM.

The CIM is essentially a generic way of describing everything associated with a computer, at both a hardware and a software level. The CIM defines many base *classes* to represent things like disks, processors, motherboards, and so forth. The CIM classes only include properties that are universal. For example, the `CIM_DiskDrive` class includes a property for `Name`, because all disk drives can be assigned a descriptive name. It also includes a property for `MaxBlockSize`, because all disk drives manufactured today have an associated maximum block size. The class doesn't include a property that indicates the file system used to format the disk, nor does it show whether a disk is basic or dynamic. Those are operating-system-specific features not addressed by the CIM.

The CIM is, however, extensible. When Microsoft created WMI, it created its own series of Win32 classes that are Windows-specific. The Win32 classes are based on, or *inherited* from, CIM classes. For example, there's a `Win32_DiskDrive` class. It includes all of the properties associated with the `CIM_DiskDrive` class, and includes additional properties—such as `PNPDeviceID`—that are specific to the Windows operating system.

---

**TIP** You might want to explore the WMI reference information online, just to see how the Win32 classes build upon their CIM counterparts. Go to http://msdn.microsoft.com/library to start. In the left-hand navigation tree, open Setup and System Administration, Windows Management Instrumentation, SDK Documentation, WMI Reference, and WMI Classes. You'll see sections for CIM classes and Win32 classes.

---

The main part of WMI is understanding that it's composed of these *classes,* which represent the hardware and software in a computer. My laptop, for example, has once *instance* of the `Win32_DiskDrive` class, which simply means that the machine contains one disk drive. My desktop machine has two instances of `Win32_DiskDrive`, which means it contains two hard disks. Absolutely everything in WMI is set up to handle multiple instances of classes. Sometimes, that doesn't seem to make any sense. After all, how many computers do you know of that contain multiple instances of a class like `Win32_MotherboardDevice`? Not many! But WMI is designed to be forward looking. Who knows; we might someday be working with computers that *do* have multiple motherboards, and so WMI is set up to deal with it.

Multiple instances can make querying WMI information seem complex. For example, suppose you want to query the IP address of a workstation's network adapter. Unfortunately, you cannot just ask for the IP address from the first adapter WMI knows about. Windows computers all contain multiple network adapters, if you stop to consider virtual VPN adapters, the virtual loopback adapter, and so forth. So, when you write WMI queries, you have to take into account the fact that the computer probably contains multiple instances of whatever you're after, and write your script accordingly. As a quick example, try the script in Listing 17.1.

**Listing 17.1** *ShowNIC.vbs.* Shows the IP address and MAC address of each network adapter you have.

```
Dim strComputer
Dim objWMIService
Dim colItems

strComputer = "."
Set objWMIService = GetObject("winmgmts:\\" & _
 strComputer & "\root\cimv2")

Set colItems = objWMIService.ExecQuery( _
 "Select * from Win32_NetworkAdapterConfiguration",,48)

For Each objItem in colItems
     WScript.Echo "IPAddress: " & objItem.IPAddress
     WScript.Echo "MACAddress: " & objItem.MACAddress
     WScript.Echo "MTU: " & objItem.MTU
Next
```

Unbelievably, WMI isn't any more complicated than that. Don't worry for now about how this script works; you'll be seeing many more like it in this and the next two chapters, along with complete explanations.

## Providers and Consumers

One pair of terms you'll run across in the WMI documentation is *providers* and *consumers*. A *consumer* is simply an application that utilizes WMI to retrieve or change system management information. Your WMI scripts, for example, are WMI consumers. A *provider* is a piece of software that makes WMI information available. Windows comes with a number of providers that make system hardware, software, and performance information available through WMI. Third-party applications can include WMI providers, which make those applications manageable through WMI.

The fact that these providers are buried within Windows disguises some of the power and flexibility of WMI. WMI isn't what I'd call an integral part of the Windows operating system; it's really an additional set of services that runs on Windows. You can even see the service on Windows 2000 and newer computers if you look in the Services control panel. I'm not suggesting that WMI isn't fully integrated with Windows; simply that Windows can run without WMI, and that WMI extends Windows' inherent capabilities. Why is this an important distinction?

First, Microsoft isn't really doing anything with WMI that you can't do in other ways. You already know how to set IP addresses, for example; you didn't need WMI to come along and give you that capability. WMI simply makes these administrative tasks available through scripts, meaning you can better automate administrative tasks than you could before. Second, Microsoft isn't doing anything with WMI that other companies can't do. WMI is completely open and extensible, and anyone can write a provider that opens up his application to your scripts.

### WMI Versions

WMI has been available in the NT and 9x product lines since Windows NT 4.0, although WMI wasn't full-featured until Windows 2000. Windows XP and Windows Server 2003 have gradually added WMI features, making more and more of the operating system accessible through WMI.

WMI is installed by default in Windows 2000, Windows XP, Windows 2003, and Windows Me. You can install WMI on Windows 95 OSR2, all editions of Windows 98, and Windows NT 4.0. I'll discuss installation requirements later in this chapter.

## Exploring WMI's Capabilities

Perhaps the easiest way to understand WMI is to simply start playing with it. Windows XP and Windows Server 2003 include `Wbemtest.exe`, a tool that can be used to test WMI functionality and explore its capabilities.

---

**NOTE** Another acronym! WBEM stands for Web-Based Enterprise Management, Microsoft's implementation of several key DMTF technologies that includes WMI. You don't see the WBEM name as much as you used to, but it still pops up in tool names and the like.

---

To run Wbemtest, simply select **Run** from the Start menu, type **wbemtest**, and click **OK.** You'll see the main Wbemtest panel, shown in Figure 17.1.

The first thing you need to do is connect to a WMI provider. Generally, that means connecting to the Windows Management Instrumentation service on your local machine or on another computer. I like to connect to the one on another computer, because it demonstrates WMI's real power as a remote administration tool. To connect, click the **Connect** button. You'll see the Connect dialog box, shown in Figure 17.2

To connect to a remote computer, type *computername***root\cimv2.** This instructs WMI to look for the specified computer name, connect to its root WMI namespace, and then switch to the cimv2 namespace. Cimv2 is simply the section that contains all of the Win32 classes, which are the ones you'll work with most often. Be sure to specify a user and password that has administrative privileges on the remote computer, because by default only administrators are allowed to work with WMI. Click **Connect** to make the connection.

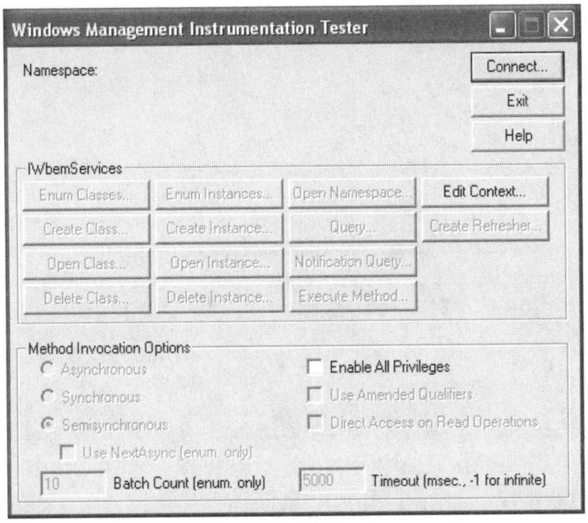

**Figure 17.1** The WMI Tester's main window

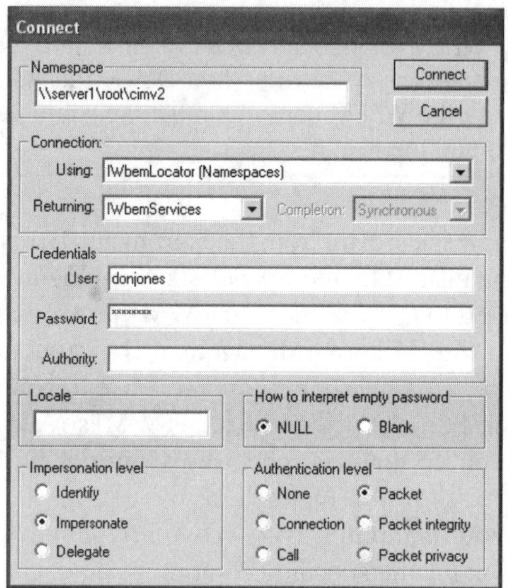


**Figure 17.2** Connecting to a remote machine's WMI namespace

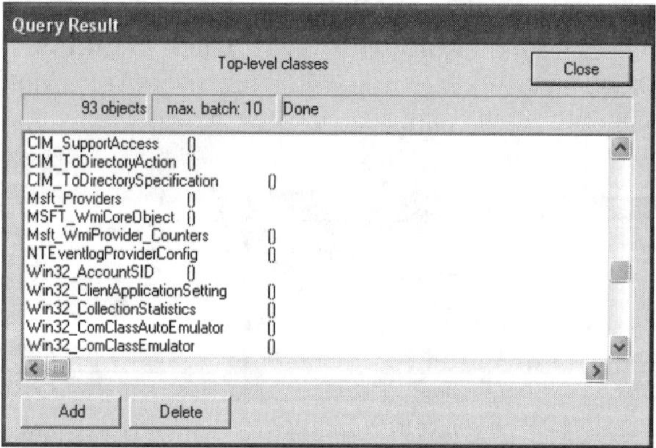


**Figure 17.3** Enumerating the classes in the remote computer's cimv2 namespace

After you're connected, click **Enum Classes** to force WMI to enumerate all available classes in the namespace. You'll be prompted for a superclass name; just leave it blank and click **OK.** You should see a dialog box like the one in Figure 17.3, listing all of the classes—both CIM and Win32 classes—that WMI found.

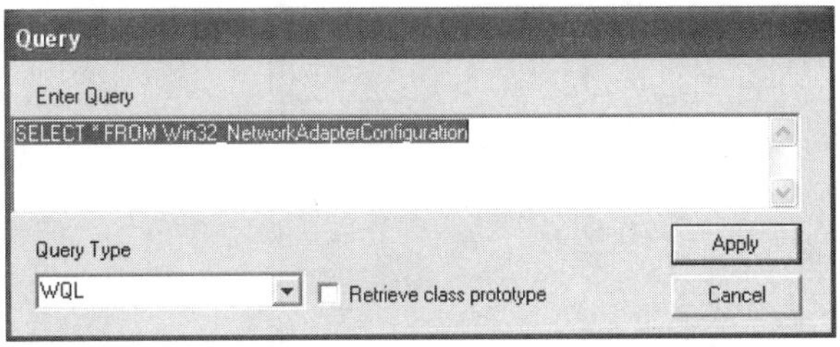

**Figure 17.4** Writing a WMI query

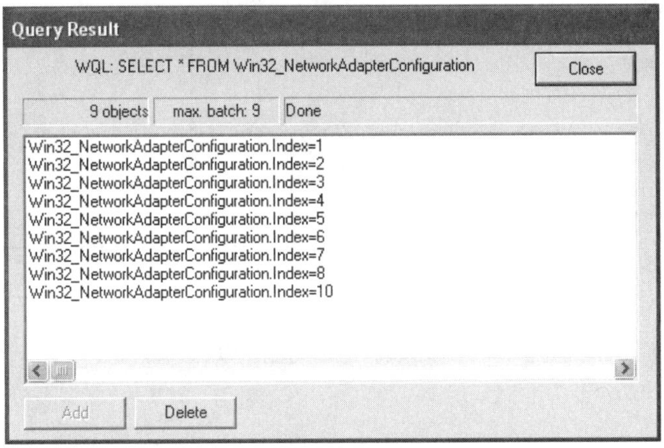

**Figure 17.5** Instances returned by the query

The next fun thing is to try querying. WMI supports a special query language called, appropriately enough, WMI Query Language, or WQL. It looks remarkably like SQL, and if you're familiar with writing SQL queries, WQL will look like an old friend. Start by clicking the **Query** button, and you'll see a dialog box like the one in Figure 17.4. Enter a query, such as **SELECT * FROM Win32_NetworkAdapter Configuration**. Be sure that **WQL** is selected for the query type, and click **Apply.** You'll see another dialog box, like the one in Figure 17.5. This dialog box lists all of the *instances* retrieved by your query. Remember, each instance represents, in this case, a single network adapter configuration. My computer, as you can see in Figure 17.5, has nine instances.

You can double-click any of the instances to display its information, as shown in Figure 17.6. This particular instance, as shown, has DHCP Enabled.

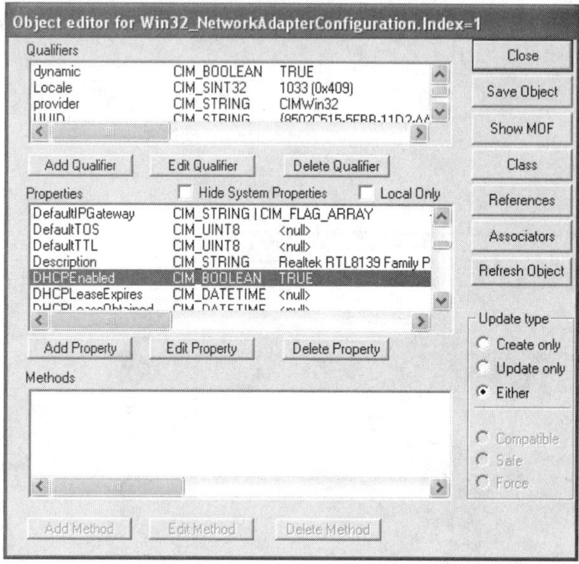


**Figure 17.6** Examining an instance's properties

Hey, you've written your first WMI query! You may not even have noticed!

## WQL Queries

Wbemtest is a great way to test WQL queries before including them in your scripts. You'll be able to immediately see what the query does, what information it returns, and so forth, which helps prevent errors in your scripts later on down the line.

WQL queries themselves are simple enough, and have five basic parts, one of which is optional.

1. `SELECT`, which must start each WQL query.
2. The properties you want to query. You can either provide a comma-separated list of property names, or if you want to retrieve all of a class' properties, specify *.
3. `FROM`, which must follow the list of properties that you want to query.
4. The name of the class you're querying.
5. Optionally, you can include `WHERE` and a conditional statement. A `WHERE` clause limits the instances returned by your query. For exam-

ple, if I include `WHERE DHCPEnabled=TRUE` in my earlier query, I receive fewer instances in the results, because only those instances of `Win32_NetworkAdapterConfiguration` that have `DHCPEnabled` set to True would be returned by the query.

Here are some sample WQL queries. If you like, try them in Wbemtest to see what they do!

- `SELECT * FROM Win32_NetworkAdapterConfiguration WHERE DHCPEnabled=TRUE`
- `SELECT Description FROM Win32_Account WHERE Name='Administrator'`
- `SELECT Freespace,DeviceID FROM Win32_LogicalDisk`

Honestly, the best advice I can offer for quickly learning WMI is to explore the WMI class reference and start writing queries in Wbemtest. You'll quickly become familiar with WQL, and you'll see what type of information is returned by WMI. In the next two chapters, I'll focus on dealing with that information, especially complex information like IP addresses. Most importantly, *do not be afraid to break something in Wbemtest.* Even if you write the worst, malformed query known to mankind, the worst that can happen is Wbemtest will crash and you'll have to re-open it. No big deal, so experiment away!

## Installing WMI

As I mentioned earlier, WMI is preinstalled on Windows 2000 and all later Windows operating systems, including Windows Me. However, if you're using anything earlier, you may need to install WMI before you can start deploying WMI scripts. WMI must be installed on every computer that you intend to query, regardless of where your scripts will actually run; WMI must also be installed on any computer that will run WMI scripts. To obtain the WMI installer, go to the Microsoft home page and select Downloads. From the left-hand menu, select the System Management Tools category. Look for the **Windows Management Instrumentation (WMI) CORE** download for WMI version 1.5. Downloads are available for Windows 9x and NT 4.0. If you cannot spot the downloads in the list, simply type **WMI** into the keyword search at the bottom of the page.

The installer is an executable, not an MSI package. Unfortunately, because these older operating systems don't support Group Policy software deployment, you'll have to manually install the package, or deploy it through alternative means such as Microsoft Systems Management Server (SMS).

I also recommend that you download and install the WMI Administrative Tools. Again, go to the Microsoft home page and select Downloads. From the left-hand menu, select the System Management Tools category. Finally, look for **WMI Administrative Tools** in the list. I'll discuss the administrative tools in the next section.

## Using the WMI Tools

I've already introduced you to Wbemtest, which is a great way to experiment with WMI and get a feel for what it can do. The WMI Administrative Tools, however, includes the WMI Object Browser, which is an exceptionally cool tool. After downloading and installing the tools, launch the Object Browser from the Start menu. Have it connect to the **root/CIMV2** namespace, and provide logon credentials if necessary. You'll see the main screen, shown in Figure 17.7.

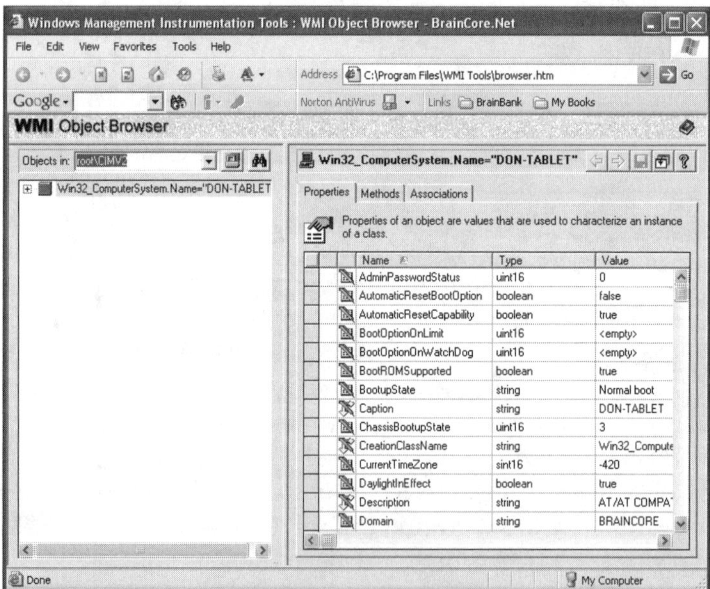


**Figure 17.7** The main Object Browser screen

The Browser lets you see all the properties associated with each class. For example, it starts connected to the `Win32_ComputerSystem` class that represents your entire computer; you can see the properties of the class—such as `AutomaticResetBootOption`—that govern many aspects of your computer's behavior.

On the Object Browser's **Methods** tab, shown in Figure 17.8, you can see the actions that the class can perform. The `Win32_ComputerSystem` class, for example, offers a `JoinDomainOrWorkgroup` method, a `Rename` method, a `SetPowerState` method, and an `UnjoinDomainOrWorkgroup` method. These methods can be programmatically called from within your scripts (which I'll explore in the next two chapters), allowing you to change the computer's configuration.

How can the Object Browser help you write WMI scripts? The Object Browser provides an easy way to see what's lurking under the hood of WMI. I've always said that the toughest part about using WMI lies in figuring out what the heck you're going to query or change; Object Browser makes it a bit easier to figure out what classes, properties, and methods you want to work with.

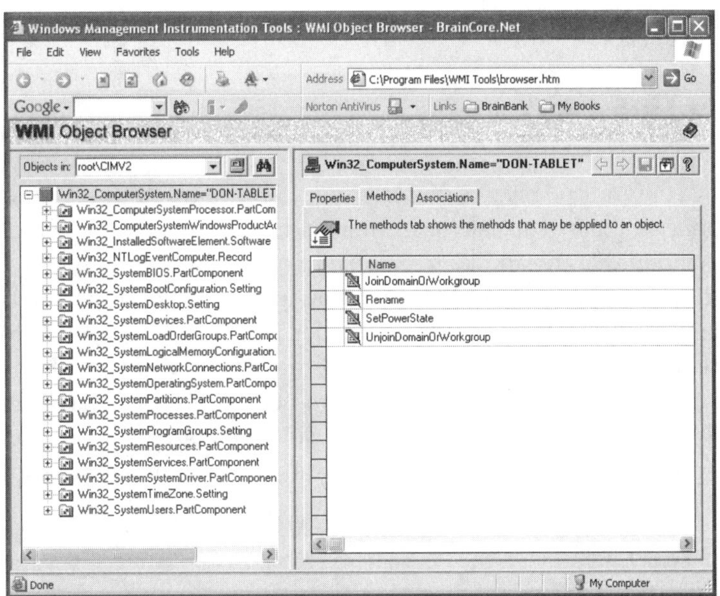


**Figure 17.8** Examining the methods of a WMI class

### Scriptomatic

There's one more WMI tool that I want to introduce: The WMI Scriptomatic. This handy tool was written by Microsoft's "Scripting Guys," who write a regular scripting column on Microsoft's TechNet Web site. You can download the Scriptomatic from http://www.microsoft.com/downloads/details.aspx?displaylang=en&familyid=9ef05cbd-c1c5-41e7-9da8-212c414a7ab0. Or, just go to the Microsoft home page, click Downloads, and look through the downloads until you find the Scriptomatic.

The Scriptomatic performs a function very similar to the WMI Query Wizard in PrimalScript, the script editor I use (available from www.sapien.com). You just pick a WMI class—like `Win32_ComputerSystem`—and the tool produces a template script that queries the class and displays all of its properties. It's a handy way to quickly see the appropriate syntax for a WMI query, but if you look at a couple of different classes you'll realize something very important: All of the scripts produced by the Scriptomatic (and the WMI Query Wizard in PrimalScript) look nearly identical. All that changes is the class name being queried, and the property names being displayed. That's because querying WMI isn't complicated! One simple, generic script—like the one I showed you in Listing 17.1—can be easily modified to query almost anything from WMI.

## Really—It's This Easy

In my conference lectures on scripting, I always try to prove how easy WMI scripting really is. I usually ask students to call out some piece of computer information that they'd like to be able to query. Believe me, I haven't memorized the hundreds of WMI classes that are available, so it's unlikely that I'll already know how to query whatever they ask for. It's a great way to show how a little documentation and a couple of tools can quickly result in a powerful WMI script. For example, suppose you need to query a server to see if any persistent routes have been added by using the `route –p add` command. No problem. Here are the four steps to writing almost any WMI script.

### Find the Class

First, I have to figure out what to query. This is easily the toughest part of the entire process. I usually start in the WMI Reference documentation, looking at the five categories of Win32 classes:

1. Computer System Hardware
2. Operating System
3. Installed Applications
4. WMI Service Management
5. Performance Counter

Of these five, Operating System seems to be the most likely choice for routing information, so I'll expand that topic. Unfortunately, that leaves me with a whole bunch of classes still to work through. Fortunately, they're alphabetical, so I can scroll right down to the R section and look for something like Win32_Route. Nope, nothing. In fact, Win32_Registry is the only thing under R, and that clearly isn't it.

Idly scrolling back up, I do see Win32_IP4RouteTable. Aha! That makes sense; Windows XP and Server 2003 both support IPv4 and IPv6; WMI clearly needs some way to distinguish between the two. Looking more closely, I also see Win32_IP4PersistedRouteTable, which looks exactly like what I want.

Here's what the Microsoft MSDN Library has to say about Win32_IP4PersistedRouteTable.

> The Win32_IP4PersistedRouteTable WMI class represents persisted IP routes. By default, the routes added to the routing table are not permanent. Rebooting the computer clears the routes from the table. However, the following Windows NT command makes the route persist after the computer is restarted:
>
> ```
> route -p add
> ```
>
> Persistent entries are automatically reinserted in the route table each time the route table is rebuilt. Windows NT stores persistent routes in the registry. This class is only applicable to IP4 and does not address IPX or IP6. An entry can be removed through the method call `SWbemServices.Delete` (in the Scripting API for WMI) or `IWbemServices::DeleteInstance` (in the COM API for WMI). This class was added for Windows Server 2003 family.

That last sentence gives me some pause: "This class was added for Windows Server 2003 family." Scrolling to the bottom of the page reveals that the class is present in Windows XP and Windows Server 2003, meaning I cannot use this on Windows 2000. That's not unusual; as WMI becomes more popular, Microsoft expands it to include more and more aspects of the operating system.

For the sake of argument, let's say I'm working entirely with Windows Server 2003 servers, which means I'll have access to this class. The documentation does imply that I can use this class to delete entries, but I'm just interested in seeing if any exist to begin with right now.

## Write the Query, Test the Query

I have to write a WQL query that will retrieve all instances of this class. Something like `SELECT * FROM Win32_IP4PersistedRouteTable` should do the trick. Time to fire up Wbemtest and try the query. After running it on my Windows XP machine, just to try it out, I get a results dialog box like the one in Figure 17.9. Sure enough, I have a persisted route on my laptop! According to the properties shown, the route's destination is for 63.171.9.180.

What if my laptop is more typical and doesn't have any persistent routes? My query would return nothing, and there's a valuable lesson: When testing your queries, always make sure there's something for them to return. In this case, *create* a persistent route, if necessary; that way, you'll be able to tell if your query is working properly.

Double-clicking the instance reveals all the properties of the class, with the values for this instance, as shown in Figure 17.10.

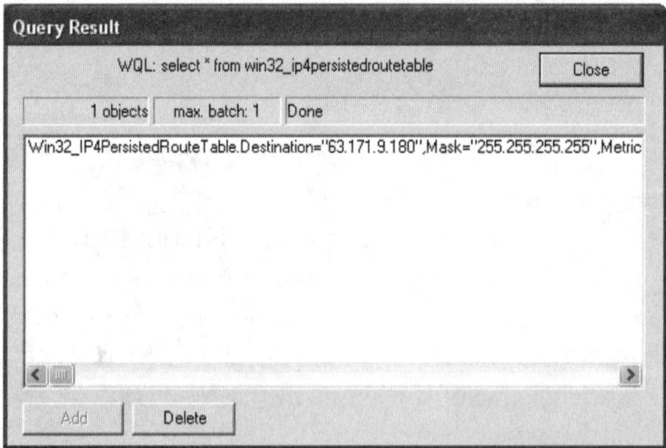


**Figure 17.9** Examining returned instances of Win32_IP4PersistedRouteTable

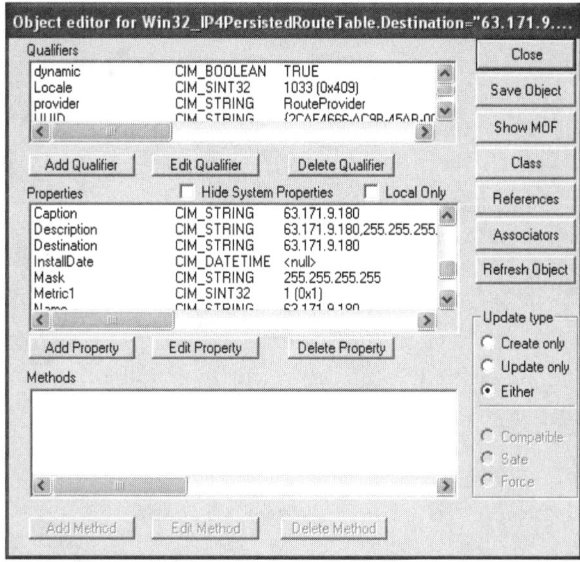


**Figure 17.10** Properties of my persisted route

## Write the Script

Remember that WMI query script I showed you in Listing 17.1? Here it is again just as a reference.

```
Dim strComputer
Dim objWMIService
Dim colItems

strComputer = "."
Set objWMIService = GetObject("winmgmts:\\" & _
 strComputer & "\root\cimv2")

Set colItems = objWMIService.ExecQuery( _
 "Select * from Win32_NetworkAdapterConfiguration",,48)

For Each objItem in colItems
 WScript.Echo "IPAddress: " & objItem.IPAddress
 WScript.Echo "MACAddress: " & objItem.MACAddress
 WScript.Echo "MTU: " & objItem.MTU
Next
```

This is a generic WMI query script, and I just need to adapt it to my current needs. I've provided you with several other template scripts in Chapter 32, which will help you get just about anything you want out of WMI. For this example, I first need to replace the query with the one I just wrote and tested.

```
Set colItems = objWMIService.ExecQuery( _
 "Select * from Win32_IP4PersistedRouteTable",,48)
```

Next, I need to modify the properties that are being used. After all, a persisted route doesn't have a MAC address or an MTU, which were both used in the original script. I want the script to display the route's caption, which tells me its destination address.

```
For Each objItem in colItems
 WScript.Echo "Route to: " & objItem.Caption
Next
```

I'd also like the script to count the persisted routes and tell me the total of how many it finds. I can add that information easily.

```
Dim iCounter
For Each objItem in colItems
 iCounter = iCounter + 1
 WScript.Echo "Route to: " & objItem.Caption
Next
WScript.Echo iCounter & " routes were found."
```

Finally, I'd like the script to connect to a specified server, not just my local machine. Again, a relatively simple change in VBScript.

```
strComputer = InputBox("Enter server name to check")
Set objWMIService = GetObject("winmgmts:\\" & _
 strComputer & "\root\cimv2")
```

That's it. Listing 17.2 shows the final, completed script that should do what I need.

**Listing 17.2** *CheckRoutes.vbs.* Checks for persisted IPv4 routes on a specified 2003 or XP machine.

```
Dim strComputer
Dim objWMIService
Dim colItems

strComputer = InputBox("Enter server name to check")
Set objWMIService = GetObject("winmgmts:\\" & _
 strComputer & "\root\cimv2")

Set colItems = objWMIService.ExecQuery( _
 "Select * from Win32_IP4PersistedRouteTable",,48)

Dim iCounter
For Each objItem in colItems
 iCounter = iCounter + 1
 WScript.Echo "Route to: " & objItem.Caption
Next
WScript.Echo iCounter & " routes were found."
```

You should be able to type this in (or copy it from the CD-ROM accompanying this book) and run it as-is.

### Try the Script

The last step, of course, is to try it. This example should work perfectly; if your future scripts don't work so well, just debug them one error at a time. Following these four simple steps, you've accomplished quite a bit: You located an appropriate WMI class, you created and tested a WQL query, you modified a template script to meet your needs, and you tested the script. That's all there is to it!

## Review

WMI *looks* complex, but that's primarily because there's so darn much of it. Boiled down, WMI isn't difficult at all, and can really be a lot of fun when you get used to it. In this chapter, you've learned how WMI works, how you can access it from your scripts, and how to methodically create WMI scripts to perform almost any task. You also learned about some of the tools that make WMI easier to work with, such as Wbemtest and the WMI Object Browser. I also introduced you to the WMI Scriptomatic from Microsoft, which makes creating new WMI scripts a real breeze.

#### COMING UP

Now that you have the WMI basics under your belt, it's time to start querying and working with basic information. In the next chapter, I'll do just that, giving you plenty of examples to work with. Afterward, I'll move on to querying more complex information, and show you how easy it can be to make even complex WMI tasks scriptable.

CHAPTER 18

# Querying Basic WMI Information

**IN THIS CHAPTER**

You've already learned how to perform very basic WMI queries; now it's time to really learn how those queries are working under the hood. I'll walk through the query-building process in more detail, and show you various ways to manipulate and work with the information you retrieve from WMI.

In the previous chapter, I showed you a standard template-style WMI query that you can modify to query almost anything from WMI. What I didn't do is show you exactly how that query works, how you can easily incorporate it into other scripts, and how to utilize the information you retrieve. If you start using WMI examples from the Web, you might even notice that different script authors write their WMI queries in completely different ways. There's nothing wrong with that, because WMI is flexible enough to work in different ways and still achieve the results you need.

## The WMI Query Language (WQL)

The WMI Query Language, or WQL, is a subset of the industry-standard Structured Query Language (SQL) defined by the American National Standards Institute (ANSI). Although there are other ways to retrieve information from WMI, writing a WQL query is probably the easiest, because WQL closely resembles normal English syntax and grammar.

In the previous chapter, you saw examples of some basic WQL queries.

- `SELECT * FROM Win32_NetworkAdapterConfiguration WHERE DHCPEnabled= TRUE`

- `SELECT Description FROM Win32_Account WHERE Name= 'Administrator'`
- `SELECT Freespace,DeviceID FROM Win32_LogicalDisk`

Queries like these will likely be the ones you use most; however, it's useful to understand what else you can do with WQL, especially when working with complex information.

Regular SQL has literally hundreds of keywords and clauses; WQL, on the other hand, has 19. That's a much more manageable number, and it means you'll be able to master WQL without rivaling your company's database administrators in SQL prowess. Of course, if you already know SQL, WQL is going to be a snap.

### Complex WMI Information

I've used the phrase *complex information* a couple of times in this and the previous chapter; the next chapter, in fact, has *complex information* right in the title. What does it mean?

I divide WMI information into two categories: simple and complex. Simple information is the kind that typically only has one instance on a computer. For example, if I want to query a computer's serial number, there's only going to be one of those. More complex information, like TCP/IP addresses, require more effort as a programmer, because each computer can have multiple network adapters, and each network adapter can have multiple addresses.

Security information can be even more complex. For example, WMI provides a way to access NTFS file permissions. Each file on the hard drive is an instance of a WMI class, and each user or group in the computer or domain is represented by a different class. In between those two classes are *access control entries,* or ACEs, which grant a specific permission on a specific file to a specific user or group. So, to access NTFS file permissions, you're dealing with at least three interrelated classes. Complex enough for you?

Properly written WQL queries can reduce this complexity by allowing you to query for specific sets of data, rather than having to wade through all the interrelated classes.

**NOTE** I'm not going to cover all 19 keywords. Several of them are intended for querying WMI events, which are special notifications generated by WMI when specific things occur, as a file being modified. Dealing with WMI events is a bit beyond the scope of this book, and better suited to traditional programming than scripting.

## The Basics

You've already met the primary players in a WQL query.

- `SELECT`, which must start each WQL query.
- The properties you want to query. You can either provide a comma-separated list of property names, or if you want to retrieve all of a class' properties, specify *.
- `FROM`, which must follow the list of properties that you want to query.
- The name of the class you're querying.
- Optionally, you can include `WHERE` and a conditional statement. A `WHERE` clause limits the instances returned by your query. For example, if I include `WHERE DHCPEnabled=TRUE` in my earlier query, I receive fewer instances in the results, because only those instances of `Win32_NetworkAdapterConfiguration` that have `DHCPEnabled` set to TRUE would be returned by the query.

`SELECT`, a property list (or *), `FROM`, and a class name are the minimum required elements for any WQL query. Everything else is optional and is used to restrict the amount of information returned by WMI. For example, `SELECT * FROM Win32_ComputerSystem WHERE Name = "Server1"` returns all instances of the `Win32_ComputerSystem` class with the appropriate server name.

**NOTE** It might seem odd to specify the computer name in a query, when you have to connect to that computer—in this example, Server1—to begin with. What other computer systems could exist on Server1, after all? However, consider so-called blade systems, where a single chassis might contain multiple independent computers. WMI is designed so that a WMI-compliant chassis could be queried for information about any of the computers it contains, although in practice I'm not aware of any chassis that can yet do so.

## Boolean Operators

Whenever you specify a `WHERE` clause in a WQL query, you have to provide some sort of logical expression. WMI returns all instances that meet your logical condition. For example, `WHERE Name = "Server1"` is a logical condition, because it includes the logical = operator.

You can specify more than one logical condition and combine them with Boolean operators. For example, `WHERE Name = "Server1" AND Domain = "MYCOMPANY"` provides two conditions that must both be matched. `AND` serves in this case as a Boolean operator.

WQL supports two primary Boolean operators.

1. `AND`. Combines two conditions, both of which must evaluate to True in order for an instance to be returned in the query results. For example, `WHERE Name = "Server1" AND Domain = "MYCOMPANY"`.
2. `OR`. Combines two conditions, either of which may evaluate to True in order for an instance to be returned in the query results. For example, `WHERE Name = "Server1" OR Domain = "MYCOMPANY"`.

Logical expressions can be grouped in parentheses. For example, suppose you're querying the `Win32_LogicalDisk` class. You might write an expression like the following.

```
SELECT * FROM Win32_LogicalDisk
  WHERE (DriveType = 2) OR
 (DriveType = 3 AND FreeSpace < 1000000)
```

This query would return all instances of `Win32_LogicalDisk` that are either removable drives (`DriveType = 2`) or fixed drives (`DriveType = 3`) with less than one megabyte free.

## Comparison Operators

Sometimes, you may need to query for instances that have a particular property set to NULL. For example, if you query `Win32_NetworkAdapterConfiguration` for a configuration that isn't set to use DHCP, the `DHCPLeaseExpires` property will be NULL. NULL is a special value, and you cannot use a query like `SELECT * FROM Win32_NetworkAdapterConfiguration WHERE DHCPLeaseExpires = NULL`. Instead, you have to use the special `IS` operator, as in `SELECT * FROM Win32_NetworkAdapterConfiguration WHERE DHCPLeaseExpires IS NULL`. To query for the opposite condition, you could use SELECT * FROM Win32_NetworkAdapterConfiguration WHERE DHCPLeaseExpires IS NOT NULL. Here they are again.

- SELECT * FROM Win32_NetworkAdapterConfiguration WHERE DHCPLeaseExpires = NULL. This doesn't work, because you cannot use normal comparison operators like = or <> in combination with NULL.
- SELECT * FROM Win32_NetworkAdapterConfiguration WHERE DHCPLeaseExpires IS NULL. This selects all instances where the property is set to a null value.
- SELECT * FROM Win32_NetworkAdapterConfiguration WHERE DHCPLeaseExpires IS NOT NULL. This selects all instances where the property is not set to a null value.

You cannot use IS or IS NOT in place of the normal comparison operators; IS and IS NOT are designed to be used only in conjunction with NULL. The normal comparison operators are

- =. Equal to
- >. Greater than
- <. Less than
- <=. Less than or equal to
- >=. Greater than or equal to
- <> or !=. Not equal to

There's one more comparison operator, LIKE, which is worth looking at. LIKE is sort of a "soft" equality operator, and allows you to use wildcards to match string data. Suppose, for example, that you want to query all network connections that have the word "Office" in their caption, such as "Office Dial-Up" or "Office VPN." You could use the following query.

```
SELECT * FROM Win32_NetworkConnection
 WHERE Caption LIKE '%Office%'
```

The LIKE operator supports several wildcard characters.

- Use % to represent zero or more characters that you don't care about. For example, %Office% returns "My Offices," "Office VPN," and "Office." On the other hand, Office% returns "Offices" and "Office VPN," but it does not return "My Offices," because there's no percent sign preceding "Office."
- Use square brackets ([ ]) to return a specific range of characters. For example, [A-Z]ars returns "Mars," "Wars," and "Tars," but not "Stars."

- Use a caret (^) to negate a character range. For example, `[^A-M]ars` returns "Wars" and "Tars," but does not return "Mars" because "M" is in the excluded range.
- Use an underscore (_) to return any single character. `M_rs` returns "Mars," "M3rs," or any other string beginning with "M," ending in "rs," and having one character in between.

Finally, you'll notice that many WMI class properties can be set to either True or False, such as the `DHCPEnabled` property of the `Win32_NetworkAdapterConfiguration` class. WQL allows you to use the keywords `TRUE` and `FALSE` to query these properties, such as:

```
SELECT * FROM Win32_NetworkAdapterConfiguration
 WHERE DHCPEnabled = TRUE
```

Don't be tempted to write the query with `DHCPEnabled IS TRUE`, because it won't work; remember that `IS` and `IS NOT` only work in conjunction with `NULL`.

### Associators, References, and Keys

If you're looking through the WMI documentation at the WQL reference, you'll notice some additional keywords: `REFERENCES OF`, `KEYS`, and `ASSOCIATORS OF`. These are all used to query more complex WMI information, and I'll cover them in the next chapter.

## Determining What to Query

I mentioned in the previous chapter that actually figuring out which WMI class to query is the truly tough part about working with WMI, and it's true. The Microsoft MSDN Library reference to the WMI classes, particularly Microsoft's Win32 classes, is the most comprehensive and useful place to start looking. The documentation can be found online at http://msdn.microsoft.com/library. Just expand Setup and System Administration in the left-hand menu, then navigate to Windows Management Instrumentation, SDK Documentation, WMI Reference, WMI Classes, and Win32Classes.

Microsoft currently divides the classes into five categories, although that will almost certainly change over time as the classes are expanded. The current categories are

- Computer System Hardware, which includes everything you can physically touch and see. This includes network adapters, the motherboard, ports, and so forth.
- Operating System, which includes everything associated with Windows itself: users and groups, file quotas, security settings, COM settings, and more.
- Installed Applications, which covers the Windows Installer subsystem and all managed applications.
- WMI Service Management, which covers the configuration and management of WMI itself.
- Performance Counter, which provides access to performance monitoring data through WMI.

After you've narrowed down the proper category, my best advice is to dive into the documentation and scroll through the class names until you find one that looks like it will do what you want. Need to force a hard drive to run CHKDSK? Hard drives are hardware, but CHKDSK is Windows-specific. After all, you don't really run CHKDSK on a hard drive, do you? You run it on a *volume,* which is a Windows thing. So, start with the Operating System category. There's the Win32_LogicalDisk category, which represents a volume like C: or D:. Lo and behold, it has a `ChkDsk` method and a `ScheduleAutoChk` method, one of which is sure to do the trick. The documentation also helpfully notes that the method is included only in Windows XP and Windows Server 2003, meaning that you'll have to find another way to handle earlier clients.

Microsoft's categorization of the WMI classes is far from consistent. For example, `Win32_NetworkAdapterConfiguration` is included in the Computer System Hardware category. Although I agree that a network adapter is definitely hardware, surely its actual configuration is part of the operating system, right? In other words, be prepared to do a little browsing to find the right classes, especially until you become accustomed to them.

---

**TIP** The Appendix of this book is a Quick Script Reference I put together to help you locate the right WMI classes more quickly. For example, if you need to write a WMI query to retrieve Windows Product Activation information, just look up "Activation" in the Quick Script Reference. You'll see a reference to WMI, an indication that it's covered in Chapters 17 through 19, and the specific classes involved: `Win32_WindowsProductActivation`, for example.

---

No matter what, *don't get discouraged.* Keep browsing through the list until you find what you want. Just so you know, WMI isn't complete, yet. Microsoft hasn't provided a WMI "hook" for each thing Windows can do. In fact, the coverage for Windows XP and Windows Server 2003 is light-years better than what's in Windows 2000, and that's better still than NT. But even Windows Server 2003's implementation of WMI doesn't let you query or control the DHCP service, modify IPv6 in any way, modify DNS server records (although you can do that through ADSI in Active Directory–integrated DNS zones), or a hundred other tasks. Eventually, you'll probably be able to do all of those things with WMI, but not today.

### Which Versions Include What?

The WMI documentation in MSDN Library is the most authoritative source for which WMI classes are included in which versions of WMI. Keep in mind that some classes gained new properties in newer versions of Windows. Near the end of each class' documentation page, you'll see something like the following:

**Client**: Included in Windows XP, Windows 2000 Professional, Windows NT Workstation 4.0 SP4, and later.

**Server**: Included in Windows Server 2003, Windows 2000 Server, Windows NT Server 4.0 SP4, and later.

Those are your official indications that the class (`Win32_SystemTimeZone`, in this example) is included in the listed versions of Windows. Take `Win32_NetworkAdapter` as a second example. The documentation indicates that it's available in Windows NT 4.0 SP4 and later, but check out the `InterfaceIndex` property. That property includes a note:

**Windows XP and earlier:** The `InterfaceIndex` property is not available.

Meaning, of course, that the property was introduced in Windows Server 2003. This particular property had to be added to `Win32_NetworkAdapter` when Microsoft added the `Win32_IP4RouteTable` class, because the route table class needed some unique number with which it could refer to network adapters. As WMI continues to grow with new classes, supporting properties will be added to existing classes to make the package complete.

Suppose you want to work with disk quotas on your Windows 2000 file servers. You find a great-looking class, `Win32_DiskQuota`, but your scripts don't seem to have any effect on your Windows 2000 machines. That's because, as the documentation notes, the class was introduced in Windows XP. How can you retrofit it to 2000? You can't. Unfair, but that's progress.

## Testing the Query

In the previous chapter, I showed you how to write and test a query using the Wbemtest tool. I recommend that you test every query you plan to write, by running Wbemtest on the target operating system. That way, you'll know your queries are returning the correct results before you spend a lot of time writing an actual script.

For specific instructions on testing a query, see "Really—It's This Easy" in Chapter 17.

If your script will run on multiple operating systems (as in a logon script or a script being used to manage multiple remote servers), be sure to test the query on each potential operating system. That way, you'll quickly spot any WMI version incompatibilities, and you can take the appropriate steps. Don't forget that you can also test your query by using a generic WMI query script, such as the kind generated by the WMI Scriptomatic or by PrimalScript's WMI Query Wizard.

For example, suppose I want to test the `Win32_QuotaSetting` query. By using PrimalScript, I just run the wizard, select **Win32_QuotaSetting** from the class list, and click **Insert**. The wizard creates the following script.

```
On Error Resume Next
Dim strComputer
Dim objWMIService
Dim colItems

strComputer = "."
Set objWMIService = GetObject( _
 "winmgmts:\\" & strComputer & "\root\cimv2")
Set colItems = objWMIService.ExecQuery( _
 "Select * from Win32_QuotaSetting",,48)
For Each objItem in colItems
 WScript.Echo "Caption: " & objItem.Caption
 WScript.Echo "DefaultLimit: " & objItem.DefaultLimit
 WScript.Echo "DefaultWarningLimit: " & _
  objItem.DefaultWarningLimit
 WScript.Echo "Description: " & objItem.Description
 WScript.Echo "ExceededNotification: " & _
  objItem.ExceededNotification
 WScript.Echo "SettingID: " & objItem.SettingID
 WScript.Echo "State: " & objItem.State
 WScript.Echo "VolumePath: " & objItem.VolumePath
```

*continues*

```
 WScript.Echo "WarningExceededNotification: " &
  objItem.WarningExceededNotification
Next
```

If I want to make a more complex query, I can just modify the template before testing the script. For example, I might change the query to something like this.

```
Set colItems = objWMIService.ExecQuery( _
 "Select * from Win32_QuotaSetting WHERE " & _
 "VolumePath = "C:\\",,48)
```

This revised query would return all quota settings affecting the C: volume, as opposed to all quota settings on the entire server. Then, I can save the query, copy it to whatever servers I plan to run the final script on, and run the query. The template scripts generated by Scriptomatic and the Query Wizard are noninvasive, meaning they only display information rather than try to change it. That makes them perfect for generating harmless test scripts that allow you to make sure your queries run without error.

Perhaps one of the most annoying aspects of troubleshooting WMI queries is that they don't often return error messages. Consider this example.

```
On Error Resume Next
Dim strComputer
Dim objWMIService
Dim colItems

strComputer = "."
Set objWMIService = GetObject("winmgmts:\\" & _
 strComputer & "\root\cimv2")
Set colItems = objWMIService.ExecQuery( _
 "Select * from Win32_Service WHERE Nmae = 'spooler'",,48)
For Each objItem in colItems
 WScript.Echo "Caption: " & objItem.Caption
Next
```

This example began life as a PrimalScript WMI Query Wizard-generated template, but I modified the WQL query. If you look closely, you'll see that I did it wrong: `Name` is spelled `Nmae`. Nonetheless, running this script as-is produces no error of any kind, from either VBScript or WMI. That's because WMI looks for all instances of Win32_Service that have a `Nmae` property set to "spooler." It doesn't find any, of course, because *no* instance of

Win32_Service has a `Nmae` property. So, the script completes cleanly without returning any information.

If your queries aren't returning instances, and you think they should, double- and triple-check the spelling of your class names and service names.

## Writing the Query in VBScript

If you're like me, you like your final scripts to be clean, consistent, and easy to read. Using the Wizard- or Scriptomatic-generated scripts isn't the best way to achieve consistency. For example, the PrimalScript Wizard always includes the following code.

```
On Error Resume Next
Dim strComputer
Dim objWMIService
Dim colItems

strComputer = "."
Set objWMIService = GetObject("winmgmts:\\" & strComputer & "\root\
  cimv2")
```

First, you might not want error-checking turned off, which is what `On Error Resume Next` does. You might use a different variable naming convention (I often do, mainly because I'm a bit too lazy to type **str** instead of just **s** for string variables and the like), or you might have already defined a variable name that the wizard is using. Understand that you can always revise and modify the template scripts to fit better within your overall scripts. Not only *can* you change them, you probably *should* change them.

Suppose you want to write a script that restarts a remote server. You've done your browsing, and `Win32_OperatingSystem` has a method named `Shutdown` that looks like it'll do the trick. Using Scriptomatic or the WMI Query Wizard, you generate code similar to the following.

```
On Error Resume Next
Dim strComputer
Dim objWMIService
Dim colItems
```

*continues*

```
strComputer = "."
Set objWMIService = GetObject("winmgmts:\\" & _
 strComputer & "\root\cimv2")
Set colItems = objWMIService.ExecQuery( _
 "Select * from Win32_OperatingSystem",,48)
For Each objItem in colItems
 WScript.Echo "BootDevice: " & objItem.BootDevice
 WScript.Echo "BuildNumber: " & objItem.BuildNumber
 WScript.Echo "BuildType: " & objItem.BuildType
 WScript.Echo "Caption: " & objItem.Caption
 WScript.Echo "CodeSet: " & objItem.CodeSet
 WScript.Echo "CountryCode: " & objItem.CountryCode
 WScript.Echo "CreationClassName: " & objItem.CreationClassName
 WScript.Echo "CSCreationClassName: " & _
  objItem.CSCreationClassName
 WScript.Echo "CSDVersion: " & objItem.CSDVersion
 WScript.Echo "CSName: " & objItem.CSName
 WScript.Echo "CurrentTimeZone: " & objItem.CurrentTimeZone
 WScript.Echo "Debug: " & objItem.Debug
 WScript.Echo "Description: " & objItem.Description
 WScript.Echo "Distributed: " & objItem.Distributed
 WScript.Echo "EncryptionLevel: " & _
  objItem.EncryptionLevel
 WScript.Echo "ForegroundApplicationBoost: " & _
  objItem.ForegroundApplicationBoost
 WScript.Echo "FreePhysicalMemory: " & _
  objItem.FreePhysicalMemory
 WScript.Echo "FreeSpaceInPagingFiles: " & _
  objItem.FreeSpaceInPagingFiles
 WScript.Echo "FreeVirtualMemory: " & objItem.FreeVirtualMemory
 WScript.Echo "InstallDate: " & objItem.InstallDate
 WScript.Echo "LargeSystemCache: " & objItem.LargeSystemCache
 WScript.Echo "LastBootUpTime: " & objItem.LastBootUpTime
 WScript.Echo "LocalDateTime: " & objItem.LocalDateTime
 WScript.Echo "Locale: " & objItem.Locale
 WScript.Echo "Manufacturer: " & objItem.Manufacturer
 WScript.Echo "MaxNumberOfProcesses: " & _
  objItem.MaxNumberOfProcesses
 WScript.Echo "MaxProcessMemorySize: " & objItem.MaxProcessMemorySize
 WScript.Echo "Name: " & objItem.Name
 WScript.Echo "NumberOfLicensedUsers: " & _
  objItem.NumberOfLicensedUsers
 WScript.Echo "NumberOfProcesses: " & objItem.NumberOfProcesses
 WScript.Echo "NumberOfUsers: " & objItem.NumberOfUsers
```

```
 WScript.Echo "Organization: " & objItem.Organization
 WScript.Echo "OSLanguage: " & objItem.OSLanguage
 WScript.Echo "OSProductSuite: " & objItem.OSProductSuite
 WScript.Echo "OSType: " & objItem.OSType
 WScript.Echo "OtherTypeDescription: " & _
  objItem.OtherTypeDescription
 WScript.Echo "PlusProductID: " & objItem.PlusProductID
 WScript.Echo "PlusVersionNumber: " & objItem.PlusVersionNumber
 WScript.Echo "Primary: " & objItem.Primary
 WScript.Echo "ProductType: " & objItem.ProductType
 WScript.Echo "QuantumLength: " & objItem.QuantumLength
 WScript.Echo "QuantumType: " & objItem.QuantumType
 WScript.Echo "RegisteredUser: " & objItem.RegisteredUser
 WScript.Echo "SerialNumber: " & objItem.SerialNumber
 WScript.Echo "ServicePackMajorVersion: " & _
  objItem.ServicePackMajorVersion
 WScript.Echo "ServicePackMinorVersion: " & _
  objItem.ServicePackMinorVersion
 WScript.Echo "SizeStoredInPagingFiles: " & _
  objItem.SizeStoredInPagingFiles
 WScript.Echo "Status: " & objItem.Status
 WScript.Echo "SuiteMask: " & objItem.SuiteMask
 WScript.Echo "SystemDevice: " & objItem.SystemDevice
 WScript.Echo "SystemDirectory: " & objItem.SystemDirectory
 WScript.Echo "SystemDrive: " & objItem.SystemDrive
 WScript.Echo "TotalSwapSpaceSize: " & _
  objItem.TotalSwapSpaceSize
 WScript.Echo "TotalVirtualMemorySize: " & _
  objItem.TotalVirtualMemorySize
 WScript.Echo "TotalVisibleMemorySize: " & _
  objItem.TotalVisibleMemorySize
 WScript.Echo "Version: " & objItem.Version
 WScript.Echo "WindowsDirectory: " & objItem.WindowsDirectory
Next
```

First, you weren't interested in querying and displaying *any* information, so you can start by wiping out all of the `WScript.Echo` lines, leaving you with the following.

```
On Error Resume Next
Dim strComputer
Dim objWMIService
Dim colItems
```

*continues*

```
strComputer = "."
Set objWMIService = GetObject("winmgmts:\\" & _
 strComputer & "\root\cimv2")
Set colItems = objWMIService.ExecQuery( _
 "Select * from Win32_OperatingSystem",,48)
For Each objItem in colItems
Next
```

Regardless of how many operating systems the computer thinks it has, the one that's running is the one you want to shut down, and that'll be the primary one. You can modify the WQL query to just retrieve that instance of the class.

```
On Error Resume Next
Dim strComputer
Dim objWMIService
Dim colItems

strComputer = "."
Set objWMIService = GetObject("winmgmts:\\" & _
 strComputer & "\root\cimv2")
Set colItems = objWMIService.ExecQuery( _
 "Select * from Win32_OperatingSystem WHERE " & _
 "Primary = TRUE",,48)
For Each objItem in colItems
Next
```

You probably don't want to shut down just the local computer, so you'll want to add some kind of prompt that collects the appropriate computer name.

```
On Error Resume Next
Dim strComputer
Dim objWMIService
Dim colItems

strComputer = InputBox("Shut down what computer?")
Set objWMIService = GetObject("winmgmts:\\" & _
 strComputer & "\root\cimv2")
Set colItems = objWMIService.ExecQuery( _
 "Select * from Win32_OperatingSystem WHERE " & _
 "Primary = TRUE",,48)
For Each objItem in colItems
Next
```

Now, let's say you want to use different variable names, and you don't want to turn off error checking. No problem—just be sure you change the variable names every time they appear in the script. A search and replace function is the most reliable way to do so, and you'll wind up with something like this.

```
Dim sComputer
Dim oWMIService
Dim oItems, oItem

sComputer = InputBox("Shut down what computer?")
Set oWMIService = GetObject("winmgmts:\\" & _
 sComputer & "\root\cimv2")
Set oItems = oWMIService.ExecQuery( _
 "Select * from Win32_OperatingSystem WHERE " & _
 "Primary = TRUE",,48)
For Each oItem in oItems
Next
```

Now, you need to add the actual `Shutdown` method.

```
Dim sComputer
Dim oWMIService
Dim oItems, oItem

sComputer = InputBox("Shut down what computer?")
Set oWMIService = GetObject("winmgmts:\\" & _
 sComputer & "\root\cimv2")
Set oItems = oWMIService.ExecQuery( _
 "Select * from Win32_OperatingSystem WHERE " & _
 "Primary = TRUE",,48)
For Each oItem in oItems
 oItem.ShutDown()
Next
```

There, you've customized the template script to meet your exact needs. Really, you're not using much of the original wizard-generated code: You kept the variable declarations, the basic WQL query, and the `For Each...Next` construct. That's about it.

---

**NOTE** It may seem odd to use a `For Each...Next` construct when you know your modified query will only return one instance. Why bother? Because the `ExecQuery` method will *always* return a collection, even if the query only returns one instance into the collection. You could have eliminated the `For Each...Next` construct and used `oItems(0).Shutdown()` instead, using the `oItems(0)` syntax to reference the first (and to your knowledge, the only) instance in the collection. Either way works fine.

## Using the Query Results

Let's look at a real-world use for WMI, and walk through the process of building the script. Suppose you want to modify a remote computer's network configuration so that all network adapters have DHCP enabled. Actually, you'll probably want to check multiple machines at once, so you'll need the script to read computer names from a text file that you'll create, using one computer name per line within the file. If the script finds that DHCP is already enabled, you want it to tell you so.

**NOTE** A slightly more real-world task might be to modify the configuration only for a specific network adapter, like the one named Local Area Network, in each machine. That requires working with WMI associator classes, which I'll cover in the next chapter.

The first part I like to handle is the WMI bit. I've found the `Win32_NetworkAdapterConfiguration` class, which has an `EnableDHCP` method that should do the job. I used the PrimalScript WMI Query Wizard to generate a template script for the class, and then trimmed it down to look like this.

```
On Error Resume Next
Dim strComputer
Dim objWMIService
Dim colItems

strComputer = "."
Set objWMIService = GetObject("winmgmts:\\" & _
 strComputer & "\root\cimv2")
Set colItems = objWMIService.ExecQuery( _
 "Select * from Win32_NetworkAdapterConfiguration",,48)
For Each objItem in colItems
 WScript.Echo "DHCPEnabled: " & objItem.DHCPEnabled
 WScript.Echo "Caption: " & objItem.Caption
Next
```

I need to have the script run through a text file, so I'll add the appropriate code. I showed you how to work with files and folders in Chapter 12.

```
Dim strComputer
Dim objWMIService
Dim colItems
Dim objFSO, objTS

Set objFSO = CreateObject("Scripting.FileSystemObject")
Set objTS = objFSO.OpenTextFile("c:\input.txt")

Do Until objTS.AtEndOfStream

 strComputer = objTS.ReadLine
 Set objWMIService = GetObject("winmgmts:\\" & _
  strComputer & "\root\cimv2")
 Set colItems = objWMIService.ExecQuery( _
  "Select * from Win32_NetworkAdapterConfiguration",,48)
 For Each objItem in colItems
  WScript.Echo "DHCPEnabled: " & objItem.DHCPEnabled
  WScript.Echo "Caption: " & objItem.Caption
 Next

Loop
```

So far, this script is just displaying the caption and current DHCP status for each network adapter configuration. I need to add some logic to enable DHCP if it isn't already enabled.

```
Dim strComputer
Dim objWMIService
Dim colItems
Dim objFSO, objTS

Set objFSO = CreateObject("Scripting.FileSystemObject")
Set objTS = objFSO.OpenTextFile("c:\input.txt")

Do Until objTS.AtEndOfStream

 strComputer = objTS.ReadLine
 Set objWMIService = GetObject("winmgmts:\\" & _
  strComputer & "\root\cimv2")
```

*continues*

```
  Set colItems = objWMIService.ExecQuery( _
   "Select * from Win32_NetworkAdapterConfiguration",,48)
  For Each objItem in colItems
   If objItem.DHCPEnabled = True Then
    WScript.Echo "DHCP Enabled for: " & objItem.Caption
   Else
    WScript.Echo "Enabling DHCP for: " & objItem.Caption
    objItem.EnableDHCP
   End If
  Next

Loop
```

This modification has an `If...Then` construct examining the `DHCPEnabled` property, rather than simply displaying the property. If the property isn't True, the script executes the `EnableDHCP` method to turn on DHCP for the network adapter configuration. In either event, an appropriate message is displayed to let me know what's happening.

## Alternative Methods

As I mentioned earlier in this chapter, you're likely to run across other ways of performing WMI queries. For example, here's a short script that returns some information about a remote machine named Server1.

```
Set System = GetObject("winmgmts:{impersonationLevel=" & _
 "impersonate}!//server1/root/cimv2:" & _
 "Win32_ComputerSystem=""SERVER1""")

WScript.Echo System.Caption
WScript.Echo System.PrimaryOwnerName
WScript.Echo System.Domain
WScript.Echo System.SystemType
```

This doesn't follow the template-style query I've been using so far; in fact, it doesn't even use WQL. However, this example is functionally the same as the following one.

```
On Error Resume Next
Dim strComputer
```

```
Dim objWMIService
Dim colItems

strComputer = "server1"
Set objWMIService = GetObject("winmgmts:\\" & _
 strComputer & "\root\cimv2")
Set colItems = objWMIService.ExecQuery( _
 "Select * from Win32_ComputerSystem WHERE " & _
 "Name = 'SERVER1'",,48)
For Each objItem in colItems
 WScript.Echo "Caption: " & objItem.Caption
 WScript.Echo "Domain: " & objItem.Domain
 WScript.Echo "PrimaryOwnerName: " & objItem.PrimaryOwnerName
 WScript.Echo "SystemType: " & objItem.SystemType
Next
```

There is practically no difference between the two. The first example uses `GetObject` to connect directly to a specified server's WMI service and retrieve a particular class (`Win32_ComputerSystem`) where the system's name is "SERVER1." The retrieved object is a WMI object, and can be used to display whatever information you want.

The second example uses the template I've used throughout this chapter (and the previous one) to fire off a WQL query, return an object collection, and then display the information. Which one is better? Technically, they're both identical. The second one has the benefit of being consistent with my other examples, and it lends itself easily to modification so that you can write more complex WQL queries to meet your specific needs. You're welcome to use either style, or even both if that's what you want to do.

## Review

You've seen several examples of how to query basic WMI information in this chapter. I showed you how to look for the proper WMI classes, write more complex WQL queries, and test your queries. I also showed you how to start with a wizard-created template script and modify it to suit your needs, even if those needs involve changing something or performing an action, rather than simply displaying or retrieving WMI information. I've shown you examples of how WMI can be queried in different ways that will help you work with the many different examples you'll find on the Web and in other publications.

All of this will help you work with most of the simpler WMI classes. Some classes, however, represent more complex bodies of information, and have to be handled a bit differently. I'll cover those in the next chapter.

**COMING UP**

Working with complex information like shares, file and folder security, and user accounts requires you to build on the basic WMI skills you've learned so far. In the next chapter, I'll introduce you to associator classes and references in WMI, and explain how to work with more complex information and interrelated WMI classes.

CHAPTER 19

# Querying Complex WMI Information

**IN THIS CHAPTER**

You've seen how to perform basic WMI queries and work with the results; in this chapter, I'll explain how more complex classes interrelate with one another and how you can work with them inside of your scripts. You'll use these techniques for working with a number of security- and configuration-related tasks, and they'll truly make WMI a powerful administrative tool.

In the previous chapter, I briefly described how some WMI classes have complex interrelationships with other classes, and promised to show you—in this chapter—how to deal with the information contained in those relationships. I even mentioned specific WQL keywords, including REFERENCES OF and ASSOCIATORS OF—that are used to query these complex classes. Now it's time to dive in and put them to work.

## Understanding WMI Relationships

Probably the best way to understand the more complex WMI classes is with an example. Take `Win32_NetworkAdapter`. This class represents a physical network adapter inside a computer, whether it's an Ethernet adapter, an IEEE 1394 (FireWire) adapter, or whatever. If you examine the class' properties in the WMI documentation, you'll see that it only includes properties that deal with the physical hardware, such as its MAC address, whether it supports media sense (which tells Windows that a cable is unplugged), its maximum speed, and so forth.

WMI also defines a class named `Win32_NetworkAdapterConfiguration`, which includes the software aspects of a network adapter, including its IP address, IPX settings, and so forth. In theory, a single hardware adapter can have multiple possible configurations, which is why these properties are split into two classes. In fact, it's theoretically possible for one configuration to be shared by two different physical adapters. WMI needs some way to relate the two classes to one another, and that way is called an *associator class.* In this case, the associator class is `Win32_NetworkAdapterSetting`, which associates a network adapter and its configuration settings.

An examination of `Win32_NetworkAdapterSetting`'s documentation reveals that it has only two properties: `Win32_NetworkAdapter` and `Win32_NetworkAdapterConfiguration`. In other words, the two properties refer back to the associated classes. The associator, then, represents a single combination of adapter and configuration, as illustrated in Figure 19.1.

You'll notice that neither the Scriptomatic nor the PrimalScript WMI Query Wizard includes `Win32_NetworkAdapterSetting` on their list of classes. That's because neither tool is designed to deal with associator classes, so you are on your own for working with them. You can get a bit of help from the Wbemtest tool, however. (I showed you how to use Wbemtest in Chapter 17.)

First, run Wbemtest and connect to your local computer's root\cimv2 namespace. Then, click **Open Class** and open the `Win32_NetworkAdapterSetting` class. You should see a dialog box like the one in Figure 19.2. Of particular interest are the two main properties: `Element` and `Setting`. According to the WMI documentation, this class' `Element` represents a `Win32_NetworkAdapter`, and the `Setting` represents an associated `Win32_NetworkAdapterConfiguration`.

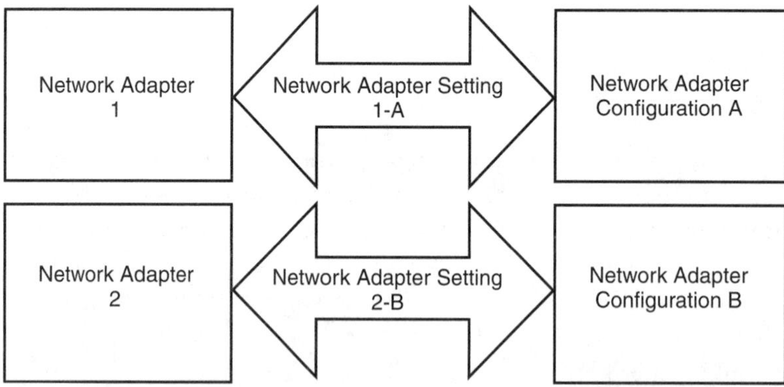


**Figure 19.1** Associating two classes

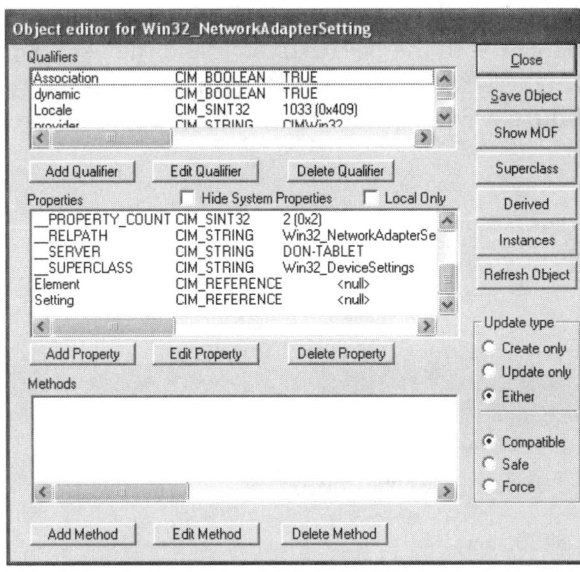


**Figure 19.2** Examining the Win32_NetworkAdapterSetting class

Click **Instances** to retrieve all instances of this class. The dialog box that appears lists one line for each combination of adapter and configuration. You'll notice that the `Element` property is listed as something like "\\\\computername\\root\\cimv2:Win32_NetworkAdapter.DeviceID=\"1\"." The `Setting` property will look something like "*computername*\\root\\cimv2:Win32_NetworkAdapterConfiguration.Index=1." Here's how to interpret that.

- First, understand that both backslashes and double quotes are illegal characters for WMI. The backslash is actually an *escape* character, meaning it's used to prefix illegal characters. So `\\` should be interpreted as a single backslash, and `\"` should be interpreted as a single quote.
- The first part of each property value is the namespace: *computername*\root\cimv2. The property's value derives from this namespace.
- The next part of each property value is the class name, followed by a period and the property name.
- The property name is followed by an equal sign, and then the associated property value.

In this example, the `Element` represents the instance of `Win32_NetworkAdapter` with the `DeviceID` of 1, and the `Setting` represents the instance of `Win32_NetworkAdapterConfiguration` with the `Index` of 1.

A quick-and-dirty way to query this information would be something like the following.

```
Dim oWMI, oSettings, oSetting
Dim oAdapter, oConfig

'connect to WMI
Set oWMI = GetObject("winmgmts:\\.\root\cimv2")

'retrieve all settings
Set oSettings = oWMI.ExecQuery( _
 "SELECT * FROM Win32_NetworkAdapterSetting")

'go through all settings
For Each oSetting in oSettings

 'get the element
 Set oAdapter = GetObject("winmgmts:" & _
  oSetting.Element)
 WScript.Echo "Adapter: " & oAdapter.Caption

 'get the setting
 Set oConfig = GetObject("winmgmts:" & _
  oSetting.Setting)
 WScript.Echo "   DHCP: " & oConfig.DHCPEnabled

 'print a divider
 WScript.Echo String(20,"-")

Next
```

This script uses a WQL query to retrieve all instances of `Win32_NetworkAdapterSetting`. Because each `Element` and `Setting` property is a complete WMI path, they are used to retrieve the appropriate `Win32_NetworkAdapter` and `Win32_NetworkAdapterConfiguration` classes. The script then prints one piece of information from each class, just to prove it's doing something. This is a standardized way that you can work with associator classes.

- Retrieve the associator class
- Use its properties, such as Element and Setting in this example, to retrieve the associated classes.
- Work with the associated classes however you like.

Not all associator classes use Element and Setting. For example, Win32_PrinterShare associates a local printer and a network share, from Win32_Printer and Win32_Share. Win32_PrinterShare uses Antecedent to refer to a Win32_Printer instance, and Dependent to refer to a Win32_Share class, instead of Element and Setting. However, you can query the associator class and its associations in exactly the same way.

```
Dim oWMI, oPShares, oPShare
Dim oPrinter, oShare

'connect to WMI
Set oWMI = GetObject("winmgmts:\\.\root\cimv2")

'retrieve all settings
Set oPShares = oWMI.ExecQuery( _
 "SELECT * FROM Win32_PrinterShare")

'go through all settings
For Each oPShare in oPShares

 'get the element
 Set oPrinter = GetObject("winmgmts:" & _
  oPShare.Antecedent)
 WScript.Echo "Printer: " & oPrinter.Name

 'get the setting
 Set oShare = GetObject("winmgmts:" & _
  oPShare.Dependent)
 WScript.Echo "  Share: " & oShare.Name

 'print a divider
 WScript.Echo String(20,"-")

Next
```

Note that all I've done in this case is change the variable names and property names. The structure of this example is identical to the first.

## Associating WMI Instances

Hopefully, my previous two examples make it easier for you to understand WMI associations. However, they're bad examples for truly working with associated classes. Why? Because you aren't ever going to begin knowing which instance of the associator class you want; you're going to begin with one of the associated classes instead. Using the preceding technique, suppose you want to find the shares for a particular printer. You'd have to

- Get the correct `Win32_Printer` class first to get its `DeviceID`.
- Query `Win32_PrinterShares` for all instances where the `Antecedent` property references the `DeviceID` you're looking for.
- Take the results of that query and retrieve all referenced instances of `Win32_Share`.

### ASSOCIATORS OF

The aforementioned technique is an awkward way to get the information, and that's why WQL offers the `ASSOCIATORS OF` command. Suppose you have a printer with a device ID of "LaserJet 5." You've created three or four shares of the printer, each with different permissions or whatever. You want to use WMI to retrieve the name of each share, and list the maximum concurrent number of users allowed to use each share. You could write a WQL query like this: `ASSOCIATORS OF {Win32_Printer.DeviceID = "LaserJet 5"}`. Note that `ASSOCIATORS OF` replaces the `SELECT`, property list, `FROM`, and class name elements of a more traditional WQL query. Also note that the class must be listed in curly braces `{}` not parentheses. That messes me up every time. Figure 19.3 shows the results of this query in Wbemtest (assuming you have a printer named LaserJet 5, that is; for this example, I used a different printer name).

It turns out there are several associated classes:

- `Win32_PrinterDriver`
- `Win32_PrinterConfiguration`
- `Win32_ComputerSystem`
- `CIM_DataFile`
- `Win32_Share`

You can restrict the list just to the `Win32_Share` class by modifying the query a bit.

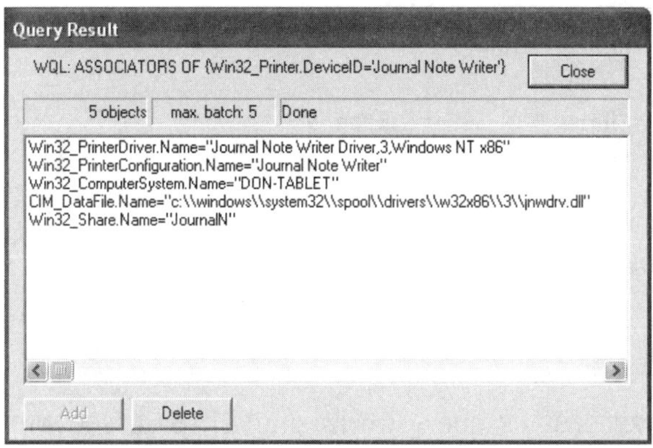


**Figure 19.3** Results of the ASSOCIATORS OF query

```
ASSOCIATORS OF {Win32_Printer.DeviceID = "LaserJet 5"}
 WHERE AssocClass = Win32_PrinterShare
```

This modified query just returns an instance of `Win32_Share` for each share that exists for the printer. Note that the query does *not* return `Win32_PrinterShare` instances; WMI is smart enough to know that although `Win32_PrinterShare` is the associator class, you're really after the other side of the relationship, which is `Win32_Share`.

The following script displays each share name for the specified printer, and the number of connections each accepts.

```
Dim oWMI, oPShares, oPShare
Dim oShare

'connect to WMI
Set oWMI = GetObject("winmgmts:\\.\root\cimv2")

'retrieve all settings
Set oPShares = oWMI.ExecQuery("ASSOCIATORS OF
  {Win32_Printer.DeviceID='LaserJet 5'} WHERE AssocClass =
  Win32_PrinterShare")

For Each oShare in oPShares

 'display share info
 If oShare.AllowMaximum = False Then
  WScript.Echo "Share " & oShare.Name & _
```

*continues*

```
    " allows " & oShare.MaximumAllowed & _
    " concurrent connections."
  Else
   WScript.Echo "Share " & oShare.Name & _
    " allows max connections."
  End If

Next
```

## REFERENCES OF

The WQL `REFERENCES OF` query works similarly to `ASSOCIATORS OF`. It's designed to return all association instances that refer to a specified source instance. However, whereas `ASSOCIATORS OF` attempts to retrieve the endpoint instances (such as mapping `Win32_Printer` all the way through to `Win32_Share`), `REFERENCES OF` only attempts to find the associator classes (such as `Win32_PrinterShare`).

For example, use Wbetmtest to execute the following query.

```
REFERENCES OF
 {Win32_Printer.DeviceID = 'printername'}
```

Of course, replace *printername* with a valid printer on your computer.

---

**NOTE** Remember, to execute a query in Wbemtest, first connect to the \default\cimv2 namespace. Then, click the **Query** button and type the query into the text box.

---

The query returns several classes:

- `Win32_DriverForDevice`
- `Win32_PrinterSetting`
- `Win32_SystemDevices`
- `Win32_PrinterShare` (if the printer is shared)
- `Win32_PrinterDriverDll`

These are all of the associator classes that refer to the specified `Win32_Printer` instance. If you want to get the endpoint of the association—in other words, the actual driver, printer setting, device, share, or driver DLL—you'd use `ASSOCIATORS OF` instead. I don't find much need for

REFERENCES OF in my administrative scripts, because I'm usually looking for the other end of the association, not the middle point.

## Using WHERE with ASSOCIATIONS OF and REFERENCES OF

Both the ASSOCIATIONS OF and REFERENCES OF queries support a WHERE clause; I showed you an example using the AssocClass keyword earlier. REFERENCES OF accepts the following keywords in its optional WHERE clause.

- ClassDefsOnly. This causes the query to return the class definition, rather than instances of the class being queried.
- RequiredQualifier. This allows you to specify a qualifier that all returned classes must meet. For example, RequiredQualifier = Dependent restricts query results to those association classes that have a property named Dependent.
- ResultClass. This allows you to restrict the query results to a particular class, such as ResultClass = Win32_PrinterShare. This cannot be used in conjunction with ClassDefsOnly.

ASSOCIATORS OF supports different WHERE options.

- AssocClass. This allows you to specify the associator class that will be used. Use this, as I did in my earlier example, to restrict your results to those from a particular class. For example, AssocClass = Win32_PrinterShare.
- ClassDefsOnly. This forces the query to return the definition for the result classes, rather than the actual instances of the class. This cannot be used with ResultClass.
- RequiredAssocQualifier. This tells the query to only return instances that are related by means of an associator class that includes the specified qualifier. Sound complex? Here's an example: RequiredAssocQualifier = Dependent. With this specified, the query only returns endpoint instances whose relationship to the queried class is through an associator class that has a property named Dependent.
- RequiredQualifier. This specifies a property that must be present in the endpoint classes returned by the query. For example, RequiredQualifier = AllowMaximum restricts the associated classes returned by the query to those with an AllowMaximum property.

- ResultClass. This specifies that the query only return specified classes. For example, ResultClass = Win32_Share ensures that only instances of Win32_Share are returned.

All of these WHERE clause keywords can be combined (except as I've noted here), and do not require commas or any other separation. For example:

```
ASSOCIATORS OF {Win32_Printer.DeviceID = 'LaserJet5'}
 WHERE
 ResultClass = Win32_Share
 RequiredQualifier = AllowMaximum
```

Don't be tempted to include an AND keyword like you would in a traditional WHERE clause, because WMI will return an error.

## Writing the Query

You've seen the whole associated class thing in action, but I want to start fresh with a new example and walk you through the entire query- and script-creation process. In the last chapter, I showed you how to set all the network adapters on a computer to use DHCP. In this chapter, I want to be more specific, and only modify the properties of a specific network adapter within the computer. More specifically, I want to

- Read a list of computer names from a text file
- Connect to WMI on each computer and locate the network adapter named "Local Area Connection"
- Ensure that each configuration for that adapter is set to use DHCP

It seems like the following query should do what I want.

```
ASSOCIATORS OF
{Win32_NetworkAdapter.NetConnectionID="Local Area Connection"}
WHERE
RESULTCLASS = Win32_NetworkAdapterConfiguration
```

That should pull all Win32_NetworkAdapter instances where the NetConnectionID is "Local Area Connection," and then retrieve the associated Win32_NetworkAdapterConfiguration instances.

## Testing the Query

Wbemtest is the place to test my new query. Unfortunately, executing it yields an error: "Invalid object path." Uh-oh.

I'm guessing the problem is that `Win32_NetworkAdapter` and `Win32_NetworkAdapterConfiguration` are associated through `Win32_NetworkAdapterSetting`, which uses `Win32_NetworkAdapter.DeviceID` and `Win32_NetworkAdapterConfiguration.Index` to perform the association. In other words, the associator class has no clue about `Win32_NetworkAdapter.NetConnectionID`.

Just to confirm that, I'll retest the query using this.

```
ASSOCIATORS OF {Win32_NetworkAdapter.DeviceID="1"} WHERE
RESULTCLASS = Win32_NetworkAdapterConfiguration
```

Sure enough, this query returns the expected instance of `Win32_NetworkAdapterConfiguration`. Here's what I'm going to have to do.

- Read a list of computer names from a text file.
- Connect to WMI on each computer and locate the network adapter named "Local Area Connection."
- Get the `DeviceID` from the `Win32_NetworkAdapter` instances returned.
- For each instance, query the associated `Win32_NetworkAdapterConfiguration` instances.
- For each of *those* instances, ensure that each configuration for that adapter is set to use DHCP.

I just need to code these actions into a script.

## Writing the Query in VBScript

Now it's time to incorporate the query into a script. This time, I'll start with the shell of the script, which will read the computer names from the text file.

```
Dim oFSO, oTS, sComputer

Set oFSO = CreateObject("Scripting.FileSystemObject")
Set oTS = oFSO.OpenTextFile("c:\input.txt")
```

*continues*

```
Do Until oTS.AtEndOfStream

 sComputer = oTS.ReadLine

Loop
```

That is easy enough. Now, for each, I need to retrieve a specified instance of `Win32_NetworkAdapter`. The caption I'm looking for—"Local Area Connection"—is stored in a property named `NetConnectionID`.

---

**TIP** How did I know which property to use? Simple: Wbemtest. I clicked **EnumInstances** and typed **Win32_NetworkAdapter** as the superclass name. Then, I double-clicked on the first instance that was returned to display its properties. I scrolled down, looking for "Local Area Connection" in the values column, and I found it in a property named `NetConnectionID`. If I hadn't found "Local Area Connection" at all, I would have tried the next instance in the list, and kept browsing until I found it.

---

Actually, I don't want to retrieve the `Win32_NetworkAdapter` instance at all. Instead, I need to retrieve all associated `Win32_NetworkAdapterConfiguration` instances. However, as I discovered earlier, I need to retrieve the `DeviceID` on my own, based on a simpler WQL query. Here's the modified script.

```
Dim oFSO, oTS, sComputer
Dim oWMI, oConfigs, oConfig, oAdapters, oAdapter

Set oFSO = CreateObject("Scripting.FileSystemObject")
Set oTS = oFSO.OpenTextFile("c:\input.txt")

Do Until oTS.AtEndOfStream

 sComputer = oTS.ReadLine

 oWMI = GetObject("winmgmts:\\" & _
  sComputer & "\root\cimv2")

 Set oAdapters = oWMI.ExecQuery( _
  "SELECT DeviceID FROM Win32_NetworkAdapter " & _
  "WHERE NetConnectionID = 'Local Area Connection')

 For Each oAdapter in oAdapters
```

```
  Set oConfigs = oWMI.ExecQuery( _
   "ASSOCIATORS OF {Win32_NetworkAdapter.DeviceID='" & _
   oAdapter.DeviceID & "'} " & _
   "WHERE RESULTCLASS = Win32_NetworkAdapterConfiguration")

 Next

Loop
```

Of course, simply retrieving the class doesn't do anything. Keep in mind that `oConfigs` will contain a collection of `Win32_NetworkAdapterConfiguration` instances, although in almost all cases the collection will only contain one instance. I'll need to loop through the instances and check each one to see if DHCP is enabled. Here's how.

```
Dim oFSO, oTS, sComputer
Dim oWMI, oConfigs, oConfig

Set oFSO = CreateObject("Scripting.FileSystemObject")
Set oTS = oFSO.OpenTextFile("c:\input.txt")

Do Until oTS.AtEndOfStream

 sComputer = oTS.ReadLine

 oWMI = GetObject("winmgmts:\\" & _
  sComputer & "\root\cimv2")

 Set oAdapters = oWMI.ExecQuery( _
  "SELECT DeviceID FROM Win32_NetworkAdapter " & _
  "WHERE NetConnectionID = 'Local Area Connection')

 For Each oAdapter in oAdapters

  Set oConfigs = oWMI.ExecQuery( _
   "ASSOCIATORS OF {Win32_NetworkAdapter.DeviceID='" & _
   oAdapter.DeviceID & "'} " & _
   "WHERE RESULTCLASS = Win32_NetworkAdapterConfiguration")

  For Each oConfig In oConfigs

   If oConfig.DHCPEnabled Then
    WScript.Echo "DHCP Enabled on " & sComputer
   Else
```

*continues*

```
    WScript.Echo "Enabling DHCP on " & sComputer
    oConfig.EnableDHCP
   End If

  Next

Next

Loop
```

That's it! The script will read the text file and set each computer's "Local Area Connection" to use DHCP. If you'd like to test it, Listing 19.1 shows the complete listing, along with in-line comments.

**Listing 19.1** *SetDHCP.vbs.* This script sets the Local Area Connection adapter to use DHCP for each computer named in text file.

```
Dim oFSO, oTS, sComputer
Dim oWMI, oConfigs, oConfig

'get a filesystemobject and open the input file
Set oFSO = CreateObject("Scripting.FileSystemObject")
Set oTS = oFSO.OpenTextFile("c:\input.txt")

'for each line of the input file...
Do Until oTS.AtEndOfStream

 'read the computer name from the file
 sComputer = oTS.ReadLine

 'connect to WMI on the remote computer
 oWMI = GetObject("winmgmts:\\" & _
  sComputer & "\root\cimv2")

 'query a collection of Win32_NetworkAdapter
 'instances that have a NetConnectionID of
 ' Local Area Connection
 Set oAdapters = oWMI.ExecQuery( _
  "SELECT DeviceID FROM Win32_NetworkAdapter " & _
  "WHERE NetConnectionID = 'Local Area Connection')

 'for each of those adapters...
 For Each oAdapter in oAdapters
```

```
  'query the associated network adapter configurations
  Set oConfigs = oWMI.ExecQuery( _
   "ASSOCIATORS OF {Win32_NetworkAdapter.DeviceID='" & _
   oAdapter.DeviceID & "'} " & _
   "WHERE RESULTCLASS = Win32_NetworkAdapterConfiguration'")

  'for each of those configurations...
  For Each oConfig In oConfigs

   'is DHCP enabled?
   If oConfig.DHCPEnabled Then

    'yes – display a message
    WScript.Echo "DHCP Enabled on " & sComputer

   Else

    'no – display a message and enable it
    WScript.Echo "Enabling DHCP on " & sComputer
    oConfig.EnableDHCP

   End If

  Next

Next

Loop
```

You'll need to provide the appropriate input file, c:\input.txt, in order to use this script.

## Another Example

This business of using associator classes is complicated, so I'm including an additional example of how they work. For this example, let's say you want to list all of the shared folders on a particular file server, along with the physical file path that each share represents. For each of those physical folders (or *directories*), you want to enable NTFS file compression. Here's what you need to do.

- Connect to WMI on a specified server.
- Retrieve a list of `Win32_Share` class instances that represent file shares (as opposed to printer or other shares)
- For each instance, retrieve the physical folder as a `Win32_Directory` class.
- For each physical folder, use the `Compress` method.

### ➤➤ Compressing All Shared Folders

Listing 19.2 shows the entire script you'll need to use.

**Listing 19.2** *CompressAll.vbs.* This script compresses all shared folders on a specified file server.

```
'get server name
strComputer = InputBox("Server name?")

'connect to WMI
Set objWMIService = GetObject("winmgmts:" & _
 "\\" & strComputer & "\root\cimv2")

'retrieve the list of shares
Set colShares = objWMIService.ExecQuery _
 ("SELECT * FROM Win32_Share WHERE " & _
 "Type = 0")

'for each share returned...
For Each objShare In colShares

 'retrieve the associated folders
 Set colFolders = objWMIService.ExecQuery _
  ("ASSOCIATORS OF {Win32_Share.Name='" & _
  objShare.Name & "'} WHERE " & _
  "AssocClass=Win32_ShareToDirectory")

 'for each folder returned...
 For Each objFolder in colFolders

  'is it already compressed?
  If objFolder.Compressed Then

   'yes - message
   Wscript.Echo objFolder.Name & " is already compressed."
```

```
    Else

     'no - message & compress it
     WScript.Echo "Compressing " & objFolder.Name
     objFolder.Comrpess

    End If

  Next

Next
```

You shouldn't need to make any modifications to this script to run it, and it should work with NT 4.0 and later servers.

### ➤➤ Compressing All Shared Folders—Explained

The script starts by simply asking for the server name. Provide the name of any NT 4.0 or later file server that's already running WMI.

```
'get server name
strComputer = InputBox("Server name?")
```

Next, the script connects to the WMI service on the remote computer.

```
'connect to WMI
Set objWMIService = GetObject("winmgmts:" & _
 "\\" & strComputer & "\root\cimv2")
```

The script now executes a simple WMI query to return all shares of type 0, which are shared folders. The WMI documentation for the `Win32_Share` class lists other types, including printers (1), devices (2), IPC shares (3), and administrative shares.

```
'retrieve the list of shares
Set colShares = objWMIService.ExecQuery _
 ("SELECT * FROM Win32_Share WHERE " & _
 "Type = 0")
```

A `For Each...Next` loop iterates through each file share.

```
'for each share returned...
For Each objShare In colShares
```

An ASSOCIATORS OF query is used to retrieve the associated folder (Win32_Directory) instances for the current Win32_Share instance. Notice that the associator class, Win32_ShareToDirectory, is specified.

```
'retrieve the associated folders
Set colFolders = objWMIService.ExecQuery _
 ("ASSOCIATORS OF {Win32_Share.Name='" & _
 objShare.Name & "'} WHERE " & _
 "AssocClass=Win32_ShareToDirectory")
```

A For Each...Next loop iterates through each folder returned. Under current Windows operating systems, this will be only one folder per share (although you might theorize that some future version would allow multiple, load-balanced physical folders per share, which is why WMI requires you to write the script this way).

```
'for each folder returned...
For Each objFolder in colFolders
```

The script checks to see if the folder is already compressed, and behaves accordingly.

```
'is it already compressed?
If objFolder.Compressed Then

 'yes - message
 Wscript.Echo objFolder.Name & " is already compressed."

Else

 'no - message & compress it
 WScript.Echo "Compressing " & objFolder.Name
 objFolder.Comrpess

End If
```

Finally, the script closes the two open For Each...Next loops.

```
    Next

Next
```

The powerful and easy `ASSOCIATORS OF` query makes scripts like this easier to write. Without it, you'd be stuck with many more `For…Next` loops and a much-harder-to-maintain script.

## Review

In this chapter, I've shown you how different WMI classes can be related to one another through associator classes. I've also introduced you to the WQL `ASSOCIATORS OF` query, which allows you to query those relationships. You've learned how to use Wbemtest to test your queries, incorporate your queries into a script, and then utilize the query results to perform administrative tasks.

By now, you should have a solid understanding of how WMI works from within a script, and how you can use it to both query and modify configuration settings within your computers. You should feel comfortable working with the simpler queries that Scriptomatic or the PrimalScript WMI Query Wizard can generate for you, and you should be comfortable writing more complex queries that utilize WMI associations and class relationships. As always, of course, the toughest part about WMI is figuring out which classes to query, but hopefully by now you're becoming comfortable with the WMI class reference in the MSDN Library, and you're able to browse through the class list and select the appropriate classes.

**COMING UP**

You've seen how to work with all kinds of WMI information, so it's time to pull everything together into a complete script. In the next chapter, I'll provide you with two complete WMI and ADSI sample scripts, so you can see how these technologies are used in real-world situations. Then, in Part IV, I'll show you how to leverage everything you've learned so far to create Web-based administrative scripts that make a great addition to your administrative utility belt.

CHAPTER 20

# Putting It All Together: Your First WMI/ADSI Script

**IN THIS CHAPTER**

It's time to leverage what you've learned about ADSI and WMI scripting. In this chapter, I'll walk you through the entire design and creation process for a new script. In addition to demonstrating a useful new purpose for WMI and ADSI, this chapter will help strengthen your script design skills.

By now, you should have a good idea of what WMI and ADSI can do for you. In this chapter, I'll walk you through the complete design process for an entirely new script. This time, I'll use both WMI and ADSI in the same script. The script's job will be to check in on every computer in an Active Directory or NT domain and query some information about its operating systems. I want the script to output this information to a text file on a file server. The information I want to collect includes operating system version, service pack level, number of processors in the machine, maximum physical memory in the machine, and so forth. This is a useful way to quickly inventory a network and see what machines might need to be upgraded before deploying a new application, or to see what machines don't have the latest service pack applied.

## Designing the Script

My script is a reasonably complex undertaking, so it helps to break it down into manageable tasks. I need the script to do three things:

1. Query a list of computers from the domain.
2. Query information from each computer.
3. Write information out to a text file.

The last bit is probably the easiest. I can use the FileSystemObject to open a text file, write information to it, and then close the text file. Something like the following would work.

```
Dim oFSO, oFile
Set oFSO = CreateObject("Scripting.FileSystemObject")
Set oFile = oFSO.CreateTextFile("output.txt")
oFile.Write "Information"
oFile.Close
```

For more information on using the FileSystemObject, refer to Chapter 12.

Querying a list of computers from the domain shouldn't be too hard, either. If I want the script to work with both NT and Active Directory domains, I need to use the WinNT ADSI provider, because only that provider works with both domains. I can query all of the objects in the domain, and then use an `If...Then` construct to work with only the computer objects. Code such as the following should do the trick.

```
Dim oDomain
Set oDomain = GetObject("WinNT://" & sDomain)
Dim oObject, sComputerName, sDetails
For Each oObject In oDomain

 'is this object a computer?
 If oObject.Class = "Computer" Then

  'yes – do something with it

 End If
Next
```

For more information on querying domains by using ADSI, see Chapter 14, and see "Querying Domain Information" in Chapter 15.

Pulling the operating system (OS) information is tougher. WMI seems like the way to go, but WMI has about three gazillion classes. Which one do I need? Fortunately, I have a way to cheat. My primary script editor is Sapien Technology's PrimalScript 3.0, and it includes a WMI Script Wizard.

**NOTE** A trial version of PrimalScript 3.0 is included on the CD that accompanies this book.

Running the wizard displays the dialog box shown in Figure 20.1. The left side of the dialog box shows a list of every WMI class that my computer knows about. Scrolling through the list, I find that there's a class named `Win32_OperatingSystem`. That seems like a good place to start.

Clicking the `Win32_OperatingSystem` class changes the dialog box to look like the one shown in Figure 20.2. Here, the wizard has filled in a sample script capable of querying information from the selected class. I see things like service pack level and operating system version, so this is probably the class I want. The wizard offers an **Insert** button to immediately insert this code into my script, and a **Copy** button to copy the code to the clipboard. Listing 20.1 shows the complete wizard code.

**NOTE** I've added line breaks and line continuation characters (_) to Listing 20.1 so that it will fit in this book.

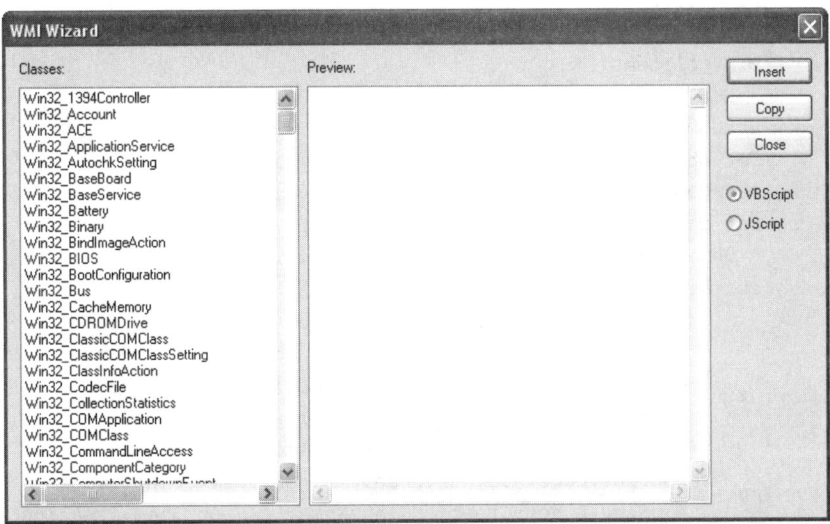


**Figure 20.1** The WMI Wizard starts with a list of all available WMI classes.

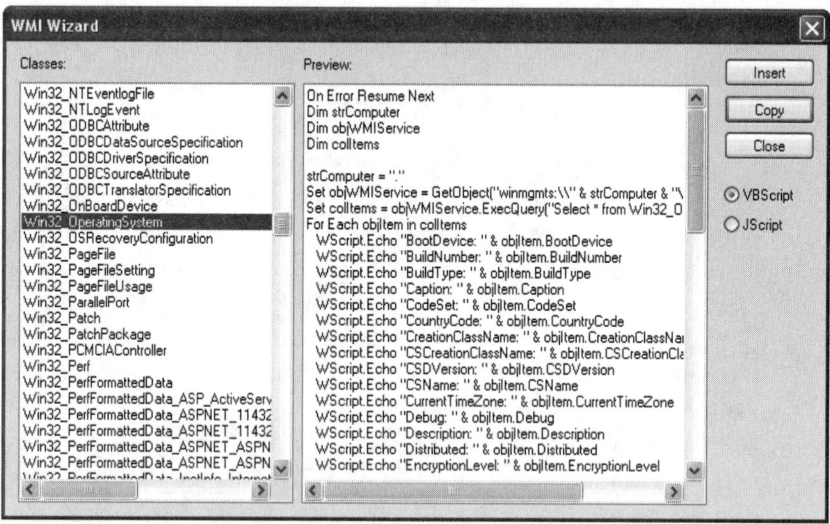

**Figure 20.2** The wizard generates sample code to query the selected class.

**Listing 20.1** *WizardCode.vbs*. This code queries the Win32_OperatingSystem class and outputs all of the class' attributes and their values.

```
On Error Resume Next
Dim strComputer
Dim objWMIService
Dim colItems

strComputer = "."
Set objWMIService = GetObject("winmgmts:\\" & _
 strComputer & "\root\cimv2")
Set colItems = objWMIService.ExecQuery( _
 "Select * from Win32_OperatingSystem",,48)
For Each objItem in colItems
      WScript.Echo "BootDevice: " & objItem.BootDevice
      WScript.Echo "BuildNumber: " & objItem.BuildNumber
      WScript.Echo "BuildType: " & objItem.BuildType
      WScript.Echo "Caption: " & objItem.Caption
      WScript.Echo "CodeSet: " & objItem.CodeSet
      WScript.Echo "CountryCode: " & objItem.CountryCode
      WScript.Echo "CreationClassName: " & objItem.CreationClassName
      WScript.Echo "CSCreationClassName: " & _
  objItem.CSCreationClassName
      WScript.Echo "CSDVersion: " & objItem.CSDVersion
```

```
    WScript.Echo "CSName: " & objItem.CSName
    WScript.Echo "CurrentTimeZone: " & objItem.CurrentTimeZone
    WScript.Echo "Debug: " & objItem.Debug
    WScript.Echo "Description: " & objItem.Description
    WScript.Echo "Distributed: " & objItem.Distributed
    WScript.Echo "EncryptionLevel: " & objItem.EncryptionLevel
    WScript.Echo "ForegroundApplicationBoost: " & _
objItem.ForegroundApplicationBoost
    WScript.Echo "FreePhysicalMemory: " & _
objItem.FreePhysicalMemory
    WScript.Echo "FreeSpaceInPagingFiles: " & _
objItem.FreeSpaceInPagingFiles
    WScript.Echo "FreeVirtualMemory: " & objItem.FreeVirtualMemory
    WScript.Echo "InstallDate: " & objItem.InstallDate
    WScript.Echo "LargeSystemCache: " & objItem.LargeSystemCache
    WScript.Echo "LastBootUpTime: " & objItem.LastBootUpTime
    WScript.Echo "LocalDateTime: " & objItem.LocalDateTime
    WScript.Echo "Locale: " & objItem.Locale
    WScript.Echo "Manufacturer: " & objItem.Manufacturer
    WScript.Echo "MaxNumberOfProcesses: " &
objItem.MaxNumberOfProcesses
    WScript.Echo "MaxProcessMemorySize: " &
objItem.MaxProcessMemorySize
    WScript.Echo "Name: " & objItem.Name
    WScript.Echo "NumberOfLicensedUsers: " &
objItem.NumberOfLicensedUsers
    WScript.Echo "NumberOfProcesses: " & objItem.NumberOfProcesses
    WScript.Echo "NumberOfUsers: " & objItem.NumberOfUsers
    WScript.Echo "Organization: " & objItem.Organization
    WScript.Echo "OSLanguage: " & objItem.OSLanguage
    WScript.Echo "OSProductSuite: " & objItem.OSProductSuite
    WScript.Echo "OSType: " & objItem.OSType
    WScript.Echo "OtherTypeDescription: " &
objItem.OtherTypeDescription
    WScript.Echo "PlusProductID: " & objItem.PlusProductID
    WScript.Echo "PlusVersionNumber: " & objItem.PlusVersionNumber
    WScript.Echo "Primary: " & objItem.Primary
    WScript.Echo "ProductType: " & objItem.ProductType
    WScript.Echo "QuantumLength: " & objItem.QuantumLength
    WScript.Echo "QuantumType: " & objItem.QuantumType
    WScript.Echo "RegisteredUser: " & objItem.RegisteredUser
    WScript.Echo "SerialNumber: " & objItem.SerialNumber
    WScript.Echo "ServicePackMajorVersion: " & _
```

*continues*

```
objItem.ServicePackMajorVersion
      WScript.Echo "ServicePackMinorVersion: " & _
  objItem.ServicePackMinorVersion
      WScript.Echo "SizeStoredInPagingFiles: " & _
  objItem.SizeStoredInPagingFiles
      WScript.Echo "Status: " & objItem.Status
      WScript.Echo "SuiteMask: " & objItem.SuiteMask
      WScript.Echo "SystemDevice: " & objItem.SystemDevice
      WScript.Echo "SystemDirectory: " & objItem.SystemDirectory
      WScript.Echo "SystemDrive: " & objItem.SystemDrive
      WScript.Echo "TotalSwapSpaceSize: " & _
  objItem.TotalSwapSpaceSize
      WScript.Echo "TotalVirtualMemorySize: " & _
  objItem.TotalVirtualMemorySize
      WScript.Echo "TotalVisibleMemorySize: " & _
  objItem.TotalVisibleMemorySize
      WScript.Echo "Version: " & objItem.Version
      WScript.Echo "WindowsDirectory: " & objItem.WindowsDirectory
Next
```

The wizard's code pulls more information than I want, and it's displaying the information in message boxes, rather than writing them to a file, but the code makes a great place to start. I can easily modify it to meet my needs.

The script is designed! I identified the three major tasks that the script needs to be able to complete, and I've created some prototype code that can be adapted to the script's exact requirements. In short, I now know how to do everything I need; I just need to rearrange it and customize it.

### What, No Wizard?

If you're not using PrimalScript, there are some other tools you can use to make WMI scripting easier. In Chapter 18, for example, I introduced Microsoft's Scriptomatic tool, which performs a similar function to the PrimalScript WMI Wizard. You can also dive into the WMI documentation in the MSDN Library (http://msdn.microsoft.com/library), which documents each WMI class and includes some scripting examples.

## Writing Functions and Subroutines

The one bit of functionality that seems to be standalone is the code generated by the wizard, which will do my WMI querying for me. I may need to use that code in another script someday, and I'll definitely be using it over and over in the script I'm writing now, so it makes sense to write it as a function.

I want the function to accept a computer name, query that computer for specific operating system information, and then compile all that information into a neatly formatted string. The function should return the string to the main script, which can then write it to a file or whatever.

Adapting the wizard's code isn't too difficult. Listing 20.2 shows my new `GetOSIno()` function. Note that this isn't intended to be run as a standalone script; as a function, it must be called by another script, which must provide the name of the computer to connect to as the function's input parameter.

**Listing 20.2** *GetOSInfo.vbs.* This function queries a computer's operating system information and returns the results in a string.

```
Function GetOSInfo(sComputer)

      'declare variables
      Dim objWMIService
      Dim colItems
      Dim strOutput

      'get WMI service
      Set objWMIService = GetObject("winmgmts:\\" & _
       strComputer & "\root\cimv2")

      'get item collection
      Set colItems = objWMIService.ExecQuery( _
       "Select * from Win32_OperatingSystem",,48)

      'init output string
      sOutput = String(70,"-")
      sOutput = sOutput & sComputer

      'append info to output string
      For Each objItem in colItems
```

*continues*

```
        strOutput = strOutput & "BuildNumber: " & _
         objItem.BuildNumber & vbCrLf
        strOutput = strOutput & "BuildType: " & _
         objItem.BuildType & vbCrLf
        strOutput = strOutput & "Caption: " & _
         objItem.Caption & vbCrLf
        strOutput = strOutput & "EncryptionLevel: " & _
         objItem.EncryptionLevel & vbCrLf
        strOutput = strOutput & "InstallDate: " & _
         objItem.InstallDate & vbCrLf
        strOutput = strOutput & "Manufacturer: " & _
         objItem.Manufacturer & vbCrLf
        strOutput = strOutput & "MaxNumberOfProcesses: " & _
         objItem.MaxNumberOfProcesses & vbCrLf
strOutput = strOutput & "MaxProcessMemorySize: " & _
         objItem.MaxProcessMemorySize & vbCrLf
 strOutput = strOutput & "Name: " & _
         objItem.Name & vbCrLf
        strOutput = strOutput & _
         "NumberOfLicensedUsers: " & _
         objItem.NumberOfLicensedUsers & vbCrLf
        strOutput = strOutput & "NumberOfProcesses: " & _
         objItem.NumberOfProcesses & vbCrLf
        strOutput = strOutput & "NumberOfUsers: " & _
         objItem.NumberOfUsers & vbCrLf
        strOutput = strOutput & "OSProductSuite: " & _
         objItem.OSProductSuite & vbCrLf
        strOutput = strOutput & "OSType: " & _
         objItem.OSType & vbCrLf
        strOutput = strOutput & "OtherTypeDescription: " & _
         objItem.OtherTypeDescription & vbCrLf
        strOutput = strOutput & "Primary: " & _
         objItem.Primary & vbCrLf
        strOutput = strOutput & "ProductType: " & _
         objItem.ProductType & vbCrLf
        strOutput = strOutput & "RegisteredUser: " & _
         objItem.RegisteredUser & vbCrLf
        strOutput = strOutput & "SerialNumber: " & _
         objItem.SerialNumber & vbCrLf
        strOutput = strOutput & _
         "ServicePackMajorVersion: " & _
         objItem.ServicePackMajorVersion & vbCrLf
        strOutput = strOutput & _
         "ServicePackMinorVersion: " & _
```

```
            objItem.ServicePackMinorVersion & vbCrLf
           strOutput = strOutput & "Version: " & _
            objItem.Version & vbCrLf
           strOutput = strOutput & "WindowsDirectory: " & _
            objItem.WindowsDirectory & vbCrLf
     Next

 'return results
     GetOSInfo = sOutput

End Function
```

I didn't have to do much to adapt the script. First, I deleted all the lines that I didn't want in my script. I changed all the `WScript.Echo` commands to `strOutput = strOutput &`, which appends the information into a string rather than displays it in a message box. I also added `& vbCrLf` to the end of each line, which adds a carriage return and linefeed character. Those help keep the final output file looking nice.

I also dressed up the code at the beginning of the function.

```
'declare variables
Dim objWMIService
Dim colItems
Dim strOutput

'get WMI service
Set objWMIService = GetObject("winmgmts:\\" & _
 strComputer & "\root\cimv2")

'get item collection
Set colItems = objWMIService.ExecQuery( _
 "Select * from Win32_OperatingSystem",,48)

'init output string
sOutput = String(70,"-")
sOutput = sOutput & sComputer
```

I added some comments to document the code—PrimalScript isn't so good about that—and I initialized my `sOutput` variable. I also started `sOut-put` off to contain a line of 70 hyphens, and the name of the computer I'm querying. These extra touches help make the final output file easier to read and more useful.

## Writing the Main Script

The function was probably the toughest part to write; with that out of the way, I can adapt my prototype code to create the main script, shown in Listing 20.3.

**Listing 20.3** *MainScript.vbs.* Queries the domain, creates the output file, and calls the custom function I already wrote.

```
Dim sDomain
sDomain = InputBox("Enter domain to inventory")

'connect to domain and retrieve
'a list of member objects
Dim oDomain
Set oDomain = GetObject("WinNT://" & sDomain)

'get the filesystemobject
Dim oFSO
Set oFSO = CreateObject("Scripting.FileSystemObject")

'open an output file
Dim oOutput
Set oOutput = oFSO.CreateTextFile("\\server1\public\output.txt")

'run through the objects
Dim oObject, sComputerName, sDetails
For Each oObject In oDomain

 'is this object a computer?
 If oObject.Class = "Computer" Then

  'yes - get computer name
  sComputerName = oObject.Name

  'get OS info
  sDetails = GetOSInfo(sComputerName)
```

```
    'write info to the file
    oOutput.Write sDetails

  End If
Next

'close the output file
oOutput.Close

'release objects
Set oOutput = Nothing
Set oFSO = Nothing
Set oObject = nothing
Set oDomain = Nothing

'display completion message
WScript.Echo "Output saved to \\server1\public\output.txt"
```

I'll provide my usual walk-through of this script in a bit; for now, try to pick out the adapted pieces of prototype code. Notice where I'm querying the domain, opening and writing to the text file, closing the text file, and calling the `GetOSInfo()` function.

## ➤➤ Inventorying the Domain

Listing 20.4 shows the complete, ready-to-run script. Get this ready to run, but don't execute it just yet. In the next section, I'll cover testing and troubleshooting this script.

**Listing 20.4** *InventoryDomain.vbs.* The complete domain inventory script.

```
'get domain name
Dim sDomain
sDomain = InputBox("Enter domain to inventory")

'connect to domain and retrieve
'a list of member objects
Dim oDomain
Set oDomain = GetObject("WinNT://" & sDomain

'get the filesystemobject
```

*continues*

```
Dim oFSO
Set oFSO = CreateObject("Scripting.FileSystemObject")

'open an output file
Dim oOutput
oOutput = oFSO.CreateTextFile("\\server1\public\output.txt")

'run through the objects
Dim oObject, sComputerName, sDetails
For Each oObject In oDomain

 'is this object a computer?
 If oObject.Class = "Computer" Then

  'yes - get computer name
  sComputerName = oObject.Name

  'get OS info
  sDetails = GetOSInfo(sComputerName)

  'write info to the file
  oOutput.Write sDetails

 End If
Next

'close the output file
oOutput.Close

'release objects
Set oOutput = Nothing
Set oFSO = Nothing
Set oObject = nothing
Set oDomain = Nothing

'display completion message
WScript.Echo "Output saved to \\server1\public\output.txt"

Function GetOSInfo(sComputer)

      'declare variables
      Dim objWMIService
      Dim colItems
      Dim strOutput
```

```
'get WMI service
Set objWMIService = GetObject("winmgmts:\\" & _
 strComputer & "\root\cimv2")

'get item collection
Set colItems = objWMIService.ExecQuery( _
 "Select * from Win32_OperatingSystem",,48)

'init output string
sOutput = String(70,"-")
sOutput = sOutput & sComputer

'append info to output string
For Each objItem in colItems
      strOutput = strOutput & "BuildNumber: " & _
       objItem.BuildNumber & vbCrLf
      strOutput = strOutput & "BuildType: " & _
       objItem.BuildType & vbCrLf
      strOutput = strOutput & "Caption: " & _
       objItem.Caption & vbCrLf
      strOutput = strOutput & "EncryptionLevel: " & _
       objItem.EncryptionLevel & vbCrLf
      strOutput = strOutput & "InstallDate: " & _
       objItem.InstallDate & vbCrLf
      strOutput = strOutput & "Manufacturer: " & _
       objItem.Manufacturer & vbCrLf
      strOutput = strOutput & "MaxNumberOfProcesses: " & _
       objItem.MaxNumberOfProcesses & vbCrLf
strOutput = strOutput & "MaxProcessMemorySize: " & _
       objItem.MaxProcessMemorySize & vbCrLf
 strOutput = strOutput & "Name: " & _
       objItem.Name & vbCrLf
      strOutput = strOutput & _
       "NumberOfLicensedUsers: " & _
       objItem.NumberOfLicensedUsers & vbCrLf
      strOutput = strOutput & "NumberOfProcesses: " & _
       objItem.NumberOfProcesses & vbCrLf
      strOutput = strOutput & "NumberOfUsers: " & _
       objItem.NumberOfUsers & vbCrLf
      strOutput = strOutput & "OSProductSuite: " & _
       objItem.OSProductSuite & vbCrLf
      strOutput = strOutput & "OSType: " & _
       objItem.OSType & vbCrLf
```

*continues*

```
            strOutput = strOutput & "OtherTypeDescription: " & _
             objItem.OtherTypeDescription & vbCrLf
            strOutput = strOutput & "Primary: " & _
             objItem.Primary & vbCrLf
            strOutput = strOutput & "ProductType: " & _
             objItem.ProductType & vbCrLf
            strOutput = strOutput & "RegisteredUser: " & _
             objItem.RegisteredUser & vbCrLf
            strOutput = strOutput & "SerialNumber: " & _
             objItem.SerialNumber & vbCrLf
            strOutput = strOutput & _
             "ServicePackMajorVersion: " & _
             objItem.ServicePackMajorVersion & vbCrLf
            strOutput = strOutput & _
             "ServicePackMinorVersion: " & _
             objItem.ServicePackMinorVersion & vbCrLf
            strOutput = strOutput & "Version: " & _
             objItem.Version & vbCrLf
            strOutput = strOutput & "WindowsDirectory: " & _
      Next            objItem.WindowsDirectory & vbCrLf

 'return results
      GetOSInfo = sOutput

End Function
```

You need to change where this script puts its output file before using it in your environment. The script prompts for the domain name, so you won't have to make any changes there.

## ➤➤ Inventorying the Domain—Explained

The script starts by prompting for the domain name. This allows the script to be used in a multidomain environment. The domain name is stored in a string variable.

```
'get domain name
Dim sDomain
sDomain = InputBox("Enter domain to inventory")
```

Next, the script uses ADSI to connect to the domain and retrieve a list of all domain objects. This may be a lengthy operation in a large domain, because computer, user, and all other objects are included in the results.

```
'connect to domain and retrieve
'a list of member objects
Dim oDomain
Set oDomain = GetObject("WinNT://" & sDomain
```

The script creates a new FileSystemObject and assigns it to a variable.

```
'get the filesystemobject
Dim oFSO
Set oFSO = CreateObject("Scripting.FileSystemObject")
```

The script now creates a new text file by using the FileSystemObject's `CreateTextFile` method. The method returns a TextStream object, which is assigned to the variable `oOutput`.

```
'open an output file
Dim oOutput
oOutput = oFSO.CreateTextFile("\\server1\public\output.txt")
```

`oDomain` now represents all of the objects in the domain; I'll use a `For Each...Next` loop to iterate through each object in turn. Within the loop, `oObject` will represent the current object.

```
'run through the objects
Dim oObject, sComputerName, sDetails
For Each oObject In oDomain
```

Because `oDomain` contains more than just computers, I need to check each object to see if its `Class` property equals "Computer." That way, I can just work with the computer objects and skip the rest.

```
 'is this object a computer?
 If oObject.Class = "Computer" Then
```

For objects that are a computer, I pull the computer name into a variable. Then, I assign the results of `GetOSInfo()` to variable `sDetails`. Finally, I write `sDetails` to the output text file using the TextStream object's `Write` method. Closing up the loop with `Next` moves on to the next object in the domain.

```
  'yes - get computer name
  sComputerName = oObject.Name

  'get OS info
  sDetails = GetOSInfo(sComputerName)

  'write info to the file
  oOutput.Write sDetails

 End If
Next
```

When I'm done with all the objects, I close the output file, release all the objects I created by setting them equal to `Nothing`, and then display a simple completion message.

```
'close the output file
oOutput.Close

'release objects
Set oOutput = Nothing
Set oFSO = Nothing
Set oObject = nothing
Set oDomain = Nothing

'display completion message
WScript.Echo "Output saved to \\server1\public\output.txt"
```

Here's that function I wrote earlier. It starts with basic variable declaration.

```
Function GetOSInfo(sComputer)

      'declare variables
      Dim objWMIService
      Dim colItems
      Dim strOutput
```

Next is pure wizard code, which uses `GetObject` to connect to the specified computer's WMI service.

```
'get WMI service
Set objWMIService = GetObject("winmgmts:\\" & _
 strComputer & "\root\cimv2")
```

After I am connected, I execute a query to retrieve the `Win32_OperatingSystem` class.

```
'get item collection
Set colItems = objWMIService.ExecQuery( _
 "Select * from Win32_OperatingSystem",,48)
```

I set up my output string to include a line of hyphens and the current computer name.

```
'init output string
sOutput = String(70,"-")
sOutput = sOutput & sComputer
```

Finally, I append the WMI information to the output string.

```
'append info to output string
For Each objItem in colItems
      strOutput = strOutput & "BuildNumber: " & _
       objItem.BuildNumber & vbCrLf
      strOutput = strOutput & "BuildType: " & _
       objItem.BuildType & vbCrLf
      strOutput = strOutput & "Caption: " & _
       objItem.Caption & vbCrLf
      strOutput = strOutput & "EncryptionLevel: " & _
       objItem.EncryptionLevel & vbCrLf
      strOutput = strOutput & "InstallDate: " & _
       objItem.InstallDate & vbCrLf
      strOutput = strOutput & "Manufacturer: " & _
       objItem.Manufacturer & vbCrLf
      strOutput = strOutput & "MaxNumberOfProcesses: " & _
       objItem.MaxNumberOfProcesses & vbCrLf
strOutput = strOutput & "MaxProcessMemorySize: " & _
       objItem.MaxProcessMemorySize & vbCrLf
```

*continues*

```
        strOutput = strOutput & "Name: " & _
              objItem.Name & vbCrLf
             strOutput = strOutput & _
              "NumberOfLicensedUsers: " & _
              objItem.NumberOfLicensedUsers & vbCrLf
             strOutput = strOutput & "NumberOfProcesses: " & _
              objItem.NumberOfProcesses & vbCrLf
             strOutput = strOutput & "NumberOfUsers: " & _
              objItem.NumberOfUsers & vbCrLf
             strOutput = strOutput & "OSProductSuite: " & _
              objItem.OSProductSuite & vbCrLf
             strOutput = strOutput & "OSType: " & _
              objItem.OSType & vbCrLf
             strOutput = strOutput & "OtherTypeDescription: " & _
              objItem.OtherTypeDescription & vbCrLf
             strOutput = strOutput & "Primary: " & _
              objItem.Primary & vbCrLf
             strOutput = strOutput & "ProductType: " & _
              objItem.ProductType & vbCrLf
             strOutput = strOutput & "RegisteredUser: " & _
              objItem.RegisteredUser & vbCrLf
             strOutput = strOutput & "SerialNumber: " & _
              objItem.SerialNumber & vbCrLf
             strOutput = strOutput & _
              "ServicePackMajorVersion: " & _
              objItem.ServicePackMajorVersion & vbCrLf
             strOutput = strOutput & _
              "ServicePackMinorVersion: " & _
              objItem.ServicePackMinorVersion & vbCrLf
             strOutput = strOutput & "Version: " & _
              objItem.Version & vbCrLf
             strOutput = strOutput & "WindowsDirectory: " & _
              objItem.WindowsDirectory & vbCrLf
       Next
```

With the main script finished, I return the output string as the function's result.

```
 'return results
      GetOSInfo = sOutput

End Function
```

There you have it—a nice, easy-to-use administrative script that uses both WMI and ADSI to accomplish a useful task.

## Testing the Script

If you jumped ahead and already tried to execute the final script, you realize that it's flawed. If you haven't, go ahead and give it a whirl now. Take a few minutes to see if you can track down the problem. There are actually three errors, and here are some hints.

- One is a simple typo.
- One is a sort of logic error, where something isn't being used properly for the situation.
- The last one is a typo, and could have been avoided if I had followed my own advice from earlier in the book.

Can you find them all? The first one is an easy mistake: I simply forgot a closing parentheses.

```
'connect to domain and retrieve
'a list of member objects
Dim oDomain
Set oDomain = GetObject("WinNT://" & sDomain
```

The correct code should be `Set oDomain = GetObject("WinNT://" & sDomain)`. The next one's a bit trickier.

```
'open an output file
Dim oOutput
oOutput = oFSO.CreateTextFile("\\server1\public\output.txt")
```

Can you see it? I'm using `oOutput` to represent an object, but I forgot to use the `Set` keyword when making the assignment. VBScript requires `Set` whenever you're assigning an object to a variable. The corrected code looks like this.

```
'open an output file
Dim oOutput
Set oOutput = oFSO.CreateTextFile("\\server1\public\
  output.txt")
```

The last error is tricky, too. It's in the `GetOSInfo()` function.

```
Function GetOSInfo(sComputer)

      'declare variables
      Dim objWMIService
      Dim colItems
      Dim strOutput

      'get WMI service
      Set objWMIService = GetObject("winmgmts:\\" & _
       strComputer & "\root\cimv2")
```

Did you find it? The problem is that I used the wizard-generated code, which uses "str" as a prefix for string variables. I'm in the habit of using the shorter prefix "s" for string variables, and that's where my problem lies. In the function definition, I declared `sComputer`, but in the line of code that connects to the WMI service, I used `strComputer`. I continued using `sComputer` elsewhere, so `strComputer` is wrong. Here's the corrected code snippet.

```
Function GetOSInfo(sComputer)

      'declare variables
      Dim objWMIService
      Dim colItems
      Dim strOutput

      'get WMI service
       Set objWMIService = GetObject("winmgmts:\\" & _
        sComputer & "\root\cimv2")
```

The problem with this error is that it doesn't cause a problem for the script; the script will execute just fine. You just won't get any results, because the script would try to connect to a computer named "". I mentioned that I could have avoided this problem by following my own advice. Had I included `Option Explicit`, VBScript would have produced an error on the offending line of code, because `strComputer` wasn't declared. `sComputer`, on the other hand, is implicitly declared because it's part of a function declaration. You'll notice that I did the same thing with `strOutput` and `sOutput`, meaning they'll have to be corrected, too.

Just to make sure you've got it all, Listing 20.5 includes the complete, corrected script. Remember that this script is also available on the CD that accompanies this book.

**Listing 20.5** *InventoryDomain2.vbs.* This corrected script produces the expected results.

```
'get domain name
Dim sDomain
sDomain = InputBox("Enter domain to inventory")

'connect to domain and retrieve
'a list of member objects
Dim oDomain
Set oDomain = GetObject("WinNT://" & sDomain)

'get the filesystemobject
Dim oFSO
Set oFSO = CreateObject("Scripting.FileSystemObject")

'open an output file
Dim oOutput
Set oOutput = oFSO.CreateTextFile("\\server1\public\output.txt")

'run through the objects
Dim oObject, sComputerName, sDetails
For Each oObject In oDomain

 'is this object a computer?
 If oObject.Class = "Computer" Then

  'yes - get computer name
  sComputerName = oObject.Name

  'get OS info
  sDetails = GetOSInfo(sComputerName)

  'write info to the file
  oOutput.Write sDetails

 End If
Next
```

*continues*

```
'close the output file
oOutput.Close

'release objects
Set oOutput = Nothing
Set oFSO = Nothing
Set oObject = nothing
Set oDomain = Nothing

'display completion message
WScript.Echo "Output saved to \\server1\public\output.txt"

Function GetOSInfo(sComputer)

      'declare variables
      Dim objWMIService
      Dim colItems
      Dim strOutput

      'get WMI service
      Set objWMIService = GetObject("winmgmts:\\" & _
       sComputer & "\root\cimv2")

      'get item collection
      Set colItems = objWMIService.ExecQuery( _
       "Select * from Win32_OperatingSystem",,48)

      'init output string
      strOutput = String(70,"-")
      strOutput = strOutput & sComputer

      'append info to output string
      For Each objItem in colItems
            strOutput = strOutput & "BuildNumber: " & _
             objItem.BuildNumber & vbCrLf
            strOutput = strOutput & "BuildType: " & _
             objItem.BuildType & vbCrLf
            strOutput = strOutput & "Caption: " & _
             objItem.Caption & vbCrLf
            strOutput = strOutput & "EncryptionLevel: " & _
             objItem.EncryptionLevel & vbCrLf
            strOutput = strOutput & "InstallDate: " & _
             objItem.InstallDate & vbCrLf
            strOutput = strOutput & "Manufacturer: " & _
```

```
                objItem.Manufacturer & vbCrLf
               strOutput = strOutput & "MaxNumberOfProcesses: " & _
                objItem.MaxNumberOfProcesses & vbCrLf
        strOutput = strOutput & "MaxProcessMemorySize: " & _
                objItem.MaxProcessMemorySize & vbCrLf
         strOutput = strOutput & "Name: " & _
                objItem.Name & vbCrLf
               strOutput = strOutput & _
                "NumberOfLicensedUsers: " & _
                objItem.NumberOfLicensedUsers & vbCrLf
               strOutput = strOutput & "NumberOfProcesses: " & _
                objItem.NumberOfProcesses & vbCrLf
               strOutput = strOutput & "NumberOfUsers: " & _
                objItem.NumberOfUsers & vbCrLf
               strOutput = strOutput & "OSProductSuite: " & _
                objItem.OSProductSuite & vbCrLf
               strOutput = strOutput & "OSType: " & _
                objItem.OSType & vbCrLf
               strOutput = strOutput & "OtherTypeDescription: " & _
                objItem.OtherTypeDescription & vbCrLf
               strOutput = strOutput & "Primary: " & _
                objItem.Primary & vbCrLf
               strOutput = strOutput & "ProductType: " & _
                objItem.ProductType & vbCrLf
               strOutput = strOutput & "RegisteredUser: " & _
                objItem.RegisteredUser & vbCrLf
               strOutput = strOutput & "SerialNumber: " & _
                objItem.SerialNumber & vbCrLf
               strOutput = strOutput & _
                "ServicePackMajorVersion: " & _
                objItem.ServicePackMajorVersion & vbCrLf
               strOutput = strOutput & _
                "ServicePackMinorVersion: " & _
                objItem.ServicePackMinorVersion & vbCrLf
               strOutput = strOutput & "Version: " & _
                objItem.Version & vbCrLf
               strOutput = strOutput & "WindowsDirectory: " & _
                objItem.WindowsDirectory & vbCrLf
        Next

    'return results
        GetOSInfo = sOutput

End Function
```

Testing a large script like this is much easier with the Script Debugger. You can spot lines that are causing trouble just by following the execution path.

For more information on the Script Debugger, see "Testing the Script" in Chapter 13. You can also read up on the Script Debugger in the VBScript documentation at http://msdn.microsoft.com/scripting.

## Review

Pulling together ADSI and WMI into a single script offers some powerful functionality. More importantly, though, the example in this chapter should make you feel more comfortable with the sometimes-daunting task of creating a script from scratch. Just break down the tasks that need to be completed, and then develop some prototype code for each task. Use wizards, examples from the Web, or samples from this book to help create prototype code. After all, there's no sense reinventing the wheel when there's a large library of samples on the Web and in this book to work with!

With your task list and prototype out of the way, you can start assembling the script. Write functions and subs to perform repetitive tasks, or tasks that you may want to reuse in future scripts. Write the main script, and then start testing. With this methodology in mind, most scripts can be whipped together quickly!

#### COMING UP

Web pages offer an exciting way to create your own centrally located, easily accessible administrative tools. In the next chapter, I'll introduce you to Active Server Pages, and in the following chapters, I'll show you how to easily and quickly apply your scripting skills to create great administrative Web pages.

PART IV

# Creating Administrative Web Pages

CHAPTER 21

# Active Server Pages Crash Course

**IN THIS CHAPTER**

You'll never bother or you'll use it all the time: Active Server Pages, Microsoft's scripted Web pages, provides a powerful way to create administrative Web pages and user self-service pages. Although making you a full ASP programmer is beyond the scope of this book, there's plenty of power available to you through the VBScript that you've already learned.

Web pages are still the hottest technology around, especially with the recent hype about Web Services and other new Web-based technologies. Web pages can have a place in administration, too. I'm not talking about creating full-fledged Web applications (although you certainly could do so by using VBScript), but you can create some great administrative utilities that are based upon Web pages. Consider the following useful, easy-to-create solutions:

- A Web page that allows Help Desk technicians to quickly check the status of a particular user account
- A Web page that retrieves inventory information about client computers on the network
- A Web page that allows users to reset their own passwords by providing some piece of personally identifiable information

The keys to the kingdom are *Active Server Pages,* or ASP, Microsoft's scripted Web development environment.

## About ASP

ASP was first introduced with Internet Information Server 3.0 (IIS 3.0), and exists in subsequent versions of IIS. It's important that you make a distinction between ASP and ASP.NET. ASP is Microsoft's original server-side scripting model, whereas ASP.NET is a completely new, .NET Framework-based technology that has nothing to do with scripting at all. IIS 5.0 and 6.0 support ASP.NET, and both of them support running both ASP and ASP.NET applications within the same Web site. Although ASP.NET is a powerful, high performance way to write Web applications, it's a bit outside the scope of administrative scripting. For instance, it doesn't use VBScript; so-called "Classic" ASP does. So, for the purposes of this book, I'll focus on the older ASP technology.

ASP is not a programming language, although that is a popular misconception. ASP is simply a specialized object model and a specialized host for VBScript. The ASP object model allows you to access information that users type into HTML input forms, and allows you to write output to HTML pages. In fact, ASP isn't particularly high-tech or fancy (although it was pretty innovative when it was introduced).

To get started with ASP, consider a basic HTML Web page.

```
<HTML>
<BODY>
<FORM ACTION="display.asp" METHOD="POST">
Computer name: <INPUT TYPE="TEXT" NAME="COMPUTERNAME"><BR>
<INPUT TYPE="SUBMIT">
</FORM>
</BODY>
</HTML>
```

Type this HTML code into Notepad and save the file as Display.asp. The file needs to be located within an IIS folder, such as C:\Inetpub\Wwwroot. If you've got the file in the correct place, you should be able to select **Run** from the Start menu, type **http://localhost/display.asp**, and see a small Web page that says "Computer name:" and has a text box and a Submit button.

Is this ASP? Not really. This is just HTML—the Web page doesn't actually do anything if you click the Submit button. You could create a page like this with any HTML editor, such as Microsoft FrontPage. In fact, I usually use FrontPage to work with ASP. You can also use higher-end script editors like PrimalScript, because they understand both ASP tags and HTML code.

### Getting Ready for Web Scripting

For this chapter and the three that follow, I'm going to assume your computer is set up to run ASP pages. You'll need a Windows 2000, Windows Server 2003, or Windows XP computer with IIS installed. You'll also need to ensure that ASP is enabled; this is the default for Windows 2000 and Windows XP, but you'll have to explicitly enable ASP in Windows Server 2003.

You should also know where the IIS root folder is. Generally, that's in C:\Inetpub\Wwwroot; you can check the properties of the Default Web Site in the Internet Services Manager console to see where the root folder is located on your computer. I'll have you place all of the sample Web pages in that root folder.

To access the Web pages you create, you need a Web browser. I use Internet Explorer, but due to the nature of ASP, you can use just about any browser you like. You should be able to point the browser to **http://localhost/*pagename.asp*** to access the various pages I'll have you create (where ***pagename.asp*** is the name of the page as saved on your computer's disk).

Finally, you may want to use a WYSIWYG (what you see is what you get) HTML editor like Microsoft FrontPage. You can use this to create your basic HTML pages (the pages I'll show you how to create will be basic indeed), rather than hand-coding the HTML tags.

## VBScript in ASP

Where's the scripting in ASP? You have to add it. Essentially, the same ASP page has a mix of both VBScript code and HTML code. The VBScript code has to be added between two special tags: `<%` and `%>`. These tags tell IIS where the script code begins and ends, and allows it to distinguish between VBScript and HTML. Consider the following revision to our running example.

```
<HTML>
<BODY>
<%
Response.Write("It is now " & Now)
%>
<FORM ACTION="display.asp" METHOD="POST">
Computer name: <INPUT TYPE="TEXT" NAME="COMPUTERNAME"><BR>
```

*continues*

```
<INPUT TYPE="SUBMIT">
</FORM>
</BODY>
</HTML>
```

Believe it or not, that's a full ASP page. The key is in the VBScript line `Response.Write("It is now " & Now)`, which is a line of VBScript that uses ASP's built-in Response object to output the current date and time to the Web page. Try running that—remember, save the page in an IIS folder and access the page by using your Web browser and the HTTP protocol—and you'll see what it looks like.

Here's how it works: When you request the file from the Web server, IIS locates the appropriate file on the hard drive. It loads the file into memory, and because the file has an .ASP filename extension, IIS hands it off to Asp.dll, which is an ISAPI plug-in that handles ASP pages. Asp.dll scans each line of the file. The first two lines obviously aren't code, because Asp.dll hasn't seen a `<%` tag; therefore, those lines are passed straight through to IIS, and IIS transmits them to your Web browser.

On the third line, ASP realizes that some script code is beginning. Asp.dll reads the fourth line, and executes it. The *results* of the code execution are passed to IIS and transmitted to your Web browser. On the fifth line of the file, Asp.dll stops looking for code and continues passing everything straight through to IIS.

---

**TIP** If you're feeling lazy, you don't have to type out `Response.Write`; you can simply use the equal sign. `<% = "Hello" %>` is functionally the same as `<% Response.Write "Hello" %>`.

---

If you've loaded this page into your Web browser, right-click the page and select **View Source** from the context menu (assuming you're using Internet Explorer, of course). You should see something like this.

```
<HTML>
<BODY>
It is now 5/26/2003 9:54:54 AM
<FORM ACTION="display.asp" METHOD="POST">
Computer name: <INPUT TYPE="TEXT" NAME="COMPUTERNAME"><BR>
<INPUT TYPE="SUBMIT">
</FORM>
</BODY>
</HTML>
```

Note that all of the HTML *outside* the `<%` and `%>` tags was transmitted to your Web browser unchanged. However, the code *inside* the tags isn't present anymore. Instead of the VBScript code and the Response object, we're simply seeing the *output* of the code. The code itself was never passed to IIS by Asp.dll, and so all the Web browser receives is a static Web page. That's exactly how ASP works.

- Code is executed on the server and never passed to the Web browser.
- Anything output by the code is passed to the Web browser.
- Any HTML outside of the special ASP code tags is passed straight through to the Web browser.

What can you do with VBScript inside an ASP page? Virtually anything. Here are two important differences between traditional VBScripting and ASP scripting.

1. You don't have access to the intrinsic WScript object. That's because ASP is an independent host for VBScript, and doesn't provide the WScript object.
2. Instead, you have access to the intrinsic ASP objects. There are five of them, but you'll spend most of your time using two of them: Response and Request.

You can continue to access WMI, ADSI, and many of the other objects that you've learned about in this book. You can use the entire VBScript language, including all of its functions, control-of-flow constructs, and so forth.

---

**TIP** If this Web page programming stuff is still a little intimidating, don't let it be! You're basically going to use HTML pages that you can create in FrontPage or another WYSIWYG editor, and you're going to learn a grand total of *two additional commands* that will accomplish 90% of the work an administrative Web page needs. Everything else will just reuse the VBScript you've already learned!

---

## The Response Object

You've already seen a quick example of the Response object and its most important method: `Write`. The Response object is used to output information to the client Web browser, including text, cookies, HTML headers, and more. In an administrative script, you're not likely to use much more than `Response.Write`, and it's one of the two additional commands that I mentioned you'd have to learn.

## Writing Output

`Response.Write` simply outputs text to the Web page. Think of it as a sort of `MsgBox` statement, or more accurately a `WScript.Echo` for Web pages. As you've seen, you can include functions and literal text, and `Response.Write` simply outputs whatever you tell it to.

Here's another example of how `Response.Write` works. Save this page as Response.asp in your computer's Web root folder, and access it via http://localhost/response.asp.

```
Response.Write Now & "<br><br>"
Response.Write "Hello!" & "<br><br>"
Response.Write "All done!"
```

Use View Source in your Web browser to see the final HTML that was transmitted to the browser.

---

**TIP** The `<br>` tags I use in this example are HTML tags for a line *break*. They're similar to using `vbCrLf` in a regular script, and tell the Web browser to insert a carriage return and linefeed. Use two of them in a row, as I've done, to create blank lines. Using `vbCrLf` doesn't work in an ASP script, because Web browsers tend to ignore incoming carriage returns and linefeeds when they display HTML.

---

## Saving Cookies

The Response object also allows you to save cookies to client computers. A *cookie* is a small collection of data, normally smaller than 1024 bytes in size. A cookie is a collection of *crumbs* (seriously), with each crumb representing one piece of data. So, if you want to save the user's name, that would be one crumb in the cookie, the user's last logon date might be another. In administrative scripts, cookies tend to have limited use. One potential use is in a Web-based wizard, such as a new user creation wizard. In that application, you might use a cookie to keep track of the settings the user enters on each page of the wizard; on the last page, you could then collect all that data together to create the new user account.

Response provides access to cookies through the `Response.Cookies` collection. It's simple to use; here's an example of setting two crumbs.

```
Response.Cookies("UserName") = "JohnD"
Response.Cookies("AcctExpires") = 0
```

The trick with cookies is that they have to be passed in the HTTP headers, not in the main HTML code. That means you have to *set* the cookies before any HTML is output to the browser. The following example works fine.

```
<%
Response.Cookies("WizardStep") = 2
Response.Cookies("UserName") = "DonJ"
%>
<HTML>
<BODY>
<!--Rest of HTML goes here-->
</BODY>
</HTML>
```

However, the following example would result in an error.

```
<HTML>
<BODY>
<%
Response.Cookies("RightNow") = Now()
%>
Thank you!
</BODY>
</HTML>
```

The error occurs because HTML has already been sent to the browser (and therefore the HTTP headers composed) by the time `Response.Cookies` is accessed. The following example will also result in an error, although for a slightly more subtle reason.

```
<%
Response.Write "Today is " & Now()
Response.Cookies("UserName") = "JohnDoe"
```

*continues*

```
%>
<HTML>
<BODY>
Hello!
</BODY>
</HTML>
```

Why the error? Because when `Response.Write` is executed, IIS realizes that this is the first HTML being output to the browser. As such, IIS automatically finalizes the HTTP headers, sends an automatic `<HTML><BODY>` tag set, and *then* executes `Response.Write`.

---

**TIP** Avoid confusion by never using `Response.Write` until *after* your `<HTML>` tag; and never use `Response.Cookies` unless it's *before* that `<HTML>` tag.

---

You'll see how to reread those cookies when I describe the Request object in the next section.

### Ending

Sometimes, you may want to tell ASP to stop processing your script and wrap things up. You can! Simply execute `Response.End`. ASP immediately will send whatever output it has already generated and won't look at your script any further.

## The Request Object

If the Response object provides a means of producing output, you might suspect that the Request object allows you to work with user input—and you'd be right. Primarily, the Request object lets you access cookies, and lets you access information entered into HTML forms.

### HTML Forms

Whenever you add an HTML form field to a Web page, you give it a name. For example, `<INPUT TYPE="TEXT" NAME="ComputerName">` creates a text box named "ComputerName." When that form is submitted back to the Web browser (when the user clicks a Submit button), whatever the user entered is paired with the form field name to make it more readily accessible to you.

ASP exposes form fields through its `Forms` collection. You can use these just like read-only variables, as shown in this snippet.

```
The computer name you entered was:
<% Response.Write Request.Forms("ComputerName") %>
```

Any fields not filled in by the user will be blank, and equal to "". You can use `Request.Forms` in logical comparisons, to produce additional output (as in the preceding example), and so forth. You'll see plenty of the Request object in the full-length sample later in this chapter.

---

**TIP** As a shortcut, you can omit `Forms` when reading forms input. For example, instead of typing **Request.Forms("ComputerName")**, you could simply type **Request("ComputerName")** and get the same results. I'll use that technique in most of my examples to save space.

---

### Cookies

Just as `Response.Cookies` allows you to write cookies to client Web browsers, `Request.Cookies` allows you to read them back out again. For example, if you've saved a crumb named "UserName," `Request.Cookies("UserName")` will read the crumb. Here's an example.

```
<HTML><BODY>
You requested account creation for user name
<% Response.Write Request.Cookies("UserName") %>.<BR>
```

`Request.Cookies` can be used anywhere in a script as it doesn't attempt to modify the HTTP headers being sent to the client.

## A Sample ASP Script

As an example, I'll show you a simple ASP script that accepts the name of a computer, and then uses Windows Management Instrumentation (WMI) to display some key information about that computer. You could expand this easily into a real-time inventory check page, usable by help desk technicians, perhaps.

Before this script will work, however, you need to make some changes to the computer running it. I'm going to list the changes needed; I'll describe the need for these changes in Chapter 23.

1. Open the Registry Editor.
2. Browse to HKEY_LOCAL_MACHINE\Software\Microsoft\WBEM\Scripting. This key should already exist.
3. Create a new DWORD value named "Enable for ASP" and set the value to 1. If the value already exists, make sure it's set to 1.
4. If you're putting this Web page in the Default Web Site, use Internet Services Manager to open the properties of that Web site. If you're using another Web site, open that site's properties.
5. On the **Directory Security** tab, disable anonymous access and ensure that **Windows Integrated Authentication** is selected.

When you attempt to access the Web page (or any other page in that Web site), you may be prompted to log on. Make sure you're doing so with a user account that's an administrator, or the script may not run properly. ASP and WMI security are complex; I'll cover them in more detail in Chapter 23 to explain what's going on.

## ➤➤ Displaying Information in a Web Page

The script in Listing 21.1 uses WMI to display information about a selected computer.

**Listing 21.1** *Display.asp.* Uses WMI to display information about a computer.

```
<%

If Request("COMPUTERNAME") <> "" Then

 Set oSystem = GetObject("winmgmts:{impersonationLevel=" & _
  "impersonate}!//" & Request("COMPUTERNAME") & _
  "/root/cimv2:Win32_ComputerSystem=" & Chr(34) & _
  Request("COMPUTERNAME") & Chr(34))

 Response.Write "System information for " & _
  Request("COMPUTERNAME") & "<HR>"
 Response.Write "Name: " & oSystem.Caption & "<BR>"
```

```
 Response.Write "Owner: " & oSystem.PrimaryOwnerName & "<BR>"
 Response.Write "Domain: " & oSystem.Domain & "<BR>"
 Response.Write "Type: " & oSystem.SystemType & "<BR>"
 Response.Write "<HR>"
 Response.End

End If

%>
<HTML>
<BODY>
<%
Response.Write("It is now " & Now)
%>
<FORM ACTION="display.asp" METHOD="POST">
Computer name: <INPUT TYPE="TEXT" NAME="COMPUTERNAME"><BR>
<INPUT TYPE="SUBMIT">
</FORM>
</BODY>
</HTML>
```

Other than the security changes I outlined previously, you shouldn't need to make any modifications to use this Web page. Keep in mind that, because it's a Web page, it should be usable by an administrator with HTTP access to the computer hosting the page.

## ➤➤ Displaying Information in a Web Page—Explained

Notice that this script begins with ASP code. The first line of code checks to see if `Request("COMPUTERNAME")` is empty. If it is, the script hasn't run before, and none of the WMI stuff is executed. Instead, the script skips directly to the HTML code.

```
<%

If Request("COMPUTERNAME") <> "" Then
 ...
End If

%>
<HTML>
<BODY>
```

The script then uses VBScript to display the current date and time.

```
<%
Response.Write("It is now " & Now)
%>
```

Finally, the script uses standard HTML to create a short input form. The form consists of a text box and a Submit button. Notice that the form's ACTION is set to submit the form to this very same page, and that the name of the text box is COMPUTERNAME. That will become important in a bit.

```
<FORM ACTION="display.asp" METHOD="POST">
Computer name: <INPUT TYPE="TEXT" NAME="COMPUTERNAME"><BR>
<INPUT TYPE="SUBMIT">
</FORM>
</BODY>
</HTML>
```

Now, the Web user can type a computer name and press **Submit**. When he does that, his browser bundles the form information (the contents of the text box) and sends it to Display.asp, which happens to be the same page. Neither the Web browser nor ASP cares that the same Web page is both displaying the form and handling it; I could have split this into two separate pages, in fact. However, keeping the form and its handling code in one page is easier for maintenance, so I did it this way.

When the code is resubmitted, ASP takes a fresh look at the page. This time, `Request("COMPUTERNAME")` isn't empty—it contains the name of a computer that the user types. The `If...Then` construct evaluates to True.

```
<%

If Request("COMPUTERNAME") <> "" Then
```

ASP evaluates the next line of code, which is a call to WMI. This call connects to the computer designated by the user and queries its `Win32_ComputerSystem` class. Actually, the query is `Win32_ComputerSystem = 'computername'`, where *computername* is whatever the user typed. This retrieves the `property` WMI class from the remote computer.

```
Set oSystem = GetObject("winmgmts:{impersonationLevel=" & _
```

```
"impersonate}!//" & Request("COMPUTERNAME") & _
"/root/cimv2:Win32_ComputerSystem=" & Chr(34) & _
Request("COMPUTERNAME") & Chr(34))
```

It's downhill from there. With `oSystem` set to the WMI class, ASP can output the information requested.

```
Response.Write "System information for " & _
 Request("COMPUTERNAME") & "<HR>"
Response.Write "Name: " & oSystem.Caption & "<BR>"
Response.Write "Owner: " & oSystem.PrimaryOwnerName & "<BR>"
Response.Write "Domain: " & oSystem.Domain & "<BR>"
Response.Write "Type: " & oSystem.SystemType & "<BR>"
Response.Write "<HR>"
Response.End
```

Did you notice `Response.End`? That prevents ASP from dropping through to the original HTML form. You could easily remove `Response.End`. The result would be a script that displays the system information, and then redisplays the original HTML form. That would be handy for immediately typing in another computer name and getting its information.

This simple example can be easily expanded to collect other information about the remote computer. In fact, this isn't unlike the WMI scripts you saw in Chapters 17 through 20; the only differences are that ASP has to be configured to work with WMI's security (and vice versa) and that you use `Response.Write` to output information instead of `MsgBox` or `WScript.Echo`.

## Testing ASP Scripts

Testing ASP scripts can be a bit of a pain. Typically, an error results in a browser window like the one shown in Figure 21.1.

The technical information in the error message breaks down as follows:

```
HTTP 500.100 - Internal Server Error - ASP error
Internet Information Services

Technical Information (for support personnel)

Error Type:
Microsoft VBScript compilation (0x800A03EE)
```

```
Expected ')'
/display.asp, line 10, column 31
Request("COMPUTERNAME" & "<HR>"
```

The important information is under "`Error Type`," and in this case, the error is that VBScript was expecting to see a closing parentheses and it didn't. The offending line of code is helpfully displayed. It looks like I forgot to include a "`)`" after `Request("COMPUTERNAME"`, and that's causing the error. It's helpful to have an editor like FrontPage or PrimalScript that displays line and column numbers. You can jump straight to the line in question, but beware of the column number: In this example, ASP is giving me column 31, which is actually at the end of the line, but the error is at column 23. ASP isn't always good about pinpointing errors.

When you encounter an error like this one, simply edit your script, save it, and click **Reload** in the Web browser. The browser should resubmit the page request, and you can try again.

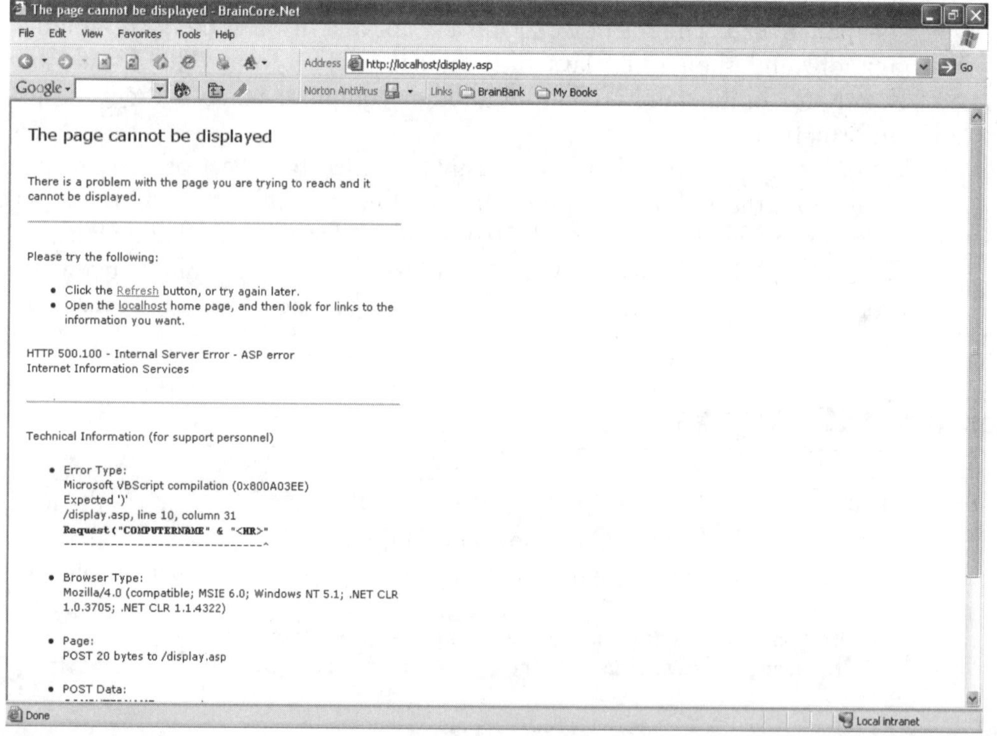


**Figure 21.1** ASP errors display in the browser window

That's pretty much how ASP testing and debugging goes: Try it, see an error, fix it, and try again. It's not unlike regular scripting, in fact. However, you don't get the advantage of a debugger with the native Windows tools (Notepad), and PrimalScript (and most third-party editors) cannot attach to ASP for debugging. Serious ASP debugging is available only in Microsoft Visual InterDev 6.0 and in Microsoft Visual Studio .NET, tools normally reserved for hardcore software developers.

## Review

ASP can be a great way to extend administrative script functionality to other administrators in your enterprise. With it, you can create Web utilities that don't necessarily require administrative privileges, and you can closely control the functionality provided by your Web tools. ASP also makes it easier to provide access: Rather than distributing scripts via e-mail or a file server, they can be centrally located and easily accessible from a single intranet Web server.

The capability of ASP to perform actions that ordinary users can't perform can also be useful. For example, I work with one company that allows department heads to submit new user account requests online. The ASP page waits for administrator approval, and then creates the new user account automatically. Administrators don't need to type in any additional information, and the approval process can be handled by a junior administrator or assistant who might not have Domain Admin privileges. ASP is a powerful way to leverage your growing scripting skills, especially in large organizations.

**COMING UP**

With the ASP basics under your belt, you're ready to build a basic static Web page and add some VBScript to it, and I'll show you how in the next chapter. After that, I'll explain some of the finer points of ASP security, and then show you how to pull everything together in a Web page designed for Help Desk technicians.

CHAPTER 22

# Adding Administrative Script to a Web Page

**IN THIS CHAPTER**

Making administrative Web pages isn't hard, but it can be tough to figure out where to start. I'll walk you through the process step-by-step, and you'll be coding your own pages before you know it.

Administrative Web pages essentially have two elements: HTML and VBScript. The two work together, and often intermingle, within a single Web page, and that can make it tough to figure out where to start when you're creating a Web page. It's easy once you get used to it, though, and in this chapter, I'll show you an example. I'll create a Web page that allows users to pull event log entries from any computer, provided they have the proper credentials to do so. The script will also allow filtering by event ID and source, making it a useful tool for combing through large event log files. While this is certainly a task you can accomplish with the Computer Management console, having this available as a Web page makes it readily accessible to network administrators, and makes it a bit more single-purpose, which can help junior administrators focus on the task at hand.

## The Basic Web Page

I always start by using FrontPage or a similar Web page layout tool to design the page's look and feel, before I add any script. Now, I'm no Web page designer, so my Web pages aren't usually super attractive, but they get the job done. Administrative scripts usually don't have to be as pretty as they do functional!

For this example, I know I'm going to need to start with some kind of HTML input form that will allow the user to specify a computer, an event log, an event ID, and other criteria. That type of form is easy enough to create in FrontPage, and here's the HTML code.

```
<FORM ACTION="event.asp" METHOD="POST">
 <Table cellpadding=2 cellspacing=2 border=0>
  <TR>
   <TD>
    <INPUT type="text" name="ComputerName"
     value="">
   </TD>
   <TD>Computer:</TD>
  </TR>
  <TR>
   <TD>
    <SELECT name="LogName">
     <OPTION value="application">Application</OPTION>
     <OPTION value="system">System</OPTION>
     <OPTION value="security">Security</OPTION>
     </SELECT>
    </TD>
    <TD>Log</TD>
   </TR>
   <TR>
    <TD><INPUT type="text" name="Source"></TD>
    <TD>Event Source</TD>
   </TR>
   <TR>
    <TD>
     <SELECT name="Type">
      <OPTION value="">All</option>
      <OPTION value="information">Information</OPTION>
      <OPTION value="warning">Warning</OPTION>
      <OPTION value="error">Error</OPTION>
     </SELECT>
    </TD>
    <TD>Type</TD>
   </TR>
  <TR>
   <TD><input type="text" name="EventCode"></TD>
   <TD>Event Code</TD>
  </TR>
  <TR>
   <TD><input type="text" name="UserName"</TD>
```

```
  <TD>User Name</TD>
 </TR>
 <TR>
  <TD><input type="password" name="Password"></TD>
  <TD>Password</TD>
 </TR>
 <TR>
  <TD COLSPAN=2 Align=center>
   <INPUT type="submit" NAME="Submit" VALUE="Submit">
  </TD>
 </TR>
 </TABLE>
</FORM>
```

---

**NOTE** Don't worry about typing these in. At the end of this chapter, I'll give you the entire script all at once (and there's a copy on the accompanying CD). Right now, just focus on what each of these different elements accomplishes.

---

That's a basic HTML form with several input fields. Notice that I used some drop-down lists—designated by the SELECT and OPTION tags—for things like the event log and the event type.

I also know that I'm going to need to display the final event log information in a table. It'll help at this point to just sort of mock up what that table will look like in HTML.

```
<TABLE cellspacing=0 cellpadding=3 border=1>
 <TR>
  <TH>Record</TH>
  <TH>Type</TH>
  <TH>Date</TH>
  <TH>Time</TH>
  <TH>Source</TH>
  <TH>Category</TH>
  <TH>Cat Strg</TH>
  <TH>Event</TH>
  <TH>Usr</TH>
  <TH>Computer</TH>
  <TH>Msg</TH>
 </TR>
</TABLE>
```

That HTML represents the first row of the table. Subsequent rows would contain actual data, and I'd use <TD> tags instead of the <TH> tags. I actually plan to have my code dynamically produce this HTML on-the-fly, so that I can produce as many data rows as necessary, but it helps to get the HTML figured out up front.

That's it! It's not going to win any design awards, but the basic HTML for the event log page is out of the way.

## Adding Functions and Subroutines

From some reading, I know that two pieces of data may cause me problems. Each event log entry has a date and time associated with it, and WMI returns those with kind of a funny format. I need to take what WMI gives me and reformat it into normal-looking dates and times. I may as well create some functions to handle the reformatting.

```
Function CDateWMI(cim_DateTime)
 'declare variables
 Dim sDateTime, iYear, iMonth, iDay

 'convert the date to a string
 sDateTime = CStr(cim_DateTime)

 'get the year, month, and day
 iYear = CInt(Mid(sDateTime, 1, 4))
 iMonth = CInt(Mid(sDateTime, 5, 2))
 iDay = CInt(Mid(sDateTime, 7, 2))

 'reformat into a normal date
 CDateWMI = CDate(Join(Array(iMonth, iDay, iYear), "/"))
End Function

Function CTimeWMI(cim_DateTime)
 'declare variables
 Dim sDateTime, iHours, iMinutes, iSeconds

 'convert the time into a string
 sDateTime = CStr(cim_DateTime)

 'get the hours, minutes, and seconds
 iHours = CInt(Mid(sDateTime, 9, 2))
```

```
iMinutes = CInt(Mid(sDateTime, 11, 2))
iSeconds = CInt(Mid(sDateTime, 13, 2))

'reformat into a normal time
CTimeWMI = TimeSerial(iHours, iMinutes, iSeconds)
End Function
```

---

**NOTE** I'll provide my usual line-by-line walk-through of these functions toward the end of this chapter.

---

So far, I have two or three files: the basic input form HTML, the prototype table HTML, and a third file containing my functions. I should be ready to start writing the main portion of the script.

## Adding Inline Script

Now it's time to start pulling everything together. In the previous chapter, I mentioned how it can save time and maintenance effort to keep a form and the handling page in the same file. I showed you an example of how to use an `If...Then` construct to tell if the form is being submitted or not.

In this page, I want to only display the HTML page if the form *isn't* being submitted. If it is being submitted, I want to take the submitted information and display the appropriate event log entries.

ASP allows you to include conditional static HTML in a Web page. It's actually harder to describe than to do it, so here's an example.

```
<%

'Was the form submitted?
If Request.Form("SUBMIT") = "" Then

%>
<FORM ACTION="event.asp" METHOD="POST">
 <Table cellpadding=2 cellspacing=2 border=0>
  <TR>
   <TD>
    <INPUT type="text" name="ComputerName"
     value="<% Response.Write CompName%>">
   </TD>
```

*continues*

```
 <TD>Computer:</TD>
</TR>
<TR>
 <TD>
  <SELECT name="LogName">
   <OPTION value="application">Application</OPTION>
   <OPTION value="system">System</OPTION>
   <OPTION value="security">Security</OPTION>
   </SELECT>
  </TD>
  <TD>Log</TD>
 </TR>
 <TR>
  <TD><INPUT type="text" name="Source"></TD>
  <TD>Event Source</TD>
 </TR>
 <TR>
  <TD>
   <SELECT name="Type">
    <OPTION value="">All</option>
    <OPTION value="information">Information</OPTION>
    <OPTION value="warning">Warning</OPTION>
    <OPTION value="error">Error</OPTION>
   </SELECT>
  </TD>
  <TD>Type</TD>
 </TR>
<TR>
 <TD><input type="text" name="EventCode"></TD>
 <TD>Event Code</TD>
</TR>
<TR>
 <TD><input type="text" name="UserName"</TD>
 <TD>User Name</TD>
</TR>
<TR>
 <TD><input type="password" name="Password"></TD>
 <TD>Password</TD>
</TR>
<TR>
 <TD COLSPAN=2 Align=center>
  <INPUT type="submit" NAME="Submit" VALUE="Submit">
 </TD>
</TR>
```

```
 </TABLE>
</FORM>

<%
'Here's the end of the original If...Then
'This is executed if the form was submitted
Else
```

Can you spot the key components? At the very start of the page, the ASP code tags indicate that VBScript is being used. The first statement is an `If…Then` construct that checks the value of the "SUBMIT" input field. If you look at the form HTML, "SUBMIT" is the name of the Submit button, and it will have a value of "SUBMIT" if it's clicked. If it's empty, the form wasn't submitted and it needs to be displayed.

```
<%

'Was the form submitted?
If Request.Form("SUBMIT") = "" Then

%>
<FORM ACTION="event.asp" METHOD="POST">
 <Table cellpadding=2 cellspacing=2 border=0>
  <TR>
   <TD>
    <INPUT type="text" name="ComputerName"
     value="<% Response.Write CompName%>">
   </TD>
...
```

Notice that the `If…Then` doesn't have an `Else` or `End If` right away. Instead, the ASP code ends with the `%>` tag, and the static HTML begins. This causes ASP only to display the static HTML if the logical condition in `If…Then` is true. There *is* an `Else` statement, all the way at the end of the static HTML.

```
  </TR>
 </TABLE>
</FORM>

<%
'Here's the end of the original If...Then
'This is executed if the form was submitted
Else
```

If the logical condition of the `If...Then` block is False, VBScript and ASP skips the static HTML and heads straight for whatever comes after the `Else`.

Speaking of that, here's the code that queries the event log and displays the information. Again, I'll walk through this line-by-line later, so for now, just see how far along you can follow.

```
'declare variables
 Dim oServices, oResultset, oRecord
 Dim sComputerName, sLogFile, sQuery
 Dim dtDate, dtTime

 'get the network object
 set oNet =CreateObject("WScript.Network")

 'get a WMI locator
 set oLocator = CreateObject("WbemScripting.SWbemLocator")

 'get the local computer name
 sComputerName = oNet.ComputerName

 'build the WMI query
 sQuery = "SELECT * FROM Win32_NTLogEvent WHERE Logfile="

 'computer name specified?
 If(Request("ComputerName") <> "") Then
  sComputerName = Request("ComputerName")
 End If

 'log filename specified?
 If(Request("LogName")<> "") Then
  sLogFile = Request("LogName")
 End If

 'append computer name and log file
 'to WMI query
 sQuery = sQuery & """" & sLogFile & """"

 'add source, type, and code to query
 If(Request("Source")<> "") Then
  sQuery = sQuery & " AND SourceName=" & """" & _
   Request("Source") & """"
 End If
 If(Request("Type") <>"") Then
```

```
 sQuery = sQuery & " AND Type=" & """" & _
  Request("Type") & """"
End If
If(Request("EventCode") <>"") Then
 sQuery = sQuery & " AND EventCode=" & _
  """" & Request("EventCode") & """"
End If

'username is blank?
If Request.form("UserName") <> "" Then
 'no - connect to local machine
 Set oServices = oLocator.ConnectServer(sComputerName, _
  "root\default", Request.form("UserName"), _
  Request.Form("Password"))

Else
 'yes = connect to local computer
 Set oServices = oLocator.ConnectServer(sComputerName )
End If

'execute query
Set oResultset = oServices.ExecQuery(sQuery)

'any results?
If(oResultset.Count = 0) Then
 'no
 Response.Write "<b>Query returned 0 records.</b>"
Else
 'yes - display results

 'build table header
 Response.Write "<TABLE cellspacing=0 cellpadding=3 border=1>"

 'build first table row
 Response.Write "<TR>"
 Response.Write "<TH>Record</TH>"
 Response.Write "<TH>Type</TH>"
 Response.Write "<TH>Date</TH>"
 Response.Write "<TH>Time</TH>"
 Response.Write "<TH>Source</TH>"
 Response.Write "<TH>Category</TH>"
 Response.Write "<TH>Cat Strg</TH>"
 Response.Write "<TH>Event</TH>"
 Response.Write "<TH>Usr</TH>"
```

continues

```
  Response.Write "<TH>Computer</TH>"
  Response.Write "<TH>Msg</TH>"
  Response.Write "</TR>"

  'go through each event entry
  For Each oRecord In oResultset
   'Format the date and time of the entry
   dtDate = CDateWMI(oRecord.TimeGenerated)
   dtTime = CTimeWMI(oRecord.TimeGenerated)


   'write row tag
   Response.Write "<TR>"

   'write cell tag & record information
   Response.Write "<TD>" & oRecord.RecordNumber &" </TD>" & _
   "<TD>" & oRecord.Type & "</TD>" & _
   "<TD>" & dtDate & "</TD>" & _
   "<TD>" & dtTime & "</TD>" & _
   "<TD>" & oRecord.SourceName & "</TD>" & _
   "<TD>" & oRecord.Category & "</TD>" & _
   "<TD>" & oRecord.CategoryString & "</TD>" & _
   "<TD>" & oRecord.EventCode & "</TD>" & _
   "<TD>" & oRecord.User & "</TD>" & _
   "<TD>" & oRecord.ComputerName & "</TD>" & _
   "<TD>" & oRecord.Message & "</TD></TR>"

  Next

   'close the table
   Response.Write "</TABLE> </FONT>"

 End If
```

There are a couple of interesting blocks of code here. Remember that prototype HTML I cooked up for the table header? Here, it's being dynamically written out by using `Response.Write` statements.

```
'build first table row
Response.Write "<TR>"
Response.Write "<TH>Record</TH>"
Response.Write "<TH>Type</TH>"
```

```
Response.Write "<TH>Date</TH>"
Response.Write "<TH>Time</TH>"
Response.Write "<TH>Source</TH>"
Response.Write "<TH>Category</TH>"
Response.Write "<TH>Cat Strg</TH>"
Response.Write "<TH>Event</TH>"
Response.Write "<TH>Usr</TH>"
Response.Write "<TH>Computer</TH>"
Response.Write "<TH>Msg</TH>"
Response.Write "</TR>"
```

A similar chunk of code writes out the data rows, using `<TD>` tags and the properties of the oRecord object, which is used to represent a single event log entry.

```
'write cell tag & record information
Response.Write "<TD>" & oRecord.RecordNumber &" </TD>" & _
"<TD>" & oRecord.Type & "</TD>" & _
"<TD>" & dtDate & "</TD>" & _
"<TD>" & dtTime & "</TD>" & _
"<TD>" & oRecord.SourceName & "</TD>" & _
"<TD>" & oRecord.Category & "</TD>" & _
"<TD>" & oRecord.CategoryString & "</TD>" & _
"<TD>" & oRecord.EventCode & "</TD>" & _
"<TD>" & oRecord.User & "</TD>" & _
"<TD>" & oRecord.ComputerName & "</TD>" & _
"<TD>" & oRecord.Message & "</TD></TR>"
```

I've now got my entire script spread throughout various files. It's time to bring them all together.

## The Result

The final script is a combination of the original static HTML, the functions I created, and the inline script code I created. Merging everything results in the working event log Web viewer.

### ➤➤ Event Log Viewer

Listing 22.1 shows the final event log viewer, in its entirety.

**Listing 22.1** *Event.asp.* Displays local and remote event logs in a Web browser.

```
<%

'Was the form submitted?
If Request.Form("SUBMIT") = "" Then

 'No - set up the form
 'Start by getting the local computer name
 Set oNet =CreateObject("WScript.Network")
 sCompName=oNet.Computername
 Response.Write "Computer: " & compname & "<BR>"
 Set oNet = Nothing

 'Now display the HTML form
%>
<FORM ACTION="event.asp" METHOD="POST">
 <Table cellpadding=2 cellspacing=2 border=0>
  <TR>
   <TD>
    <INPUT type="text" name="ComputerName"
     value="<% Response.Write CompName%>">
   </TD>
   <TD>Computer:</TD>
  </TR>
  <TR>
   <TD>
    <SELECT name="LogName">
     <OPTION value="application">Application</OPTION>
     <OPTION value="system">System</OPTION>
     <OPTION value="security">Security</OPTION>
     </SELECT>
    </TD>
    <TD>Log</TD>
   </TR>
   <TR>
    <TD><INPUT type="text" name="Source"></TD>
    <TD>Event Source</TD>
   </TR>
   <TR>
    <TD>
     <SELECT name="Type">
      <OPTION value="">All</option>
```

```
      <OPTION value="information">Information</OPTION>
      <OPTION value="warning">Warning</OPTION>
      <OPTION value="error">Error</OPTION>
     </SELECT>
    </TD>
    <TD>Type</TD>
   </TR>
  <TR>
   <TD><input type="text" name="EventCode"></TD>
   <TD>Event Code</TD>
  </TR>
  <TR>
   <TD><input type="text" name="UserName"</TD>
   <TD>User Name</TD>
  </TR>
  <TR>
   <TD><input type="password" name="Password"></TD>
   <TD>Password</TD>
  </TR>
  <TR>
   <TD COLSPAN=2 Align=center>
    <INPUT type="submit" NAME="Submit" VALUE="Submit">
   </TD>
  </TR>
 </TABLE>
</FORM>

<%
'Here's the end of the original If...Then
'This is executed if the form was submitted
Else

 'declare variables
 Dim oServices, oResultset, oRecord
 Dim sComputerName, sLogFile, sQuery
 Dim dtDate, dtTime

 'get the network object
 set oNet =CreateObject("WScript.Network")

 'get a WMI locator
 set oLocator = CreateObject("WbemScripting.SWbemLocator")
```

continues

```
'get the local computer name
sComputerName = oNet.ComputerName

'build the WMI query
sQuery = "SELECT * FROM Win32_NTLogEvent WHERE Logfile="

'computer name specified?
If(Request("ComputerName") <> "") Then
 sComputerName = Request("ComputerName")
End If

'log filename specified?
If(Request("LogName")<> "") Then
 sLogFile = Request("LogName")
End If

'append computer name and log file
'to WMI query
sQuery = sQuery & """" & sLogFile & """"

'add source, type, and code to query
If(Request("Source")<> "") Then
 sQuery = sQuery & " AND SourceName=" & """" & _
  Request("Source") & """"
End If
If(Request("Type") <>"") Then
 sQuery = sQuery & " AND Type=" & """" & _
  Request("Type") & """"
End If
If(Request("EventCode") <>"") Then
 sQuery = sQuery & " AND EventCode=" & _
  """" & Request("EventCode") & """"
End If

'username is blank?
If Request.form("UserName") <> "" Then
 'no - connect to local machine
 Set oServices = oLocator.ConnectServer(sComputerName, _
  "root\default", Request.form("UserName"), _
  Request.Form("Password"))

Else
 'yes = connect to local computer
 Set oServices = oLocator.ConnectServer(sComputerName )
End If
```

```
'execute query
 Set oResultset = oServices.ExecQuery(sQuery)

 'any results?
 If(oResultset.Count = 0) Then
  'no
  Response.Write "<b>Query returned 0 records.</b>"
 Else
  'yes - display results

  'build table header
  Response.Write "<TABLE cellspacing=0 cellpadding=3 border=1>"

  'build first table row
  Response.Write "<TR>"
  Response.Write "<TH>Record</TH>"
  Response.Write "<TH>Type</TH>"
  Response.Write "<TH>Date</TH>"
  Response.Write "<TH>Time</TH>"
  Response.Write "<TH>Source</TH>"
  Response.Write "<TH>Category</TH>"
  Response.Write "<TH>Cat Strg</TH>"
  Response.Write "<TH>Event</TH>"
  Response.Write "<TH>Usr</TH>"
  Response.Write "<TH>Computer</TH>"
  Response.Write "<TH>Msg</TH>"
  Response.Write "</TR>"

  'go through each event entry
  For Each oRecord In oResultset
   'Format the date and time of the entry
   dtDate = CDateWMI(oRecord.TimeGenerated)
   dtTime = CTimeWMI(oRecord.TimeGenerated)


   'write row tag
   Response.Write "<TR>"

   'write cell tag & record information
   Response.Write "<TD>" & oRecord.RecordNumber &" </TD>" & _
   "<TD>" & oRecord.Type & "</TD>" & _
   "<TD>" & dtDate & "</TD>" & _
   "<TD>" & dtTime & "</TD>" & _
   "<TD>" & oRecord.SourceName & "</TD>" & _
```

continues

```
   "<TD>" & oRecord.Category & "</TD>" & _
   "<TD>" & oRecord.CategoryString & "</TD>" & _
   "<TD>" & oRecord.EventCode & "</TD>" & _
   "<TD>" & oRecord.User & "</TD>" & _
   "<TD>" & oRecord.ComputerName & "</TD>" & _
   "<TD>" & oRecord.Message & "</TD></TR>"

  Next

   'close the table
   Response.Write "</TABLE> </FONT>"

 End If

'custom functions
Function CDateWMI(cim_DateTime)
 'declare variables
 Dim sDateTime, iYear, iMonth, iDay

 'convert the date to a string
 sDateTime = CStr(cim_DateTime)

 'get the year, month, and day
 iYear = CInt(Mid(sDateTime, 1, 4))
 iMonth = CInt(Mid(sDateTime, 5, 2))
 iDay = CInt(Mid(sDateTime, 7, 2))

 'reformat into a normal date
 CDateWMI = CDate(Join(Array(iMonth, iDay, iYear), "/"))
End Function

Function CTimeWMI(cim_DateTime)
 'declare variables
 Dim sDateTime, iHours, iMinutes, iSeconds

 'convert the time into a string
 sDateTime = CStr(cim_DateTime)

 'get the hours, minutes, and seconds
 iHours = CInt(Mid(sDateTime, 9, 2))
 iMinutes = CInt(Mid(sDateTime, 11, 2))
 iSeconds = CInt(Mid(sDateTime, 13, 2))
```

```
 'reformat into a normal time
 CTimeWMI = TimeSerial(iHours, iMinutes, iSeconds)
 End Function

End If
%>
```

You shouldn't have to make any changes to this code to get it running in your environment. Just make sure you're using the appropriate user credentials.

**NOTE** This script transmits passwords in clear text from your Web browser to the Web server. I don't advise using this script outside of a lab environment unless you secure the connection with a VPN or by using SSL encryption on the Web server. Because you'll be providing administrative passwords, anyone with a network sniffer could intercept the password and wreak havoc on your network.

## ➤➤ Event Log Viewer—Explained

The script starts out by seeing whether the form was submitted.

```
<%

'Was the form submitted?
If Request.Form("SUBMIT") = "" Then
```

If the form wasn't submitted, I first retrieve the local computer name. This allows me to display that as a default selection. To get the name, I use the WScript.Network object.

```
 'No - set up the form
 'Start by getting the local computer name
 Set oNet =CreateObject("WScript.Network")
 sCompName=oNet.Computername
 Response.Write "Computer: " & compname & "<BR>"
 Set oNet = Nothing
```

The script continues by displaying the main HTML form. Notice that I've inserted the local computer name as the default value for the "ComputerName" text box. I've highlighted that code in boldface. I often make little tweaks like this to my static HTML just to make a page a bit easier to use, if I can.

```
 'Now display the HTML form
%>
<FORM ACTION="event.asp" METHOD="POST">
 <Table cellpadding=2 cellspacing=2 border=0>
  <TR>
   <TD>
    <INPUT type="text" name="ComputerName"
     value="<% Response.Write CompName%>">
   </TD>
   <TD>Computer:</TD>
  </TR>
  <TR>
   <TD>
    <SELECT name="LogName">
     <OPTION value="application">Application</OPTION>
     <OPTION value="system">System</OPTION>
     <OPTION value="security">Security</OPTION>
     </SELECT>
    </TD>
    <TD>Log</TD>
   </TR>
   <TR>
    <TD><INPUT type="text" name="Source"></TD>
    <TD>Event Source</TD>
   </TR>
   <TR>
    <TD>
     <SELECT name="Type">
      <OPTION value="">All</option>
      <OPTION value="information">Information</OPTION>
      <OPTION value="warning">Warning</OPTION>
      <OPTION value="error">Error</OPTION>
     </SELECT>
    </TD>
    <TD>Type</TD>
   </TR>
  <TR>
   <TD><input type="text" name="EventCode"></TD>
   <TD>Event Code</TD>
  </TR>
  <TR>
```

```
  <TD><input type="text" name="UserName"</TD>
  <TD>User Name</TD>
 </TR>
 <TR>
  <TD><input type="password" name="Password"></TD>
  <TD>Password</TD>
 </TR>
 <TR>
  <TD COLSPAN=2 Align=center>
   <INPUT type="submit" NAME="Submit" VALUE="Submit">
  </TD>
 </TR>
</TABLE>
</FORM>

<%
'Here's the end of the original If...Then
'This is executed if the form was submitted
Else
```

This is the end of the static HTML. If the form wasn't submitted, this is the last thing the script executes. On the other hand, if the form *was* submitted, everything after `Else` is the *first* thing that is executed.

I start by declaring a handful of variables that I'll use later.

```
'declare variables
Dim oServices, oResultset, oRecord
Dim sComputerName, sLogFile, sQuery
Dim dtDate, dtTime
```

Next, I get a reference to the WScript.Network object. Didn't I already do this? Yes, but in the section of code that is called when the form *wasn't* submitted. That code hasn't executed this time around, because the form was submitted. Therefore, I need to get the object reference.

```
'get the network object
set oNet =CreateObject("WScript.Network")
```

I also need to get a WMI locator so that I can find whatever computer I plan to connect to.

```
 'get a WMI locator
set oLocator = CreateObject("WbemScripting.SWbemLocator")
```

Now I can use the WScript.Network object to retrieve the local computer name.

```
'get the local computer name
sComputerName = oNet.ComputerName
```

I've declared a string variable to store the WMI query; I'll populate that variable with the first part of the query. Notice how I leave the query hanging at the end; I'll append more information as the script runs.

```
'build the WMI query
sQuery = "SELECT * FROM Win32_NTLogEvent WHERE Logfile="
```

If the user provides a computer name in the form, I want to pull that into a variable. Similarly, if the user specifies a log name, I want to pull that into a variable, too.

```
'computer name specified?
If(Request("ComputerName") <> "") Then
 sComputerName = Request("ComputerName")
End If

'log filename specified?
If(Request("LogName")<> "") Then
 sLogFile = Request("LogName")
End If
```

Now I can add on to the WMI query by adding the log filename.

```
'append computer name and log file
'to WMI query
sQuery = sQuery & """" & sLogFile & """"
```

The user can optionally specify an event source, type, and event code to filter on. If any of those three are specified, I need to add the appropriate criteria to the query.

```
'add source, type, and code to query
If(Request("Source")<> "") Then
 sQuery = sQuery & " AND SourceName=" & """" & _
  Request("Source") & """"
End If
```

```
If(Request("Type") <>"") Then
 sQuery = sQuery & " AND Type=" & """" & _
  Request("Type") & """"
End If
If(Request("EventCode") <>"") Then
 sQuery = sQuery & " AND EventCode=" & _
  """" & Request("EventCode") & """"
End If
```

Next, I need to see whether the user name was filled in. If it wasn't, I use the WMI locator to connect to the appropriate remote machine, providing the user name and password that the user typed. Otherwise, I force WMI to connect to the local computer, using the computer name I got from the WScript.Network object.

```
'username is blank?
If Request.form("UserName") <> "" Then
 'no - connect to machine
 Set oServices = oLocator.ConnectServer(sComputerName, _
  "root\default", Request.form("UserName"), _
  Request.Form("Password"))

Else
 'yes = connect to local computer
 Set oServices = oLocator.ConnectServer(sComputerName )
End If
```

Now I can execute the WMI query against the computer I connected to. This returns a WMI result set, hopefully consisting of one or more event log entries.

```
'execute query
Set oResultset = oServices.ExecQuery(sQuery)
```

I cannot safely assume that any entries came back. After all, the log might be empty, or perhaps no entries matched the criteria provided. So, I check to see if the result set is empty, and if it is, I display a message to that effect. If the result set isn't empty, the script continues to execute.

```
'any results?
If(oResultset.Count = 0) Then
 'no
```

*continues*

```
  Response.Write "<b>Query returned 0 records.</b>"
Else
  'yes - display results
```

First, I have to write out the HTML table header. I already worked out this HTML code earlier; this is using `Response.Write` to produce the code into the stream of HTML being sent to the Web browser.

```
 'build table header
Response.Write "<TABLE cellspacing=0 cellpadding=3 border=1>"

'build first table row
Response.Write "<TR>"
Response.Write "<TH>Record</TH>"
Response.Write "<TH>Type</TH>"
Response.Write "<TH>Date</TH>"
Response.Write "<TH>Time</TH>"
Response.Write "<TH>Source</TH>"
Response.Write "<TH>Category</TH>"
Response.Write "<TH>Cat Strg</TH>"
Response.Write "<TH>Event</TH>"
Response.Write "<TH>Usr</TH>"
Response.Write "<TH>Computer</TH>"
Response.Write "<TH>Msg</TH>"
Response.Write "</TR>"
```

Next, I'll use a `For Each...Next` loop to go through each result in the result set. Each result represents a single *record,* or event log entry.

```
'go through each event entry
For Each oRecord In oResultset
```

Each entry has a `TimeGenerated` property that's a combination date and time. I already wrote functions to reformat this data into something more legible, so I'll call those functions now.

```
'Format the date and time of the entry
dtDate = CDateWMI(oRecord.TimeGenerated)
dtTime = CTimeWMI(oRecord.TimeGenerated)
```

Now I can write the HTML code for the data row. I'll just write out the appropriate `<TD>` and `</TD>` tags, along with the desired properties from the oRecord object, which is used to represent the current event log entry.

```
'write row tag
Response.Write "<TR>"

'write cell tag & record information
Response.Write "<TD>" & oRecord.RecordNumber &" </TD>" & _
"<TD>" & oRecord.Type & "</TD>" & _
"<TD>" & dtDate & "</TD>" & _
"<TD>" & dtTime & "</TD>" & _
"<TD>" & oRecord.SourceName & "</TD>" & _
"<TD>" & oRecord.Category & "</TD>" & _
"<TD>" & oRecord.CategoryString & "</TD>" & _
"<TD>" & oRecord.EventCode & "</TD>" & _
"<TD>" & oRecord.User & "</TD>" & _
"<TD>" & oRecord.ComputerName & "</TD>" & _
"<TD>" & oRecord.Message & "</TD></TR>"
```

That's almost it. I can close up the `For Each` loop, and after all records have been processed, write out the HTML tags that close the table.

```
 Next

  'close the table
  Response.Write "</TABLE> </FONT>"

End If
```

Finally, I've thrown in the two custom functions I wrote. These were used earlier in the script. The first one simply starts by pulling the date and time data into a string variable. Then, it uses substring functions (`Mid()`) to pull out the year, month, and day. It ends by using string array functions to create a normal-looking date from the results.

```
'custom functions
Function CDateWMI(cim_DateTime)
 'declare variables
 Dim sDateTime, iYear, iMonth, iDay
```

*continues*

```
 'convert the date to a string
 sDateTime = CStr(cim_DateTime)

 'get the year, month, and day
 iYear = CInt(Mid(sDateTime, 1, 4))
 iMonth = CInt(Mid(sDateTime, 5, 2))
 iDay = CInt(Mid(sDateTime, 7, 2))

 'reformat into a normal date
 CDateWMI = CDate(Join(Array(iMonth, iDay, iYear), "/"))
End Function
```

For more information on substrings, see "Working with Substrings" in Chapter 8. For more information on array handling, see "Working with Arrays" in Chapter 9.

The next function does substantially the same thing, only it pulls data from different locations to get the hours, minutes, and seconds portion of the event entry's creation date.

```
Function CTimeWMI(cim_DateTime)
 'declare variables
 Dim sDateTime, iHours, iMinutes, iSeconds

 'convert the time into a string
 sDateTime = CStr(cim_DateTime)

 'get the hours, minutes, and seconds
 iHours = CInt(Mid(sDateTime, 9, 2))
 iMinutes = CInt(Mid(sDateTime, 11, 2))
 iSeconds = CInt(Mid(sDateTime, 13, 2))

 'reformat into a normal time
 CTimeWMI = TimeSerial(iHours, iMinutes, iSeconds)
 End Function

End If
%>
```

That's it! One complete Web page script, ready to go.

## Review

I hope that the example in this chapter has shown you how easy it can be to create useful administrative Web pages. Start by designing the Web page itself in FrontPage or another editor. Don't worry about producing a beautiful page, just get the elements in place that you need. Then, add functions and subroutines as necessary to support the script you'll write. Finally, add any inline code that you need. Keep in mind that ASP allows static HTML to be conditional if placed within an `If...Then` construct.

### COMING UP

ASP, IIS, WMI, ADSI, and the other technologies used in scripting can conspire to create real security vulnerabilities—or security hassles, depending on how you look at it. In the next chapter, I'll explain the pros and cons of ASP scripting security and show you how to configure your machines to provide functionality with minimal vulnerabilities.

CHAPTER 23

# Web Page Security Overview

**IN THIS CHAPTER**

IIS' built-in security model can make administrative Web pages a bit more difficult to write. I'll explain how IIS handles security, and how your scripts and Web servers need to be configured in order to enable scripting functionality.

Administrative Web pages must comply with IIS' security features. Those features differ a bit from version to version; in this chapter, I'm assuming that you're using Internet Information Server (IIS) 4.0 (Windows NT), IIS 5.0 (Windows 2000), IIS 5.1 (Windows XP), or IIS 6.0 (Windows Server 2003). IIS 6.0 differs the most from a security standpoint, so I'll spend extra time discussing those differences.

Bear in mind that IIS' entire security makeup is designed to prevent you from doing what administrative Web pages do, particularly working with ADSI and WMI. That's OK, though, because it's configurable, and I'll show you how to make it work.

## The ASP Security Context

ASP pages run under a specific security context, and the identity of that context depends on a few factors. First, bear in mind that the IIS service itself runs under the LocalSystem account. As the name implies, LocalSystem has almost complete control over all local resources, and practically no authority to access network resources. However, although IIS *runs* under the LocalSystem account, actions performed by Web pages (including ASP pages) do *not* have LocalSystem privileges. That's because IIS uses a system of *impersonations* to grant security privileges to Web pages.

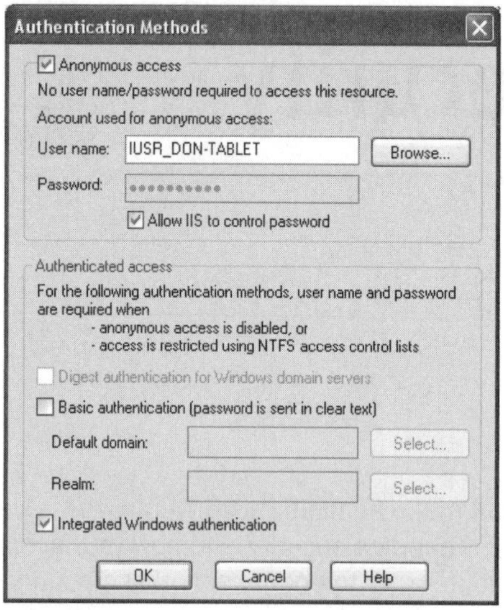

**Figure 23.1** Enabling anonymous access for a Web site

The first impersonation IIS does is the Anonymous user account. That's the IUSR_*machinename* user account that's created when IIS is installed. It's a local account, not a domain account, and it isn't a member of the machine's Users group—it's a member of the Guests group. That membership severely restricts the functionality that the account has, and pretty much limits it to reading Web pages. IIS performs this impersonation whenever anonymous access is enabled for a Web site, as shown in Figure 23.1.

**NOTE** Windows Server 2003 doesn't use the IUSR_*machinename* account by default. Instead, it uses a special new built-in user account named Network Service. Regardless, many administrators commonly change IIS to use a more restricted user account, which may affect what your scripts can do.

Note that you can change the user account used to grant anonymous access. I don't recommend ever using a more powerful account, though, as you enable completely unauthenticated users to perform some powerful operations. For example, the Anonymous user account doesn't have permission to run WMI scripts or queries; you could configure IIS to use the local Administrator account for anonymous access instead. That would get your WMI scripts running, but it would also allow complete strangers to have full control over your Web server. Not a good idea!

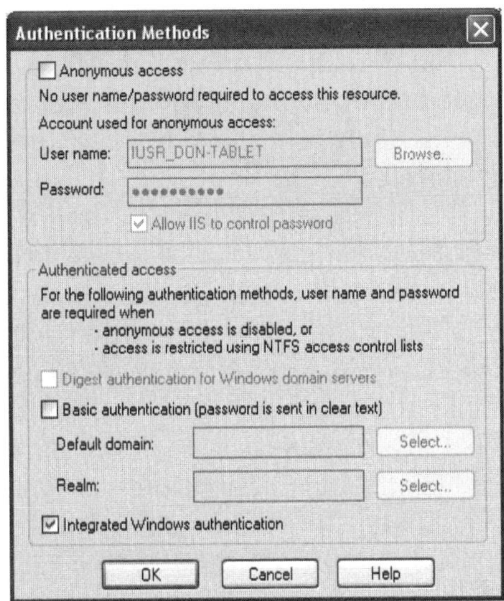


**Figure 23.2** Disabling anonymous access for a Web site

Remember, IIS uses the Anonymous user account whenever anonymous access is allowed, and when there are no special NTFS permissions on the Web page a user requests. If you want to force IIS to use another form of impersonation, you have to disable anonymous access, as shown in Figure 23.2, or apply restrictive NTFS permissions to the Web pages. Those permissions must not allow the Anonymous user account, meaning you'll have to remove the Everyone group from the NTFS permissions, and ensure that neither the Anonymous user account nor the Guest group has permissions.

When anonymous access is disabled (either through the Web site or by NTFS permissions to the Web page), IIS requires the user to provide logon credentials. The Web site's Authentication Methods properties (shown in Figure 23.2) allow you to determine which methods are available.

- Digest authentication is available for domain member servers and domain controllers. This authentication is reasonably secure, but isn't supported by a very wide range of Web browsers.
- Basic authentication passes logon credentials in clear text. This is compatible with most Web browsers, although it should only be used when the Web server offers HTTPS encrypted connections. Clear text passwords can be easily intercepted when they're not encrypted by HTTPS.

- Integrated Windows authentication works primarily with Internet Explorer, and provides the most transparent and secure authentication. Domain users logged on to a domain member workstation generally don't have to retype their user name or password when this type of authentication is used.

When any of these types of authentication are enabled, IIS impersonates the user indicated by the logon credentials. For example, suppose you configure only Integrated Windows authentication, and then log on to your workstation as a member of the Domain Admins group. If you access a Web page, the Web page will be able to execute with Domain Admin privileges. If another non-administrator user accesses the same Web page, the page will only execute with normal Domain User permissions.

---

**TIP** Most administrative Web pages need administrative privileges to execute properly. To accommodate them, I generally set up a separate, dedicated intranet Web site—either on a standalone small Web server or in a separate Web site—to host my administrative Web pages. That way, I can configure the site to require Integrated Windows authentication, and use NTFS permissions to restrict access to only administrators.

---

Understanding the security context that your scripts are using is important for troubleshooting purposes. I always recommend running complicated scripts as a regular VBS script (which you run under `Wscript.exe`) before incorporating them into a Web page. Doing so allows you to ensure that the scripts are working correctly; any errors that crop up when you move the script into a Web page is likely to be a security context problem. If you're having problems and you suspect that authentication security is the issue, try running the Web page shown in Listing 23.1. You'll immediately see what user IIS is trying to impersonate when running ASP pages.

**Listing 23.1** *WhoAmI.asp.* Shows the user account IIS is using for security impersonation.

```
<%

Dim sUser
sUser = Request.ServerVariables("LOGON_USER")

If sUser = "" Then
 Response.Write("ANONYMOUS")
```

```
Else
 Response.Write("Logged on as " & sUser)
End If

%>
```

Obviously, you need to make sure this Web page resides in the same Web site as the one you're testing. Different Web sites can have different authentication settings.

## Prohibited Behaviors

To protect your computers and your network, the Anonymous IIS user account is not a member of the local Users group; it's a member of the Guests user group. By default, a large number of useful scripting features and operating system functionality aren't available to members of the Guests group:

- WMI.
- Most ADSI functions; only general LDAP queries are allowed for most directory services. Active Directory doesn't usually allow anonymous LDAP queries by default.
- Most operations that use the FileSystemObject (FSO).
- Most operations using Windows Script Host (WSH) objects, including the Network and Shell objects.
- Almost all network operations, including using any components that require network access.

The Anonymous user account is a local account on the Web server, and as such has no privileges or capabilities across the network or within a domain. Essentially, you can use intrinsic and custom VBScript functions and features, the intrinsic ASP objects (including Request and Response), and that's about it.

**NOTE** IIS itself doesn't impose many restrictions on functionality; it's the user context being used to execute ASP pages that can be restricted. The Anonymous account can't do much, whereas an administrator account can do anything. Always keep that simple rule in mind as you write administrative Web pages.

## IIS 4.0, 5.0, and 5.1 versus IIS 6.0

IIS 6.0 is the first time Microsoft has tried to create a more secure IIS "out of the box," as opposed to a more *functional* IIS. That's led to a lot of misconceptions, but keep in mind that IIS 6.0 isn't necessarily more secure than earlier versions—it's just that most of the functionality that includes security vulnerabilities is disabled by default on a new IIS 6.0 installation. Upgrades from previous versions are *not* necessarily more secure out of the box, as they inherit the settings from the old version being upgraded.

One of the first things you need to know about IIS 6.0 is that ASP is not installed by default. In other words, if you just select the **Application Server** component in Add/Remove Windows Components, IIS 6.0 will be installed *without* the ASP ISAPI filter, meaning ASP pages won't be executed. You must go into the **Details** of the component installation to enable ASP, as shown in Figure 23.3.

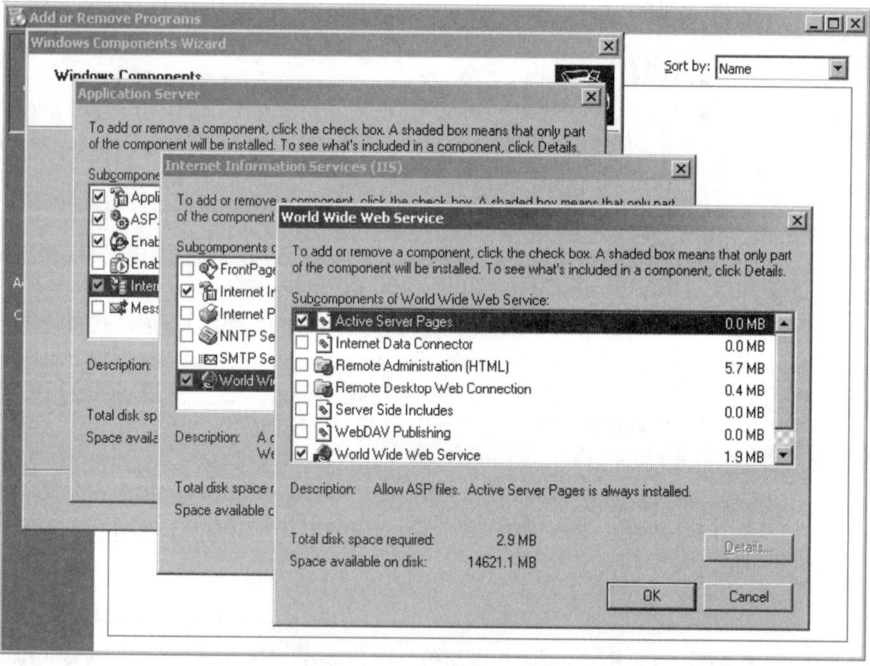


**Figure 23.3** Installing ASP support with IIS 6.0

IIS 6.0 also adds another authentication choice: Microsoft .NET Passport authentication. This authentication type requires special setup and developer support, as well as a paid license to the .NET Passport system. It's not something you'll typically use in an administrative script.

Much of IIS 6.0's new security features aren't actually part of IIS 6.0 at all; they're part of the .NET Framework, including ASP.NET, which is bundled with Windows Server 2003. However, "classic" ASP doesn't utilize any of the Framework's security features, so I won't cover them here.

---

**NOTE** If you're an experienced IIS administrator and you'd like to learn more about what's new and changed in IIS 6.0, check out *Microsoft® IIS 6.0 Delta Guide* by Martin C. Brown, published by Sams Publishing.

---

IIS 6.0 does have an interesting new concept called *application pools*, which have their own security features. The application pools play into IIS 6.0's new architecture. First, each application pool has its own memory space, meaning a crash in one pool won't affect applications running in other pools. From a security standpoint, each pool has its own security context. By defaultthis is a network service account, but you can also configure it to be a local system account or any specific user account you prefer, as shown in Figure 23.4.

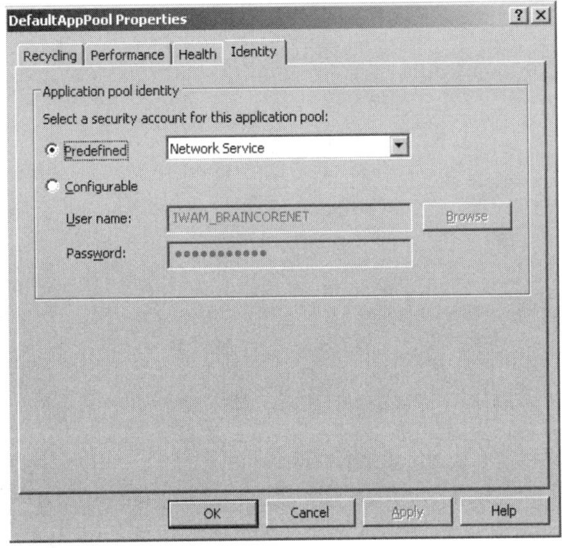


**Figure 23.4** Configuring application pool identity

You can configure as many application pools as you like, and each Web site is configured to run in a specific application pool. A pool can thus contain several Web sites, one site, or no sites. Figure 23.5 shows how a Web site is configured to exist within a specific application pool.

If you're trying to configure IIS 6.0 to run your administrative Web pages, I recommend switching the application pool to use the Local System identity, and then disabling anonymous access. This provides a security model much like IIS 5.0, and will allow most administrative Web pages to run without errors.

---

**TIP** Don't change the configuration of the default application pool (**Default–AppPool**), because that will change the security for any other sites using that pool. Instead, create a new pool, modify its identity, and assign the Web site containing your administrative Web pages to the new pool.

---

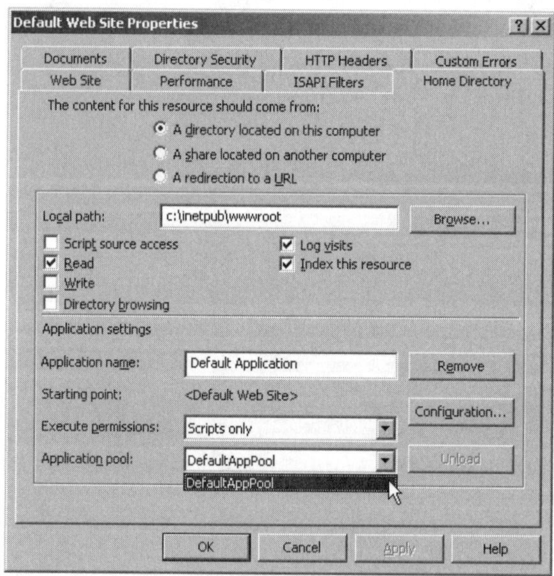


**Figure 23.5** Configuring a site's application pool

## NTFS and IIS Security

IIS is fully integrated with the Windows operating system, which means it respects and obeys Windows' security constraints. In particular, IIS respects the permissions assigned to files and folders that reside on NTFS-formatted volumes.

---

**TIP** Because FAT (and its variants, like FAT32) doesn't provide any file-level security, I don't recommend using it to store Web site content. Always store Web site content—especially administrative Web pages—on an NTFS volume.

---

The bottom line is this: IIS won't allow any user to access a Web page unless that user has at least Read permissions to the Web page file. You can use this to your advantage when you create administrative Web pages. Simply edit the security properties of your Web pages, and ensure that *only authorized users* have Read access. Remove the Everyone group, for example, and add the Domain Admins group. Doing so forces IIS to authenticate any user requesting the page—even if anonymous access is enabled—and prevents unauthorized access.

## Writing Secure ASP Code

Obviously, I recommend using NTFS permissions to secure your administrative Web pages. Grant permissions *only* to administrators that are allowed to use the pages, and completely remove the Everyone group from the permissions. Also, ensure that the Guest group doesn't have permissions. After you've done that, IIS won't allow anyone who isn't authorized to even see the pages, let alone try to execute them.

You can use a couple of other techniques to improve the security of your administrative Web pages. First, authenticate your users. For example, if you've written a script that only members of the Help Desk group should be able to execute, use a function like the one in Listing 23.2.

**Listing 23.2** *CheckMembership.vbs.* This function ensures a user is a member of a particular group.

```
Function AllowUser(sDomain, sAuthorizedGroup)

 Dim sUserADPath, bLoggedOn
 sUserADPath = "WinNT://" & sDomain & _
  "/" & Request.ServerVariables("LOGON_USER")

 'change backslashes to slashes for ADSI
 sUserADPath = Replace(sUserADPath, "\", "/")

 'get the group
 Set oGroup = GetObject("WinNT://DON-TABLET/" & _
  sAuthorizedGroup & ",group")

 'is the user a member?
 For Each oMember in oGroup.Members
  If LCase(oMember.ADsPath) = LCase(sUserADPath) Then
   bLoggedOn = True
   Exit for
  End If
 Next

 AllowUser = bLoggedOn
End Function
```

This function accepts a domain name and a group name, and returns True if the current user is a member of that group. Use it as follows.

```
If Not AllowUser("MyDomain","Help Desk") Then
 Response.Write "You do not have permissions."
 Response.End
End If
```

Another technique is to check for spoofed form submissions. Whenever a user fills out an HTML form and submits it, the receiving page can check the source of the submission. For administrative scripts, you can check to make sure the form was submitted from the Web page you intended. This prevents hackers from trying to create their own substitute form, inserting bogus values, and submitting the form to the processing page. For example, the following code makes sure that the form was posted from a page named Admin.asp.

```
If Request.ServerVariables("HTTP_REFERRER") <> _
 "http://myserver/admin.asp" Then
 Response.Write "Unauthorized submission."
 Response.End
End If
```

One form of IIS attack that's been successful in the past is tricking scripts into writing command code. It's a complex tactic, but easy to defend against. Instead of using `Response.Write` to create output, use `Response.Write Server.HTMLEncode(`*`whatever`*`)`. By forcing any output to be coded as HTML, you can eliminate most forms of this attack.

Some attacks try to insert special characters into your script's input parameters, causing it to crash or to perform unexpected functions. You can use VBScript's regular expressions capability, along with the `Replace()` function, to easily strip out these special characters. For example, this script isn't secure.

```
Dim sUser, sDomain
sUser = Request("UserName")
sDomain = Request("DomainName")
```

Why is this not secure? Because the values are taken from the Request object and put into variables with no checking. Presumably, those variables are used to control the script's actions, but the variables could contain characters that, especially if output through `Response.Write`, make IIS perform actions that a user wouldn't ordinarily be able to perform. Instead of moving data directly into variables, consider testing the input data first, to ensure it doesn't contain any suspicious characters. The script in Listing 23.3 illustrates the technique.

**Listing 23.3** *Checkinput.vbs.* Checking input for special characters.

```
Dim sUser, sDomain
sUser = SafetyCheck(Request("UserName"))
sDomain = SafetyCheck(Request("DomainName"))

Function SafetyCheck(sString)
```

*continues*

```
    Dim o
    Set o = CreateObject("VBScript.RegExp")

    'define bad characters
         Dim sBadChars
         sBadChars = "(<\s*(script|object|applet|embed|form)\s*>)"
         sBadChars = sBadChars & "|" & "(<.*>)"
         sBadChars = sBadChars & "|" & "(&.{1,5};)"
         sBadChars = sBadChars & "|" & "eval\s*\("
         sBadChars = sBadChars & "|" & "(event\s*=)"

         'Remove character encoding
         sBadChars = Replace(sBadChars,"<", "(<|%60|<)")
         sBadChars = Replace(sBadChars,">", "(>|%62|>)")

    'set case and global options
         o.IgnoreCase = True
         o.Global =False

         'insert the bad characters pattern
    o.Pattern = sBadChars

    'test for bad characters
    Dim bValid
    bValid = o.Test(sString)

    'release expression object
         Set o = Nothing

    'if no bad characters, return original string
    'otherwise, return an empty string
    If bValid Then
     SafetyCheck = sString
    Else
     SafetyCheck = ""
    End If

End Function
```

The `SafetyCheck()` function returns an empty string if there are any special characters, and returns the original string if it appears to be safe.

**NOTE** VBScript regular expressions are beyond the scope of this chapter, but you can read more about them in the VBScript documentation. They provide a powerful way to search, match, and manipulate strings, beyond VBScript's built-in string-handling functions.

## Review

Understanding ASP and IIS security isn't difficult, and you need to master the basic concepts in this chapter before you can start effectively using administrative Web pages. The most important lesson, as in any security discussion, is to *trust no one.* Always check input values and parameters to make sure they're what you expected, and always validate user identity before performing any tasks. ASP and VBScript provide some functionality to make identity validation and data scrubbing easy, and IIS itself provides a number of features to help secure and protect your administrative Web pages.

### COMING UP

In the next chapter, I'll help you put it all together with two complete, systematic examples of designing and writing administrative Web pages. I'll build on the examples in Chapters 13 and 20, where you practiced your script design skills, and show you how to start with a basic static HTML page and create a functional, useful Web-based administrative tool.

CHAPTER 24

# Putting It All Together: Your First Administrative Web Pages

**IN THIS CHAPTER**

It's time to take everything you've learned and create a complete, administrative Web page from scratch. The two step-by-step examples in this chapter will include the design process, as well as some cool ADSI code that queries domain information.

It's time to take everything you've learned about scripting and Web pages and merge them. In this chapter, I'm going to walk you through two complete examples. The first example will be a simple one: creating a Web page that allows junior administrators to quickly and easily check the status of a user account in a domain. The second example will be a bit more complicated, and will allow an administrator to automatically create new IIS virtual directories. That example will show you how to check a user's identity from within a script—a useful trick in any administrative Web page.

Most importantly, these examples will walk you through the complete Web page design process, so that you'll feel more comfortable embarking on your own projects in the future.

## Checking User Account Status

The business requirements for this example aren't complex. I want to have a simple Web page that accepts a user ID, and then queries a predetermined NT or Active Directory domain to see if that user account is locked out or disabled. I want the results to be displayed on the bottom of the page, so that an administrator can quickly enter another user ID to check its status.

## Designing the Page

I use Microsoft FrontPage to produce most of my Web page designs. It's easy, and with FrontPage 11, you don't get a lot of extraneous fancy HTML formatting, so it's easier to see what's going on.

Listing 24.1 shows the simple HTML form I cooked up in FrontPage.

**Listing 24.1** *Userprops.htm*. This is a static HTML page that will be adapted to ASP later.

```
<html>
<head><title>Check User Account Status</title></head>
<body>
<p align="center"><b>Check User Account Status</b><i><br>
This page will work only for domain administrators
or account operators.</i></p>
<form method="POST" action="userprops.asp">
 <p align="center">User ID:<br>
 <input type="text" name="UserID" size="20"></p>
 <p align="center"><input type="submit"
 value="Submit" name="Submit"></p>
 <hr noshade color="#000000">
</form>
<p align="center"><b>Status for<br>
<u>xx<br>
</u>yy</b></p>
</body>
</html>
```

If you open the page in FrontPage or even a Web browser, you'll notice that I've included some placeholder information. The "xx" and "yy" at the bottom of the page are where I want my script to insert the user ID and its account status. I find that including placeholder information like this helps me figure out exactly where in the HTML code my script needs to insert stuff. It also lets me apply formatting—such as boldfacing and underlining—by using FrontPage's excellent formatting tools, so that I don't have to worry about what the underlying HTML codes are.

**TIP** Don't forget that you can load these listings from the CD accompanying this book. Try making your own customizations to Listing 24.1, perhaps changing colors or dressing up the formatting a bit. Leave the placeholder information alone, and you'll be able to easily incorporate the script code I'll show you later.

## Writing Functions and Subroutines

There's not much code required for this example, but there's no reason not to write it as a function or subroutine. Why bother? Because it'll make the code easier to pull out and reuse in future scripts.

When I'm writing scripts for Web pages, I often like to start by writing a plain script in Notepad or another editor. This allows me to test the script code on its own, without fussing with the Web page stuff. After the script is working, I can incorporate it into the Web page easily enough.

Listing 24.2 shows the test script I wrote for this example. Notice that almost the entire script is a function; there's only one line of code outside the function, and that line of code simply calls the function to test it. By including all the code in a function (or sub), I can easily paste it into my Web page later.

**Listing 24.2** *TestUserAcct.vbs.* This script checks the status of a particular user account.

```
MsgBox UserStatus("donjones")

Function UserStatus(sUser)

 'bind to the provider
 On Error Resume Next
 Dim oUser
 Set oUser = GetObject("WinNT://server1/" & _
  sUser & ",user")

 'user found?
 If Err <> 0 Then

  'no!
  sMsg = "USER NOT FOUND"

 Else
```

*continues*

```
    'user was found
    'is this account disabled?
    If oUser.AccountDisabled = "True" Then
     sMsg = sMsg & " Disabled"
    End If

    'is this account locked?
    If oUser.IsAccountLocked = "True" Then
     sMsg = sMsg & " Locked Out"
    End If

    'neither?
    If sMsg = "" Then
     sMsg = "Normal"
    End If

  End If

  'return result
  UserStatus = sMsg

End Function
```

There are a couple of important things to notice about this script.

- I've hard-coded a user name—donjones—to test with. That's outside of the main function, though, so I won't have to make a change when I move this script into the Web page.
- The domain is hard-coded within the function. In this case, it's "server1," which is actually the name of a particular domain controller. You'll want to change that to be a valid domain controller name or domain name in your environment.

Try using this script with several user accounts, including some that don't exist, some that are locked out, and some that are disabled. Ensure the script returns an appropriate response for each. Keep in mind that you can use the Windows Script Debugger and editors like VBSEdit or PrimalScript, making it easier to write and debug the bulk of your code.

## Writing the Main Script

Now it's time to merge the script and the Web page. I'm going to use a slightly different technique than I've used in previous Web page examples. Check out Listing 24.3.

### ➤➤ User Properties

This script prompts for a user ID, and then connects to a domain controller named Server1 to check on the status of the user ID. It can display a message if the user ID isn't found, if the ID is locked out and/or disabled, or if the account's status is normal.

**Listing 24.3** *UserProps.asp.* The merged script and Web page.

```
<%

Function UserStatus(sUser)

 'bind to the provider
 On Error Resume Next
 Dim oUser
 Set oUser = GetObject("WinNT://server1/" & _
  sUser & ",user")

 'user found?
 If Err <> 0 Then

  'no!
  sMsg = "USER NOT FOUND"

 Else

  'user was found
  'is this account disabled?
  If oUser.AccountDisabled = "True" Then
   sMsg = sMsg & " Disabled"
  End If

  'is this account locked?
  If oUser.IsAccountLocked = "True" Then
   sMsg = sMsg & " Locked Out"
  End If
```

*continues*

```
  'neither?
  If sMsg = "" Then
   sMsg = "Normal"
  End If

 End If

 'return result
 UserStatus = sMsg

End Function

%>
<html>
<head><title>Check User Account Status</title></head>
<body>
<p align="center"><b>Check User Account Status</b><i><br>
This page will work only for domain administrators
or account operators.</i></p>
<form method="POST" action="userprops.asp">
 <p align="center">User ID:<br>
 <input type="text" name="UserID" size="20"></p>
 <p align="center"><input type="submit"
 value="Submit" name="Submit"></p>
 <hr noshade color="#000000">
</form>
<%
If Request("Submit") <> "" Then
%><p align="center"><b>Status for<br>
<u><% Response.Write Request("UserID") %><br>
</u><% Response.Write UserStatus(Request("UserID")) %></b></p>
<%
End If
%>
</body>
</html>
```

Notice that I plugged the actual function in at the start of the page. The main script code doesn't start until the middle of the actual HTML: I use an `If…Then` construct to see whether the form is being submitted. If it is, I display the second part of the HTML, replacing my placeholder "xx" and "yy" with `Response.Write` commands that display the appropriate information.

## ➤➤ User Properties—Explained

I'll walk through what the script is doing. I start with the `UserStatus` function, which accepts a user ID as its only input.

```
<%

Function UserStatus(sUser)
```

Next, I bind to the WinNT ADSI provider. Remember, this allows the script to work with older NT domains as well as Active Directory domains. I plug the name of the user ID in the `sUser` variable. Note that you'll need to change server1 to either a domain controller or a domain that exists in your environment.

```
'bind to the provider
On Error Resume Next
Dim oUser
Set oUser = GetObject("WinNT://server1/" & _
 sUser & ",user")
```

Did you notice the `On Error Resume Next`? If the user ID provided doesn't exist, ADSI won't be able to bind to it, and will return an error. I've told VBScript to ignore the error and resume executing code. In the next line of code, I check to see if the special Err object has a value of zero. If it does, no error occurred; if it's not zero, an error occurred and I can set an output message to indicate that the user wasn't found.

```
'user found?
If Err <> 0 Then

 'no!
 sMsg = "USER NOT FOUND"

Else
```

Now that the user was found, I can check its `AccountDisabled` and `IsAccountLocked` properties, which are set by the WinNT provider. If either is true, I concatenate an appropriate message to `sMsg`. I concatenate so that both "Disabled" and "Locked Out" can appear in the same message, because an account can be both locked out and disabled.

```
'user was found
'is this account disabled?
If oUser.AccountDisabled = "True" Then
 sMsg = sMsg & " Disabled"
End If

'is this account locked?
If oUser.IsAccountLocked = "True" Then
 sMsg = sMsg & " Locked Out"
End If
```

If sMsg is still empty at this point, the account was neither locked out nor disabled, so I set sMsg to include a message indicating that the account is normal.

```
'neither?
If sMsg = "" Then
 sMsg = "Normal"
End If

End If
```

Finally, the function returns sMsg as its output.

```
'return result
UserStatus = sMsg

End Function
```

That's all of the function code, and now the regular text of the Web page begins.

```
%>
<html>
<head><title>Check User Account Status</title></head>
<body>
<p align="center"><b>Check User Account Status</b><i><br>
This page will work only for domain administrators
or account operators.</i></p>
<form method="POST" action="userprops.asp">
 <p align="center">User ID:<br>
```

```
  <input type="text" name="UserID" size="20"></p>
  <p align="center"><input type="submit"
  value="Submit" name="Submit"></p>
  <hr noshade color="#000000">
</form>
```

Here's where the main script picks up. I check to see if the submit button was pushed. If it wasn't, this entire block of code—down to `</body>`—is skipped. The practical effect of the `If...Then` construct, then, is to not display any of the ASP code's output HTML the first time this page is displayed.

```
<%
If Request("Submit") <> "" Then
```

Although the next few lines are a mix of static HTML and VBScript code, none of these lines display if the logical condition for the `If...Then` construct isn't true. If the form was submitted, this code will output the user ID entered into the form, as well as the results of the `UserStatus()` function.

```
%><p align="center"><b>Status for<br>
<u><% Response.Write Request("UserID") %><br>
</u><% Response.Write UserStatus(Request("UserID")) %></b></p>
```

Finally, I'll wrap up the `If...Then` construct with an `End If` statement, and finish the static HTML for the page.

```
<%
End If
%>
</body>
</html>
```

This is a straightforward page, and it should run as-is, after you've corrected "server1" to be a domain controller or domain name that exists on your network.

---

**NOTE** You can also point this script to a particular server and use the script to check local user accounts.

---

## Testing the Page

I didn't include any tricky bugs in this page, so it should work as-is. If you're getting errors, or if you're getting "USER NOT FOUND" responses when you shouldn't, check to ensure that your ADSI connection path is correct, including the server or domain name. Also, make sure that you're authenticating to the domain as a member of the Domain Admins or Account Operators groups, because only those groups have permission to query the information that the script is trying to retrieve.

If you're having other types of problems with the Web page, go back to your Notepad version of the script (see Listing 24.2), and get that working first. You should be able to run it on the Web server as an administrator. If that works, and the Web page still doesn't, here are some possible areas for troubleshooting.

- IIS may not allow ASP pages. This can be especially true on IIS 6.0, which doesn't enable ASP by default.
- IIS may be configured to allow anonymous authentication. IIS won't check your domain credentials if anonymous users are allowed, so you'll need to disable anonymous access to force IIS to recognize you as an administrator.
- ADSI might not be installed. It's installed by default on Windows 2000 and later, so make sure you're running on at least that operating system.

### Setting Up the Environment

Before this script will work, you need to make sure that you have your IIS environment set up correctly. For this chapter, I assume that you're placing your ASP pages in an IIS folder, such as C:\Inetpub\Wwwroot. I also assume that you've configured the Web site to disallow anonymous authentication and to allow only Windows Integrated authentication. This configuration will ensure that only authorized users have access to the page. If unauthorized users gain access to the page, they still won't be able to use it, but they will receive an error message that might be confusing. Better to keep them out of areas where they don't belong!

## Administering IIS

Suppose you want to make it easy for junior administrators to create new virtual directories under IIS. You need a tool that will create the virtual directory, and automatically assign the designated Web developer as the owner of the new directory. This would be a great tool in a Web development shop, and can save a lot of mouse clicking. Suppose you also want to make sure that only members of a special Web Operators group on the Web server can use the page.

**NOTE** This code is adapted in part from the IIS Admin Web site included with IIS 4.0 and 5.0. That site and its source are great examples of how to use the IIS administration object, which is utilized within this script.

### Designing the Page

As usual, I start with FrontPage to make the basic HTML. In this case, it's pretty simple, and it's shown in Listing 24.4.

**Listing 24.4** *IIS.htm.* Static HTML for the IIS administration page.

```
<HTML>
<BODY>
<CENTER>
 <FORM ACTION="iis.asp" METHOD="POST">
  <INPUT type="text" name="VirtualDir">
  <SELECT size=1 name="Developer">
   <OPTION VALUE="test">TEST</OPTION>
  </SELECT>
  <INPUT type="checkbox" name="AllowScript">
  <INPUT type="submit" value="Submit" name="Submit">
 </FORM>
</CENTER>
</BODY>
</HTML>
```

Not much to it. The only placeholder information is the TEST option in the drop-down list box; I'll want to populate the list with the members of the Web Developers group.

For a script this complex, I also want to lay out the tasks that I need to accomplish.

- Create an IIS virtual directory.
- Set properties on a virtual directory.
- Create a physical file folder.
- Set permissions on a physical file folder.
- Check to make sure the user logged on.
- Check to make sure the user is in the Web Operators group.
- Get a membership list from a local computer group.

You should know how to do all but the first two. Excuse me? You don't know how to set permissions on a folder from within a script? Sure, you do—you just have to be creative. You've probably used, or at least heard of, `Cacls.exe`, Microsoft's command-line utility for setting NTFS permissions. I'll just use that within my script. Yes, I could use WMI, but working with permissions from within WMI is insanely complicated. I'm not after an "elegant" script, I'm out to get a job done as quickly as possible. Therefore, `Cacls.exe` it is.

---

**TIP** When you don't know how to do something in script, be creative! If you have free time later—and who does?—you can always use a "prettier" method, but when there's work to be done, just do it in whatever way you know how. If it works, it isn't wrong.

---

## Writing Functions and Subroutines

I've identified several tasks that can be broken up into functions or subroutines. These include creating the IIS virtual directory, creating the physical folder on the hard drive, and a couple of others. Listing 24.5 has the list of functions and subs.

**Listing 24.5** *IISFandS.vbs.* These functions and subs will be called from the main script.

```
Function IISDirExists(sVirtualDir)

 On Error Resume Next
```

```
 Dim bExists

 'create an IIS admin object
 'assumes Default Web Site
 Set oIISAdmin = GetObject("IIS://localhost/W3SVC/1/Root/"
  & sVirtualDir)

 'if there's no error, the dir exists
 'display message and end
 If Err.Number = 0 Then
  bExists = True
 Else
  bExists = False
 End If

 'release IIS admin object
 Set oIISAdmin = Nothing

 IISDirExists = bExists

End Function

Function CreateFolder(sVirtualDir)

 'get another admin object first
 Set oIISAdmin = GetObject("IIS://localhost/W3SVC/1/Root")
 sVDirPath  = oIISAdmin.Path & "\" & sVirtualDir

 'get a filesystemobject
 Set oFSO = Server.CreateObject("Scripting.FileSystemObject")

 'create the folder on disk if it
 'doesn't exist already
 If Not oFSO.FolderExists(sVDirPath) Then
    oFSO.CreateFolder sVDirPath
 End If

 'release the filesystemobject
 Set oFSO = Nothing

 'return the path to the folder
 CreateFolder = sVDirPath

End Sub
```

*continues*

```
Sub CreateIISVDir(sVirtualDir, bAllowScript, sVDirPath, _
 bInProcess)

 Set oVirtualDir = oIISAdmin.Create("IISWebVirtualDir",
   sVirtualDir)
 oVirtualDir.AccessScript = bAllowScript
 oVirtualDir.Path = sVDirPath
 oVirtualDir.SetInfo
 oVirtualDir.AppCreate bInprocess

End Sub

Sub CheckAuth()

 If Request.ServerVariables("LOGON_USER") = "" Then
  Response.Status = "401 Authorization Required"
  Response.End
 End If

End Sub
```

These probably deserve some explanation. I'll start with `IISDirExists()`, which checks to see if a virtual directory with a specified name already exists in IIS' Default Web Site.

```
Function IISDirExists(sVirtualDir)

 On Error Resume Next
 Dim bExists

 'create an IIS admin object
 'assumes Default Web Site
 Set oIISAdmin = GetObject("IIS://localhost/W3SVC/1/Root/"
  & sVirtualDir)

 'if there's no error, the dir exists
 'display message and end
 If Err.Number = 0 Then
  bExists = True
 Else
  bExists = False
 End If
```

```
 'release IIS admin object
 Set oIISAdmin = Nothing

 IISDirExists = bExists

End Function
```

This function uses the IIS Administration object. Notice that it works a lot like ADSI: You connect to it using the `IIS:` provider, specify the server name ("localhost"), the service ("W3SVC"), the instance ("1" is the Default Web Site), and then specify "Root" to connect to the root level. Finally, I tacked on the name of the virtual directory I'm checking on. This call to `GetObject` fails if the virtual directory doesn't exist, so I issue `On Error Resume Next` to start with. If the call does fail, I catch it with the `If Err.Number = 0` statement. Here's how it works.

- If there's no error, the directory exists, and I set `bExists` to True.
- If there's an error, the directory doesn't exist, so I set `bExists` to False.

Finally, I release the Administration object and return my result.

The next function creates a new physical file folder. It accepts the name of the virtual directory, though, and uses an IIS admin object to figure out the correct physical file path. This ensures that the new folder will be created under the Default Web Site's physical root folder (usually C:\Inetpub\Wwwroot).

```
Function CreateFolder(sVirtualDir)

 'get another admin object first
 Set oIISAdmin = GetObject("IIS://localhost/W3SVC/1/Root")
 sVDirPath  = oIISAdmin.Path & "\" & sVirtualDir

 'get a filesystemobject
 Set oFSO = Server.CreateObject("Scripting.FileSystemObject")

 'create the folder on disk if it
 'doesn't exist already
 If Not oFSO.FolderExists(sVDirPath) Then
    oFSO.CreateFolder sVDirPath
 End If
```

*continues*

```
 'release the filesystemobject
 Set oFSO = Nothing

 'return the path to the folder
 CreateFolder = sVDirPath

End Sub
```

At the completion of this function, I return the full path of the new folder. I'll use that information again in the next routine, which is a sub. This routine creates the IIS virtual directory and sets its scripting permissions property, its physical path, and its status as an in-process IIS application.

```
Sub CreateIISVDir(sVirtualDir, bAllowScript, sVDirPath, _

 bInProcess)

 Set oVirtualDir = oIISAdmin.Create("IISWebVirtualDir",
   sVirtualDir)
 oVirtualDir.AccessScript = bAllowScript
 oVirtualDir.Path = sVDirPath
 oVirtualDir.SetInfo
 oVirtualDir.AppCreate bInprocess

End Sub
```

I need one more sub. This one just checks to make sure the current user authenticated and has a user name; if he doesn't, I set `Response.Status` equal to the "Authorization Required" error message and end the script.

```
Sub CheckAuth()

 If Request.ServerVariables("LOGON_USER") = "" Then
  Response.Status = "401 Authorization Required"
  Response.End
 End If

End Sub
```

That's the bulk of the script's heavy lifting. There are a couple of other tasks I'll write in the main script, mainly because they require a lot of input parameters and aren't worth writing as a separate function or sub.

### Writing the Main Script

Time to add the main script. I still need to populate that drop-down list with members of the Web Developers group, run CACLS, and make sure the current user belongs to the Web Operators group.

#### ➤➤ IIS Administration

Listing 24.6 shows the full, complete Web page code.

**Listing 24.6** *IIS.asp.* You'll need to make some changes to get this working in your environment.

```
<%

Function IISDirExists(sVirtualDir)

 On Error Resume Next
 Dim bExists

 'create an IIS admin object
 'assumes Default Web Site
 Set oIISAdmin = GetObject("IIS://localhost/W3SVC/1/Root/"
  & sVirtualDir)

 'if there's no error, then the dir exists
 'display message and end
 If Err.Number = 0 Then
  bExists = True
 Else
  bExists = False
 End If

 'release IIS admin object
 Set oIISAdmin = Nothing

 IISDirExists = bExists

End Function
```

*continues*

```
Function CreateFolder(sVirtualDir)

 'get another admin object first
 Set oIISAdmin = GetObject("IIS://localhost/W3SVC/1/Root")
 sVDirPath  = oIISAdmin.Path & "\" & sVirtualDir

 'get a filesystemobject
 Set oFSO = Server.CreateObject("Scripting.FileSystemObject")

 'create the folder on disk if it
 'doesn't exist already
 If Not oFSO.FolderExists(sVDirPath) Then
    oFSO.CreateFolder sVDirPath
 End If

 'release the filesystemobject
 Set oFSO = Nothing

 'return the path to the folder
 CreateFolder = sVDirPath

End Sub

Sub CreateIISVDir(sVirtualDir, bAllowScript, sVDirPath, _
 bInProcess)

 Set oVirtualDir = oIISAdmin.Create("IISWebVirtualDir",
   sVirtualDir)
 oVirtualDir.AccessScript = bAllowScript
 oVirtualDir.Path = sVDirPath
 oVirtualDir.SetInfo
 oVirtualDir.AppCreate bInprocess

End Sub

Sub CheckAuth()

 If Request.ServerVariables("LOGON_USER") = "" Then
  Response.Status = "401 Authorization Required"
  Response.End
 End If

End Sub
```

```
'Ensure authentication occurs
CheckAuth

'handle submitted form
If Request("Submit") <> "" Then

 Dim sVirtualDir, bInprocess
 Dim oIISAdmin, sVDirPath
 Dim oFSO, sDeveloper
 Dim oVirtualDir, bAllowScript
 Dim sServer, oWSH
 Dim oReturnCode, sCmdLine

 'get submitted information
 sVirtualDir = Request.Form("VirtualDir")
 sDeveloper = Request.Form("Developer")

 If Request.Form("AllowScript") = "on" Then
  bAllowScript = "True"
 Else
  bAllowScript = "False"
 End If

 'see if virt dir exists already
 If IISDirExists(sVirtualDir) = True Then
  Response.Write "That directory exists."
  Response.End
 End If

 'Create the directory in the file system
 sVDirPath = CreateFolder(sVirtualDir)

 'Create the folder in IIS
 CreateIISVDir(sVirtualDir, bAllowScript, sVDirPath, bInProcess)

 'build a command line for CACLS
 sCmdLine = "cmd /c echo y| CACLS "
 sCmdLine = sCmdLine & sVDirPath
 sCmdLine = sCmdLine & " /g "
   & sDeveloper & ":C"

 'create a WSH shell object
 Set oWSH = Server.CreateObject("WScript.Shell")
```

*continues*

```
  'execute CACLS
  oReturnCode = oWSH.Run (sCmdLine , 0, True)

  'release the shell object
  Set oWSH = Nothing

  'report
  Response.Write("Done.")
  Response.End

End If



%>
<HTML>
<BODY>
<%
Dim sUserADSI, oMachine
Dim oMember, oGroup
Dim sADSI, bLoggedOn
Dim sMember

'get current user
sUserADSI = "WinNT://BRAINCORE/" & _
 Request.ServerVariables("LOGON_USER")

'change backslashes to slashes for ADSI
sUserADSI = Replace(sUserADSI, "\", "/")

'get the group
Set oGroup = GetObject("WinNT://DON-TABLET/Web Operators,group")

'is the user a member?
For Each oMember in oGroup.Members
 If LCase(oMember.ADsPath) = LCase(sUserADSI) Then
  bLoggedOn = True
  Exit for
 End If
Next

Set oGroup = Nothing
If bLoggedOn = True Then
%><CENTER>
 <FORM ACTION="iis.asp" METHOD="POST">
```

```
  <INPUT type="text" name="VirtualDir">
  <SELECT size=1 name="Developer">
<%

'make a list of Web Developers members
Set oGroup = _
 GetObject("WinNT://don-tablet/Web Developers,group")

For Each oMember in oGroup.Members
 sMember = Replace(oMember.ADsPath, "/", "\")
 sMember = Mid(sMember, 9, Len(sMember))
 Response.Write "<OPTION VALUE=" & sMember & ">"
 Response.Write sMember
 Response.Write "</OPTION>"
Next
Set oGroup = Nothing
%>
  </SELECT>
  <INPUT type="checkbox" name="AllowScript">
  <INPUT type="submit" value="Submit" name="Submit">
 </FORM>
</CENTER>
<%
Else
%>Your user account:
 <% Response.Write sUserADSI %>
 does not have access to this page.
 <%
End If
%>
</BODY>
</HTML>
```

You need to make a number of changes to get this to work.

- Change “don-tablet” to the name of the local Web server.
- Change “BRAINCORE” to the name of the domain or workgroup that the Web server belongs to.
- Make sure the “Web Operators” and “Web Developers” user groups all exist.
- Make sure the Default Web Site exists in IIS.

### ➤➤ IIS Administration—Explained

This page starts with the functions and subs I outlined earlier.

```
<%

Function IISDirExists(sVirtualDir)

 On Error Resume Next
 Dim bExists

 'create an IIS admin object
 'assumes Default Web Site
 Set oIISAdmin = GetObject("IIS://localhost/W3SVC/1/Root/"
  & sVirtualDir)

 'if there's no error, then the dir exists
 'display message and end
 If Err.Number = 0 Then
  bExists = True
 Else
  bExists = False
 End If

 'release IIS admin object
 Set oIISAdmin = Nothing

 IISDirExists = bExists

End Function

Function CreateFolder(sVirtualDir)

 'get another admin object first
 Set oIISAdmin = GetObject("IIS://localhost/W3SVC/1/Root")
 sVDirPath  = oIISAdmin.Path & "\" & sVirtualDir

 'get a filesystemobject
 Set oFSO = Server.CreateObject("Scripting.FileSystemObject")

 'create the folder on disk if it
 'doesn't exist already
 If Not oFSO.FolderExists(sVDirPath) Then
   oFSO.CreateFolder sVDirPath
 End If
```

```
 'release the filesystemobject
 Set oFSO = Nothing

 'return the path to the folder
 CreateFolder = sVDirPath

End Sub

Sub CreateIISVDir(sVirtualDir, bAllowScript, sVDirPath, _
 bInProcess)

 Set oVirtualDir = oIISAdmin.Create("IISWebVirtualDir",
   sVirtualDir)
 oVirtualDir.AccessScript = bAllowScript
 oVirtualDir.Path = sVDirPath
 oVirtualDir.SetInfo
 oVirtualDir.AppCreate bInprocess

End Sub

Sub CheckAuth()

 If Request.ServerVariables("LOGON_USER") = "" Then
  Response.Status = "401 Authorization Required"
  Response.End
 End If

End Sub
```

Next, I call the `CheckAuth` routine. This ensures that the user has authenticated; if he hasn't, the sub takes care of sending an appropriate error message and ending the script.

```
'Ensure authentication occurs
CheckAuth
```

Now, I need to see if the form has been submitted. For now, let's assume it has been, so the following code will evaluate to a True logical condition.

```
'handle submitted form
If Request("Submit") <> "" Then
```

I'll dimension some variables, and then pull information from the Request object into variables. Pulling the information into variables just makes it easier to work with, so I don't have to keep retyping **Request("VirtualDir")** and so forth.

```
Dim sVirtualDir, bInprocess
Dim oIISAdmin, sVDirPath
Dim oFSO, sDeveloper
Dim oVirtualDir, bAllowScript
Dim sServer, oWSH
Dim oReturnCode, sCmdLine

'get submitted information
sVirtualDir = Request.Form("VirtualDir")
sDeveloper = Request.Form("Developer")

If Request.Form("AllowScript") = "on" Then
 bAllowScript = "True"
Else
 bAllowScript = "False"
End If
```

Now, use the `IISDirExists()` function to see if the specified virtual directory already exists. If it does, write an error message and end the script.

```
'see if virt dir exists already
If IISDirExists(sVirtualDir) = True Then
 Response.Write "That directory exists."
 Response.End
End If
```

If you've made it this far, you know the directory doesn't already exist in IIS. Call the routine to create the folder in the file system. Note that this function actually checks to see if the folder exists, and only tries to create it if it doesn't exist.

```
'Create the directory in the file system
sVDirPath = CreateFolder(sVirtualDir)
```

Because the physical folder exists, the virtual directory can be created in IIS.

```
'Create the folder in IIS
CreateIISVDir(sVirtualDir, bAllowScript, sVDirPath, bInProcess)
```

Next, assemble a command-line string to execute CACLS. This makes the designated developer the owner of the physical folder, so that he or she can manipulate the files in the folder.

```
'build a command line for CACLS
sCmdLine = "cmd /c echo y| CACLS "
sCmdLine = sCmdLine & sVDirPath
sCmdLine = sCmdLine & " /g "
  & sDeveloper & ":C"
```

To launch the command line, you need a reference to the Windows Script Host's Shell object.

```
'create a WSH shell object
Set oWSH = Server.CreateObject("WScript.Shell")
```

Use the Shell object to execute CACLS.

```
'execute CACLS
oReturnCode = oWSH.Run (sCmdLine , 0, True)
```

Finish the script and write a completion message.

```
'release the shell object
Set oWSH = Nothing

'report
Response.Write("Done.")
Response.End

End If
```

Everything up to now only executes when the script is completed. If the script *wasn't* submitted, the following is executed.

```
%>
<HTML>
<BODY>
<%
```

*continues*

```
Dim sUserADSI, oMachine
Dim oMember, oGroup
Dim sADSI, bLoggedOn
Dim sMember
```

That gets variable definitions out of the way. Because the first thing we need to do is make sure the user is a member of Web Operators, we need to get the user's logon name. The Request object provides a `ServerVariables` collection, which provides access to a number of useful data—including the name of the logged-on user. I'm prefixing that logon name with a string that will turn it into an ADSI path.

```
'get current user
sUserADSI = "WinNT://BRAINCORE/" & _
 Request.ServerVariables("LOGON_USER")
```

We're going to be feeding that path to ADSI, so we need to flip any backslashes into regular slashes. The `LOGON_USER` variable returns something to the effect of `domain\user`, but ADSI expects to see `domain/user` instead. The `Replace()` function accomplishes the switch in one step.

```
'change backslashes to slashes for ADSI
sUserADSI = Replace(sUserADSI, "\", "/")
```

I use ADSI to get a reference to the Web Operators group.

```
'get the group
Set oGroup = GetObject("WinNT://DON-TABLET/Web Operators,group")
```

Now, I iterate through each member of the group. For each one, I check to see if the member's ADSI path matches the one I built for the user. If it does match, I set a variable to True and exit the `For Each...Next` loop.

```
'is the user a member?
For Each oMember in oGroup.Members
 If LCase(oMember.ADsPath) = LCase(sUserADSI) Then
  bLoggedOn = True
  Exit for
 End If
Next
```

I can now release the ADSI group object. If `bLoggedOn` equals True, I know the user logged on as a member of the Web Operators group, and I can continue.

```
Set oGroup = Nothing
If bLoggedOn = True Then
```

The next few lines are straight from my original static Web page design.

```
%><CENTER>
 <FORM ACTION="iis.asp" METHOD="POST">
  <INPUT type="text" name="VirtualDir">
  <SELECT size=1 name="Developer">
```

It's time to fill in that drop-down list of Web Developer members. I use code similar to what I just used to check the Web Operators group: query ADSI for the group, and add each member as an `<OPTION>` to the drop-down list box.

```
<%

'make a list of Web Developers members
Set oGroup = GetObject("WinNT://don-tablet/Web Developers,group")

For Each oMember in oGroup.Members
 sMember = Replace(oMember.ADsPath, "/", "\")
 sMember = Mid(sMember, 9, Len(sMember))
 Response.Write "<OPTION VALUE=" & sMember & ">"
 Response.Write sMember
 Response.Write "</OPTION>"
Next
Set oGroup = Nothing
%>
```

Finishing the static HTML also finishes the code that executes if the user is a member of Web Operators.

```
  </SELECT>
  <INPUT type="checkbox" name="AllowScript">
  <INPUT type="submit" value="Submit" name="Submit">
 </FORM>
</CENTER>
<%
```

Now, I include an `Else` and the code to execute if the user *isn't* a member of Web Operators.

```
Else
%>Your user account:
 <% Response.Write sUserADSI %>
 does not have access to this page.
 <%
End If
%>
</BODY>
</HTML>
```

That's it! The script should execute perfectly, after you make the minor changes I mentioned earlier. This should also serve as a great example of working with IIS from script, and of how to design an administrative Web page.

## Review

The example in this chapter should help you see how a typical administrative Web page is designed, created, tested, and used. Although this was a relatively simple example, it offers powerful functionality. You could expand this example to work in a multiple-domain environment, perhaps offering a drop-down list of available domains, or even a drop-down list of users (although that might take a while to populate in a large domain). The point is that Web pages offer an exciting, easy-to-use alternative interface for junior administrators, can be made as secure as other types of administrative utilities, and are easy to create by using the same techniques that you use for other scripts.

**COMING UP**

Enough of Web pages—it's time to move on to more advanced general scripting techniques. In the next chapter, I'll introduce you to modular programming, including script packaging and Windows Script Components. In following chapters, you'll see how to protect scripts by using encryption, and you'll learn more about scripting and security.

PART V

# Advanced Scripting Techniques

CHAPTER 25

# Modular Script Programming

**IN THIS CHAPTER**

Want to do more scripting in less time? Then you need to get modular, which is what this chapter is all about. You'll learn to create code in an easy-to-reuse fashion, enabling future scripts to leverage the work you've done in the past.

Throughout this book, I advocate the use of functions and subs to encapsulate useful script routines. This type of encapsulation makes it easy to cut and paste functions and subs into future scripts, allowing you to easily reuse script code that may have taken you a while to write and debug. Cutting and pasting is great, but it has some fundamental flaws. For example, if you decide to improve a particular function, you have to improve every copy of it that you've ever made, one copy at a time. Fortunately, VBScript provides a more efficient way to reuse the functions and subs you write: Windows Script Components (WSC).

## Introduction to Windows Script Components

To properly introduce WSC, I need to dive a bit deeper into developer-speak than I'm accustomed to doing; so bear with me. First, you should realize that you're already using programming objects in your scripts. Specifically, you're using objects—or *components*—written to Microsoft's Component Object Model, or COM. I briefly touched on COM in Chapter 5, but here's a quick refresher on what it does for you.

When you create, or *instantiate*, a COM class in a script, you do so by using the `CreateObject` statement. For example, `CreateObject("Scripting.FileSystemObject")` creates a new FileSystemObject. When VBScript executes that command, it asks COM to load "Scripting.FileSystemObject" into memory and make it available to VBScript. COM looks up the class "Scripting.FileSystemObject" in the registry. You can open the registry yourself, using Regedit or another editor, and search for "Scripting.FileSystemObject." You'll find that it has a globally unique identifier (GUID) of "{0D43FE01-F093-11CF-8940-00A0C9054228}" and that it's *in-process server* (InprocServer32) is C:\Windows\System32\scrrun.dll, which is the Microsoft Scripting Runtime DLL. COM loads that DLL into memory when you ask for a FileSystemObject.

All COM components must have an in-process server. When you create a new WSC, you're essentially creating a script that *pretends* to be a COM component. That pretense is helped by Scrobj.dll, which is the WSC in-process server. You can create instances of WSCs within scripts, and when you do so, COM loads Scrobj.dll, which in turn loads the actual WSC script and executes it. So a WSC is a regular VBScript masquerading as a DLL! In fact, any programming language that uses DLLs—including Visual Basic, Delphi, VBScript, C++, and more—can use a WSC, because WSCs meet all of the requirements for regular COM components.

Okay, that's enough developer-*ese* for one chapter. It's time to start looking at how you create these things.

### In- and Out-of-Process

What, exactly, is the difference between in-process and out-of-process? In IIS 5.0 (and earlier), each Web site on a server runs in a separate instance of `Inetinfo.exe`. Each `Inetinfo.exe` has its own memory space, and any COM objects that an ASP page instantiates generally run inside that memory space. It's easy for programmers, but if a COM object causes a problem, it can take down the entire Web site. Almost all objects you'll use in ASP run in process; out-of-process components run in their own memory space, and must implement special techniques to allow communications between their own space and `Inetinfo.exe`'s.

IIS 6.0 introduces a slightly new model called worker process isolation. Without going into the gory detail of IIS 6.0's architecture, it works something like this: Only one copy of `Inetinfo.exe` runs on the server. It spawns several subordinate worker processes, each with its own memory space, to execute Web sites. In-process servers run in these worker process spaces, effectively protecting different Web sites from a crash in any one site.

## Scripting and XML

WSCs are regular text files, but they require a special XML formatting to contain the script. The XML helps describe what the WSC does, and how it is activated and used. Probably the easiest way to see how it works is to see an example, so take a look at Listing 25.1. This is a sample WSC that performs several Windows Management Instrumentation (WMI) functions. I adapted the script from one first provided on www.wshscripting.com, an unfortunately now-defunct Web site that offered scripting examples.

**Listing 25.1** *WMIFunctions.wsc.* Example WSC.

```
<?xml version="1.0"?>
<package>
 <comment>
 WMI Management Library
 </comment>
 <component id="WMILIB">
  <?component error="true" debug="true" ?>
  <registration progid="WMILIB.WSC"
  classid="{61E6E0DC-4554-4D12-A9F4-D8E70DBCF318}"
  description="WMI Library" remotable="no" version="1.00">
  </registration>
  <public>
   <method name="Shutdown">
    <parameter name="Host"/>
   </method>
   <method name="Reboot">
    <parameter name="Host"/>
   </method>
   <method name="StartProcess">
    <parameter name="Host"/>
    <parameter name="CommandLine"/>
    <parameter name="StartDirectory"/>
   </method>
   <method name="Processes">
    <parameter name="Host"/>
   </method>
   <method name="EndProcess">
    <parameter name="Host"/>
    <parameter name="ProcessID"/>
   </method>
```

*continues*

```
  </public>
  <implements id="ASP" type="ASP"/>
  <reference guid="{00000205-0000-0010-8000-00AA006D2EA4}"
  version="2.0"/>
  <object id="Recordset" progid="ADODB.Recordset"/>
  <script id="Implementation" language="JScript">
<![CDATA[
var description = new WMILIB;

function WMILIB()
{
 this.Processes = Processes;
 this.StartProcess = StartProcess;
 this.EndProcess = EndProcess;
 this.Reboot = Reboot;
 this.Shutdown = Shutdown;
}

function Shutdown(Host)
{
 try
 {
  var wql = "SELECT * FROM Win32_OperatingSystem WHERE
  Primary=True";
  var os = GetObject("winmgmts://" + Host +
  "/root/cimv2").ExecQuery(wql);
  for(var en = new Enumerator(os); !en.atEnd();
  en.moveNext())
   en.item().ShutDown();
  return true;
 }
 catch(e)
 {
  return false;
 }
}

function Reboot(Host)
{
 try
 {
  var wql = "SELECT * FROM Win32_OperatingSystem WHERE
  Primary=True";
  var os = GetObject("winmgmts://" + Host +
```

```
  "/root/cimv2").ExecQuery(wql);
  for (var en = new Enumerator(os); !en.atEnd();
  en.moveNext())
   en.item().Reboot();
  return true;
 }
 catch(e)
 {
  return true;
 }
}

function StartProcess(Host, CommandLine, StartDirectory)
{
 try
 {
  var ProcID;
  var Proc = GetObject("WinMgmts://" + Host +
  "/root/cimv2").Get("Win32_Process");
  Proc.Create(CommandLine, StartDirectory, ProcID);
  return true;
 }
 catch(e)
 {
  return false;
 }
}

function EndProcess(Host, ProcessID)
{
 try
 {
  var wql = "SELECT * FROM Win32_Process WHERE ProcessId="
  + ProcessID;
  var procs = GetObject("WinMgmts://" + Host +
  "/root/cimv2").ExecQuery(wql);
  for(var en = new Enumerator(procs); !en.atEnd();
  en.moveNext())
   en.item().Terminate;
  return true;
 }
 catch(e)
 {
  return false;
```

continues

```
 }
}

function Processes(Host)
{
 try
 {
  var wql = "SELECT * FROM Win32_Process";
  var procs = GetObject("WinMgmts://" + Host +
  "/root/cimv2").ExecQuery(wql);
  var values = new ActiveXObject("Scripting.Dictionary");
  for(var en = new Enumerator(procs); !en.atEnd();
  en.moveNext())
   values.Add(en.item().ProcessId, en.item().Description);
  return values;
 }
 catch(e)
 {
  return new Array(e.description);
 }
}
]]>
  </script>
 </component>
</package>
```

This particular WSC is actually written in JScript (also called JavaScript or ECMAScript), not VBScript. That's an important thing to note, because it doesn't matter what language the WSC is in. You can still use it in your own VBScript files. For this example, I ignore the actual script code and focus just on the XML packaging that makes this a WSC.

All WSCs need to start with a basic XML declaration, and a `<package>` tag. This tag marks the beginning of the WSC package.

```
<?xml version="1.0"?>
<package>
```

Next, the script includes a comment contained in `<comment>` tags. The comment provides a helpful description of what the WSC does. Notice the closing `</comment>` tag; all XML tags must come in pairs. Therefore, `<comment>` is paired by `</comment>`. Tags must also be nested, which means the

`</comment>` tag *must* appear before a `</package>` tag, thus fully enclosing the comment within the package.

```
<comment>
WMI Management Library
</comment>
```

Next, the script creates an actual component. Note that each WSC file can contain multiple components within a single package, but a single file can only contain a single package. This component also contains a special tag that specifies how errors will be handled. Setting `error` equal to `true` forces errors that occur within the WSC to be displayed; setting `debug` to `true` allows the component to be debugged using the Windows Script Debugger.

```
<component id="WMILIB">
 <?component error="true" debug="true" ?>
```

Next is an important piece of the WSC: the registration. Just as the FileSystemObject has a class ID and GUID, so must your WSCs. Most importantly, these must be unique. There are a number of parameters required.

- `Progid` is optional, but provides other programmers with a friendly way of referencing your WSC. "Scripting.FileSystemObject" is an example of a `progid`.
- `Classid` is required, and must be a unique GUID. Microsoft provides utilities such as `Uuidgen.exe` to produce unique GUIDs that you can use. Editors like PrimalScript can also make one up for you.
- `Description` is optional, and provides a brief description of the component. This description appears in certain visual development tools when your component is loaded.
- `Version` is also optional, and should be a numeric version number as shown here.
- `Remotable` is optional, and indicates whether the script can be running remotely using Distributed COM. I won't be covering remoted WSCs in this book, although you can read more about them at http://msdn.microsoft.com/scripting.

```
<registration progid="WMILIB.WSC"
classid="{61E6E0DC-4554-4D12-A9F4-D8E70DBCF318}"
description="WMI Library" remotable="no" version="1.00">
</registration>
```

Next, your WSC needs to advertise the functions and subs it offers. These are referred to using the COM term, *method.* As you can see here, each method has its own name and list of parameters, which correspond to the input parameters of the appropriate functions or subs. These are all contained with a `<public>` section, indicating that these methods can be used by other scripts.

```
<public>
 <method name="Shutdown">
  <parameter name="Host"/>
 </method>
 <method name="Reboot">
  <parameter name="Host"/>
 </method>
 <method name="StartProcess">
  <parameter name="Host"/>
  <parameter name="CommandLine"/>
  <parameter name="StartDirectory"/>
 </method>
 <method name="Processes">
  <parameter name="Host"/>
 </method>
 <method name="EndProcess">
  <parameter name="Host"/>
  <parameter name="ProcessID"/>
 </method>
</public>
```

This WSC specifies an `<implements>` tag, which in this case grants it access to the ASP object model. This isn't necessary unless you want the WSC to be accessible from ASP pages. The `<reference>` tag specifies an external type library used by the script; this is also optional. In this case, the external type library is Microsoft's ActiveX Data Objects (ADO), so an `<object>` tag is used to reference it.

```
<implements id="ASP" type="ASP"/>
<reference guid="{00000205-0000-0010-8000-00AA006D2EA4}"
version="2.0"/>
<object id="Recordset" progid="ADODB.Recordset"/>
```

Next comes the actual script, enclosed by a `<script>` tag that includes the language. Following that are the actual functions and subs that make up the script—in this case, all Jscript, but they could be VBScript just as easily. Notice that the parameters of each correspond to the parameters specified for the `<method>` tags earlier.

```
  <script id="Implementation" language="JScript">
<![CDATA[
var description = new WMILIB;

function WMILIB()
{
 this.Processes = Processes;
 this.StartProcess = StartProcess;
 this.EndProcess = EndProcess;
 this.Reboot = Reboot;
 this.Shutdown = Shutdown;
}

function Shutdown(Host)
{
 try
 {
  var wql = "SELECT * FROM Win32_OperatingSystem WHERE
  Primary=True";
  var os = GetObject("winmgmts://" + Host +
  "/root/cimv2").ExecQuery(wql);
  for(var en = new Enumerator(os); !en.atEnd();
  en.moveNext())
   en.item().ShutDown();
  return true;
 }
 catch(e)
 {
  return false;
 }
}

function Reboot(Host)
{
 try
 {
  var wql = "SELECT * FROM Win32_OperatingSystem WHERE
  Primary=True";
  var os = GetObject("winmgmts://" + Host +
  "/root/cimv2").ExecQuery(wql);
```

*continues*

```
  for (var en = new Enumerator(os); !en.atEnd();
  en.moveNext())
   en.item().Reboot();
  return true;
 }
 catch(e)
 {
  return true;
 }
}

function StartProcess(Host, CommandLine, StartDirectory)
{
 try
 {
  var ProcID;
  var Proc = GetObject("WinMgmts://" + Host +
  "/root/cimv2").Get("Win32_Process");
  Proc.Create(CommandLine, StartDirectory, ProcID);
  return true;
 }
 catch(e)
 {
  return false;
 }
}

function EndProcess(Host, ProcessID)
{
 try
 {
  var wql = "SELECT * FROM Win32_Process WHERE ProcessId="
  + ProcessID;
  var procs = GetObject("WinMgmts://" + Host +
  "/root/cimv2").ExecQuery(wql);
  for(var en = new Enumerator(procs); !en.atEnd();
  en.moveNext())
   en.item().Terminate;
  return true;
 }
 catch(e)
 {
  return false;
 }
```

```
}

function Processes(Host)
{
 try
 {
  var wql = "SELECT * FROM Win32_Process";
  var procs = GetObject("WinMgmts://" + Host +
  "/root/cimv2").ExecQuery(wql);
  var values = new ActiveXObject("Scripting.Dictionary");
  for(var en = new Enumerator(procs); !en.atEnd();
  en.moveNext())
   values.Add(en.item().ProcessId, en.item().Description);
  return values;
 }
 catch(e)
 {
  return new Array(e.description);
 }
}
]]>
```

The script winds up by closing the open <script>, <component>, and <package> tags. That's it!

```
  </script>
 </component>
</package>
```

To make the WSC usable on your computer, there are two additional steps you need to take. First, you should generate a type library. This enables editors like PrimalScript to display pop-up help when using the WSC in another script; you can use tools like PrimalScript to generate the type library file, which is saved in a file with a TLB filename extension. Generally, you can also right-click the WSC file itself and select **Generate type library** from the context menu.

You also need to register the library. This adds it to the system registry by using Regsvr32, in much the same way that new DLLs are registered with the system. Again, right-clicking the WSC file usually displays a **Register component** option on the context menu, and tools like PrimalScript also offer registration menu options. You can also manually register the component from the command line:

```
Regsvr32 scrobj.dll /n /i:file:\\path\filename.wsc
```

After the WSC is properly registered, you can start using it within your scripts. For the example in this chapter, you would use something like this.

```
Dim oWMILib
Set oWMILib = CreateObject("WMILIB.WSC")
```

If a WSC isn't registered, you can still get to it. You just have to use a slightly different method. If the WSC file is named WMILib.wsc, and stored in C:\My Documents, you could use the following.

```
Dim oWMILib
Set oWMILib = GetObject("script:c:\My Documents\WMILib.wsc")
```

This technique locates and loads the script, without having the WSC actually listed in the system registry. However, you do have to know the exact location of the WSC file.

## Review

Windows Script Components, or WSCs, are special scripts that can be executed like COM components. They make it easy to package, redistribute, and reuse scripts and routines that have taken you a long time to perfect, thus making your scripting efforts faster and more efficient. WSCs are written much like normal scripts, but have a special XML layout that allows them to be executed by Scrobj.dll.

**COMING UP**

With the fundamentals of Windows Script Components under your belt, you're ready to start reusing code in your scripts. In the next chapter, I'll show you how to use components in a real script, and I'll show you how you can integrate other modular programming techniques.

CHAPTER 26

# Using Script Components

**IN THIS CHAPTER**

You've seen how to create script components; in this chapter, I'll show you how to utilize them in your own scripts. There's a ton of script components on the Web that serve valuable functions, and you don't need to know much about how they work to use them in your own scripts.

In the previous chapter, I showed you how you can create your own script components. They're a great way to modularize and encapsulate your code, allowing you to easily reuse it in other scripts. However, for administrators, the real value of script components is the ease with which they allow you to use other people's work in your own scripts. In this chapter, I'll guide you through the process of locating, registering, and utilizing the script components that have been written by hundreds of other script programmers and made available on the Web.

## Obtaining the Component

Hop on Google and find the component you need. I usually try to come up with some keywords that match the task I'm trying to do, and then throw "script component" in quotes, along for the ride. That usually delivers some good results in a page or two of hits.

For this walk-through, I've selected a component that allows me to display a more complex dialog box than VBScript provides. You can get the component's source code from http://cwashington.netreach.net/depo/view.asp?Index=409&ScriptType=component; you need to download it onto your local computer to use it. The component is credited to Micheal Harris.

## Reviewing the Component

Given the nasty things people can do with script viruses, I never run a component without looking at it first. Opening MSG.wsc in PrimalScript, or simply reviewing the source code online, reveals a relatively simple script. It's in VBScript, so I can more or less follow what it's doing. I don't see any FileSystemObject calls to delete everything on the computer, any code that looks like it's going to send an e-mail to everyone in my address book, and so forth.

Reviewing the component also allows me to see what methods and properties it offers. In this case, I can get that information from the Web site where the component is found, but that might not be the case for every component you run across. Looking through this component in PrimalScript, I can see its interfaces. As shown in Figure 26.1, PrimalScript lists each method and property in its left-hand tree. You can click on any one to jump straight to the code that implements each. This script appears to implement the following:

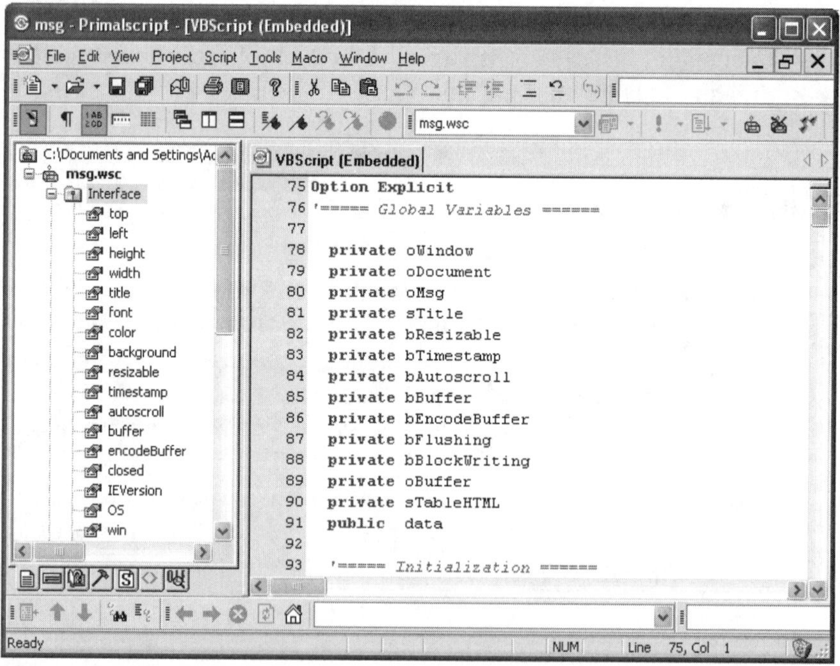


**Figure 26.1** Reviewing a script component's interfaces

- A `Show` method
- A `Write()` method, which accepts a line of text as a parameter
- A `Clear` method
- Several properties such as `Top` and `Left`, which appear to set the size of the dialog box
- A number of other useful-looking properties and methods

## Using the Component

Next, I need to register the component, which is easy enough. Right-click it in Explorer and select **Register** from the Context menu. Now I'm ready to use the component in a script.

### ➤➤ Showing a Message Box

Listing 26.1 shows the script I wrote that uses the MSG.wsc component.

**Listing 26.1** *ShowMessageBox.vbs.* Displaying a progress bar.

```
'show the message box
     dim oMsgBox
     set oMsgBox = createobject("msg.wsc")
     oMsgBox.show


     oMsgBox.write "Custom text goes here"
     oMsgBox.write "Close this box to continue"

oMsgBox.complete
```

This script should work fine, provided you've downloaded and registered the component.

### ➤➤ Showing a Message Box—Explained

This script starts simply enough, by declaring a variable and creating an object reference to the MSG.wsc component that I downloaded and registered.

```
'show the message box
dim oMsgBox
set oMsgBox = createobject("msg.wsc")
```

Next, I simply show the message box and use its `WriteLine` method to display some text.

```
oMsgBox.show


oMsgBox.write "Custom text goes here"
oMsgBox.write "Close this box to continue"
```

I then call the component's `Complete` method. Looking at the component's source code, this appears to actually write all the text I've told it to.

```
oMsgBox.complete
```

As you can see, the script component is utilized just like any other object. The difference with the script component is that I can review its source code to see what it does and discover its methods and properties. This is a great way to obtain functionality—like a graphical progress display—that I ordinarily wouldn't want to take the time to write myself.

I don't want to delve into how this particular component functions; the point is that it's very easy to download components like this from the Web and put them into use in your own environment. This particular component is well documented and comes with several examples of how to use it, which is an added bonus. The Web site at http://cwashington.netreach.net/main/default.asp includes several other components that you can download, such as components that provide the following capabilities:

- File and folder access.
- Binary comparisons of files
- Send a "magic packet" to remote computers to wake them up (Wake-on-LAN)
- Generate a progress bar display

As I mentioned earlier, you can also use Google to search for script components from other Web sites. Finally, the companion Web site to this book, www.adminscripting.com, hosts a script library where you may find additional useful components (or add your own).

## Review

Script components are easy to create, and even easier to use. By using script components, you can leverage your own past work as well as the work of others to create more powerful, professional, and flexible scripts—all much faster than if you had to do everything on your own from scratch. Also, keep in mind that I'll provide links to additional components as I find them (and as you suggest them) on this book's companion Web site, www.adminscripting.com.

**COMING UP**

If you're interested in protecting your scripts and creating a safer scripting environment, the next two chapters are for you. I'll cover script encoding and scripting security issues, along with suggestions for configuring your environment for safer scripting.

CHAPTER 27

# Encoded Scripts

**IN THIS CHAPTER**

Looking to protect the intellectual property or the integrity of your scripts? Encoding is the way to go, and WSH supports a complete script encoding technology. You'll learn how to use it, and how it can benefit your administrative scripts.

Do you ever worry about your users seeing your script source code and somehow learning more than they should? Or, perhaps you just want to ensure that your scripts aren't modified and run by someone who shouldn't be doing so. Encrypted or encoded scripts offer a solution to these problems, and Microsoft offers a Script Encoder tool to use with your administrative scripts. The Encoder can take a script and turn it into something like this.

```
//**Start
Encode**#@~^QwIAAA==@#@&0;mDkWP7nDb0zZKD.n1YAMGhk+Dvb`@#@&P,kW`UC7kLlDG
Dcl22gl:n~{'~Jtr1DGkW6YP&xDnD+OPA62sKD+ME#@#@&P,~~k6PvxC\rLmYGDcCwa.n.k
kWUbx[+X66Pcr*cJ#,@*{~!*P~P,P~. YEMU`DDE bIP,P,+s/n@#@&P~P,~PM+O;Mx`WC^
/n#pN6EU1YbWx,o Obaw.WaDrCD+nmL+v#@#@&~P7lMPdY.q,'~J_CN,Y4rkP4nnPCx,C1Y
;mV, +(PkrY ~~l,wCL PmKhwmYk(snPSkDt~JI@#@&P~\m.PkY.+,'PE8MWA/ .kPGDt D
PDtmUPri@#@&,P-CMP/D.&,'Pr\rmMWkWWY~(YnDnY,2a2^WDn.,*!,Ep@#@&,P7lD,/D.
c,'~JSW;s9Ptm-+,4+ U~VKl9+[REI,Pr0,c\ DrWHZW.. mOAMGS/nM`*#@#@&P,
~P9W^Es+UOchDbO+v/YMq~_,/DDfPQ~kY.c*IP,+sd @#@&~~,P[W1;s+UDRSDkD+vdYMF
~_,/O.yP_,dYM&P3~dYMc*iNz&R @*^#~@
```

Although it looks like gibberish, it still runs perfectly. You can be assured that nobody will change the script, because changing a single character of the encoded script will render it useless.

## Installing the Script Encoder

Microsoft's Script Encoder can be downloaded from the Scripting Web site at http://msdn.microsoft.com/scripting. Just click the **Download** link and look for the Script Encoder. You can find complete documentation online at http://msdn.microsoft.com/library/default.asp?url=/library/en-us/script56/html/seconscriptencoderoverview.asp.

The Script Encoder is a command-line tool, and is designed to run against an already-written and debugged script. After you encode the script, you cannot change it; if you do need to make changes, you have to work with the original unencoded version and then re-encode the changed script.

### Encoded versus Encrypted

The Script Encoder *looks* like a form of encryption. In a way, in fact, it is a form of encryption: Clear-test script code is run through a mathematical algorithm and the result is illegible (at least to humans). The Windows Script Host understands how to decode the script, though, allowing it to retrieve the original script code and execute it. Therefore, the Encoder can be said to use a form of encryption.

However, the Encoder isn't designed to foil all attempts at accessing your source code. *All* scripts are encoded using the same algorithm, so that any copy of the Windows Script Host can decode and execute the script. That means it isn't impossible—or even necessarily difficult—for a clever person to figure out the encoding algorithm used and create his own decoder.

You can rely on the Encoder to stop casual access to your source code, and to stop casual users from attempting to modify your scripts. However, you cannot rely on the Encoder to provide absolute protection for your scripts.

## Writing Encoded Scripts

You write encoded scripts the same way you would almost any script, at least to start. Listing 27.1 shows an example.

**Listing 27.1** *ResetPW.vbs.* An unencoded administrative script written in VBScript.

```
'get user account
varUserID = inputbox ("Reset password for what user ID?")

'bind to domain user
set objUser = GetObject("WinNT://MyDomain/" & varUserID & _
 ",user")

'make up a random password
varPass = DatePart( "y", Date() )
varPass = varPass & left(varUserID, 2)

'set password
objUser.SetPassword varPass

'show password
WScript.echo "New password is " & varPass
```

You don't need to add anything special to the file; the Script Encoder recognizes the VBS filename extension and deals with the file appropriately. To encode the file, simply run `SCRENC /f resetpw.vbs`. The Encoder produces a file named ResetPW.vbe, which is an encoded VBScript file. Here's what it will look like.

```
#@~^pAEAAA==@#@&BL Y,E/ D,Cm1W;xD@#@&-
mDjknD&fP{~rxaED4G6~crIn/ OPalddSWD[~6W.PS4mY~!/ DP&fQE#@#@&@#@&E4rU9PY
K~NK:lbU~Ek+M@#@&/nO,W8L`d+MPx~V+Y68N+^YvEqkUgK=zztXGG:mkUzrP'~7lD`d+Mq
f,'~JBEk+.Jb@#@&@#@&BsC3 P;2,lP.C
      NG:,2m/dSWMN@#@&\m.nm/dP{P9CD+nm.YvPJHESPGlD+c#~b@#@&-
lMKlk/~x,\l.Km/dPL~^+WD`7lD`/ .qG~~ *@#@&@#@&B/ OPal/kAGD9@#@&W8Lid D
? Onm/dAKDN~-mDKlkd@#@&@#@&BktWSPaC/khGD9@#@&
      UmDb2Yc+m4G~Jg+SP2lddSW.N,r/,J~',\l.Km/d@#@&@#@&2HoAAA==^#~@
```

You can also run the Script Encoder with the following syntax: `SCRENC` *`inputfile outputfile`*, in which case you can specify an output filename. The Script Encoder also supports the following command-line parameters:

- `/s`. Silent operation, with no feedback to the screen.
- `/f`. Instructs the Encoder to overwrite the input file with the output file.

- /l *language*. Specifies a new default language, either JScript or VBScript. Overrides the filename extension VBS or JS.

If you're writing scriptlets, you need to add some extra code to your scripts. Scriptlets contain `<SCRIPT>` and `</SCRIPT>` tags, as shown here.

```
<SCRIPT>
'get user account
varUserID = inputbox ("Reset password for what user ID?")

'bind to domain user
set objUser = GetObject("WinNT://MyDomain/" & varUserID & _
 ",user")

'make up a random password
varPass = DatePart( "y", Date() )
varPass = varPass & left(varUserID, 2)

'set password
objUser.SetPassword varPass

'show password
WScript.echo "New password is " & varPass
</SCRIPT>
```

You need to provide the Encoder with some cue as to how to process the file.

```
<SCRIPT LANGUAGE="VBSCRIPT">
'**Start Encode**
'get user account
varUserID = inputbox ("Reset password for what user ID?")

'bind to domain user
set objUser = GetObject("WinNT://MyDomain/" & varUserID & _
 ",user")

'make up a random password
varPass = DatePart( "y", Date() )
varPass = varPass & left(varUserID, 2)

'set password
objUser.SetPassword varPass
```

```
'show password
WScript.echo "New password is " & varPass
</SCRIPT>
```

These additions, shown in boldface, tell the Encoder which language to use and where to begin the encoding process. Anything before the `**Start Encode**` comment line won't be encoded, allowing you to preserve copyright statements and other comments. For example:

```
<SCRIPT LANGUAGE="VBSCRIPT">
'copyright (c)2003 Don Jones
'**Start Encode**
'get user account
varUserID = inputbox ("Reset password for what user ID?")

'bind to domain user
set objUser = GetObject("WinNT://MyDomain/" & varUserID & _
 ",user")

'make up a random password
varPass = DatePart( "y", Date() )
varPass = varPass & left(varUserID, 2)

'set password
objUser.SetPassword varPass

'show password
WScript.echo "New password is " & varPass
</SCRIPT>
```

The Encoder can also bulk-encode scripts. Simply provide a wildcard as the input file and a folder name as the output: `SCRENC *.vbs c:\encoded`. The Encoder encodes each script and places the encoded version in the specified folder.

## Running Encoded Scripts

Encoded scripts can normally be executed just like any other script, with a couple of caveats. First, if your scripts don't include `<SCRIPT>` tags, the filename extensions must be either VBE (for VBScript) or JSE (for Jscript). The different filename extension tells WSH that it needs to decode the script before executing it; if you change the filename extension to VBS (or JS), you receive a runtime error when executing the script.

When the Encoder goes to work on a file that does use `<SCRIPT>` tags, it changes the `LANGUAGE` attribute. `<SCRIPT LANGUAGE="VBScript">` becomes `<SCRIPT LANGUAGE="VBScript.Encode">`, for example, giving WSH the cue it needs to decode the script before trying to execute it.

## Review

Script encoding offers a way to protect the source code of your scripts from prying eyes, and a way to ensure that your scripts aren't modified. Encoding doesn't provide any kid of runtime security; in other words, by default, Windows Script Host will execute *any* encoded script it's asked to execute. In the next chapter, I'll show you how to lock down WSH so that only your authorized scripts execute in your environment.

**COMING UP**

Encoding is a great way to secure and protect your scripts. In the next chapter, I'll explain how scripting itself can be made safer and more secure. Even in this age of script-borne computer viruses, you can still allow administrative scripts to run in your environment. After that, Part VI of this book will present several more full-length example scripts to start you toward your own administrative scripts!

CHAPTER 28

# Scripting Security

**IN THIS CHAPTER**

Chances are that you've had to completely disable scripts in your environment, thanks to the number of abusive scripts out there. Making scripting a safe part of your environment can be difficult, so in this chapter, I'll give you some pointers for doing so.

Scripting has two primary security issues associated with it. First, the Windows Script Host (WSH) is included with just about every version of Windows since Windows 98. Second, WSH associates itself with a number of filename extensions, making it very easy for users to click an e-mail file attachment and launch unauthorized scripts. The knee-jerk reaction of many administrators is to simply disable scripting altogether, which also removes a beneficial administrative tool from the environment. In this chapter, I'll focus on ways to address the two primary security issues associated with scripting, helping you to configure a safer scripting environment.

## Why Scripting Can Be Dangerous

"Why can scripting be dangerous?" isn't a question many administrators have to ask. Something like 70% of all new viruses, according to some authorities, are script based; certainly some of the most devastating viruses, including Nimda, Melissa, and others, propagate at least partially through scripts sent via e-mail. Even internally produced scripts can be dangerous, as scripts can delete users, create files, and perform any number—in fact, an almost unlimited number—of tasks. There's little question about the damage scripts can do, making it vitally important that your environment be secured to allow *only* those authorized, tested scripts that you or your fellow administrators authorize.

Perhaps the most dangerous aspect of administrative scripting is the easy accessibility scripts have to the system. Users can launch scripts without even realizing that they're doing so; a large number of file extensions are registered to the Windows Script Host, and double-clicking any file with one of those extensions launches the script. In Windows XP, the default script extensions are

- JS for JScript files
- JSCRIPT for Jscript files
- JSE for Jscript encoded files
- VBE for VBScript encoded files
- VBS for VBScript files
- WSC for Windows Script Components
- WSF for Windows Script Files

Note that older computers may also register VB for VBScript files, SCR for script files, and other extensions; Windows XP cleaned up the filename extension list a bit. Don't forget, of course, static HTML files—with HTML or HTM filename extensions—which can contain embedded client-side script.

---

**NOTE** Other types of scripts exist, such as the Visual Basic for Applications (VBA) embedded into Microsoft Office documents. However, I'm going to focus this discussion on scripts associated or executed by the Windows Script Host.

---

The goal of any security program should be to allow beneficial, authorized scripts to run, while preventing unauthorized scripts from running.

## Security Improvements in Windows XP and Windows Server 2003

Windows XP and Windows Server 2003 introduce a new concept called *software restriction policies.* These policies, which are part of the computer's local security settings and can be configured centrally through Group Policy, define the software that may and may not run on a computer. By default, Windows defines two possible categories that software can fall into: *disallowed,* meaning the software won't run, and *unrestricted,* meaning the software will run without restriction. Unrestricted is the default system security level, meaning that by default all software is allowed to run without restriction.

Windows also defines *rules,* which help to categorize software into either the disallowed or unrestricted categories. By default, Windows comes with four rules, defining all system software—Windows itself, in other words—as unrestricted. This way, even if you set the default security level to disallowed, Windows will continue to be categorized as unrestricted.

You can define your own rules, as well.

- Certificate rules identify software based on the digital certificate used to sign the software.
- Hash rules identify software based on a unique checksum, which is different for any given executable file.
- Path rules identify software based on its file path. You can also specify an entire folder, allowing all software in that folder to run or to be disallowed.
- Internet Zone rules identify software based on its Internet zone location.

Therefore, you create rules that allow Windows to identify software. The rules indicate if the identified software belongs to the unrestricted or disallowed categories. Software not specifically identified in a rule belongs to whichever category is set to be the system default.

Suppose, for example, that you set the system default level to disallowed. From then on, no software will run unless it is specifically identified in a rule and categorized as unrestricted. Although it takes a lot of configuration effort to make sure everything is listed as allowed, you can effectively prevent any unauthorized software—such as scripts—from running on your users' computers.

Software restriction policies also define a list of filename extensions that are considered by Windows to be executable, and the list includes (by default) many standard WSH scripting filename extensions. The DLL filename extension is notably absent from the list. That's because DLLs never execute by themselves; they must be called by another piece of software. By allowing DLLs to run unrestricted, you avoid much of the configuration hassle you might otherwise expect. For example, you can simply authorize `Excel.exe` to run, and not have to worry about the dozens of DLLs it uses, because they aren't restricted. The default filename extension list does *not* include JS, JSCRIPT, JSE, VBE, VBS, or WSF, and I heartily recommend that you add them. For example, Figure 28.1 shows that I've added VBS to the list of restricted filenames, forcing scripts to fall under software restriction policies.

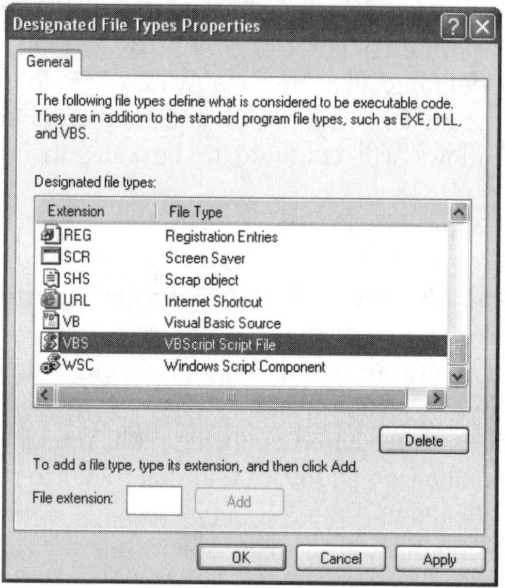


**Figure 28.1** Placing VBS files under software restriction policy control

With effective use of software restriction policies, you can gain immediate and effective control over which scripts run in your environment, as well as control other types of executable software. One of the most effective ways to ensure that only *your* scripts run is to sign them, and then create a software restriction policy rule that identifies your scripts by their digital signature.

## Digitally Signing Scripts

A signed script includes a digital signature as a block comment within the file. You need to be using the WSH 5.6 or later XML format, because it contains a specific element for storing the certificate. Take Listing 28.1 as an example.

### ➤➤ Script Signer

This script signs another script for you. Just run it with the appropriate command-line parameters shown, or run it with no parameters to receive help on the correct usage.

**Listing 28.1** *Signer.vbs.* This script signs another one.

```
<job>
 <runtime>
  <named name="file" helpstring="The script file to sign"
   required="true" type="string" />
  <named name="cert" helpstring="The certificate name"
   Required="true" type="string" />
  <named name="store" helpstring="The certificate store"
   Required="false" type="string" />
 </runtime>
 <script language="vbscript">

  Dim Signer, File, Cert, Store
  If Not WScript.Arguments.Named.Exists("cert") Or _
   Not WScript.Arguments.Named.Exists("file") Then

   WScript.Arguments.ShowUsage()
   WScript.Quit

  End If

  Set Signer = CreateObject("Scripting.Signer")
  File = WScript.Arguments.Named("file")
  Cert = WScript.Arguments.Named("cert")

  If WScript.Arguments.Named.Exists("store") Then
   Store = WScript.Arguments.Named("store")
  Else
   Store " "
  End If

  Signer.SignFile(File, Cert, Store)

 </script>
</job>
```

## ➤➤ Script Signer—Explained

This script is stored in an XML format, which describes its command-line parameters. That's what the first block of XML does.

```
<job>
 <runtime>
  <named name="file" helpstring="The script file to sign"
   required="true" type="string" />
  <named name="cert" helpstring="The certificate name"
   Required="true" type="string" />
  <named name="store" helpstring="The certificate store"
   Required="false" type="string" />
 </runtime>
```

Then, the actual script begins. It checks first to see that both the "cert" and "file" command-line arguments were provided; if they weren't, the script displays the help information and exits.

```
 <script language="vbscript">

  Dim Signer, File, Cert, Store
  If Not WScript.Arguments.Named.Exists("cert") Or _
   Not WScript.Arguments.Named.Exists("file") Then

   WScript.Arguments.ShowUsage()
   WScript.Quit

  End If
```

Assuming everything was provided, the script creates a new Scripting.Signer object and passes it the file and certificate command-line arguments.

```
  Set Signer = CreateObject("Scripting.Signer")
  File = WScript.Arguments.Named("file")
  Cert = WScript.Arguments.Named("cert")
```

If a specific certificate store is specified, that's passed to the Signer objects, too.

```
  If WScript.Arguments.Named.Exists("store") Then
   Store = WScript.Arguments.Named("store")
  Else
   Store " "
  End If
```

Finally, the Signer's `SignFile` method is called to actually sign the target script file. The file is opened, and its signature is written to a comment block.

```
  Signer.SignFile(File, Cert, Store)

 </script>
</job>
```

Note that anyone can get into the file and modify its signature. However, the signature no longer matches the script, and it cannot pass the trust test conducted by WSH. Similarly, any changes to the script's code, after it is signed, fail the trust test.

## Running Only Signed Scripts

If you don't want to mess around with software restriction policies, you can also rely on WSH's own built-in form of security policy. This policy allows you to specify that only signed scripts will be run; unsigned scripts won't be. This is probably the easiest and most effective way to prevent most unauthorized scripts.

To set the policy, open the registry key HKEY_CURRENT_USER\SOFTWARE\Microsoft\Windows Script Host\Settings\TrustPolicy. Set the value to 0 to run all scripts, 1 to prompt the user if the script is untrusted, and 2 to only run trusted scripts. What's a *trusted* script? Any script that has been digitally signed by a certificate that the user's computer is configured to trust. For example, if you purchase a certificate from VeriSign (which all Windows computers trust by default), and use that certificate to sign your scripts, they'll run. Unfortunately, a hacker could do the same thing—but you could easily investigate the source of the certificate, because it's a way to uniquely identify the signer.

Using this built-in trust policy allows you to run only signed scripts no matter what version of Windows your users have, provided you've deployed WSH 5.6 or later to all computers. Note that this technique, because it relies on WSH and not the operating system, works on all operating systems capable of running WSH. Many of the other techniques in this chapter—such as Software Restriction Policies—run only on Windows XP, Windows Server 2003, and later.

## Ways to Implement Safe Scripting

Although Software Restriction Policies offer a promising way to control what runs on your users' computers, it's only available on XP and 2003, and does require some pretty significant planning before you can roll it out. Are there any alternatives to safely scripting? Absolutely.

### The Filename Extension Game

One of the easiest ways is to configure your users' computers to no longer associate VBS, SCR, WSF, and other filename extensions with the `WScript.exe` executable. Removing these file associations prevents users from double-clicking any script files and having them automatically run. To keep your own scripts running, simply associate a new filename extension—such as CORPSCRIPT—with `WScript.exe`. Name trusted scripts appropriately, and they'll run. It's unlikely a hacker can guess your private filename extension, making this a simple, reasonably effective means of establishing a safer scripting environment.

### Script Signing

As I described earlier in this chapter, signing your scripts is a simple and effective way to guarantee their identity. By globally setting the WSH trust policy, you can prevent your computers from running untrusted scripts. There doesn't have to be much expense associated with this technique: You can establish your own Certification Authority (CA) root, use Group Policy to configure all client computers to trust that root, and then use the root to issue yourself a code-signing certificate.

### Antivirus Software

Most modern antivirus software watches for script launches and displays some kind of warning message. I don't consider this an effective means of protecting your enterprise from unauthorized scripts; it's difficult to communicate to your users which scripts are "good" and which are "bad," putting them into just as much trouble as before the antivirus solution stepped in to help. However, such software can provide an easy-to-deploy means of protecting against scripts, especially if you aren't planning to use your own scripts on users' machines (as in logon scripts).

### Defunct Techniques

Some popular techniques have been used in the past to control scripting that I want to discuss very briefly. I don't consider these methods reliable, secure, or desirable.

- Removing `WScript.exe` and `Cscript.exe`. Under Windows 2000 and later, these two files are under Windows File Protection and are not easily removed to begin with. Plus, doing so completely disables scripting, which probably isn't a goal if you're reading this book.
- Disassociating the VBS, WSF, and other filename extensions. Scripts can still be executed by running `Wscript.exe` *scriptname*, because that doesn't require a filename extension. In other words, it doesn't require much effort for hackers to e-mail shortcuts that do precisely that, thus defeating this technique as a safety measure.
- Renaming `WScript.exe` to something else. This is ineffective. Although it prevents the existing file extensions (VBS, etc.) from launching `WScript.exe`, it doesn't necessarily prevent scripts from running. Additionally, because `WScript.exe` is under Windows File Protection on Windows 2000 and later, the file may eventually wind up being replaced under your nose.

## Review

Scripting *can* be made safe in almost any environment. The capability of WSH to spot signed scripts and execute them, combined with your ability as an administrator to customize the filename extensions on client and server computers, can provide an effective barrier against unauthorized scripts, still allowing your own scripts to run.

**COMING UP**

You're all finished! If you've read this book straight through, you've learned how to program in VBScript, use ADSI and WMI, create administrative Web pages, and even secure your environment for safer scripting. In the next part, I'll wrap up with some longer examples of administrative scripts that you can use as references or start running in your environment right away.

PART VI

# Ready-to-Run Examples

CHAPTER 29

# Logon and Logoff Scripts

**IN THIS CHAPTER**

Both NT and Active Directory domains allow you to specify logon scripts; Active Directory also allows you to specify a logoff script for users and computers. I'll provide some sample logon and logoff scripts that you can use as a starting point for building your own.

Perhaps one of the most common uses for scripting is the creation of logon (and, for Active Directory domains, logoff) scripts. A number of scripting languages have been created almost exclusively for use in these scripts, including Microsoft's unsupported Kixtart, the more general-purpose WinBatch, and many others. Dozens of command-line utilities exist that allow batch files to stand in as logon scripts. Although VBScript has a steeper learning curve than these other products, it also offers unmatched power and flexibility. VBScript's capability to use COM objects and directly access many operating system features allows it to immediately take advantage of new technologies and techniques.

Because every environment requires a unique logon script, it's impossible to offer examples that you can truly use without modification. Instead, I've tried to create examples that are modular, allowing you to pick and choose the various tasks you need for your own logon scripts. As a result, some of the tasks my examples perform are slightly less than real world. For example, you'll see examples where I'm using script to execute a relatively useless command-line utility. The point of the example isn't the utility itself, but rather the ability to execute external commands. You should be able to quickly modify the pieces of these examples to assemble your own highly useful scripts.

---

**NOTE** I'm assuming that you know how to designate logon (and logoff) scripts for whatever domain environment you're working in. If you don't, consult the operating system's documentation for more information.

---

## NT and Active Directory Logon Scripts

The first example script works in either an Active Directory (AD) or NT domain environment. It includes a number of common logon script tasks.

---

**NOTE** One thing to be careful of: Windows 9x scripts actually execute before the operating system finishes the user logon process. As a result, the technique I use to retrieve the current user's name won't always work properly. There's no pretty workaround for this; I'll show you one example of how to make your script essentially sit and wait until Windows finishes and the user name becomes available.

---

### ➤➤ Logon Script One

Listing 29.1 shows the script code. I've included comments to help identify each task, so that you can easily break this apart and reuse various bits in your own scripts.

**Listing 29.1** *Logon1.vbs.* This script includes most common logon script tasks.

```
' sample logon script

' first let's create the objects we'll be using
dim objShell, objNetwork
set objShell = WScript.CreateObject("WScript.Shell")
set objNetwork = WScript.CreateObject("WScript.Network")

' let's display a welcome message
dim strDomain, strUser
strDomain = objNetwork.UserDomain
strUser = objNetwork.UserName
msgbox "Welcome to the " & strDomain & ", " & strUser & "!"


'we'll map the Z: drive to a network location
objNetwork.MapNetworkDrive "Z:", "\\Server\Share"


'let's connect to a network printer and make it
' the default - we'll capture LPT2:
```

```
objNetwork.AddPrinterConnection "LPT2", "\\Server\Print1"


'connect a second printer without capturing a printer port
objNetwork.AddWindowsPrinterConnection _
"\\server\print2", "Lexmark Optra S 1650"


'let's make that the default printer
objNetwork.SetDefaultPrinter "\\Server\Print2"


'now let's see if this fellow is a Domain Admin
dim objAdmins, user, IsMember
IsMember = False
set objAdmins = GetObject("WinNT://Domain1/Domain Admins")
for each user in objAdmins.members
 if user.name = strUser then
  IsMember = True
 end if
next

'if user is Domain Admin map the Y: drive
if IsMember = true then
 objNetwork.MapNetworkDrive "Y:", "\\Server\C$"
end if
```

You obviously need to adjust server names, domain names, and so forth to make this run in your environment. However, rather than getting *this* script to run in your environment, I recommend pulling out the pieces you like and building your own script from scratch.

## ➤➤ Logon Script One—Explained

I begin by creating the various objects I need to use and assigning them to variables. If you break apart this script, be sure to pull out the appropriate object creation statements.

```
' sample logon script

' first let's create the objects we'll be using
dim objShell, objNetwork
```

*continues*

```
set objShell = WScript.CreateObject("WScript.Shell")
set objNetwork = WScript.CreateObject("WScript.Network")
```

I use `MsgBox()` to display a friendly welcome message that includes the domain name and user name.

```
' let's display a welcome message
dim strDomain, strUser
strDomain = objNetwork.UserDomain
strUser = objNetwork.UserName
msgbox "Welcome to the " & strDomain & ", " & strUser & "!"
```

I mentioned earlier that this doesn't work so well on Windows 9x computers, because `UserName` isn't available right away. If you need to ensure that this will work properly on 9x machines, try adding the following modification.

```
' let's display a welcome message
dim strDomain, strUser
Do Until objNetwork.UserName <> ""
 WScript.Sleep(5000)
Loop
strDomain = objNetwork.UserDomain
strUser = objNetwork.UserName
msgbox "Welcome to the " & strDomain & ", " & strUser & "!"
```

This modification (shown in boldface) has the script sleep in five-second increments, and then check to see if Windows has finished logging on and populated the `UserName` property of the Network objects.

Moving on, I next map a drive to a network location. Easily the single most common logon script task, this is accomplished in just one line of code.

```
'we'll map the Z: drive to a network location
objNetwork.MapNetworkDrive "Z:", "\\Server\Share"
```

Next, I capture the LPT2 port to a network printer. This is less common nowadays, because so few of us are running old DOS applications that require captured printer ports, but here it is in case you need it.

```
'let's connect to a network printer - we'll capture LPT2:
objNetwork.AddPrinterConnection "LPT2", "\\Server\Print1"
```

Far more common is the need to map a network printer. Note that this only works if Windows "Point and Print" is enabled. In other words, if you run this command and the print server doesn't have the appropriate printer drivers for your client, the command fails. Generally, NT-based clients printing to same-generation NT-based servers (such as XP printing to Windows 2000 or 2003) use the server's printer drivers, and this command works fine.

The second parameter defines the name of the printer as you want it to appear in the client's Printers and Faxes folder.

```
'connect a second printer without capturing a printer port
objNetwork.AddWindowsPrinterConnection "\\server\print2", _
 "Lexmark Optra S 1650"
```

You can make a mapped printer the default, as shown here. Just specify the UNC. Note that the printer should already be mapped for this to work best.

```
'let's make that the default printer
objNetwork.SetDefaultPrinter "\\Server\Print2"
```

Checking for group membership is the roughest thing a logon script has to do. I start by defining a variable, `IsMember`, and setting it to False. Then, I use ADSI to query for the domain's Domain Admins group.

```
'now let's see if this fellow is a Domain Admin
dim objAdmins, user, IsMember
IsMember = False
set objAdmins = GetObject("WinNT://Domain1/Domain Admins")
```

Next, I run through each member of the group to see if the current user is a member of the group. If I find the current user in the group, I set `IsMember` to True.

```
for each user in objAdmins.members
 if user.name = strUser then
  IsMember = True
 end if
next
```

The preceding routine is just a tad inefficient; after I locate the current user in the group, there's no need to continue checking other members. The routine can be made just a bit more efficient by adding one line, shown here in boldface.

```
for each user in objAdmins.members
 if user.name = strUser then
  IsMember = True
  Exit Sub
 end if
next
```

My last action is to map a drive to a server's administrative share if the user is, in fact, a domain administrator. Checking for membership first ensures that this command runs without error, because only domain admins (by default) have permission to server administrative shares.

```
'if user is Domain Admin map the Y: drive
if IsMember = true then
      objNetwork.MapNetworkDrive "Y:", "\\Server\C$"
end if
```

One thing this script doesn't accommodate is nested group membership. For example, if the user is a member of a group, and the group is a member of Domain Admins, this script doesn't pick up on that. Checking for nested group membership is a bit more complex; for scripts like this, I usually don't worry about it because for security reasons, I try to avoid including other groups in Domain Admins.

## ➤➤ Logon Script Two

Listing 29.2 shows another logon script that runs in any domain environment. This one performs a few more advanced tasks, such as writing to the registry and running a command-line utility. This script also checks to see if it was run from `Cscript.exe` (rather than `WScript.exe`), and exits if it wasn't.

**Listing 29.2** *Logon2.vbs.* This logon script performs more advanced logon tasks.

```
Dim oShell
Dim oNetwork
```

```
Set oShell  = WScript.CreateObject ("WScript.shell")
Set oNetwork = WScript.CreateObject("WScript.Network")

'ensure this was run by using Cscript
Dim oRegExp, bIsCScript
Set oRegExp = New RegExp
oRegExp.IgnoreCase  = true
oRegExp.Pattern = "cscript.exe$"
bIsCScript = oRegExp.Test(WScript.FullName)
Set oRegExp = Nothing
If Not bIsCScript() Then
  Wscript.echo WScript.FullName & _
   " must be run with CScript."
  Wscript.Quit
End If

'run command line
oShell.Run "NET TIME /RTSDOMAIN:BRAINCORE /SET"

'write registry key
oShell.RegWrite "HKLM\Software\Company" & _
 "\Software\Key\Value", 1, "REG_DWORD"
```

## ➤➤ Logon Script Two—Explained

As usual, I start by declaring variables and creating the objects I'll use in the script.

```
Dim oShell
Dim oNetwork

Set oShell  = WScript.CreateObject ("WScript.shell")
Set oNetwork = WScript.CreateObject("WScript.Network")
```

The next bit of code uses a regular expression to see if the script was executed via `Cscript.exe`. I start by creating the regular expression object.

```
'ensure this was run by using  Cscript
Dim oRegExp, bIsCScript
Set oRegExp = New RegExp
```

Next, I tell it to ignore upper- and lower-case differences in the comparison I'll have it make, and I tell it that I'm looking for a string that starts with "cscript.exe" and ends with anything.

```
oRegExp.IgnoreCase  = true
oRegExp.Pattern = "cscript.exe$"
```

I test the comparison pattern against the full name of the currently running script. If the result comes back empty (`Nothing`), I know the script wasn't run with `Cscript.exe`, so I display a message and quit. This is a useful technique if you want to ensure command-line output formatting or some other feature unique to `Cscript.exe`.

```
bIsCScript = oRegExp.Test(WScript.FullName)
Set oRegExp = Nothing
If Not bIsCScript() Then
  Wscript.echo WScript.FullName & _
   " must be run with CScript."
  Wscript.Quit
End If
```

Next, I have the script execute a command-line utility. In this case, it's the `NET TIME` command, used to set the local computer's clock. This demonstrates how to run external command-line utilities from within a script. This is also a good reason to run the script from Cscript, so that a new command-line window doesn't pop open just to execute this command, which is what would happen if you used WScript.

```
'run command line
oShell.Run "NET TIME /RTSDOMAIN:BRAINCORE /SET"
```

Finally, I write a registry value. You could also write operating system values to force SMB signing or other features.

```
'write registry key
oShell.RegWrite "HKLM\Software\Company" & _
 "\Software\Key\Value", 1, "REG_DWORD"
```

This script is another example of the flexibility VBScript can bring to your logon scripts.

### Calling VBScript Logon Scripts in NT Domains

NT wasn't built to understand VBScript, and its ability to define logon scripts is pretty much limited to executable (EXE) and batch (BAT) files. Fortunately, those are enough to get VBScript scripts up and running.

One option is to define the logon script for your users as `Wscript.exe` *`scriptname.vbs`*, calling `WScript.exe` directly and passing the name of the script to run. That technique has problems with some clients, however, because they aren't expecting a space in the logon script name.

Another technique is to create a simple batch file that launches `WScript.exe` and the appropriate logon script. You can then define that batch file as users' actual logon script, and it'll get your code up and running appropriately.

Keep in mind that all users expected to run your script must have the Windows Script Host (WSH) installed, and that the latest version (5.6 as of this writing) is preferred.

## Active Directory–Specific Logon Scripts

If you're in an AD domain, you can take advantage of AD's newer technologies and built-in scripting interfaces, such as ADSI, to perform more powerful and flexible tricks in your logon scripts.

### ➤➤ AD Logon Script

Listing 29.3 shows a sample logon script designed to run within an AD environment.

**Listing 29.3** *ADLogon1.vbs.* This script requires Active Directory to run.

```
Const G_SALES = "cn=sales"
Const G_MARKETING = "cn=marketing"
Const G_EXECS = "cn=executives"

Set oNetwork = CreateObject("WScript.Network")
oNetwork.MapNetworkDrive "h:", "\\FileServer\Users\" & _
 oNetwork.UserName
```

*continues*

```
Set oADSystemInfo = CreateObject("ADSystemInfo")
Set oUser = GetObject("LDAP://" & oADSystemInfo.UserName)
sGroups = LCase(Join(oUser.MemberOf))

If InStr(sGroups, G_SALES) Then
 oNetwork.MapNetworkDrive "S:", "\\FileServer\SalesDocs\"
 oNetwork.AddWindowsPrinterConnection "\\PrintServer\Quotes"
 oNetwork.SetDefaultPrinter "\\PrintServer\Quotes"
End If

If InStr(sGroups, G_MARKETING) Then
 oNetwork.MapNetworkDrive "M:", "\\FileServer\MarketingDocs\"
 oNetwork.AddWindowsPrinterConnection "\\PrintServer\ColorLaser"
 oNetwork.AddWindowsPrinterConnection "\\PrintServer\BWLaser"
 oNetwork.SetDefaultPrinter "\\PrintServer\BWLaser"
End If

If InStr(sGroups, G_EXECS) Then
 oNetwork.MapNetworkDrive "X:", "\\FileServer\ExecDocs\"
 oNetwork.AddWindowsPrinterConnection "\\PrintServer\Execs"
 oNetwork.SetDefaultPrinter "\\PrintServer\Execs"
End If
```

As with the other scripts in this chapter, you need to rename the server and share names appropriately.

## ➤➤ AD Logon Script—Explained

I start by creating constants for each user group I want to check the membership of. These constants make it easier to read the rest of the script. Notice that I'm using AD-style naming, specifying the *cn*, or common name, of each group.

```
Const G_SALES = "cn=sales"
Const G_MARKETING = "cn=marketing"
Const G_EXECS = "cn=executives"
```

The next bit of code creates a WScript.Network object, and maps a single drive to the user's home directory. The earlier caveat about Win9x machines applies: `UserName` isn't populated right away so you need to add some wait time into the code.

```
Set oNetwork = CreateObject("WScript.Network")
oNetwork.MapNetworkDrive "h:", "\\FileServer\Users\" & _
 oNetwork.UserName
```

Next, I use ADSI to retrieve the current domain information and logged on user name. Then, I connect to ADSI via LDAP to retrieve the list of groups the user belongs to. This information is returned in a string, which I've stored in `sGroups`.

```
Set oADSystemInfo = CreateObject("ADSystemInfo")
Set oUser = GetObject("LDAP://" & oADSystemInfo.UserName)
sGroups = LCase(Join(oUser.MemberOf))
```

Checking for group membership is now as easy as seeing if `sGroups` contains the group name, which I can do by using the `InStr()` function. For each group the user belongs to, I map the appropriate network drives and printers. Because users may belong to more than one group (an executive could also be in sales or marketing, for example), each group is handled individually.

```
If InStr(sGroups, G_SALES) Then
 oNetwork.MapNetworkDrive "S:", "\\FileServer\SalesDocs\"
 oNetwork.AddWindowsPrinterConnection "\\PrintServer\Quotes"
 oNetwork.SetDefaultPrinter "\\PrintServer\Quotes"
End If

If InStr(sGroups, G_MARKETING) Then
 oNetwork.MapNetworkDrive "M:", "\\FileServer\MarketingDocs\"
 oNetwork.AddWindowsPrinterConnection "\\PrintServer\ColorLaser"
 oNetwork.AddWindowsPrinterConnection "\\PrintServer\BWLaser"
 oNetwork.SetDefaultPrinter "\\PrintServer\BWLaser"
End If

If InStr(sGroups, G_EXECS) Then
 oNetwork.MapNetworkDrive "X:", "\\FileServer\ExecDocs\"
 oNetwork.AddWindowsPrinterConnection "\\PrintServer\Execs"
 oNetwork.SetDefaultPrinter "\\PrintServer\Execs"
End If
```

That's easy enough! This is a great way to build a logon script that maps several different drives. Note that this same technique doesn't work as well in an NT domain, because NT domains don't provide an easy way to retrieve all of a user's groups into a single, convenient string variable.

## ➤➤ AD Logon Script Two

You can also create site-aware logon scripts. This is especially useful for mapping printers, as it allows you to map a *local* printer for the user. Roaming users who travel between sites appreciate always having a nearby printer to print to. Listing 29.4 shows a script that does just this, as well as maps a drive to the logon server's Utilities share. This might be a means of providing users with local access to a set of company-wide utilities or document templates, for example.

**Listing 29.4** *ADLogon2.vbs.* This script is site and logon server–aware.

```
Dim oSystemInfo
Dim oShell
Dim sLogonServer, sSiteName

'get logon server
Set oShell = Wscript.CreateObject("Wscript.Shell")
sLogonServer = oShell.ExpandEnvironmentStrings("%LOGONSERVER%")

'get AD site name
Set oSystemInfo = CreateObject("ADSystemInfo")
sSiteName = oSystemInfo.SiteName

'map printer based on site
Select Case sSiteName
 Case "Boston"
  oNetwork.AddWindowsPrinterConnection "\\BOS01\Laser1"
  oNetwork.SetDefaultPrinter "\\BOS01\Laser1"
 Case "New York"
  oNetwork.AddWindowsPrinterConnection "\\NYC02\LaserJet"
  oNetwork.SetDefaultPrinter "\\NYC02\LaserJet"
 Case "LA"
  oNetwork.AddWindowsPrinterConnection "\\LASrv\HP2"
  oNetwork.SetDefaultPrinter "\\LASrv\HP2"
 Case "Las Vegas"
  oNetwork.AddWindowsPrinterConnection "\\VEG4\LaserJet"
  oNetwork.SetDefaultPrinter "\\VEG4\LaserJet"
 Case "Houston"
  oNetwork.AddWindowsPrinterConnection "\\TX2\HP03"
```

```
  oNetwork.SetDefaultPrinter "\\TX2\HP03"
End Select

'show message
MsgBox "Your default printer has been " & _
 "set to a printer at the local office."

'map L: drive to logon server's
'UTILITIES share
oNetwork.MapNetworkDrive "L:", sLogonServer & _
 "\Utilities\"
```

Again, to pull bits of this script into your own, you need to modify the UNCs to suit your environment.

## ➤➤ AD Logon Script Two—Explained

I start by declaring variables.

```
Dim oSystemInfo
Dim oShell
Dim sLogonServer, sSiteName
```

Next, I create a WScript Shell object to retrieve the logon server name. This information is stored in an environment string; note that this technique can be used to retrieve any environment string, such as the system temp folder.

```
'get logon server
Set oShell = Wscript.CreateObject("Wscript.Shell")
sLogonServer = oShell.ExpandEnvironmentStrings("%LOGONSERVER%")
```

I use the AD System Info object to retrieve the current site name. This is only available on AD clients, including downlevel (9x and NT) clients running the Directory Services client.

```
'get AD site name
Set oSystemInfo = CreateObject("ADSystemInfo")
sSiteName = oSystemInfo.SiteName
```

Next, the script uses a **Select...Case** construct to map a printer based on the current site location. The printer is made the default, making it easier for users to just click Print in their applications.

```
'map printer based on site
Select Case sSiteName
 Case "Boston"
  oNetwork.AddWindowsPrinterConnection "\\BOS01\Laser1"
  oNetwork.SetDefaultPrinter "\\BOS01\Laser1"
 Case "New York"
  oNetwork.AddWindowsPrinterConnection "\\NYC02\LaserJet"
  oNetwork.SetDefaultPrinter "\\NYC02\LaserJet"
 Case "LA"
  oNetwork.AddWindowsPrinterConnection "\\LASrv\HP2"
  oNetwork.SetDefaultPrinter "\\LASrv\HP2"
 Case "Las Vegas"
  oNetwork.AddWindowsPrinterConnection "\\VEG4\LaserJet"
  oNetwork.SetDefaultPrinter "\\VEG4\LaserJet"
 Case "Houston"
  oNetwork.AddWindowsPrinterConnection "\\TX2\HP03"
  oNetwork.SetDefaultPrinter "\\TX2\HP03"
End Select
```

I also notify the users that this printer assignment has been made. That way, they know what to expect when printing. For large offices, you might want the message to include the printer name and location, so the user knows where to find his hard copy.

```
'show message
MsgBox "Your default printer has been " & _
 "set to a printer at the local office."
```

Finally, I map a drive to the Utilities share of the authenticating domain controller.

```
'map L: drive to logon server's
'UTILITIES share
oNetwork.MapNetworkDrive "L:", sLogonServer & _
 "\Utilities\"
```

You now have another useful script that leverages VBScript's access to domain information like the logon server and site name!

## Active Directory Logoff Scripts

Keep in mind that AD actually offers four types of automated scripts: logon, startup, logoff, and shutdown. *Logon* scripts execute when a user logs on, whereas *startup* scripts execute when a computer starts. Startup scripts are a good place to perform configuration changes, such as changing a computer's IP address. Logon scripts, which are what I've shown you so far in this chapter, make changes to the user's environment.

AD also supports *logoff* scripts, which execute when a user logs off, and *shutdown* scripts, which execute when a computer shuts down. It's tougher to find practical applications for these scripts, but there definitely are some. For example, you might copy a custom application's database file to a network server, if the server is available when the user logs off. That would provide a convenient, automated backup for laptop users. If you're mapping drive letters and printers in a logon script, you might unmap those in a logoff script. That way, mobile users won't see those resources if they log on to their machines while they are disconnected from the network.

### ➤➤ Logoff Script

Listing 29.5 shows a sample logoff script that unmaps a network printer, which was mapped in a logon script. Note that I use `On Error Resume Next` in this script, so that the script doesn't generate an error if the printer isn't already mapped (which would be the case if the user had manually deleted the mapping already). Note that this is essentially a reverse script of Listing 29.4, and undoes everything that script accomplishes.

**Listing 29.5** *Logoff.vbs.* This script is designed to run when a user logs off his computer.

```
Dim oSystemInfo
Dim oShell
Dim sLogonServer, sSiteName

'get logon server
Set oShell = Wscript.CreateObject("Wscript.Shell")
sLogonServer = oShell.ExpandEnvironmentStrings("%LOGONSERVER%")

'get AD site name
Set oSystemInfo = CreateObject("ADSystemInfo")
sSiteName = oSystemInfo.SiteName
```

*continues*

```
'turn off error checking
On Error Resume Next

'unmap printer based on site
Select Case sSiteName
 Case "Boston"
  oNetwork.RemovePrinterConnection "\\BOS01\Laser1"
Case "New York"
  oNetwork.RemovePrinterConnection "\\NYC02\LaserJet"
Case "LA"
  oNetwork.RemovePrinterConnection "\\LASrv\HP2"
Case "Las Vegas"
  oNetwork.RemovePrinterConnection "\\VEG4\LaserJet"
Case "Houston"
  oNetwork.RemovePrinterConnection "\\TX2\HP03"
End Select

'unmap L: drive to logon server's
'UTILITIES share
oNetwork.RemoveNetworkDrive "L:", True
```

This script obviously needs to be modified with the correct UNCs and site names before it can be used.

## ➤➤ Logoff Script—Explained

I start as usual, by declaring variables. As in the earlier logon script example, I use an environment variable to retrieve the name of the logon server, and use the AD client to discover the current site name.

```
Dim oSystemInfo
Dim oShell
Dim sLogonServer, sSiteName

'get logon server
Set oShell = Wscript.CreateObject("Wscript.Shell")
sLogonServer = oShell.ExpandEnvironmentStrings("%LOGONSERVER%")

'get AD site name
Set oSystemInfo = CreateObject("ADSystemInfo")
sSiteName = oSystemInfo.SiteName
```

Because any of these printer or drive connections could already be gone, I disable error checking. This allows the script to continue even if it encounters an error.

```
'turn off error checking
On Error Resume Next
```

Based on the site name, I remove the printer connection. Note that `RemovePrinterConnection` undoes mappings created with both `AddPrinterConnection` and `AddWindowsPrinterConnection`.

```
'unmap printer based on site
Select Case sSiteName
 Case "Boston"
  oNetwork.RemovePrinterConnection "\\BOS01\Laser1"
Case "New York"
  oNetwork.RemovePrinterConnection "\\NYC02\LaserJet"
Case "LA"
  oNetwork.RemovePrinterConnection "\\LASrv\HP2"
Case "Las Vegas"
  oNetwork.RemovePrinterConnection "\\VEG4\LaserJet"
Case "Houston"
  oNetwork.RemovePrinterConnection "\\TX2\HP03"
End Select
```

Finally, I remove the drive L: mapping created in the logon script. Notice the `True` parameter, which forces the drive to be unmapped even if the computer is using resources located on that drive; we're logging off, so it doesn't matter if there's a file open. It won't be open for long.

```
'unmap L: drive to logon server's
'UTILITIES share
oNetwork.RemoveNetworkDrive "L:", True
```

Other uses of logoff scripts might include copying instant messenger contact lists to a central location, for later retrieval by a logon script. Alternatively, you might kick off a database replication process between a central database and a local copy, causing sales orders or whatever to be updated. Logoff scripts are most useful in implementing these kinds of automated business processes, rather than performing the configuration changes we usually associate with logon scripts.

## Review

You've seen several examples of how logon (and logoff) scripts can be used in both AD and NT domains to provide automated client computer configuration. Don't forget, though, that servers are computers, too; using startup and shutdown scripts can be a great way to start third-party utilities on servers, collect software or hardware inventory information, and so forth. In any case, VBScript provides the flexibility and power you need to perform just about any task automatically at startup, logon, logoff, and shutdown.

**COMING UP**

In the next chapter, I'll provide some example domain administration scripts. You'll see how VBScript can be used to manage users, groups, and domains, and how you can automate processes like adding new users. After that, I'll show you some general network administration samples, and in Chapter 32 show you some all-purpose ADSI and WMI scripts that you can use to start writing your own scripts.

CHAPTER 30

# Windows and Domain Administration Scripts

**IN THIS CHAPTER**

In this chapter, I provide a few Windows and domain administration scripts, along with the line-by-line explanations I've used throughout this book. These samples are intended to be immediately useful in your own environment, and they provide a great way to see specific scripting features in action so that you can use them more effectively in your own scripts.

A number of different tasks exist within a domain that you may want to automate. Some that pop into mind are automating the process of creating new user accounts, finding users who haven't logged on in a long time and disabling their accounts, and collecting information from the computers in your domain. Whatever your needs, scripting is an excellent solution, and the three sample scripts in this chapter should give you a good idea of what you can accomplish.

## Automating User Creation

In this example, I'll show you how to use ActiveX Data Objects (ADO) to query information from an Excel spreadsheet, put that information into script variables, and use those variables to create and configure new domain user objects.

**NOTE** I've not covered ADO, and I find it doesn't come up often in many administrative scripts. I don't provide a comprehensive explanation of it here, but this example should give you a starting point if you have a need for a similar script in the future.

To run this script, you're going to need to create an Excel spreadsheet. Leave the first sheet named Sheet1, which is the default, and enter the following column headers on row 1:

- UserID
- FullName
- Description
- HomeDirectory
- Groups
- DialIn

Populate the remaining rows as follows.

- UserID: Enter the unique user ID you want this user to have. Note that the script doesn't do any error checking, and Windows lets you create users with duplicate names in a script. Be careful, though, because user accounts with duplicate names don't behave properly.
- FullName: The full name of the user.
- Description: Optionally, a description of the user.
- HomeDirectory: This needs to be a subfolder under a file server's root folder. You'll see how this gets used later.
- Groups: A comma-delimited list of groups the user should be placed in.
- DialIn: "Yes" or "No" describing whether the user should have dial-in permissions.

---

**TIP** This script is designed to work in any Windows domain, from Windows NT to Active Directory.

---

## ➤➤ Automating User Creation

Automating the creation of new user accounts is a must-have administrative utility in many environments, because it helps reduce administrative time and improve the consistency of the created accounts. Listing 30.1 shows a script that reads user information from an Excel spreadsheet and creates the appropriate domain user accounts.

**Listing 30.1** *AddUsers.vbs.* This script pulls new user information from an Excel spreadsheet and creates the user accounts.

```
' PART 1: Open up the Excel spreadsheet
' using ActiveX Data Objects
Dim oCN
Set oCN = CreateObject("ADODB.Connection")
oCN.Open "Excel"

Dim oRS
Set oRS = oCN.Execute("SELECT * FROM [Sheet1$]")


' PART 2: Get a reference to the
' Windows NT domain using ADSI
Dim oDomain
Set oDomain = GetObject("WinNT://NT4PDC")


' PART 3: Open an output text file
' to store users' initial passwords
Dim oFSO, oTS
Set oFSO = CreateObject("Scripting.FileSystemObject")
Set oTS = oFSO.CreateTextFile("c:\passwords.txt",True)


' PART 4: For each record in the recordset,
' add the user, set the correct user
' properties, and add the user to the
' appropriate groups

' create the necessary variables
Dim sUserID, sFullName, sDescription
Dim sHomeDir, sGroups, sDialIn
Dim sPassword, oUserAcct, oFolder
Dim sGroupList, iTemp, oGroup

' define the base path for the home
' directories to be created in
Dim sHomePath
sHomePath = "\\iridis1\c$\users\"
```

*continues*

```
' now go through the recordset one
' row at a time
Do Until oRS.EOF

  ' get the user information from this row
  sUserID = oRS("UserID")
  sFullName = oRS("FullName")
  sDescription = oRS("Description")
  sHomeDir = oRS("HomeDirectory")
  sGroups = oRS("Groups")
  sDialIn = oRS("DialIn")

  ' make up a new password
  sPassword = Left(sUserID,2) & DatePart("n",Time) & _
   DatePart("y",Date) & DatePart("s",Time)

  ' create the user account
  Set oUserAcct = oDomain.Create("user",sUserID)

  ' set account properties
  oUserAcct.SetPassword sPassword
  oUserAcct.FullName = sFullName
  oUserAcct.Description = sDescription
  oUserAcct.HomeDirectory = sHomeDir

  ' set RAS permission
  If sDialIn = "Y" Then
    oUserAcct.RasPermissions = 9
  Else
    oUserAcct.RasPermissions = 1
  End If

  ' save the account
  oUserAcct.SetInfo

  ' get a reference to the new account
  ' this gets us a valid SID & other info
  Set oUserAcct = GetObject("WinNT://NT4PDC/" & _
   sUserID & ",user")

  ' write password to file
  oTS.Write sUserID & "," & sPassword & vbCrLf
```

```
' PART 4A: Add user account to groups
' use the Split function to turn the
' comma-separated list into an array
sGroupList = Split(sGroups, ",")

' go through the array and add the user
' to each group
For iTemp = 0 To uBound(sGroupList) - 1

   ' get the group
   Set oGroup = GetObject("WinNT://NT4PDC/" & _
    sGroupList(iTemp) & ",group")

   ' add the user account
   oGroup.Add oUserAcct.ADsPath

   ' release the group
   Set oGroup = Nothing

Next


' PART 4B: Create the user's Home Directory
' (append UserID to the Home Path variable)
Set oFolder = oFSO.CreateFolder(sHomePath & sUserID)


' PART 5: All done!
' release the user account
Set oUserAcct = Nothing

' move to the next row in the recordset
oRS.MoveNext

Loop


' PART 6: Final clean up, close down
oRS.Close
oTS.Close
WScript.Echo "Passwords have been written to c:\passwords.txt."
```

Before you can run this script, you need to create a System ODBC DSN named Excel that points to your Excel spreadsheet. You'll also need to edit the server and domain names in the script to match your environment.

## ➤➤ Automating User Creation—Explained

This is a hard-working script that has quite a bit of functionality. It starts by defining an ADO connection, and then opening it. Note that for the script to work, a System ODBC DSN named Excel must exist, and it must point to a spreadsheet matching the description I gave you earlier.

```
' PART 1: Open up the Excel spreadsheet
' using ActiveX Data Objects
Dim oCN
Set oCN = CreateObject("ADODB.Connection")
oCN.Open "Excel"
```

Next, the script creates an ADO recordset—a set of database records—by querying the rows from the Excel spreadsheet.

```
Dim oRS
Set oRS = oCN.Execute("SELECT * FROM [Sheet1$]")
```

Now, the script uses ADSI to get a reference to the Windows domain. In this example, I'm connecting directly to an NT 4.0 PDC; you could specify an Active Directory domain name or an Active Directory domain controller, if you want. For more on using ADSI to connect to a domain, see Chapter 15.

```
' PART 2: Get a reference to the
' Windows NT domain using ADSI
Dim oDomain
Set oDomain = GetObject("WinNT://NT4PDC")
```

The last preliminary step is to create an output text file, where I store the new users' passwords. For more information on how to create and write to text files, turn to Chapter 12.

```
' PART 3: Open an output text file
' to store users' initial passwords
Dim oFSO, oTS
```

```
Set oFSO = CreateObject("Scripting.FileSystemObject")
Set oTS = oFSO.CreateTextFile("c:\passwords.txt",True)
```

The script can begin its real work. The first step is to define several variables, which are used to store information about each user as we create each user's account.

```
' PART 4: For each record in the recordset,
' add the user, set the correct user
' properties, and add the user to the
' appropriate groups

' create the necessary variables
Dim sUserID, sFullName, sDescription
Dim sHomeDir, sGroups, sDialIn
Dim sPassword, oUserAcct, oFolder
Dim sGroupList, iTemp, oGroup
```

Next, I define a variable for where I want the users' home directories created. Note that I'm using the C$ administrative share of a particular server. Whatever information is in the HomeDirectory column for each user will be appended to this file path, and the user's User ID will be appended to that. For example, if I want my own home directory to be \\BrainCore1\C$\Users\DonJ, I'd leave the HomeDirectory column blank in the spreadsheet.

```
' define the base path for the home
' directories to be created in
Dim sHomePath
sHomePath = "\\BrainCore1\C$\Users\"
```

Now, I use a `Do...Loop` to go through each row in the recordset—meaning each row in the Excel spreadsheet—one at a time. The recordset is an `EOF` property that will be set to True when I reach the end of the recordset, so having the loop check that keeps everything running smoothly.

```
' now go through the recordset one
' row at a time
Do Until oRS.EOF
```

I pull information from the current row into variables, just to make the information easier to work with. Notice that I simply tell the recordset object which column's information I want, and the information is retrieved.

```
' get the user information from this row
sUserID = oRS("UserID")
sFullName = oRS("FullName")
sDescription = oRS("Description")
sHomeDir = oRS("HomeDirectory")
sGroups = oRS("Groups")
sDialIn = oRS("DialIn")
```

I need to make up a new password for the user. I'm using the leftmost two characters of the user ID, and the current minutes, Julian date, and seconds from the system clock. It's not a great password, but it's reasonably unique, tough to guess, and easy to communicate to the user when he shows up for his first day of work.

```
' make up a new password
sPassword = Left(sUserID,2) & DatePart("n",Time) & _
 DatePart("y",Date) & DatePart("s",Time)
```

Next, I ask ADSI to create a new user account.

```
' create the user account
Set oUserAcct = oDomain.Create("user",sUserID)
```

The account isn't created yet, but I can still set its initial properties, based on the values in the variables.

```
' set account properties
oUserAcct.SetPassword sPassword
oUserAcct.FullName = sFullName
oUserAcct.Description = sDescription
oUserAcct.HomeDirectory = sHomeDir
```

The ADSI documentation tells me that the `RasPermissions` property should be set to 9 if the user should have dial-in permissions, and 1 otherwise—that's how I'll set the property.

```
' set RAS permission
If sDialIn = "Yes" Then
```

```
  oUserAcct.RasPermissions = 9
Else
  oUserAcct.RasPermissions = 1
End If
```

I need to tell ADSI to save the information, which creates the user account. This also creates the account's unique Security Identifier (SID).

```
' save the account
oUserAcct.SetInfo
```

I'm going to need that SID in a minute, so I need to tell ADSI to get the new user account again. I just use an ADSI query to pull the user account by using its User ID, which I already know. I'll use a variable, `oUserAcct`, to reference the new account.

```
' get a reference to the new account
' this gets us a valid SID & other info
Set oUserAcct = GetObject("WinNT://NT4PDC/" & _
 sUserID & ",user")
```

Before I forget, I should write that new password out to a file, so that I can tell the user what it is.

```
' write password to file
oTS.Write sUserID & "," & sPassword & vbCrLf
```

Now comes the fun part: adding the user to groups. First, I'm going to use the `Split` function to change that comma-delimited list into a string array. Each element in the array holds one group name.

```
' PART 4A: Add user account to groups
' use the Split function to turn the
' comma-separated list into an array
sGroupList = Split(sGroups, ",")
```

I use a `For…Next` loop to go through the array of group names. Notice that the array starts at zero. I can use the `Ubound()` function to find out how big the array is, although the biggest element I can access is `Ubound() – 1`, because the array starts numbering at zero, not one.

```
' go through the array and add the user
' to each group
For iTemp = 0 To Ubound(sGroupList) - 1
```

Now, I have one specific group name to work with, so I can ask ADSI to get a reference to that group.

```
  ' get the group
  Set oGroup = GetObject("WinNT://NT4PDC/" & _
   sGroupList(iTemp) & ",group")
```

Then, I can use the group's `Add` method to add the user's SID to the group. This is why I needed the user's SID; groups are nothing but lists of SIDs.

```
  ' add the user account
  oGroup.Add oUserAcct.AdsPath
```

Just to be tidy, I can release the group object when I'm finished with it.

```
  ' release the group
  Set oGroup = Nothing

Next
```

To create the user's home directory, I use the FileSystemObject (FSO) to create the appropriate folder. I might also need to set NTFS permissions; I could use WMI to do that, but it's beyond the scope of this example.

```
' PART 4B: Create the user's Home Directory
' (append UserID to the Home Path variable)
Set oFolder = oFSO.CreateFolder(sHomePath & sUserID)
```

I'm finished! I can release the user account and move on to the next record.

```
' PART 5: All done!
' release the user account
Set oUserAcct = Nothing
```

```
  ' move to the next row in the recordset
  oRS.MoveNext

Loop
```

When I've made it through all of the records, I can shut down the recordset and the output file, and display an informative message.

```
' PART 6: Final clean up, close down
oRS.Close
oTS.Close
WScript.Echo "Passwords have been written to c:\passwords.txt."
```

That's it! You have a fully functional script to add users to your domain automatically.

## Finding Inactive Users

This is a script I like to run from time to time, just to find out how many user accounts haven't logged on for a while. Often, they're accounts of employees who have left, but another administrator (certainly not me!) forgot to remove the accounts. Because the accounts represent a potential security threat, I like to disable them until I can figure out if they're still needed for something.

**NOTE** This script works reliably only in Active Directory domains that use Windows Server 2003 domain controllers. Unfortunately, the attribute in Active Directory that stores the last logon date is not reliably updated and replicated in NT or Windows 2000 domains. The only way to use this script in older domains is to run it independently against each domain controller and then compare the results, because each domain controller maintains an independent list of last logon times.

### ➤➤ Finding Inactive Users

Listing 30.2 demonstrates how to use ADSI to locate users who haven't logged on in a while.

**Listing 30.2** *FindOldUsers.vbs.* This script checks the LastLogin date to see when users last logged into the domain.

```
Dim dDate
Dim oUser
Dim oObject
Dim oGroup
Dim iFlags
Dim iDiff
Dim iResult
Const UF_ACCOUNTDISABLE = &H0002

'Set this to TRUE to enable Logging only mode –
'no changes will be made
CONST LogOnly = TRUE

'Point to oObject containing users to check
Set oGroup = _
 GetObject("WinNT://MYDOMAINCONTROLLER/Domain Users")
On error resume next
For each oObject in oGroup.Members

 'Find all User Objects Within Domain Users group
 '(ignore machine accounts)
 If (oObject.Class = "User") And _
  (InStr(oObject.Name, "$") = 0) Then
  Set oUser = GetObject(oObject.ADsPath)
 End If

 dDate = oUser.get("LastLogin")
 dDate = Left(dDate,8)
 dDate = CDate(dDate)

'find difference in weeks between then and now
 iDiff = DateDiff("ww", dDate, Now)

 'if 6 weeks or more then disable the account
 If iDiff >= 6 Then
  iFlags = oUser.Get("UserFlags")
 End If

 If (iFlags AND UF_ACCOUNTDISABLE) = 0 Then

  ' Only disable accounts if LogOnly set to FALSE
```

```
  If LogOnly = False Then
   oUser.Put "UserFlags", iFlags OR UF_ACCOUNTDISABLE
   oUser.SetInfo
  End if

  sName = oUser.Name
  iResult = Log(sName,iDiff)
 End If
Next

Set oGroup = Nothing
MsgBox "All Done!"

Function Log(sUser,sDate)

 'Constant for Log file path
 CONST StrLogFile = "C:\UserMgr1.txt"

 Set oFS = CreateObject("Scripting.FileSystemObject")
 Set oTS = oFS.OpenTextFile(strLogFile, 8, True)
 oTS.WriteLine("Account:" & vbTab & sUser & vbTab & _
  "Inactive for:" & vbTab & sDate & vbTab & "Weeks" & _
  vbTab & "Disabled on:" & vbTab & Date & vbTab & "at:" & _
  vbTab & Time)
  oTS.Close
  Set oFS = Nothing
  Set oTS = Nothing

End Function
```

You need to set the domain controller name to one that's within your environment. You can also customize the script to specify the number of weeks that can go by before you consider a user inactive. Finally, as-is, the script only tells you which accounts it would like to disable; you need to make one minor modification, which I discuss below, to have it make the change.

## ➤➤ Finding Inactive Users—Explained

I start the script by defining a bunch of variables and a couple of constants. *Constants,* you may recall, are simply friendly names for difficult-to-remember values. In this case, I define one constant to be the value that a user account's flags take on when the account is disabled. I use another constant to tell the script whether to simply log its recommendations or disable old accounts; edit the script and change the constant to False if you want the script to disable accounts for you. See Chapter 5 for more coverage of variables and constants.

```
Dim dDate
Dim oUser
Dim oObject
Dim oGroup
Dim iFlags
Dim iDiff
Dim iResult
Const UF_ACCOUNTDISABLE = &H0002

'Set this to TRUE to enable Logging only mode –
'no changes will be made
CONST LogOnly = TRUE
```

The script now needs to connect to the domain using ADSI and retrieve the Domain Users group. Look to Chapter 15 for more on connecting to domains.

```
'Point to oObject containing users to check
Set oGroup = GetObject("WinNT://MYDOMAINCONTROLLER/Domain Users")
```

Now, I use a `For Each…Next` loop to go through each user in the domain, one at a time.

```
On error resume next
For Each oObject in oGroup.Members
```

Even in NT, groups can technically contain computers as well as users. To make sure I'm only dealing with users, I add an `If…Then` to test the current account's object class.

```
 'Find all User Objects Within Domain Users group
 '(ignore machine accounts)
 If (oObject.Class = "User") And _
  (InStr(oObject.Name, "$") = 0) Then
  Set oUser = GetObject(oObject.ADsPath)
 End If
```

I want the script to pull in the `LastLogin` date.

---

**NOTE** Microsoft almost always uses the term *logon* rather than *login,* because login was what you did in a Novell NetWare environment. But the folks who wrote the underlying code never got the message, and so it's Last*Login.*

---

After getting the date, I'm going to grab just the leftmost eight characters. That's because `LastLogin` also includes time information, which I don't need. I end by converting the information to an actual, formatted date.

```
dDate = oUser.get("LastLogin")
dDate = Left(dDate,8)
dDate = CDate(dDate)
```

I use the `DateDiff()` function to find the difference between the last login date and today. The "ww" tells `DateDiff()` that I want the difference expressed in weeks, instead of days or some other interval.

```
'find difference in weeks between then and now
iDiff = DateDiff("ww", dDate, Now)
```

If the difference is six weeks or more, I retrieve the user's existing `UserFlags` property, which includes whether the account is disabled.

```
'if 6 weeks or more then disable the account
If iDiff >= 6 Then
 iFlags = oUser.Get("UserFlags")
End If
```

If the user account isn't already disabled, I disable it—*if* that constant is set to False.

```
If (iFlags AND UF_ACCOUNTDISABLE) = 0 Then

 ' Only disable accounts if LogOnly set to FALSE
 If LogOnly = False Then
  oUser.Put "UserFlags", iFlags OR UF_ACCOUNTDISABLE
  oUser.SetInfo
 End if
```

Whether I disable the account or not, I use a function named `Log` to add this user account to the log file.

```
  sName = oUser.Name
  iResult = Log(sName,iDiff)
 End If
Next
```

At this point, I've run through all of the accounts and I can display a message indicating that the script is finished.

```
Set oGroup = Nothing
MsgBox "All Done!"
```

The last thing in the script is the `Log` function. It accepts two parameters: the user's name and a date. This information is saved to a text file, and the name of that file is defined in a constant. Chapter 5 covers custom functions and subroutines.

```
Function Log(sUser,sDate)

 'Constant for Log file path
 CONST StrLogFile = "C:\UserMgr1.txt"
```

You might notice that the function opens the text file each time the function is called. That's because I also close the file each time the function is finished. It may seem inefficient, but this ensures that the file is safely closed if the script crashes in the middle for some reason. Note that the "8" used in the `OpenTextFile` method opens the file for appending. See Chapter 12 for more on reading and writing to text files.

```
 Set oFS = CreateObject("Scripting.FileSystemObject")
 Set oTS = oFS.OpenTextFile(strLogFile, 8, True)
```

All that's left now is to write the information into the log file, close the file, and release the objects I've created.

```
 oTS.WriteLine("Account:" & vbTab & sUser & vbTab & _
  "Inactive for:" & vbTab & sDate & vbTab & "Weeks" & _
  vbTab & "Disabled on:" & vbTab & Date & vbTab & "at:" & _
  vbTab & Time)
```

```
  oTS.Close
  Set oFS = Nothing
  Set oTS = Nothing

End Function
```

This is a great script to run on a regular basis, and you can even use Task Scheduler to automate it. Just make sure it's running under an administrator's account if you want it to actually disable the inactive user accounts.

## Collecting System Information

Software like Microsoft Systems Management Server (SMS) does a great job of collecting information from all of the computers in your environment. However, it's an expensive, complicated product, and sometimes you might just need a quick-and-dirty means of collecting the same information. This script is a great starting point for an inventory collection system that you can make a part of your users' logon scripts.

### ➤➤ Collecting System Information

Listing 30.3 shows how a WMI script can be used to inventory information from a computer. For example, you could modify this script to run against multiple machines at once, letting you know what servers are running particular types of hardware.

**Listing 30.3** *CollectSysInfo.vbs.* This script inventories a computer and displays the information.

```
Set oSystemSet = _
GetObject("winmgmts:").InstancesOf("Win32_ComputerSystem")

For Each oSystem in oSystemSet
 system_name = oSystem.Caption
 system_type = oSystem.SystemType
 system_mftr = oSystem.Manufacturer
 system_model = oSystem.Model
Next
```

*continues*

```
Set oProcSet = _
GetObject("winmgmts:").InstancesOf("Win32_Processor")

For Each oSystem in oProcSet
 proc_desc = oSystem.Caption
 proc_mftr = oSystem.Manufacturer
 proc_mhz = oSystem.CurrentClockSpeed
Next

Set oBiosSet = _
 GetObject("winmgmts:").InstancesOf("Win32_BIOS")

For Each oSystem in oBiosSet
      bios_info = oSystem.Version
Next

Set oZoneSet = _
 GetObject("winmgmts:").InstancesOf("Win32_TimeZone")

For Each oSystem in oZoneSet
      loc_timezone = oSystem.StandardName
Next

Set oOSSet = _
 GetObject("winmgmts:").InstancesOf("Win32_OperatingSystem")

For Each oSystem in oOSSet
 os_name = oSystem.Caption
 os_version = oSystem.Version
 os_mftr = oSystem.Manufacturer
 os_build = oSystem.BuildNumber
 os_dir = oSystem.WindowsDirectory
 os_locale = oSystem.Locale
 os_totalmem = oSystem.TotalVisibleMemorySize
 os_freemem = oSystem.FreePhysicalMemory
 os_totalvirmem = oSystem.TotalVirtualMemorySize
 os_freevirmem = oSystem.FreeVirtualMemory
 os_pagefilesize = oSystem.SizeStoredInPagingFiles
Next

sMsg = ("OS Name:  " & os_name & Chr(10))
sMsg = sMsg & _
 ("Version:  " & os_version & " Build " & os_build & _
 Chr(10))
```

```
sMsg = sMsg & _
 ("OS Manufacturer:  " & os_mftr & Chr(10))
sMsg = sMsg & _
 ("oSystem Name:  " & system_name & Chr(10))
sMsg = sMsg & _
 ("oSystem Manufacturer:  " & system_mftr & Chr(10))
sMsg = sMsg & _
 ("oSystem Model:  " & system_model & Chr(10))
sMsg = sMsg & _
 ("oSystem Type:  " & system_type & Chr(10))
sMsg = sMsg & _
 ("Processor:  " & proc_desc & " " & proc_mftr & _
 " ~" & proc_mhz & "Mhz" & Chr(10))
sMsg = sMsg & _
 ("BIOS Version:  " & bios_info & Chr(10))
sMsg = sMsg & _
("Windows Directory:  " & os_dir & Chr(10))
sMsg = sMsg & _
 ("Locale:  " & os_locale & Chr(10))
sMsg = sMsg & _
("Time Zone:  " & loc_timezone & Chr(10))
sMsg = sMsg & _
("Total Physical Memory:  " & os_totalmem & "KB" & _
 Chr(10))
sMsg = sMsg & _
 ("Available Physical Memory:  " & os_freemem & "KB" & _
 Chr(10))
sMsg = sMsg & _
("Total Virtual Memory:  " & os_totalvirmem & "KB" & _
 Chr(10))
sMsg = sMsg & _
 ("Available Virtual Memory:  " & _
 os_freevirmem & "KB" & Chr(10))
sMsg = sMsg & _
 ("Page File Space : " & os_pagefilesize & "KB" & _
 Chr(10))

MsgBox sMsg, 0,"System Summary Information"
```

This script is ready to run as-is on any system that supports WMI. Right now, the script is programmed to display its information in a message box. However, if you want to collect remote computer information, you could make this script part of a logon script and rewrite it to save its information to a file or database located on a file server. After all of your users log on and run the script, you'll have a complete central inventory of your computers!

## ➤➤ Collecting System Information—Explained

To save space, I've left out the variable declarations in this script. That's normally a poor programming practice, but I hope you'll forgive me in light of the length of the script. Rather than declaring variables, this script jumps right in by using WMI to connect to the local management provider. You can learn more about WMI starting in Chapter 17.

```
Set oSystemSet = _
GetObject("winmgmts:").InstancesOf("Win32_ComputerSystem")
```

Next, I loop through each system instance that WMI found and retrieve its caption, system type, manufacturer, and model. Normally, there will only be one of these per computer. However, the WMI specification supports multiple "machines within a machine," so to speak, and that's why I've created a loop.

```
For Each oSystem in oSystemSet
 system_name = oSystem.Caption
 system_type = oSystem.SystemType
 system_mftr = oSystem.Manufacturer
 system_model = oSystem.Model
Next
```

Processors are next, and I save their caption, manufacturer, and clock speed.

```
Set oProcSet = _
GetObject("winmgmts:").InstancesOf("Win32_Processor")

For Each oSystem in oProcSet
 proc_desc = oSystem.Caption
 proc_mftr = oSystem.Manufacturer
 proc_mhz = oSystem.CurrentClockSpeed
Next
```

Now for the BIOS; I just retrieve the version.

```
Set oBiosSet = _
 GetObject("winmgmts:").InstancesOf("Win32_BIOS")

For Each oSystem in oBiosSet
      bios_info = oSystem.Version
Next
```

It might be useful to see which time zone your computers are configured for. Remember that some applications use time stamps for auditing purposes; having all of your computers in one time zone (at least, the ones that really are in the same time zone) makes that auditing information more accurate.

---

**NOTE** Time zones don't affect domain operations, which all use Universal (Greenwich) time.

---

```
Set oZoneSet = _
 GetObject("winmgmts:").InstancesOf("Win32_TimeZone")

For Each oSystem in oZoneSet
      loc_timezone = oSystem.StandardName
Next
```

Next, I query a bunch of information about the operating system, including its name, version, manufacturer, build number, the location of the Windows folder, the language locale, and stats on the system's memory configuration.

```
Set oOSSet = _
 GetObject("winmgmts:").InstancesOf("Win32_OperatingSystem")

For Each oSystem in oOSSet
 os_name = oSystem.Caption
 os_version = oSystem.Version
 os_mftr = oSystem.Manufacturer
 os_build = oSystem.BuildNumber
 os_dir = oSystem.WindowsDirectory
 os_locale = oSystem.Locale
 os_totalmem = oSystem.TotalVisibleMemorySize
 os_freemem = oSystem.FreePhysicalMemory
```

*continues*

```
 os_totalvirmem = oSystem.TotalVirtualMemorySize
 os_freevirmem = oSystem.FreeVirtualMemory
 os_pagefilesize = oSystem.SizeStoredInPagingFiles
Next
```

Now, I format all of the information I've collected into a string variable.

```
sMsg = ("OS Name:  " & os_name & Chr(10))
sMsg = sMsg & _
 ("Version:  " & os_version & " Build " & os_build & _
 Chr(10))
sMsg = sMsg & _
 ("OS Manufacturer:  " & os_mftr & Chr(10))
sMsg = sMsg & _
 ("oSystem Name:  " & system_name & Chr(10))
sMsg = sMsg & _
 ("oSystem Manufacturer:  " & system_mftr & Chr(10))
sMsg = sMsg & _
 ("oSystem Model:  " & system_model & Chr(10))
sMsg = sMsg & _
 ("oSystem Type:  " & system_type & Chr(10))
sMsg = sMsg & _
 ("Processor:  " & proc_desc & " " & proc_mftr & _
 " ~" & proc_mhz & "Mhz" & Chr(10))
sMsg = sMsg & _
 ("BIOS Version:  " & bios_info & Chr(10))
sMsg = sMsg & _
("Windows Directory:  " & os_dir & Chr(10))
sMsg = sMsg & _
 ("Locale:  " & os_locale & Chr(10))
sMsg = sMsg & _
("Time Zone:  " & loc_timezone & Chr(10))
sMsg = sMsg & _
("Total Physical Memory:  " & os_totalmem & "KB" & _
 Chr(10))
sMsg = sMsg & _
 ("Available Physical Memory:  " & os_freemem & "KB" & _
 Chr(10))
sMsg = sMsg & _
("Total Virtual Memory:  " & os_totalvirmem & "KB" & _
 Chr(10))
sMsg = sMsg & _
 ("Available Virtual Memory:  " & _
 os_freevirmem & "KB" & Chr(10))
```

```
sMsg = sMsg & _
 ("Page File Space : " & os_pagefilesize & "KB" & _
 Chr(10))
```

Finally, I finish by using a message box to display the information. As I pointed out earlier, you could modify this to write the information to a central file or database.

```
'display results
MsgBox sMsg, 0,"System Summary Information"
```

This script is a great example of how WMI can save you time and effort when you need to perform enterprise-wide operations in a limited amount of time or on a limited budget. It is not SMS, but it's free, easy to write yourself, and can help solve a similar problem.

## Review

Managing domains and Windows by using scripts is an effective, efficient use of your VBScript skills. You'll probably find that a good half of the scripts you write, in fact, are designed for Windows or domain management, since those tasks are most often in need of automation. The samples in this chapter provide a great jump-start for improving your environment's security, consistency, and maintainability, all with a few lines of script code!

**COMING UP**

In Chapter 32, I'll present several network administration scripts. These scripts make heavy use of complicated WMI and ADSI queries, making them great examples for getting started on your own high-end administrative scripts.

CHAPTER 31

# Network Administration Scripts

**IN THIS CHAPTER**

These are among the most common scripts you'll probably write and run, so I've assembled quite a few ready-to-run examples. You can use these in your environment right now, or you can modify them for your own purposes. I've included line-by-line explanations for each so that you can figure out what they do.

Administrative scripts can be some of the most useful tools in your administrator's toolbox. Perhaps the scripts automate some repetitive task; perhaps they enable you to remotely accomplish tasks that would otherwise require a visit to a user's desktop; or, perhaps they simply allow you to accomplish something that would otherwise be too difficult. In any case, the examples in this chapter cover a wide range of uses, and should give you a better idea of what scripts can help you accomplish.

## Shutting Down Remote Computers

This is always a useful trick to have up your sleeve. After you've figured out how to do it, you can perform a number of other useful tricks with remote computers.

### ➤➤ Shutting Down Remote Computers

Listing 31.1 shows the basic script. You are prompted for a computer name, and then that computer is shut down. This script does use WMI, so both your computer and the one you're shutting down must support WMI, and your user credentials must be accepted on the remote machine as an administrator.

**Listing 31.1** *Shutdown.vbs.* Shuts down a remote computer by using WMI.

```
'get machine to shut down
Dim sMachine
sMachine = InputBox("Shut down what computer?")

'create WMI query
Dim sWMI
sWMI = "SELECT * FROM Win32_OperatingSystem WHERE" & _
 "Primary = True"

'Contact specified machine
Dim oOS
Set oOS = GetObject("winmgmts://" & sMachine & _
 "/root/cimv2".ExecQuery(sWMI))

'run through all returned entries
Dim oItem
For Each oItem in oOS
 oItem.Shutdown
Next
```

You don't need to make any changes to this script to get it to run.

## ➤➤ Shutting Down Remote Computers—Explained

This script is typical of most WMI scripts you've seen, except that it uses a method of the queried WMI instance instead of simply querying information. The script starts by getting the name of the computer you want to work with.

```
'get machine to shut down
Dim sMachine
sMachine = InputBox("Shut down what computer?")
```

Next, the script creates a basic WMI query to get all instances of `Win32_OperatingSystem` that are the primary operating system on the remote machine. I'm not aware of any circumstances under which this query could return more than one operating system, but it's theoretically possible.

```
'create WMI query
Dim sWMI
sWMI = "SELECT * FROM Win32_OperatingSystem WHERE" & _
 "Primary = True"
```

Next, the script executes the WMI query to obtain a list of results.

```
 'Contact specified machine
Dim oOS
Set oOS = GetObject("winmgmts://" & sMachine & _
 "/root/cimv2".ExecQuery(sWMI)
```

Finally, because it's theoretically possible for a machine to have more than one primary operating system installed, I run through each one and use its `Shutdown` method to tell it to shut down. This performs a clean shutdown, meaning applications are asked to exit.

```
'run through all returned entries
Dim oItem
For Each oItem in oOS
 oItem.Shutdown
Next
```

That's all there is to it. The WMI documentation says that the `Win32_OperatingSystem` class exposes three methods associated with rebooting and shutting down. They are

1. `Shutdown`, which I've used here. This is a basic clean shutdown.
2. `Win32Shutdown`, which provides more control over the shutdown process. You can pass this method a flag indicating what type of shutdown you'd like. For example, 0 is a logoff, 1 is a shutdown, 2 is a reboot, and 8 is a power off. Add 4 to any value to force the action, making 6, for example, a forced reboot.
3. `Reboot`, which is a simple, clean reboot cousin of `Shutdown`.

You can modify the example script here to use any one of these. For example, to implement a forced shutdown:

```
'run through all returned entries
Dim oItem
For Each oItem in oOS
 oItem.Win32Shutdown(5,0)
Next
```

I'm often asked if there's a way to automatically log users off their computers at a specific time; many organizations want to use this capability to better manage software deployments as well as keep workstations more secure. There is a way! Just use `Win32Shutdown` with the appropriate parameter and run the script from Task Scheduler. Provided the script runs under the credentials of a domain administrator, it should be able to force all machines in the domain to remotely log off, if desired. Just provide it with a list of computers, either from a file or from the results of a domain query.

## Listing Remote Shares

Ever wonder what shares are available on a remote file server? I've often needed a complete list. Yes, you can use `NET VIEW` or another command-line utility, but what if you want to list several servers at once, or have the list of shares output to a text file, or used by another script? Having a script capable of generating this list can be a handy tool.

### ➤➤ Listing Shares

Listing 31.2 shows how to pull a list of shares from any remote computer, using ADSI.

**Listing 31.2** *Shares.vbs.* Listing remote shares.

```
sServerName = _
 InputBox("Enter name of server to list shares for.")

Set oFS = GetObject("WinNT://" & sServerName & _
 "/LanmanServer,FileService")
For Each sSh In oFS
      WScript.Echo sSh.name
Next
```

Not very complicated, is it? That's the power of ADSI. You shouldn't have to make any changes to run this script, and it will run on NT, 2000, XP, and 2003 systems.

### ➤➤ Listing Shares—Explained

This script starts out by simply asking for the name of the server that you want to list shares for.

```
sServerName = InputBox("Enter name of server to list shares for.")
```

Next, it queries ADSI. The ADSI query connects to the specified server's LanManServer, which is a file service. Physically, the Server service is present on all Windows NT-based computers, including NT, 2000, XP, and 2003.

```
Set oFS = GetObject("WinNT://" & sServerName & _
 "/LanmanServer,FileService")
```

The file service has a collection of shares, and this next loop simply iterates each of them and displays each in a message box (or outputs to the command line, if you're running through `Cscript.exe`).

```
For Each sSh In oFS
      WScript.Echo sSh.name
Next
```

You can customize this script easily. For example, to output the server's shares to a text file, just modify the latter half of the script as follows.

```
Dim oFSO, oTS
Set oFSO = CreateObject("Scripting.FileSystemObject")
Set oTS = oFSO.CreateTextFile("c:\shares")

oTS.WriteLine "Shares for server " & sServerName
For Each sSh in oFS
 oTS.WriteLine sSh.Name
Next
oTS.Close
```

You can modify the script to read a list of servers and output each of their file share lists. Listing 31.3 shows the complete script.

**Listing 31.3** *ListShares.vbs.* Listing shares for servers from a text file.

```
Dim oFSO, oTSIn, oTSOut
Set oFSO = CreateObject("Scripting.FileSystemObject")

'Create output file
Set oTSOut = oFSO.CreateTextFile("C:\shares.txt")

'Open input file
Set oTSIn = oFSO.OpenTextFile("c:\servers.txt")

'go through servers
Do Until oTSIn.AtEndOfStream

'get server name
Dim sServerName
sServerName = oTSIn.ReadLine

 Dim oFS, sSH
 Set oFS = GetObject("WinNT://" & sServerName & _
  "/LanmanServer,FileService")

 'go through shares
 For Each sSh in oFS
  oTSOut.WriteLine sSh.Name
 Next

 Set oFS = Nothing

Loop

'close files
oTSIn.Close
oTSOut.Close

'finished!
MsgBox "Finished!"
```

The input file in this example should list one server name per line, with as many servers as you like.

# Finding Out Who Has a File Open

### ➤➤ Who Has a File

Listing 31.4 shows the script.

**Listing 31.4** *WhoHas.vbs.* Shows who has a particular file open.

```
' first, get the server name we want to work with
varServer = InputBox ("Server name to check")

' get the local path of the file to check
varFile= _
 InputBox ("Full path and filename of the file on the" & _
 "server (use the local path as if you were " & _
 "at the server console)")

' bind to the server's file service
set objFS = GetObject("WinNT://" & varServer & _
 "/lanmanserver,fileservice")

' scan through the open resources until we
' locate the file we want
varFoundNone = True

' use a FOR...EACH loop to walk through the
' open resources
For Each objRes in objFS.Resources

      ' does this resource match the one we're looking for?
      If objRes.Path = varFile Then

            ' we found the file - show who's got it
            varFoundNone = False
            WScript.Echo objRes.Path & " is opened by " & _
             objRes.User
      End If
Next

' if we didn't find the file open, display a msg
If varFoundNone = True Then
      WScript.Echo "Didn't find that file opened by anyone."
End If
```

To operate this script, simply type the name of a server and the full path and filename of a file. This path must be the local path on the server; typing a UNC doesn't work. For example, suppose ServerA has a folder named C:\SalesDocs, which contains a file named Sales.doc. The folder is shared as Sales, and you want to find out who has the file \\ServerA\Sales\Sales.doc open. You'd enter **ServerA** for the server name, and **C:\SalesDocs\Sales.doc** as the file path and name.

## ➤➤ Who Has a File—Explained

As with most scripts, this one begins by collecting some basic information: in this case, the name of a server and the complete path and name of a file.

```
' first, get the server name we want to work with
varServer = InputBox ("Server name to check")

' get the local path of the file to check
varFile= _
 InputBox ("Full path and filename of the file on the" & _
 "server (use the local path as if you were " & _
 "at the server console)")
```

Next, the script uses ADSI to bind to the specified server's Server service.

```
' bind to the server's file service
set objFS = GetObject("WinNT://" & varServer & _
 "/lanmanserver,fileservice")
```

In Listings 31.2 and 31.3, you saw how to iterate through the Server services' shares; this script iterates through open resources instead. First, the script sets a variable indicating that the requested file hasn't yet been found.

```
' scan through the open resources until we
' locate the file we want
varFoundNone = True
```

Now the script uses a `For Each...Next` construct to iterate through the open files.

```
' use a FOR...EACH loop to walk through the
' open resources
For Each objRes in objFS.Resources
```

Each resource is checked to see if its path matches the specified file path and filename.

```
' does this resource match the one we're looking for?
If objRes.Path = varFile Then
```

If there's a match, the variable is set to False, meaning the file was found. The name of the user who has the file open is displayed in a message box. Notice that the script doesn't use `Exit For` at this point; more than one user can have a file open, so the script needs to continue looking for other open resources matching the specified file path. There is one resource for each user that has the file open.

```
            ' we found the file - show who's got it
            varFoundNone = False
            WScript.Echo objRes.Path & " is opened by " & _
             objRes.User
      End If
Next
```

Finally, the script displays a message if that variable still equals True. This tells you that the script has finished running, but didn't find any open resources matching the file you specified.

```
' if we didn't find the file open, display a msg
If varFoundNone = True Then
      WScript.Echo "Didn't find that file opened by anyone."
End If
```

Because this script uses the WinNT ADSI provider, it works with Windows NT 4.0, 2000, XP, and 2003.

## Uninstall Remote MSI Packages

Using WMI to interact with MSI packages seems tricky, but it's not too complicated. Wouldn't it be nice to have a script that shows you which MSI packages are installed on a remote computer, and lets you selectively uninstall one? You could remotely weed out unapproved applications on users' machines, maintain servers, and a host of other useful tasks.

## ➤➤ Remote MSI Uninstall

Listing 31.5 shows the script. It prompts you for a machine name, and then shows you which packages are installed. Note that the one thing this script doesn't do is work against the machine it's running on; that's because WMI doesn't allow you to specify alternate user credentials when accessing the local machine. If you want to uninstall something locally, use the Control Panel!

---

**NOTE** This script runs on Windows NT 4.0, Windows XP, and Windows 2000. However, Windows Server 2003 requires the optional Windows Installer provider, which is included on the Windows Server 2003 CD-ROM.

---

**Listing 31.5** *Uninstall.vbs.* Uninstalls a remote MSI package.

```
'get remote computer name
Dim sMachine
sMachine = InputBox("Computer name?")

'get admin credentials
Dim sAdminUser, sPassword
sAdminUser = InputBox("Enter the admin user name.")
sPassword = InputBox("Enter the users password. ")

'get a WMI Locator
Dim oLocator
Set oLocator = CreateObject("WbemScripting.SWbemLocator")

'connect to remote machine
Dim oService
Set oService = oLocator.ConnectServer(sMachine, "root\cimv2", _
    sAdminUser, sPassword)

'get a list of installed products
Dim sMsg, sName
For Each oProduct in GetObject( _
 "winmgmts:{impersonationLevel=impersonate,(Debug)}" _
 ).InstancesOf("win32_Product")

 'is this the product we want?
 sMsg = "Product: " & vbCrLf
 sMsg = sMsg & oProduct.Name
      sMsg = sMsg & vbCrLf & "Uninstall this product?"
```

```
 If MsgBox(sMsg, 4) = 6 Then
  sName = oProduct.Name
  Exit For
 End If

Next

'Get the named package
For each oProduct in GetObject( _
 "winmgmts:{impersonationLevel=impersonate}" _
 ).ExecQuery _
     ("Select * from Win32_Product where Name='" & sName & "'")

 'uninstall it
     oProduct.Uninstall

     'done!
     MsgBox "Uninstalled " & sName

Next
```

This script should run with no alterations in your environment.

## ➤➤ Remote MSI Uninstall—Explained

This script begins by collecting the computer name and administrative credentials. Note that your admin password is displayed in clear text on the screen, but that it isn't transmitted in clear text across the network.

```
'get remote computer name
Dim sMachine
sMachine = InputBox("Computer name?")

'get admin credentials
Dim sAdminUser, sPassword
sAdminUser = InputBox("Enter the admin user name.")
sPassword = InputBox("Enter the users password. ")
```

Next, the script fires up WMI and creates a locator. Then, it uses the locator to connect to the specified machine by using the specified credentials. This bit makes the script throw an error if you try to run it against your local machine.

```
'get a WMI Locator
Dim oLocator
Set oLocator = CreateObject("WbemScripting.SWbemLocator")

'connect to remote machine
Dim oService
Set oService = oLocator.ConnectServer(sMachine, "root\cimv2", _
    sAdminUser, sPassword)
```

The script now queries WMI for a list of installed packages, or products.

```
'get a list of installed products
Dim sMsg, sName
For Each oProduct in GetObject( _
 "winmgmts:{impersonationLevel=impersonate,(Debug)}" _
 ).InstancesOf("win32_Product")
```

The script builds a message that displays the name of the current product.

```
 'is this the product we want?
 sMsg = "Product: " & vbCrLf
 sMsg = sMsg & oProduct.Name
      sMsg = sMsg & vbCrLf & "Uninstall this product?"
```

The script uses `MsgBox()` to ask if this is the product you want to uninstall. If it is, the script sets the product's name into a variable for later use, and stops going through products.

```
 If MsgBox(sMsg, 4) = 6 Then
  sName = oProduct.Name
  Exit For
 End If

Next
```

Now, the script gets the named package through another WMI query.

```
      'Get the named package
For each oProduct in GetObject( _
 "winmgmts:{impersonationLevel=impersonate}" _
 ).ExecQuery _
      ("Select * from Win32_Product where Name='" & sName & "'")
```

The script executes the package's `Uninstall` method, which remotely runs the uninstall. Normally, the user on the remote computer doesn't see a thing, although that can differ from package to package.

```
'uninstall it
    oProduct.Uninstall
```

Finally, the script displays a message to let you know it finished.

```
    'done!
    MsgBox "Uninstalled " & sName

Next
```

Notice that the uninstall routine occurs inside a `For Each...Next` loop; this uninstalls any packages with the same name as the name you selected. Normally, each package has a unique name, so just one package is uninstalled each time you run this script.

## Adding Users from Excel

Adding users to your domain in bulk can be a great timesaver, especially in rapidly growing organizations. This example lists users in an Excel spreadsheet, and actually uses ActiveX Data Objects (ADO) to read information from the spreadsheet.

You need to do a bit of preparation to use this script. First, create a new Excel spreadsheet. The spreadsheet should look something like Table 31.1.

Notice that the Groups column is a comma-delimited list of group names, with no spaces after the commas.

**Table 31.1** Sample Excel Spreadsheet for Adding Users

| UserID | FullName | Description | Home Directory | Groups | DialIn |
|---|---|---|---|---|---|
| DonJ | Don Jones | Administrator | donj | Domain Admins | Y |
| GregM | Greg Marino | Sales | gregm | Sales,Execs | N |

You also need to create an ODBC DSN (Data Source Name) that points to the spreadsheet. On Windows XP, open the Administrative Tools program group, and select the Data Sources item. Create a new System DSN that uses the Microsoft Excel driver. Name the DSN "Excel." When you make the Excel spreadsheet, be sure to create your columns and rows on Sheet1, and don't change the sheet name.

## ➤➤ Adding Users

Listing 31.6 shows the complete script, which uses the Excel sheet and DSN you set up earlier.

**Listing 31.6** *AddUsers.vbs.* Adds users in bulk from an Excel spreadsheet.

```
' PART 1: Open up the Excel spreadsheet
' using ActiveX Data Objects
Dim oCN
Set oCN = CreateObject("ADODB.Connection")
oCN.Open "Excel"

Dim oRS
Set oRS = oCN.Execute("SELECT * FROM [Sheet1$]")


' PART 2: Get a reference to the
' Windows NT domain using ADSI
Dim oDomain
Set oDomain = GetObject("WinNT://NT4PDC")


' PART 3: Open an output text file
' to store users' initial passwords
Dim oFSO, oTS
Set oFSO = CreateObject("Scripting.FileSystemObject")
Set oTS = oFSO.CreateTextFile("c:\passwords.txt",True)


' PART 4: For each record in the recordset,
' add the user, set the correct user
' properties, and add the user to the
' appropriate groups

' create the necessary variables
```

```
Dim sUserID, sFullName, sDescription
Dim sHomeDir, sGroups, sDialIn
Dim sPassword, oUserAcct, oFolder
Dim sGroupList, iTemp, oGroup

' define the base path for the home
' directories to be created in
Dim sHomePath
sHomePath = "\\iridis1\c$\users\"

' now go through the recordset one
' row at a time
Do Until oRS.EOF

  ' get the user information from this row
  sUserID = oRS("UserID")
  sFullName = oRS("FullName")
  sDescription = oRS("Description")
  sHomeDir = oRS("HomeDirectory")
  sGroups = oRS("Groups")
  sDialIn = oRS("DialIn")

  ' make up a new password
  sPassword = Left(sUserID,2) & DatePart("n",Time) & _
   DatePart("y",Date) & DatePart("s",Time)

  ' create the user account
  Set oUserAcct = oDomain.Create("user",sUserID)

  ' set account properties
  oUserAcct.SetPassword sPassword
  oUserAcct.FullName = sFullName
  oUserAcct.Description = sDescription
  oUserAcct.HomeDirectory = sHomeDir

  ' set RAS permission
  If sDialIn = "Y" Then
    oUserAcct.RasPermissions = 9
  Else
    oUserAcct.RasPermissions = 1
  End If

  ' save the account
  oUserAcct.SetInfo
```

*continues*

```
    ' get a reference to the new account
    ' this gets us a valid SID & other info
    Set oUserAcct = GetObject("WinNT://NT4PDC/" & sUserID & _
     ",user")

    ' write password to file
    oTS.Write sUserID & "," & sPassword & vbCrLf

    ' PART 4A: Add user account to groups
    ' use the Split function to turn the
    ' comma-separated list into an array
    sGroupList = Split(sGroups, ",")

    ' go through the array and add the user
    ' to each group
    For iTemp = 0 To uBound(sGroupList)

      ' get the group
      Set oGroup = GetObject("WinNT://NT4PDC/" & _
       sGroupList(iTemp) & ",group")

      ' add the user account
      oGroup.Add oUserAcct.ADsPath

      ' release the group
      Set oGroup = Nothing

    Next


    ' PART 4B: Create the user's Home Directory
    ' (append UserID to the Home Path variable)
    Set oFolder = oFSO.CreateFolder(sHomePath & sUserID)


    ' PART 5: All done!
    ' release the user account
    Set oUserAcct = Nothing

    ' move to the next row in the recordset
    oRS.MoveNext

Loop
```

```
' PART 6: Final clean up, close down
oRS.Close
oTS.Close
WScript.Echo "Passwords have been written to c:\passwords.txt."
```

You need to adjust the server names and domain to suit your environment, but otherwise this script should run unaltered in either an NT or Active Directory domain.

## ➤➤ Adding Users—Explained

The script starts by creating an ADO connection object and opening the "Excel" DSN. Because the DSN is tied to your spreadsheet, the connection object now represents that spreadsheet.

```
' PART 1: Open up the Excel spreadsheet
' using ActiveX Data Objects
Dim oCN
Set oCN = CreateObject("ADODB.Connection")
oCN.Open "Excel"
```

Next, the script queries all rows from Sheet1 into a Recordset object. The recordset treats the first row as a column header, which sets up the column names.

```
Dim oRS
Set oRS = oCN.Execute("SELECT * FROM [Sheet1$]")
```

Now, all of the users you want to create are in the Recordset. Each record in the Recordset represents a single user. The next preparatory step is to connect to a domain or domain controller by using ADSI.

```
' PART 2: Get a reference to the
' Windows NT domain using ADSI
Dim oDomain
Set oDomain = GetObject("WinNT://NT4PDC")
```

oDomain now represents the domain, or a domain controller. Finally, the script opens up an output text file. Because we'll be creating new users, they need passwords; the script generates unique passwords for each user and saves them to this file.

```
' PART 3: Open an output text file
' to store users' initial passwords
Dim oFSO, oTS
Set oFSO = CreateObject("Scripting.FileSystemObject")
Set oTS = oFSO.CreateTextFile("c:\passwords.txt",True)
```

The script needs to define a number of variables that will hold information about the user being created.

```
' PART 4: For each record in the recordset,
' add the user, set the correct user
' properties, and add the user to the
' appropriate groups

' create the necessary variables
Dim sUserID, sFullName, sDescription
Dim sHomeDir, sGroups, sDialIn
Dim sPassword, oUserAcct, oFolder
Dim sGroupList, iTemp, oGroup
```

This is where you define the base path for your users' home directories. Typically, this is a shared folder. Note that one thing this script does not do is apply NTFS permissions; that's an enhancement you can make using WMI, if you like.

```
' define the base path for the home
' directories to be created in
Dim sHomePath
sHomePath = "\\iridis1\c$\users\"
```

The script now uses a `Do...Loop` construct to go through each record in the Recordset. The loop stops executing when the last row is passed, setting the Recordset object's `EOF` property to True.

```
' now go through the recordset one
' row at a time
Do Until oRS.EOF
```

Within the loop, the script first pulls information from the Recordset into variables, making the information a bit easier to access and work with. Notice that the Recordset object allows you to refer to each column of information by name, based on the names defined in the header row of the spreadsheet.

```
' get the user information from this row
sUserID = oRS("UserID")
sFullName = oRS("FullName")
sDescription = oRS("Description")
sHomeDir = oRS("HomeDirectory")
sGroups = oRS("Groups")
sDialIn = oRS("DialIn")
```

The new user needs a password, so the script makes one up. This takes the first two characters of the user's ID, the current minutes from the system clock, the current Julian date, and the current seconds. Not a fantastic password, but should be unique for each user.

```
' make up a new password
sPassword = Left(sUserID,2) & DatePart("n",Time) & _
 DatePart("y",Date) & DatePart("s",Time)
```

Now, the script can create the user account. This uses the domain object's `Create` method to create a new object of the "user" class, having the user ID specified as the new object's name.

```
' create the user account
Set oUserAcct = oDomain.Create("user",sUserID)
```

Several properties of the new account can be set up right away, including its password, full name, home directory, and description.

```
' set account properties
oUserAcct.SetPassword sPassword
oUserAcct.FullName = sFullName
oUserAcct.Description = sDescription
oUserAcct.HomeDirectory = sHomeDir
```

The dial-in permissions flag can also be set.

```
' set RAS permission
If sDialIn = "Y" Then
  oUserAcct.RasPermissions = 9
Else
  oUserAcct.RasPermissions = 1
End If
```

Finally, the new object's `SetInfo` method saves the new object and its properties. This is necessary before the domain will assign a unique security identifier (SID) to the account. Remember that, in a domain, groups contain the SIDs for the member accounts, not the member accounts' names. To update group membership for this user, then, the script has to save the user object and then retrieve its new SID. That SID can be added to the group membership lists.

```
' save the account
oUserAcct.SetInfo
```

Requerying ADSI for the user that was just created makes the SID available when we need it.

```
' get a reference to the new account
' this gets us a valid SID & other info
Set oUserAcct = GetObject("WinNT://NT4PDC/" & sUserID & _
 ",user")
```

Writing the password to a file allows someone to communicate it to the new user.

```
' write password to file
oTS.Write sUserID & "," & sPassword & vbCrLf
```

Now, it's time to add the user to groups. Because there can be more than one group, the `Split()` function is used to create an array of group names.

For more on the `Split()` function, refer to Chapter 9, "Working with Arrays."

```
' PART 4A: Add user account to groups
' use the Split function to turn the
' comma-separated list into an array
sGroupList = Split(sGroups, ",")
```

Now the script can examine each element of the array one at a time. Each element contains a single group name.

```
' go through the array and add the user
' to each group
For iTemp = 0 To uBound(sGroupList)
```

The script first queries ADSI to get a reference to the specified group.

```
  ' get the group
  Set oGroup = GetObject("WinNT://NT4PDC/" & _
   sGroupList(iTemp) & ",group")
```

Then, the script uses the group's `Add` method to add the user's `ADsPath` property, which is the user's SID.

```
  ' add the user account
  oGroup.Add oUserAcct.ADsPath
```

Finally, the group object is released so that the next group in the list can be retrieved.

```
  ' release the group
  Set oGroup = Nothing

Next
```

With the groups out of the way, the script can create the user's home directory folder. This is created under the base path specified earlier.

```
' PART 4B: Create the user's Home Directory
' (append UserID to the Home Path variable)
Set oFolder = oFSO.CreateFolder(sHomePath & sUserID)
```

That's all the user object is needed for. It can be released, and the script can move on to the next user.

```
' PART 5: All done!
' release the user account
Set oUserAcct = Nothing
```

*continues*

```
  ' move to the next row in the recordset
  oRS.MoveNext

Loop
```

When all of the users are processed, the script closes the Recordset object, closes the output text file, and reminds you where you can find the text file containing the new users' passwords.

```
' PART 6: Final clean up, close down
oRS.Close
oTS.Close
WScript.Echo "Passwords have been written to c:\passwords.txt."
```

It's a powerful script that not only demonstrates how to effectively use ADSI, but also how to use ADO for simple data-retrieval operations. Believe it or not, you could easily modify this script to use Access databases instead of Excel. Simply change the "Excel" DSN to point to an Access database, and change one line of code.

```
Dim oRS
Set oRS = oCN.Execute("SELECT * FROM [Sheet1$]")
```

Change "[Sheet1$]" to the name of the Access database table containing your users. As long as the table's column names match the ones I used in the Excel spreadsheet, this script will work just fine.

## Listing Hot Fixes and Software

Wouldn't it be nice to have a script that you could run on each computer in your enterprise to get an inventory of hot fixes and software applications? It's not hard! Rather than showing you a single sample script, though, I want to walk through this example a bit more modularly. The first thing I need is a routine that determines the local computer's name, and then opens an output text file on a file server somewhere.

```
Dim oNetwork
Set oNetwork = CreateObject("WScript.Network")

Dim sLocal
```

```
sLocal = oNetwork.ComputerName

Dim oFSO, oTS
Set oFSO = CreateObject("Scripting.FileSystemObject")
Set oTS = oFSO.CreateTextFile("\\server\" & _
 sLocal & ".txt")
```

This results in an object `oTS`, which is a TextStream object representing an output text file. The file is named after the computer on which it runs, and you can modify the location to be a file server in your environment.

I just need to find a list of hot fixes and applications, and I don't need to turn any further than the Scriptomatic tool, or the WMI Query Wizard in PrimalScript. Hot fixes are formally known as QFEs, or Quick Fix Engineering patches, and there's a WMI class just for them. The following wizard-generated code queries it for me.

```
On Error Resume Next
Dim strComputer
Dim objWMIService
Dim colItems

strComputer = "."
Set objWMIService = GetObject("winmgmts:\\" & strComputer & "\root\
  cimv2")
Set colItems = objWMIService.ExecQuery("Select * from
  Win32_QuickFixEngineering",,48)
For Each objItem in colItems
 WScript.Echo "Caption: " & objItem.Caption
 WScript.Echo "CSName: " & objItem.CSName
 WScript.Echo "Description: " & objItem.Description
 WScript.Echo "FixComments: " & objItem.FixComments
 WScript.Echo "HotFixID: " & objItem.HotFixID
 WScript.Echo "InstallDate: " & objItem.InstallDate
 WScript.Echo "InstalledBy: " & objItem.InstalledBy
 WScript.Echo "InstalledOn: " & objItem.InstalledOn
 WScript.Echo "Name: " & objItem.Name
 WScript.Echo "ServicePackInEffect: " & _
  objItem.ServicePackInEffect
 WScript.Echo "Status: " & objItem.Status
Next
```

Similarly, I can query for installed products (software packages) with the following code.

```
On Error Resume Next
Dim strComputer
Dim objWMIService
Dim colItems

strComputer = "."
Set objWMIService = GetObject("winmgmts:\\" & strComputer & "\root\
  cimv2")
Set colItems = objWMIService.ExecQuery("Select * from
  Win32_Product",,48)
For Each objItem in colItems
 WScript.Echo "Caption: " & objItem.Caption
 WScript.Echo "Description: " & objItem.Description
 WScript.Echo "IdentifyingNumber: " & objItem.IdentifyingNumber
 WScript.Echo "InstallDate: " & objItem.InstallDate
 WScript.Echo "InstallDate2: " & objItem.InstallDate2
 WScript.Echo "InstallLocation: " & objItem.InstallLocation
 WScript.Echo "InstallState: " & objItem.InstallState
 WScript.Echo "Name: " & objItem.Name
 WScript.Echo "PackageCache: " & objItem.PackageCache
 WScript.Echo "SKUNumber: " & objItem.SKUNumber
 WScript.Echo "Vendor: " & objItem.Vendor
 WScript.Echo "Version: " & objItem.Version
Next
```

Again, that's straight from the wizard, so there's not much effort involved. Now, PrimalScript's WMI Query Wizard generates code that echoes to the command line or a message box; to write to my output file I can just replace the `Wscript.Echo` with `oTS.WriteLine`. I can eliminate any queried information that I don't care about, and eliminate redundant lines in the two segments of wizard-generated code. Listing 31.7 shows the completed script.

**Listing 31.7** *Inventory.vbs.* Lists all hot fixes and software on the local computer and outputs the list to a text file.

```
Dim oNetwork
Set oNetwork = CreateObject("WScript.Network")

Dim sLocal
sLocal = oNetwork.ComputerName

Dim oFSO, oTS
```

```
Set oFSO = CreateObject("Scripting.FileSystemObject")
Set oTS = oFSO.CreateTextFile("\\server\" & _
 sLocal & ".txt")

On Error Resume Next
Dim strComputer
Dim objWMIService
Dim colItems

oTS.WriteLine
oTS.WriteLine "INSTALLED HOTFIXES"
oTS.WriteLine

strComputer = "."
Set objWMIService = GetObject("winmgmts:\\" & strComputer & "\root\
  cimv2")
Set colItems = objWMIService.ExecQuery("Select * from
  Win32_QuickFixEngineering",,48)
For Each objItem in colItems
 oTS.WriteLine "HotFixID: " & objItem.HotFixID
 oTS.WriteLine "ServicePackInEffect: " & _
  objItem.ServicePackInEffect
 oTS.WriteLine "Status: " & objItem.Status
 oTS.WriteLine
Next

oTS.WriteLine
oTS.WriteLine "INSTALLED SOFTWARE"
oTS.WriteLine

strComputer = "."
Set objWMIService = GetObject("winmgmts:\\" & strComputer & "\root\
  cimv2")
Set colItems = objWMIService.ExecQuery("Select * from
  Win32_Product",,48)
For Each objItem in colItems
 oTS.WriteLine "Caption: " & objItem.Caption
 oTS.WriteLine "Version: " & objItem.Version
 oTS.WriteLine
Next
```

I added a few extra lines to the text file to make it easier to read. You could modify this script to use ADO to write to a database or Excel spreadsheet, if you want, or to some other format.

## Review

Administration can be faster and easier with scripting in your bag of tricks. In this chapter, you've seen how to combine basic VBScript, the FileSystemObject, WMI, ADSI, and other components to create effective, automated administration tools. This is truly the essence of administrative scripting: gluing together these various components with the help of VBScript to create tools you'll use over and over again.

**COMING UP**

In the last chapter of this book, I'll present more examples of scripts that utilize WMI and ADSI. Although you've already seen several examples that use WMI and ADSI, they can be difficult-to-approach technologies, so I figure a few more examples can't hurt.

CHAPTER 32

# WMI and ADSI Scripts

**IN THIS CHAPTER**

Although I've shown a dozen example scripts for WMI and ADSI, you may still feel like both technologies are a bit complex—they certainly look complex. My goal here is to provide some examples that will help take the mystery out of them.

WMI and ADSI both come across as incredibly complex. It's not surprising; the official Microsoft documentation doesn't help make them any more approachable. However, I've found that a few generic WMI and ADSI scripts can show you how to do just about anything with either of the two technologies. That's what this chapter is all about: providing you with some templates that you can use to write your own WMI and ADSI scripts to do anything you need.

## The All-Purpose WMI Query Script

About 75% of my time with WMI is spent querying information. Fortunately, there's a very simple template you can use. In fact, this is identical to the code produced by PrimalScript's WMI Query Wizard and by the Microsoft Scriptomatic tool. The fact that those tools exist goes to show how generic and all-purpose WMI scripting really can be.

Start by finding the WMI class that you need to query. This isn't hard, but it can be time-consuming because there are so many classes to choose from. I usually use PrimalScript or the Scriptomatic to browse through the classes until I see one I want.

Next, define the three variables you need to query WMI.

```
Dim strComputer
Dim objWMIService
Dim colItems
```

Then, write the actual query.

```
strComputer = "."
Set objWMIService = GetObject("winmgmts:\\" & _
 strComputer & "\root\cimv2")
Set colItems = objWMIService.ExecQuery( _
 "Select * from class_name_here",,48)
```

Notice that you can change the value assigned to `strComputer` to query a remote machine. Insert the appropriate class name. Next, write a `For Each...Next` loop that iterates through the classes that you queried.

```
For Each objItem in colItems
Next
```

Finally, insert the appropriate lines within the construct to work with the class' properties.

```
 WScript.Echo objItem.property_name_here
 WScript.Echo objItem.property_name_here
```

If you don't want to display the information, write it to a text file, assign it to a variable, or do whatever you like. For example, let's say you want to limit the number of class instances returned by your query. When querying `Win32_QuickFixEngineering`, you receive *all* installed hot fixes. What if you just want a particular one? No problem. Modify your query appropriately.

```
strComputer = "."
Set objWMIService = GetObject("winmgmts:\\" & _
 strComputer & "\root\cimv2")
Set colItems = objWMIService.ExecQuery( _
 "Select * from Win32_QuickFixEngineering " & _
 "WHERE HotFixID = 'Q123456'", _
 ,48)
```

You can specify a `WHERE` clause and indicate any property you want, listing the desired value for that property. WMI obeys, and returns only the instances that match your query. Pretty simple! This all-purpose query template can be adapted to almost any purpose. For example, the following script lists various properties of a network adapter configuration. The boldfaced elements are the class and property names I plugged into the generic template.

```
Dim strComputer
Dim objWMIService
Dim colItems

strComputer = "."
Set objWMIService = GetObject( _
 "winmgmts:\\" & strComputer & "\root\cimv2")
Set colItems = objWMIService.ExecQuery( _
 "Select * from Win32_NetworkAdapterConfiguration",,48)

For Each objItem in colItems
      WScript.Echo "ArpAlwaysSourceRoute: " &
  objItem.ArpAlwaysSourceRoute
      WScript.Echo "ArpUseEtherSNAP: " & objItem.ArpUseEtherSNAP
      WScript.Echo "Caption: " & objItem.Caption
      WScript.Echo "DatabasePath: " & objItem.DatabasePath
      WScript.Echo "DeadGWDetectEnabled: " & _
       objItem.DeadGWDetectEnabled
      WScript.Echo "DefaultIPGateway: " & _
       objItem.DefaultIPGateway
      WScript.Echo "DefaultTOS: " & objItem.DefaultTOS
      WScript.Echo "DefaultTTL: " & objItem.DefaultTTL
      WScript.Echo "Description: " & objItem.Description
      WScript.Echo "DHCPEnabled: " & objItem.DHCPEnabled
      WScript.Echo "DHCPLeaseExpires: " & _
       objItem.DHCPLeaseExpires
      WScript.Echo "DHCPLeaseObtained: " & _
        objItem.DHCPLeaseObtained
Next
```

This template makes a nice, easy way to work with just about any type of WMI query you need to write.

## The All-Purpose WMI Update Script

Querying is easy, but what about updating information in WMI? Just as easy. Start with the basic query template. Instead of echoing property information, however, simply use one of the class' methods, which are documented in the MSDN Library. Here's how to find the Library.

1. Go to http://msdn.microsoft.com/library.
2. In the left-hand menu tree, expand **Setup and System Administration**.
3. Expand **Windows Management Instrumentation**.
4. Expand **SDK Documentation**.
5. Expand **WMI Reference**.
6. Expand **WMI Classes**.
7. Expand **Win32 Classes**.
8. Expand the appropriate category, such as Computer System Hardware Classes, for the class you're interested in.
9. Expand the class itself for a listing of methods, or click on the class for a list of properties.

Take the `Win32_NetworkAdapterConfiguration` class as an example. This class has a property named `DHCPEnabled`, which reads True or False. It seems that setting this to True would enable DHCP, but reading the documentation indicates that this particular property is read-only. However, expanding the class definition shows a method named `EnableDHCP` that looks like just the thing. The following script would enable DHCP on the network adapters in a computer.

```
Dim strComputer
Dim objWMIService
Dim colItems

strComputer = "."
Set objWMIService = GetObject( _
 "winmgmts:\\" & strComputer & "\root\cimv2")
Set colItems = objWMIService.ExecQuery( _
 "Select * from Win32_NetworkAdapterConfiguration",,48)

For Each objItem on colItems
 objItem.EnableDHCP
Next
```

Notice that this updated script looks a *lot* like the query script. In fact, I started with the exact same code. That's how easy it can be to update computer configurations by using WMI.

## The All-Purpose ADSI Object Creation Script

Creating objects in ADSI doesn't require a lot of code, either. Here's a generic, all-purpose script for creating a user.

```
strContainer = ""
strName = "UserName"

'generic part
Set objRootDSE = GetObject("LDAP://rootDSE")
If strContainer = "" Then
  Set objContainer = GetObject("LDAP://" & _
    objRootDSE.Get("defaultNamingContext"))
Else
  Set objContainer = GetObject("LDAP://" & _
    strContainer & "," & _
    objRootDSE.Get("defaultNamingContext"))
End If

'create the object
Set objUser = objContainer.Create("user", "cn=" & strName)
objUser.Put "sAMAccountName", strName
objUser.SetInfo
```

This script is pretty much exactly what the Microsoft EZADScriptomatic tool generates for you. Just fill in the container name with an organizational unit (OU) name or some other container name; otherwise, the user is created in the default location for your domain. Do you need to create a computer instead? Just change the last three lines of code to read like this.

```
Set objComputer = objContainer.Create("computer", "cn=" & strName)
objComputer.SetInfo
```

Do you want a new contact object? Here are the last couple of lines of code.

```
Set objContact = objContainer.Create("contact", "cn=" & strName)
objContact.SetInfo
```

New OUs are easy, too.

```
Set objOrganizationalunit = _
 objContainer.Create("organizationalUnit", "ou=" & strName)
objOrganizationalunit.SetInfo
```

Groups are only a bit tougher. Because there are multiple types of groups, you need to add this code to the beginning of your script.

```
ADS_GROUP_TYPE_GLOBAL_GROUP = &h2
ADS_GROUP_TYPE_LOCAL_GROUP = &h4
ADS_GROUP_TYPE_UNIVERSAL_GROUP = &h8
ADS_GROUP_TYPE_SECURITY_ENABLED = &h80000000
```

These definitions are Active Directory's standard numeric codes for group types. The last lines of code in the script would then be

```
Set objGroup = objContainer.Create("group", "cn=" & strName)
objGroup.Put "sAMAccountName", strName
objGroup.Put "groupType", ADS_GROUP_TYPE_GLOBAL_GROUP Or _
  ADS_GROUP_TYPE_SECURITY_ENABLED
objGroup.SetInfo
```

Replace the boldfaced bit with the appropriate group type from the list you added to the beginning of your script.

## The All-Purpose ADSI Object Query Script

Querying information is just as easy. Your script starts out with some generic object-retrieval code.

```
strContainer = ""
strName = "UserName"

'generic part
Set objRootDSE = GetObject("LDAP://rootDSE")
If strContainer = "" Then
  Set objItem = GetObject("LDAP://" & _
    objRootDSE.Get("defaultNamingContext"))
Else
```

```
  Set objItem = GetObject("LDAP://cn=" & strName & "," & _
   strContainer & "," & _
   objRootDSE.Get("defaultNamingContext"))
End If
```

Then, you add code depending on what type of object you're querying. For example, to get a user's name, just access `objItem.Get("Name")`. For the user's display name, it's just `objItem.Get("displayName")`. For an exhaustive list of properties of users, contacts, groups, computers, and organizational units, see the ADSI documentation, or just use the EZADScriptomatic, which you can download from www.microsoft.com/scripting.

## The All-Purpose ADSI Object Deletion Script

This template script looks a lot like the object creation script to start with.

```
strContainer = ""
strName = "UserName"

'generic part
Set objRootDSE = GetObject("LDAP://rootDSE")
If strContainer = "" Then
  Set objContainer = GetObject("LDAP://" & _
    objRootDSE.Get("defaultNamingContext"))
Else
  Set objContainer = GetObject("LDAP://" & _
    strContainer & "," & _
    objRootDSE.Get("defaultNamingContext"))
End If
```

This code simply connects to a container, such as an OU. After you're connected, you can delete the object, such as a user.

```
objContainer.Delete "user", "cn=" & strName
```

You can reuse this line of code to delete a contact, computer, or group just by replacing "user" with "contact", "computer", or "group" as appropriate. Nothing could be simpler.

## Mass Password Changes with ADSI

One cool use for ADSI that folks don't often think of is using it to manage the local Security Accounts Manager (SAM) of member computers. I have a useful script I run every 30 days or so to change the local Administrator passwords on all my machines; I use the same script to also change some other special user accounts I've created.

### ➤➤ Mass Password Changes

Listing 32.1 shows the script. Note that it reads the computer names from a text file, which lists one computer name per line. This way, I just have to maintain the text file list. You could also write the script to first query all of the computer names in the domain if you want a higher level of automation with less maintenance.

**Listing 32.1** *MassPass.vbs.* Changes local Administrator passwords.

```
Dim oFSO, oTSIn
Dim sComputer, sUser, oUser, sDSPath
Dim sNewPass

sUser = "Administrator"
sNewPass = "pA55w0Rd!"

Set oFSO = CreateObject("Scripting.FileSystemObject")
Set oTSIn = oFSO.OpenTextFile("c:\machines.txt")

Do Until oTSIn.AtEndOfStream
 sComputer = oTSIn.ReadLine
 sDSPath = "WinNT://" & sComputer & "/" & sUser & ",user"

 Set oUser = GetObject(sDSPath)
  If Err Then
   WScript.Echo sComputer & " could not be contacted"
   Err.Clear
  Else
   oUser.SetPassword newPassword
  End If
Loop
```

```
MsgBox "Complete"
oTSIn.Close
```

The only change you may need to make is to change the new password, and to change the location of the input file c:\machines.txt.

## ➤➤ Mass Password Changes—Explained

This script starts by defining several variables.

```
Dim oFSO, oTSIn
Dim sComputer, sUser, oUser, sDSPath
Dim sNewPass
```

Next, the user name that will be changed and the new password are defined.

```
sUser = "Administrator"
sNewPass = "pA55w0Rd!"'
```

A FileSystemObject is created and used to open the input text file. This text file contains the computer names on which I want to modify the Administrator password.

```
Set oFSO = CreateObject("Scripting.FileSystemObject")
Set oTSIn = oFSO.OpenTextFile("c:\machines.txt")
```

The script simply reads in computer names by using a `Do...Loop` construct.

```
Do Until oTSIn.AtEndOfStream
 On Error Resume Next
 sComputer = oTSIn.ReadLine
```

For each computer, the script attempts to connect to the specified user account.

```
 sDSPath = "WinNT://" & sComputer & "/" & sUser & ",user"

 Set oUser = GetObject(sDSPath)
```

If the computer is contacted, the password is changed; if the computer cannot be contacted or the Administrator account has been renamed, an error message is displayed.

```
  If Err Then
   WScript.Echo sComputer & " could not be contacted"
   Err.Clear
  Else
   oUser.SetPassword newPassword
  End If
Loop
```

The script closes the input text file and displays a completion message.

```
MsgBox "Complete"
oTSIn.Close
```

ADSI scripts don't have to be fancy or complicated to be useful; this tool can save hours of manual labor and help create a more secure environment.

## Review

Hopefully, the examples in this chapter—particularly the generic WMI and ADSI scripts—will help you conquer any lingering fears or misgivings about becoming a power scripter. Both WMI and ADSI are incredibly useful technologies, and with the examples I've provided in this chapter and elsewhere in this book, you should be able to do just about anything you want with them.

**ALL FINISHED!**

Welcome to the end! I've provided you with an appendix that you can use to learn more about scripting technologies, and to help you as a quick reference for future scripts. However, you should be ready to start scripting on your own. Have fun, experiment a lot, and don't be afraid to steal ideas or code from the examples in this book! Good luck!

PART VII

# Appendix

APPENDIX

# Administrator's Quick Script Reference

One of the toughest parts about scripting, at least for administrators, can be figuring out which VBScript command or object to use for a particular purpose. I've created this appendix to help with that problem. If you need to do something in particular with VBScript, but don't know exactly how, this appendix is where you need to be. Look up the task you're trying to perform, and I'll provide you with the specific VBScript statement, function, object, or other element that you need to use. I'll also provide you with a cross-reference to the chapter in this book that covers the particular element. Don't forget that you can also use Google and other Web-based resources to figure out how to perform specific tasks.

I cover some tips for using Google as a scripting resource in Chapter 4. Here's a sample entry:

Files, working with: FileSystemObject (12)

This entry indicates that you can use the FileSystemObject to work with files, and that you can find more information about the FileSystemObject in Chapter 12. I don't provide a chapter for every feature, generally because I don't cover them all in detail. When there's no chapter reference, simply refer to the feature's documentation in the main VBScript documentation. Sometimes, I provide a chapter reference when I've discussed similar features. For example, if you look up "Rounding" in this index you'll find a reference to Chapter 7. I don't specifically discuss rounding in Chapter 7, but I do discuss similar functions. In this index, I provide the name of appropriate VBScript functions—such as Round()—and you can look them up in Microsoft's documentation. The idea is just to give you a pointer to the functions and objects you'll need, so that you don't have to wander aimlessly through the documentation.

I've tried to list each feature with as many descriptions as I could think of. For example, if you're trying to figure out a way to trap or handle errors, you could look for "Trapping," "Handling," or just "Errors" and find what you're looking for.

---

**NOTE** For Windows Management Instrumentation (WMI), I've also provided the name of appropriate WMI classes in italics. That will direct you to the appropriate class reference in the WMI documentation more quickly.

---

1394: WMI (17-19) *Win32_1394Controller, Win32_1394ControllerDevice*

**A**

Accounts, users and groups: WMI (17–19) *Win32_Account, Win32_Group, Win32_GroupInDomain, Win32_GroupUser, Win32_LogonSession, Win32_LogonSessionMappedDisk, Win32_NetworkLoginProfile, Win32_SystemAccount, Win32_UserAccount, Win32_UserInDomain*
Activating an application: WSH Shell object (11)
Activation, Windows Product: WMI (17–19) *Win32_ComputerSystemWindowsProductActivationSetting, Win32_Proxy, Win32_WindowsProductActivation*
Active Directory, querying: ADSI (14–16)
Active Directory: ADSI (14–16)
Addition: + (7)
Application, activating: WSH Shell object (11)
Applications, executing: WSH Shell object (11)
Arguments, command-line, named: WSH Named object (11)
Arguments, command-line: WSH Arguments object
Arrays, lower bounds: LBound
Arrays, upper bounds: UBound
Arrays, working with: UBound, LBound
Auditing, security: WMI (17–19) *Win32_AccountSID, Win32_ACE, Win32_LogicalFileAccess, Win32_LogicalFileAuditing, Win32_LogicalFileGroup, Win32_LogicalFileOwner, Win32_LogicalShareAccess, Win32_LogicalFileSecuritySetting, Win32_LogicalShareAuditing, Win32_LogicalShareSecuritySetting, Win32_SecurityDescriptor, Win32_SecuritySetting, Win32_SecuritySettingAccess, Win32_SecuritySettingAuditing, Win32_SecuritySettingGroup, Win32_SecuritySettingOfLogicalFile, Win32_SecuritySettingOfLogicalShare, Win32_SecuritySettingOfObject, Win32_SecuritySettingOwner, Win32_SID, Win32_Trustee*

## B



## C

### D



### E

**F**

**G**

Gathering input: InputBox (6)
Getting an object: GetObject (14)
Group membership: ADSI (14–16)
Groups and users: WMI (17–19) *Win32_Account, Win32_Group, Win32_GroupInDomain, Win32_GroupUser, Win32_LogonSession, Win32_LogonSessionMappedDisk, Win32_NetworkLoginProfile, Win32_SystemAccount, Win32_UserAccount, Win32_UserInDomain*
Groups, creating: ADSI (14–16)
Groups, deleting: ADSI (14–16)
Groups, modifying: ADSI (14–16)
Groups, working with: ADSI (14–16)

**H**

Handling errors: On Error
Hardware settings: WMI (17–19)
Hives, registry: WSH Shell object (11)
Hot fix: WMI (17–19) *Win32_OperatingSystemQFE, Win32_QuickFixEngineering*

**I**

Input devices: WMI (17–19) *Win32_Keyboard, Win32_PointingDevice*
Input, user: InputBox (6)

**J**

Jobs: WMI (17–19)

**K**

Keys, registry: WSH Shell object (11)
Keystrokes, sending: WSH Shell object (11)

**L**

LDAP: ADSI (14–16)
Local users: WMI (17–19) *Win32_SystemUsers*
Logging events: WSH Shell object (11)
Logical disks: WMI (17–19) *Win32_LogicalDisk, Win32_MappedLogicalDisk*
Logs, event: WMI (17–19) *Win32_NTEventLogFile, Win32_NTLogEvent, Win32_NTLogEventComputer, Win32_NTLogEventLog, Win32_NTLogEventUser*
Loops: Do…Loop, For…Next, For Each…Next (10)

**M**

Manipulating shortcuts: WSH Shortcut object (11)
Mapping drives: WSH Network object (11)
Mapping printers: WSH Network object (11)

## N

## O



## P

## Q



## R

Routes: WMI (17–19) *Win32_ActiveRoute, Win32_IP4PersistedRouteTable, Win32_IP4RouteTable, Win32_IP4RouteTableEvent*

Running scripts remotely: WSH Controller object

## S

Scheduler: WMI (17–19) *Win32_CurrentTime, Win32_ScheduledJob*

Scripts, remote: WSH Controller object

Security: WMI (17–19) *Win32_AccountSID, Win32_ACE, Win32_LogicalFileAccess, Win32_LogicalFileAuditing, Win32_LogicalFileGroup, Win32_LogicalFileOwner, Win32_LogicalShareAccess, Win32_LogicalFileSecuritySetting, Win32_LogicalShareAuditing, Win32_LogicalShareSecuritySetting, Win32_SecurityDescriptor, Win32_SecuritySetting, Win32_SecuritySettingAccess, Win32_SecuritySettingAuditing, Win32_SecuritySettingGroup, Win32_SecuritySettingOfLogicalFile, Win32_SecuritySettingOfLogicalShare, Win32_SecuritySettingOfObject, Win32_SecuritySettingOwner, Win32_SID, Win32_Trustee*

Sending keystrokes: WSH Shell object (11)

Serial port: WMI (17–19) *Win32_SerialPort*

Services, background: WMI (17–19) *Win32_DependentService, Win32_LoadOrderGroup, Win32_BaseService, Win32_Service*

Set default printer: WSH Network object (11)

Share and file security: WMI (17–19) *Win32_AccountSID, Win32_ACE, Win32_LogicalFileAccess, Win32_LogicalFileAuditing, Win32_LogicalFileGroup, Win32_LogicalFileOwner, Win32_LogicalShareAccess, Win32_LogicalFileSecuritySetting, Win32_LogicalShareAuditing, Win32_LogicalShareSecuritySetting, Win32_SecurityDescriptor, Win32_SecuritySetting, Win32_SecuritySettingAccess, Win32_SecuritySettingAuditing, Win32_SecuritySettingGroup, Win32_SecuritySettingOfLogicalFile, Win32_SecuritySettingOfLogicalShare, Win32_SecuritySettingOfObject, Win32_SecuritySettingOwner, Win32_SID, Win32_Trustee*

Shares: WMI (17–19) *Win32_ServerConnection, Win32_ServerSession, Win32_ConnectionShare, Win32_PrinterShare, Win32_SessionConnection, Win32_SessionProcess, Win32_ShareToDirectory, Win32_Share*

Shortcuts, URL: WSH UrlShortcut object (11)

Shortcuts, working with: WSH Shortcut object (11)

Special folders: WSH SpecialFolders method (11)

Start menu: WMI (17–19) *Win32_LogicalProgramGroup, Win32_LogicallProgramGroupDirectory, Win32_LocalProgramGroupItem, Win32_LogicalProgramGroupItemDataFile, Win32_ProgramGroup, Win32_ProgramGroupContents, Win32_ProgramGroupOrItem*

Startup commands: WMI (17–19) *Win32_StartupCommand*

**T**



**U**

## V



## W

# Index

# CD-ROM Warranty

Addison-Wesley warrants the enclosed CD-ROM to be free of defects in materials and faulty workmanship under normal use for a period of ninety days after purchase (when purchased new). If a defect is discovered in the CD-ROM during this warranty period, a replacement CD-ROM can be obtained at no charge by sending the defective CD-ROM, postage prepaid, with proof of purchase to:

Disc Exchange
Addison-Wesley Professional
Pearson Technology Group
75 Arlington Street, Suite 300
Boston, MA 02116
Email: AWPro@aw.com

Addison-Wesley makes no warranty or representation, either expressed or implied, with respect to this software, its quality, performance, merchantability, or fitness for a particular purpose. In no event will Addison-Wesley, its distributors, or dealers be liable for direct, indirect, special, incidental, or consequential damages arising out of the use or inability to use the software. The exclusion of implied warranties is not permitted in some states. Therefore, the above exclusion may not apply to you. This warranty provides you with specific legal rights. There may be other rights that you may have that vary from state to state. The contents of this CD-ROM are intended for personal use only.

More information and updates are available at:
http://www.awprofessional.com/